Child of God & are greatly loved by Your Father. God bless You! K—

I See Him... I See Him...

God's Word to Witness By

By Ken Kreh

xulon PRESS

I See Him!...I See Him!...
God's Word to Witness By
by Ken Kreh

Printed in the United States of America

ISBN 1-59781-966-2

www.xulonpress.com

Dedication

Most importantly, this book is dedicated to my Lord Jesus Christ who died on the cross for my sins. I serve a loving Father in heaven, and I am thankful He has filled me with His Spirit.

I want to remember my earthly father, Kenneth A. Kreh, who died and went to be with the Lord in 1977. Dad was my best friend and taught me much about life.

I want to thank my wife, Helen, for putting up with me all these years with her love and encouragement. Thank you to my children, Colin and Courtney, for inspiring me to become the best father that I can be.

Thank you to my brothers Jim and Greg for sharing the good news of salvation back in the early 1970's. I would not know and have a personal relationship with Jesus without your testimonies and pointing the way. Bill and Gary, thank you for being brothers I could look up to.

Lastly, I want to thank my mother, Valeria Kreh, for bringing me up in knowledge that there is a God and instilling him into my life at an early age. I love you so much for always being there for me.

Contents

God loves you and so do I!

Preface

I see Jesus everywhere I look in the holy word of the Bible. I love to meditate on Him and all He has done.

Psalm 145: 5: [5] They will speak of the glorious splendor of your majesty, and I will meditate on your wonderful works. **(NIV)**

The first thing I wrote was, "The Toughest Teacher?" It came to me while I was meditating on God and His word. It was in the summer of 2001. I had just finished the book, "The Spiritual Man," by Watchman Nee (I highly recommend its reading.), and I was deeply affected by Watchman's writing on meditating.

Watchman warns that while meditating on God and His word, you must have an active, not a passive mind. A passive mind leads to deception. He shares that Satan can deceive you if you do not engage your mind while meditating on God. That is his only weapon: filling your mind with deception, turning you away from the truth. You must keep your mind active during meditation. You must search for the truth by testing all thought through scripture.

So, while in the shower, I began meditating on God for the first time using an active mind. Thoughts of having tough teachers in school, tough teachers to earn a good grade from, filled my mind. Then God showed me that the Bible is "the textbook of life." God led me into the Old Testament showing me He is the teacher, and He is a very tough teacher. Then he led me into the New Testament and showed me the loving and caring teacher that He is and that it is possible to get an "A" in His class. My mind was filled with scripture; and at the end, God spoke into my spirit and said, "Write this down!" At that moment, I did not realize why I was writing it down; that came much later. But I said, "Okay Lord, I will write it down." And I did.

Over the years, I continued to write each new idea down and accumulated the pages. I began to realize God was working a plan. He could use my writings for his purpose.

My reason for writing this book is that I want to witness about my Lord and Savior Jesus Christ and help other believers do the same with their faith. As a young babe in Christ—and I was a babe in Christ for a long, long time—I found it difficult to share my faith with others, even those I was close to. I guarantee you my best buddies did not have a clue I had faith in Jesus because my light did not shine very brightly.

The first time I shared my faith, I was kind of forced to. I would not have been able to live with myself if I hadn't, and I felt the urging of the Holy Spirit to do so. You see, my best golfing buddy and dear friend, Jay, was dying of cancer. While at his house visiting and knowing I may lose him, I opened up to Jay and told him about my faith. It was hard and awkward. After I was finished, he thanked me and said he would give it some thought. I know that other mutual friends and acquaintances of both Jay and I came forth and shared with him also. Jay lost his battle to cancer at the young age of 43. It is my hope I will be reunited with Jay some day in Heaven.

I want to aid fellow Christians in sharing their faith with others. Maybe they are babes in Christ as I once was. Sharing one's faith with others, especially to his or her loved ones and friends is so very important. When it comes to sharing my own faith, I tell others I am like Moses, tripping over God's words and lacking confidence; and maybe you are like me. God has given me a chance to share and to point to His scripture, and just maybe, by someone reading this book, others will come to know Jesus as Lord. If you are a believer who is having a hard time sharing your faith, get this book into the hands of a non-believer and suggest chapters that you think might speak to him or her; and let the Holy Spirit do His work. I pray it will plant a seed.

I wrote this book with the unbelieving skeptic in mind. I wrote it for the intellectual and the atheist who says there is no God. If you are such a person, give this book—and, more importantly, the Bible—a chance to convince you otherwise. Nothing is more important than where you will spend eternity. Give yourself a chance of being convinced you are wrong about your beliefs. If I am wrong about what God has shown to all of us in scripture and you are right, I lose nothing; and neither do you. But if I am right and you are wrong, I gain everything. I gain eternity with a loving Father in Heaven; and you will lose everything. The unbeliever has no hope: he or she will spend eternity separated from our loving Father.

Some people think they are not bad people and can earn their way into heaven. Many choose to believe in a heaven, but not in a hell. They are wishing there is a heaven and hoping there isn't a hell. They want to believe all roads will lead to heaven. This is not what the Bible teaches. All opinions cannot be right. There are thousands of religions out there to choose from. Where do your beliefs come from? The Bible declares itself to be the word of God. I highly recommend you check out the Bible and see for yourself that only God can have absolute wisdom and truth.

How would God, who might want to reveal himself to his creation, go about introducing himself?Would God reveal himself to only one human and let that person dictate to you what God is like?Or would God reveal himself to many, each person revealing more about him, all in continuity with no contradictions. That is exactly what has happened in the Bible! From the first chapter and first verse in Genesis to the last verse in the last chapter of Revelation, with many authors over thousands of years, God has told us this truth: the Bible is the biography of Jesus Christ. This is His story.

I want you to see Jesus; I use plenty of scripture so you can see him. In fact, scripture is telling the story, and I am only pointing to what God reveals. Because there is so much scripture in this book, you may want to have your own Bible nearby to follow along with what I have written.

It is God's word in scripture that fills me with so much hope. It is why I have hope in eternity. It is the reason why I say 70 years,

80 years, 90 years, 100 years, or 1,000 years is not enough; I want more. The Bible gives us this hope. It says in **Ecclesiastes 3: 11:**

> "He has made everything beautiful in its time. He has also set **eternity in the hearts of men**; yet **they cannot fathom what God has done from beginning to end."** (NIV)

It is my hope and desire that this book will be used by God to be a blessing for those who read it.

> **Romans 15: 13:** [13]Now the **God of hope** fill you with all joy and peace in believing, that ye may **abound in hope**, through the power of the Holy Ghost.

God loves you and so do I!

Introduction

This book is written for the seeker of the truth found in the Bible. Most of the chapters were written independent of the other chapters in this book. Each chapter can stand on its own writing. This book will show God is revealing himself not only in scripture, but also in creation and nature, in human nature, in pain and suffering, in human relationships, and many other ways. The bible is written in layer upon layer of revelation of God's truth. The Bible is unique from all other books ever written. When you bring all of scripture together, with all of the books and many authors of the Old and New Testament...it is my belief that the Bible is the biography of Jesus Christ. No matter if I read from the Old Testament or if I am reading in the New Testament, **I see Jesus.**

God had me write this book so you can do your own research and decide if you can see him for yourself. I have included almost 100 percent of the Bible verses in each chapter of this book so you do not have to have to look up verses yourself. Most verses in this book are taken from the King James Version. I have also used the New International Version (**NIV**) and the New American Standard Bible (**NASB**) at times in my book. Because there are many versions of the Bible, **I strongly urge you to have your own Bible with you so you can confirm and understand what I am writing from scripture.** I feel I am only bringing God's word together from both the Old and the New Testaments and pointing to the truth in the Bible and what it is showing mankind. If at any time you cannot see what I am trying to show in my limited abilities (I am only a man), pray about it and ask God to reveal you the truth. I believe the Holy Spirit will reveal the truth to you if you seek the truth and God earnestly.

If at anytime you are convicted by the Holy Spirit that you are a sinner and need to be forgiven and would want to begin a personal relationship with your Creator, please go to **Chapter 38** for the steps to follow in becoming a follower of Jesus Christ... our Lord, Redeemer, Savior, and Creator.

Remember while reading this book that the Bible is a Jewish book with mostly Jewish authors. They write in the style their Eastern Culture would have had their minds trained in. It is completely different than how our Western culture would describe things. The writers of the Bible describe by painting pictures so you can see pictures of what is taking place. May you see the picture God has painted in His revelation to man: His word, the Bible.

God loves you and so do I!

"I SEE HIM.... I SEE HIM!"

Chapter 1

Revelations 4:8 *"...Holy, holy, holy, LORD God Almighty, which was, and is, and is to come."*

It is early morning, and I am standing at the top steps of the church of my childhood. I love this old church that was built in the late 1800's. It is an Old Catholic church, with a wide and high stairway to the center entrance and beautiful carved wooden doors to enter from. Also, it has two smaller carved wooden doors on each side of the main entrance. They are at ground level. The church itself is tall and long with a high steeple with a cross on the top that can be seen from all around. The church inside is beautiful, with sculptures of saints, and the Blessed Mary, and Jesus hanging on the cross. It has beautiful, stained-glass windows on both sides of the church; and I am in awe of the "Stations of the Cross" that are wood carvings hanging on the walls that present different times of Jesus' march up the hill of Calvary. Off to the sides are rows of candles that you pay for and you light in remembrance of a loved one who has passed away. Where you enter into the Sanctuary, there are bowls of Holy Water that you make the "Sign of the Cross" with your hand as for to receive a blessing.

The bells at the top of the steeple ring out loud and powerful. As a young boy, the caretaker of the church, Mr. Mann, allowed me to ring them. The bells would ring out to call people to church. As I pulled the ropes, it would lift me off the ground; and they hadn't even started ringing yet. As the bells began to move more and more, they would lift me higher and higher, and they began to ring. The bells ringing kept lifting me high in the air and back down again, over and over again... as Mr. Mann made sure I did not fall from the ropes as they lifted me high into the air.

The church organ is magnificent. The pipes for the organ are up in the steeple. Once Mr. Mann took me up there to see them as well as the large bells I rang. The view from the top was awesome. You could see in all directions, above all of the trees in the area, above all of the buildings.

Lastly, the altar is beautiful. It was like "Holy Ground" to me as a child where the priest led us in worship, and I served as an altar boy. Yes, I love this old church and all of my fond childhood memories of it.

And now I am grown and stand at the top of the steps. It is a different kind of morning than normal; I feel a little eerie and a little edgy. People are beginning to come into church, one and two here and another one there. It is not Sunday, yet people are coming to church anyway. It seems for not to worship, but because they are scared and are trying to find sanctuary in the church. More people are coming.

Now, my two brothers Jim and Greg come up to me, with smiles on their faces. They are so happy. They are anticipating something wonderful. They do not utter a single word to me, and more people are coming to church, hurrying past us, anxious to get into church.

As I stand there with my brothers, I feel anxiety coming over me. I am beginning to feel afraid. There is something going on that is scary, and I do not know what it is. More and more people are streaming into church now. They are afraid. I become more frightened.

I look at my brothers; I see no fear in them. They are smiling and joyful and anticipating something. More and more people are coming now, and they are afraid. They are looking for a place to hide and in this large, old church; they come ... **to hide**. I am so scared, but I do not feel the need to run and hide as the people going into church do. I am frozen in place wondering what is happening.

Now, people are running into church. They are so frightened and must get into church **...now.** I am so frightened, to the point I want to flee, but for some reason I cannot. The people are pouring into church now; it is a stampede.

I look at my brothers, and they are unafraid and excited. They stand at the church, not seeing the people stream by, but looking up into the sky.... I am so frightened.

Suddenly, my brothers point to the sky and shout out, **"I see him...I see him"** and start running towards what they see. People are now frantic and running into church to hide, but not me.

I look up to see what my brothers are running toward, and I see the clouds part and the **brightest light, as bright as the sun, coming to earth; and inside the light is a figure of a man.** I can make out that he is in a white gown and wearing sandals. I cannot look upon his face; it is so bright a light surrounding him. I am so scared, but I do not feel the need to run and hide. Yet, I do not want to run towards the light as my brothers do. I am caught in between... not needing to run and hide, but also not wanting to go and greet this man in the light my brothers are so joyful to see. I am stuck in my tracks. **I am stuck on a fence.**

What you have just read is a dream my Lord and God sent me when I was 21 years old. He sent me this dream, and as soon as I awoke from this dream, I knew the message it brought. God allowed me to see the **triumphant return** of Jesus because of his love **for me, unconditional, before I knew him and had a true relationship with him.** The message was clear.

> **Revelation 3:15-16** 15 'I know your deeds, that you are **neither cold nor hot**; I wish that you were cold or hot.
>
> 16 'So because you are **lukewarm**, and neither hot nor cold, **I will spit you out of My mouth. (NASB)**

God was telling me I was lukewarm, and I was not hot or cold for him. I was on the fence and that just does not make it to heaven. **God was telling me to accept him or deny him... do something!** If I stay where I am I would be denied in heaven at Judgment Day.

> **Luke 9:26** [26]For whosoever shall be **ashamed of me** and of **my words**, of him shall the **Son of man (Jesus-insert added by writer) be ashamed**, when he shall come in his own glory, and in his Father's, and of the holy angels.

You see, my brothers Jim and Greg knew Jesus as Lord and Savior and were unafraid. I believed in God and that Jesus died on the Cross for mankind, but I knew him not because I did not have a personal relationship with him. I had not invited him into my life, and therefore what Jesus did on the cross for mankind was not **given to me as yet. I had not accepted the free gift of salvation, I had not trusted in him... I was trying to do it on my own.**

> **Revelation 3:20** [20]Behold, I stand at the door, and knock: **if any man hear my voice, and open the door, I will come in to him**, and will sup with him, and he with me.

Jesus is asking you to invite him in and **do it now: Do not hesitate or wait.** Do not be lukewarm as I was, in danger of losing my salvation forever.

I wish I could write that after this dream God sent, I repented of my sins and invited God into my heart and life. I did not. You see, I believed my brothers' witness about Jesus. I read the entire New Testament and came to the conclusion the Bible is true and Jesus is the Son of God and died for my sins...but I was deceived by Satan and could not make that commitment. I was deceived into thinking I was going to have to give up something in my life, lose control. I was scared to make a commitment...until two years later.

It was February 1977, and I was 23 years old. While my father was walking back to the house from the mailbox, he experienced chest pains; and we thought he was having a heart attack. As he lay in the hospital, waiting for test results and the doctors to do exploratory surgery over a period of a few days, God was faithful and allowed my brother Jim to witness the salvation message to him once again. It was the first time in a long time my father allowed any one to speak to him about God because he was angry with Him. This night, his heart was softened and so thankfully, he accepted Jesus into his heart and believed.

Afterwards, the test results came in: **terminal lung cancer, 3 to 6 months to live**.

I came to Jesus Christ shortly thereafter, no longer afraid. So did my (at the time) fiancé and now wife Helen. My brother Bill, who like my Father was hardened and angry with God and his church, accepted Jesus. It changed my brother Gary. My mother entered into a deeper relationship with Jesus. God used this most painful experience and brought an entire family to Him.

My father went home to the Lord in October 1977 at the age of 58. Generations of my Father... his five sons, grandchildren, and some day great grandchildren will be blessed with the salvation message because of God's faithfulness.

> **Psalm 22: 30 – 31** "...future generations will be told about the Lord. They will proclaim his righteousness to a people **yet unborn** for he has done it." **(NIV)**

Are you ready? Do not wait...do not be caught on the fence...it is time.

God loves you and so do I!

THE TOUGHEST TEACHER?

Chapter 2

2 Timothy 3: 16 [16]***All scripture** is given by **inspiration of God**, and is profitable **for doctrine**, for reproof, for correction, **for instruction** in righteousness."*

I was meditating on God when I began to think about my kids' school and how there can be a tough teacher to get a good grade from. No matter how hard you try, there is no pleasing that teacher. Nothing is good enough; a passing grade is hard to come by.

As I continued my meditation, I began to think about God as our teacher. And the subject we are taking from him is the "**Class of Life.**" The textbook is the Bible, and this class is **mandatory**; all are required to pass this class in order to receive their diplomas. Compared to any earthly teacher we ever had or our children will have, **no teacher would or will ever be tougher than God!**

Why do I say that? Well, let's delve into the textbook (Bible). God demands perfection. There are only two grades possible in God's Class.

1) **A= Perfect in every way.**
2) **F= Failure.**

Further, if you receive a failing grade, there are no make-ups; and you cannot retake the class. You only have one chance at this class. You fail for eternity with no hope of having a **second chance**. And by the way, it is **impossible** to get an **A** in this class, so **everyone fails—No one ever has or ever will pass this class.** God is the toughest-grading teacher we can ever face, and the Class of Life is the toughest class.

In the textbook **(Bible),** we will find the requirements to pass the "Class of Life":

1) You must keep his Commandments. In **Exodus 20: 1-17** are the listed commandments given to us by God. There are **only ten.**
2) In **Matthew 5: 48** you will see written: [48]**Be ye therefore perfect**, even as your Father which is in heaven is perfect. **(You must be perfect as God!)**
3) If you can do **#1,** you pass the class with flying colors: **you get an A.**
4) In order to do **#1,** you must first be as **# 2.**

Yes, the textbook (Bible) is tough, and God is one tough teacher; but we cannot blame God for failing his class. The reason all fail this "Class of Life" is found in the textbook.

> **1 Kings 8:46** "for there is **no man** that sinneth not!" **(All have sinned.)**
>
> **Romans 3:10** " [10]As it is written, There is **none righteous**, no, **not one**."
>
> **Romans 3:12** "there is **none that doeth good**, no, not one."
>
> **Romans 3:23** " [23]For **all have sinned**, and **come short** of the glory of God."

And in **James 2 verse 10** is why we all surely fail God's class.

"[10]For whosoever shall keep the whole law (**Commandments**), and yet **offend in one point, he is guilty of all.**"

God demands perfection. One slip, one mistake and you fail the Class of Life. Is there a man alive who can pass this class... **can you?** How utterly impossible it is for any person to pass this class on his or her own merits. No matter how much good work you do, it is never good enough. Even Mother Teresa could not pass this class on her own with such high standards God requires.

God's righteousness condemns us all, and we all fail the class. God is a loving God, but he is also righteous; and he must judge us all by his standards. Our hearts love the sin that is in us and therefore it is our own doing that we fail his class.

As I continued my thinking of God as our teacher, I started thinking about the **true God**, the **easiest and most loving Teacher** for those of us who know him. **Before time began** God knew we would never be able to pass the "Class of Life." God had to **meet** the requirements for passing this class **for us** or **all would fail and perish** as the punishment for failure.

2 Timothy 1: 9 [9]**Who hath saved us**, and called us with an holy calling, **not according to our works**, but according to **his own purpose and grace**, which was given us in **Christ Jesus before the world began**"

Before time began God knew we could never live up to his requirements and pass, so he made a plan so **no one** would ever need fail his class.

God's plan was simple. All you had to do was accept a **free gift** from God. You **do not and cannot earn** this gift...**God freely offers it to all.** Now, the class is possible to pass; there is **no reason** for anyone to fail his class. **All that is required is to accept God's free**

gift of life, a gift that is everlasting. It was given to us before the beginning of time, and it lasts forever.

God reveals what the free gift is in the textbook, his holy word, the Bible:

> **John 3: 16-18** reads: [16]For **God so loved** the world, that **he gave** his only begotten Son (**Jesus is our free gift**), that **whosoever believeth in him** should not perish, but **have everlasting life.**
>
> [17]For God sent not his Son into the world to condemn the world; but that **the world through him might be saved.**
>
> [18]**He that believeth on him is not condemned**: but he that believeth not is condemned already, because he hath not believed in the name of the only begotten Son of God.

Further writings in the textbook (Bible) reveal:

> **Romans 8:3** [3]For what the law was powerless to do in that it was weakened by the **sinful nature, God did by sending his own Son** in the likeness of sinful man to be a **sin offering.** And so he condemned sin in sinful man **(NIV)**
>
> **Romans 3: 23-24** reads: [23]For all have sinned, and come short of the glory of God; [24]Being **justified freely by his grace (as if we had never sinned)** through the **redemption that is in Christ Jesus.**"

You see, the textbook and class we have been taking is the biography of Jesus Christ. From the very first book of the Bible to the last is the fulfillment of the Scriptures through Jesus Christ.

> **Genesis 3:15** [15]And I will put enmity between thee and the woman, and between thy seed and **her seed (Jesus)**; it shall bruise thy head, and thou **(Satan)** shalt bruise his heel.

In Isaiah 53, written nearly 745 years before Christ, Isaiah prophesied of the crucifixion of Jesus.

> But he was **pierced for our transgressions,**
> he was crushed for our iniquities;
> the punishment that brought us peace was upon him, and
> by his wounds we are healed. **(NIV)**

In Psalm 22 written in 1000 B.C., you will see another accurate description of Jesus' crucifixion.

> [16]For dogs have compassed me: the assembly of the wicked have inclosed me: **they pierced my hands and my feet.**

Who is Jesus Christ?Not only is Jesus with God... **He is God!** He is the perfect sacrifice who can take away the sins of the world: yours and mine.

John 1: 1-2 The Word Became Flesh– God comes to us!

> [1]In the beginning was the Word, and the Word was with God, and the **Word was God**. [2]The same was in the beginning with God.

John 1: 29 Jesus the Lamb of God- He takes our sins away!

> [29]The next day John seeth Jesus coming unto him, and saith, Behold the Lamb of God, **which taketh away the sin of the world.**

All through the textbook (Bible), God's plan for our salvation is revealed. God sent his only Son Jesus to die in the place of us. Through this free gift, we can pass God's class and have everlasting life. And **receiving his free gift is the only way to pass.**

> **John 14: 6-7** [6]Jesus saith unto him, I am the way, the truth, and the life: **no man cometh unto the Father, but by me.**
>
> **[7]If ye had known me, ye should have known my Father also**: and from henceforth ye know him, and **have seen him.**

Jesus above is saying I am the only way to come to the Father, our God. He is also saying that **if you know him, you also know the Father. Jesus says, "I am the Father, you know him, and have seen him."** You see, Jesus Christ is our **Free Gift.** You must receive him into your life and begin a relationship with the living Christ to pass the class and receive your reward, **eternal life.** This is why God is the easiest, most loving and only Teacher there is.

God made his "Class of Life," which was impossible for us to pass on our own works (good deeds, keeping his commandments, and loving one another, etc.), and made the requirements a **free gift. God says,** "Come and get **your A. All you have to do is accept my free gift, my Son Jesus Christ, and you pass.**

The Steps to follow to receive your "A" are as follows:

1) **You must repent.** You must admit you are a sinner; you have rebelled against a holy and loving God. There must be a change of heart, a genuine sorrow and shame for your sin.
2) **You must have faith in Jesus Christ.** You must accept that Jesus is the Christ, the Son of the Living God, and Christ died for the ungodly and sinners. It means to believe in the power and love of Jesus to save you. It means trusting Jesus to make you right with God.

3) **You must confess.** The Bible says that if you confess with your mouth, **"Jesus is Lord,"** and believe in your heart that God raised him from the dead- you will be saved.
4) **Pray.** You are now able to speak to God as **your Father**, something that you have never been able to do before.

One last thing: Begin a relationship with fellow believers by attending church and getting involved in Christ's ministry and work. You will be truly blessed by seeking a strong relationship with your Savior, Jesus Christ.

P.S., God loves you and so do I.

"GOD'S LOVING ARMS"

Chapter 3

Isaiah 40:11 *"He tends his flock like a shepherd: he gathers the* ***lambs*** *in his* ***arms*** *and* ***carries*** *them close to his* ***heart****..."* **(NIV)**

I was on the Internet, searching for web sites about God. I had been doing this on a regular basis, and AOL had one you could click on and have instant access. The slogan to this site is, "Everyone believes in something." At this site, every main religion from atheism to Buddhism to Islam to Judaism to New Age religions to Christianity was represented, all in this one site. It is an attempt by the host site to make all religions the same; all are on the same playing field, and all lead to the same God. This is not what the Bible teaches. In fact, most main religions do not teach that either, including Islam.

I was curious to find out what was on the Islam site, so I clicked on it. There, you could find out much about this religion from the perspective of its followers. After reading many of the pages of information on Islam, I noticed they had chat rooms, so I decided to enter and see what they would be chatting about. There were many persons there, and the main topic they were discussing seemed to be the Christian belief in the Trinity and the falsehood of such teachings according to Islam. I saw there was another person chatting who was defending the teachings of the Bible; he was all alone in challenging their beliefs. Others were discussing whether it was all right to have friendships with infidels (those who are unbelievers in Islamic teachings). Some were moderate and spoke that they should befriend infidels, and others spoke harshly against having friendship with them. It was interesting to just sit and watch.

I decided to chime in about the Trinity issue and got out my Bible and began quoting scripture for them to read. I was completely ignored. I would chime in again with other verses and again silence...no response. I had forgotten the Bible bears no weight with Muslims, for they believe Christians and Jews have changed verses and meanings in the Bible and therefore corrupted the word of God. Finally, one of the chat room participants from the Islamic faith sent me an instant message asking me, "Brother, are you searching?" I responded, "No, but I am interested in learning a little about what you believe."

We began a lengthy (approximately one-and-a-half hour) discussion on what his faith is as a Muslim and what my faith as a Christian is. There are strong differences in our beliefs. The Muslim religion does not believe we are serving the same God. I would agree. **The differences are too great, and the teachings contradict each other.**

Also, the salvation message the Holy Bible gives is unknown in the Islamic faith. The way to heaven Muhammad taught in writing the Koran is totally different. Both faiths would agree it is very dangerous to one's salvation if he or she chooses the wrong message.

It all boils down to this: Islam teaches the five pillars of faith. In the book I read, "Unveiling Islam," which was written by two Muslim (turned Christian) brothers, Ergrun & Emir Caner. The writers proclaim these five pillars are non-negotiable, cannot be questioned, and must be believed. It is disrespectful and blasphemous to criticize the teachings of the five pillars. The writers share that to criticize its teachings is punishable by imprisonment or worse in many Muslim nations.

Please read "Unveiling Islam" for an in-depth study. But what it all boils down to is this: Islam teaches that there are scales Allah uses. It teaches that somehow if the good I do outweighs the bad I do, **I might** be given mercy. **If I am a good Muslim or if I am good enough, then I might (a Muslim can never be assured) get to heaven.** This is what my good friend who called me brother kept trying to tell me while we sent instant messages to each other. He kept telling me **you must work your way into heaven,** and I kept telling my Muslim friend the **good news** taught in the Holy Bible. **God is love and by his grace** we are saved.

> **Ephesians 2: 8-9** [8]For **by grace are ye saved through faith**; and that **not of yourselves**: it is **the gift of God:** [9]**Not of works**, lest any man should boast.
>
> **Ephesians 2: 4-7** further says: [4]But God, who is rich in mercy, **for his great love** wherewith **he loved us,** [5]**Even when we were dead in sins**, hath quickened us together with Christ, (**by grace ye are saved**;)
>
> [6]And hath raised us up together, and made us sit together in heavenly places in **Christ Jesus**: **(Scripture is speaking in past tense that we already sit with Christ in heaven. His work is done!)** [7]That in the ages to come he might **shew (show)** the **exceeding riches of his grace** in his **kindness toward us** through **Christ Jesus.**

Oh, how God loves us even though we do not deserve any mercy for our sins. The Bible teaches we can never be good enough to earn heaven, as my Muslim friend tried to tell me. I know this is a hard concept for some of us to accept because we are brought up in a society where we must work in order to earn anything. It is human nature to want to return the favor if someone does anything good for us. Salvation is a free gift of love given to us by a heavenly Father who loves us! Our heavenly Father gives us this free gift through his son Jesus Christ, who took the place for us at the cross and died for our sins. **He who believes in God's son Jesus will have eternal life.** Eternal life is our free gift that is given to us **without works.** The laws given by God to Moses were to show mankind our inability to keep God's ways and laws. **The scales of good and bad are thrown away.**

As I shared this good news with my Muslim friend, he became increasingly annoyed with me and made one final attempt to see God his way. He shared:

"It's like you and I are in the middle of the ocean; our boat went down, and we are both drowning. God sees us and has mercy on us and throws us each a life jacket. We both put them on. The seas are rough, and we still might drown so I **(the Muslim)** start kicking as hard as I can towards shore, trying to save myself with the life jacket God gave me. If I work hard enough and don't give up, **I might make it to shore. There is no guarantee, but I might make it."**

He continued, "On the other hand, the life jacket God gave you**, you do nothing with it**. You stay where you are and do not try to save yourself, and **you drown**." I replied to my Muslim friend, "No, **my God wraps me in his loving arms and carries me to shore." (He did this by dying on the cross for me.)**

> **Mark 10: 16** [16]And he took them **up in his arms**, put his hands upon them, and blessed them.

You see, Mohammad taught that you must save yourself. Islam does not teach that God is love. There is no description of God being love in the Koran. God is to be feared, and he will have mercy on those he chooses to have mercy on. The Bible teaches the total opposite:

> **John 3:16-18 shows that God is "love":** [16]For **God so loved** the world, that he gave his only begotten Son, that **whosoever believeth in him should not perish, but have everlasting life.**
>
> [17]For God sent not his Son into the world to condemn the world; but that **the world through him might be saved. [18]He that believeth on him is not condemned**: but he that believeth not is condemned already, because he hath not believed in the name of the only begotten Son of God.

Many say Christians are intolerant of other religious beliefs, that we feel we are superior to other people and what they believe. That we are judgmental. Let it be made clear: it is not intolerance, but **love for all sinners; we cannot deny the truth**. This is the truth: **Jesus Christ DID NOT come into the world to save Christians;** He came to **save the world...all persons, everyone, all**. God is love and that is why God died on the cross for our sins. Jesus is God in the flesh whose one purpose in life was to die a sinner's death even though **he was perfect. It took a perfect sacrifice to deliver us from sin, and only God could do that for us...and he did: Jesus.... at the cross...the perfect lamb...pure love for us...God!** We will build on this truth in coming chapters.

It is up to us to choose to accept or reject the free gift of salvation. Which God (god) do you choose to serve? Do you want to serve a god that you must fear?Must you want to serve a god in a religion with tenets that teach God does not love you?Must you want to serve in a religion that teaches if the good that you do somehow outweighs the bad that you do, **you might see heaven. There is no guarantee.** This is the teaching of the Koran and Islam. Mohammad taught he himself had no guarantee.

Or do you want to serve the **God that loves you** just the way you are, no strings attached, who accepts you no matter what, no matter what you have done. He is the Father who loves us with an everlasting love. **This is the God of the Bible** and the one who wants a personal relationship with you. **Why? Because he loves you!** He wants you to know we are his sons and daughters and loves us dearly. **Yes, there is a difference in the God you choose to serve.** Which one do you want to serve? **Which one sounds better to you?**

> **John 1: 12** [12]**But as many as received Him**, to them He gave the right to **become children of God**, even to those who believe in His name, **(NASB)**

> **Romans 8: 16-17** [16]The Spirit itself beareth witness with our spirit, **that we are the children of God:**

[17]And if children, **then heirs**; **heirs of God**, and **joint-heirs with Christ**; if so be that we suffer with him, that **we may be also glorified together.**

Joshua 24: 15 "but as for me and my house, **we will serve the LORD**."

God loves you and so do I!

Is there really a Hell?

Chapter 4

Many people choose not to believe in a place called hell. They hope there is a place called heaven but they pray there isn't a place called hell. They want to believe a loving God will not send them there. **They are correct**. But a righteous God who is perfect and cannot be with sinful persons can. The Bible is clear in its teachings that there are two natures of **God. He is both:**

1) **Righteous;** judging **each person** for his or her sins
2) **Loving**; redeeming us from the penalty of sin.

Lets deal with the question of hell. **Is there really a place called hell?** Both the Old and New Testaments say **YES.** There is more scripture written warning us of eternal damnation than there is about heaven. In **chapter 5**, "Did Jesus Spend Time in Hell" we will deal further with this subject. We will learn in the next chapter the Hebrew language does not have a word for hell. The word **"Sheol"** is used, which translates in English as "**grave**"; but it's meaning is much more than that.

Old Testament scripture makes it clear—there is a hell. A sampling from various writers proclaim:

> **Isaiah 5: 14** 14 Therefore **hell (Sheol)** hath enlarged herself, and opened her mouth without measure: and their glory,

and their multitude, and their pomp, and he that rejoiceth, **shall descend into it.**

Isaiah 14: 15 [15]Yet thou shalt be brought down to **hell (Sheol)**, to the sides of the pit.

Psalm 55:15 [15]Let death seize upon them, and let them go down quick into **hell (Sheol)**: for wickedness is in their dwellings, and among them.

Psalm 9: 17 [17]The wicked shall be turned into **hell (Sheol)**, and all the nations **(Unbelievers- "nations" is used for Gentiles)** that forget God

Proverbs 15: 24 [24]The way of life is **above (Heaven)** to the **wise (Believers)**, that he may depart from **hell (Sheol)** beneath.

The prophet Daniel warns there are two ways to go when we die:

Daniel 12: 2 [2]And many of them that sleep in the dust of the earth shall awake, some to **everlasting life**, and some to **shame and everlasting contempt.**

The Old Testament is full of warnings about hell, but in the New Testament, it gets more descriptive. These passages below are all **words spoken by Jesus.** The New Testament was originally written in Greek and the word used for hell is "**Hades.**" **Jesus believed in hell and warned us about it:**

Matthew 5: 29 [29]And if thy right eye offend thee, pluck it out, **(Do not take this literally; it is just a warning what sin will cost us—hell)** and cast it from thee: for it is profitable for thee that one of thy members should perish, and **not that thy whole body should be cast into hell (Hades).**

Matthew 10: 28 [28]And fear not them which kill the body, but are not able to kill the soul: but rather **fear him which is able to destroy both soul and body in hell (Hades).**

Matthew 23: 33 [33]Ye serpents, ye generation of vipers, how can ye escape the **damnation of hell (Hades)? (Do not let this warning go unheeded by you!)**

Luke 12: 5 [5]But I will **forewarn** you whom ye shall fear: Fear him, which after he hath killed **hath power to cast into hell (Hades)**; yea, I say unto you, Fear him.

By Jesus own words he forewarns that God has the power to cast evil into hell. Sin is evil, and God will sit in judgment over us for our own sins if we die in them. God does have a plan; we can escape judgment for our sins, but we must trust the one who has the power over us.

Other New Testament scripture confirms there is a hell.

James 3: 6 [6]And the tongue is a fire, **a world of iniquity**: so is the tongue among our members, that it **defileth the whole body**, and setteth on fire the course of nature; and **it is set on fire of hell (Hades).**

2 Peter 2: 4 [4]For if God spared not the **angels that sinned**, but **cast them down to hell (Hades)**, and delivered them into chains of darkness, to be reserved unto judgment;

The Bible teaches there is a hell. God would not spare Satan and the fallen angels that sinned from hell. What about us? Who will be punished?The Old and New Testament both gives us the answer.

2 Peter 2: 9 [9]The Lord knoweth how to **deliver the godly** out of temptations, and to **reserve the unjust unto the day of judgment to be punished**:

Psalm 81: 15 Those **who hate the LORD** would cringe before him, and their **punishment would last forever. (NIV)**

Psalm 91: 7-9 [7] A thousand may fall at your side, ten thousand at your right hand, **but it will not come near you (Those who are saved!).** [8]You will only observe with your eyes and **see the punishment of the wicked.** [9] **If you make the Most High your dwelling**— even the LORD, who is my refuge-" **(NIV)**

Proverbs 10: 16 The wages of the righteous bring them life, **but the income of the wicked** brings them **punishment. (NIV)**

Jeremiah 4: 18 "Your own conduct and actions have brought this upon you. This is your **punishment**. How bitter it is! How it pierces to the heart!" **(NIV)**

Ezekiel 18: 4 [4]Behold, **all souls are mine**; as the soul of the father, so also the soul of the son is mine: **the soul that sinneth, it shall die.**

In the Old Testament, there is passage after passage warning of punishment for those in their sins all warning us of a certain everlasting punishment. **The New Testament even makes it a clearer warning:**

Matthew 25: 46 [46]And these shall go away into **everlasting punishment**: but the **righteous into life eternal**.

Luke 21: 22-23 [22]**For this is the time of punishment in fulfillment of all that has been written.** [23]**How dreadful it will be in those days for pregnant women and nursing mothers! There will be great distress in the land and wrath against this people. (NIV)**

Jude 1: 7 [7]Even as Sodom and Gomorrha (**examples of sexual sin**), and the cities about them in like manner, giving themselves over to fornication, and going after strange flesh, are set forth for an example, **suffering the vengeance of eternal fire.**

Please pay attention to the warnings below:

Hebrews 2: 3 [3]**How shall we escape, if we neglect so great salvation**; which at the first began to be spoken by the Lord, and was confirmed unto us by them that heard him;

God has given us a great gift of **salvation!** The Bible declares we can escape from punishment if we do not neglect this gift. The prophets and the eyewitnesses have declared what was spoken by Jesus is true. We can escape through faith in Jesus Christ.

Revelation 20: 14-15 [14]And **death and hell were cast into the lake of fire**. This is the second death.

[15]And **whosoever was not found written in the book of life** was cast **into the lake of fire.**

Scripture upon scripture, Old Testament and New Testament alike, layer upon layer, all warning us, all giving us a chance to seek God and turn away from sin.

Who goes to Heaven?

It says in **Romans 3: 23:** [23]For **all have sinned (We all start here!)**, and come short of the glory of God;

All have sinned, and we all deserve the same punishment—**eternal separation for our Father, our Creator God.** But wrapped around this Bible verse is the good news of salvation. It is what the Bible has been teaching from the beginning.

Romans 3: 22-24 [22]**Even the righteousness of God** which is **by faith of Jesus Christ** unto all and upon all them that believe: for **there is no difference**:

[23]For all have sinned, and come short of the glory of God;

[24]**Being justified freely by his grace** through **the redemption that is in Christ Jesus:**

What the above verses are teaching is **righteousness comes to those who have faith in Jesus Christ! It is by grace and the redemption given to us through Jesus!**

In **John 6: 46-48,** Jesus declares: [46]No one has seen the Father except the one who is from God; only he has seen the Father. [47]I tell you the truth, **he who believes has everlasting life.** [48]**I am the bread of life. (NIV)**

Ephesians 2: 5 [5]even when we were dead in our transgressions, made us alive together with **Christ (by grace you have been saved), (NASB)**

God warns us about the bad news throughout scripture. He is righteous, and he will judge us accordingly. He will be sending the lost to an everlasting place called hell, guilty for the sins they have committed. Let us not dwell on this fact, **let us dwell on the fact that God loves us!** God put a plan into place before time that did redeem us. He loved us so much that he came into this world to take the punishment for our sins in our place. Through faith in Jesus, we can be saved and have eternal life. It is the good news of the Bible.

God loves you and so do I!

Jesus spent time in "Sheol" "Hades" "Hell" "Grave"

Chapter 5

I wrote this chapter because a friend of our family had her daughter ask her if Jesus ever spent time in hell after he died on the cross.

Finding if Jesus spent time in hell before his resurrection, you need to go to the Hebrew text of the Old Testament and the Greek text of the New Testament. You will discover through studying God's word what happened to Jesus at the time of his death and resurrection in both the Old and New Testaments.

We begin our search with **Psalm 16**. King David is speaking prophetic words of the Messiah. He foresees the death and resurrection of our Lord Jesus Christ as the apostle Peter in the New Testament in the book of Acts affirms it.

> **Psalm 16: 8-11** 8I have set the LORD always before me: because **he is at my right hand**, I shall not be moved.
>
> 9Therefore my heart is glad, and my glory rejoiceth: my flesh also shall rest in hope.
>
> **10For thou wilt not leave my soul in hell; neither wilt thou suffer thine Holy One (Jesus!) to see corruption.**

> [11]Thou wilt shew me the path of life: in thy presence is fulness of joy; at **thy right hand there are pleasures for evermore. (Jesus sits at the right hand of God forever and ever.)**

We know that Peter in **Acts 2: 25-35** is quoting **Psalm 16: 8-11** when he speaks of the resurrection of Jesus Christ. **Peter confirms the resurrection of Jesus that David foresaw:**

> [25]For David speaketh concerning him **(Jesus)**, I **foresaw** the Lord always before my face, for **he is on my right hand**, that I should not be moved:
>
> [26]Therefore did my heart rejoice, and my tongue was glad; moreover also my flesh shall rest in hope:
>
> **[27]Because thou wilt not leave my soul in hell**, neither wilt thou suffer **thine Holy One (Jesus) to see corruption. (Through a miracle his body saw no decay while in the grave for three days!)**
>
> [28]Thou hast made known to me the ways of life; thou shalt make me full of joy with thy countenance.
>
> [29]Men and brethren, **let me freely speak unto you of the patriarch David, that he is both dead and buried, and his sepulcher (tomb) is with us unto this day.**

Peter is confirming this is Jesus and not David scripture is speaking about in Psalm 16—David to this day is buried in his sepulcher (**tomb**).

> **[30]Therefore being a prophet**, and knowing that **God had sworn with an oath to him,** that of the fruit of his loins, according to the flesh, **he would raise up Christ to sit on his throne;**

> [31]**He seeing this before spake of the resurrection of Christ, that his soul was not left in hell, neither his flesh did see corruption.**

Verses 30 and 31 are so very important to understand. God himself **swore with an oath** to King David that an heir of his would be born and sit on his throne forever.

> **2 Samuel 7: 11- 14 the LORD telleth thee** that he will make thee an house.
>
> [12]And **when thy days be fulfilled**, and **thou shalt sleep with thy fathers, I will set up thy seed after thee**, which shall proceed out of thy bowels, and **I will establish his kingdom**.
>
> [13]He shall build an house for my name, **(King Solomon is the son who built the temple for God)** and **I will stablish the throne of his kingdom for ever.**
>
> [14]**I will be his father, and he shall be my son. (Jesus is the heir of David who's Kingdom will last forever.)**
>
> **Verse 16:** [16]And thine house and thy kingdom shall be established for ever before thee: **thy throne shall be established for ever**.

No question God is saying the one who sits on the throne that will last forever is a man being that he is in the line of David; **but he is much more**. Further revelation from scripture reveals:

> **Jeremiah 23: 5-6** [5]Behold, the days come, saith the LORD, **that I will raise unto David a righteous Branch,** and a King shall reign and prosper, and shall execute judgment and justice in the earth.

6In his days Judah shall be saved, and Israel shall dwell safely: and **this is his name whereby he shall be called, THE LORD OUR RIGHTEOUSNESS. ("YHWH"; another Hebrew name for God.)**

It is Jesus Christ that David foresaw and whom he wrote about in Psalm 16—his resurrection, and **he is God.** Jesus fulfilled the prophecy of Jeremiah in the Old Testament that an heir of King David would be born **(a man)** who will reign forever and be **YHWH**- the Hebrew word for God.

Important: The chosen people are still looking for their Messiah to come. Scripture reveals that the Messiah must come from the line of David. No longer is this possible to prove. The Romans have long destroyed the records of the genealogy for the Jews when in 70 A.D they destroyed the temple where the records were kept. Jesus genealogy was established before this happened and his family tree from both his mother Mary and his Step Father Joseph is shown in the gospels of Matthew and Luke and both family trees trace back to King David.

Returning to **Acts 32- 35**:

32**This Jesus hath God raised up**, whereof we all are witnesses.

33Therefore **being by the right hand of God exalted**, and having received of the Father the promise of the Holy Ghost, he hath shed forth this, which ye now see and hear.

34**For David is not ascended into the heavens**: but he saith himself, The Lord said unto my Lord, **Sit thou on my right hand, (Peter is confirming this is Jesus and not David who sits at the right hand of God and Jesus is God!)**

35**Until I make thy foes thy footstool.**

Take special note of verse 35. This fulfills the very first prophecy given to us in God's own words. It fulfills what God said in **Genesis 3: 15:** [15]And I will put enmity between thee and the woman, and between thy seed and her seed; it shall bruise thy head, and **thou shalt bruise his heel.**

When Jesus died on the cross as the "Suffering Messiah," it only bruised him. It was so God could show us his power by resurrecting the "Triumphant Messiah." Jesus is no longer the Lamb of God who was sacrificed for sin, but is now—the Lion, the King and He has made Satan his footstool by conquering death and sin. In order to do this, Jesus was willing to spend time in Sheol for us:

In **Psalm 16:10**, The Holy Spirit **(speaking through David's prophetic words)** knows what David could not describe in his own limited understanding. David sees the Messiah spending time in Sheol. **Verse 10** reads: [10]For You will not abandon my soul to **Sheol**" **(Hell) (NASB).** The Hebrew word in the original text is **"Sheol"** which in English, we translate as **"grave."**

Switching to the New Testament, Peter confirms this teaching in **Acts 2: 31** we see Peter quoting **Psalm 16** and confirming it to be Christ's resurrection and explaining that Jesus did spend time in Hades. **Acts 2:31** reads, [31]he **(David)** looked ahead and spoke of the **resurrection of the Christ**, that **HE WAS NEITHER ABANDONED TO HADES (Hell), NOR DID His flesh SUFFER DECAY. (NASB)**

The original Greek word used is **"Hades"** in the New Testament and is translated in English as **"grave"** just as **"Sheol"** is in Hebrew. So the words **Sheol** and **Hades** are the equivalent of the same word, the first being a Hebrew word and the later being a Greek word.

The Hebrew word **Sheol** used by David in **Psalm 16** was a very indefinite, imprecise word. It's meaning was not precise enough to tell us what happened after death. A good description of Sheol is that it is the abode of the dead, it is the grave, it is the pit, and it is the underworld. That was the vantage point of where David was looking from—and peering into the future, seeing Jesus' death and resurrection.

As God continues to reveal truth, we learn from the New Testament more about hell. The apostle Peter uses the Greek word **"Hades"** in the place of the Hebrew word "Sheol" in the book of Acts. Hades is used **only for unbelievers** and it is a place of torment.

Luke 16:23 [23]"In **Hades** he lifted up his eyes, **being in torment**... ((**NASB**))

Luke above is describing Hades as a place of torment, plain and simple. Since humans are made with a spirit, a soul, and a body (**1 Thessalonians 5: 23**) the unbeliever's spirit and soul go to the place of suffering called Hades when he dies, and his body goes to the grave and does see decay.

The result of Jesus dying on the cross for our sins was that he spent time in the grave as well as Hades. David describes it as **Sheol in Psalm 16:10,** Peter describes it as **Hades** in **Acts 2:23,** and the English language describes it as **grave. Christ's body** spent time in the **grave** while his **soul** spent time in **Sheol (Hades) (Hell) (all the same, in three different languages).**

What David foresaw in Psalm 16 was Jesus would not remain in this disembodied state with his **body in grave and his spirit and Soul in Sheol.**

Though he entered **Sheol (Hades) (Hell), Jesus did not remain there;** and his body was miraculously preserved for three days and night and did not decay.

As "believers," we can have the same assurance. **At the death of a believer**, scripture teaches his or her **spirit and soul** will go to be home with Christ in Heaven, while his or her earthly **body** goes to the **grave.**

2 Corinthians 5: 6-8 [6]Therefore we are always confident, knowing that, whilst **we are at home in the body, we are absent from the Lord:**

[7](For we walk by faith, not by sight:)

[8]We are confident, I say, and **willing rather to be absent from the body, and to be present with the Lord.**

The apostle Paul longed to depart from this earth and be with Jesus. Paul had no fear of dying. He knew he would be going to be with Jesus and a much better place:

> **Philippians 1:23** [23]For I am in a strait betwixt two, **having a desire to depart, and to be with Christ; which is far better:**

In Closing:

In chapters 4 and 5, we can see clearly that the Bible does teach us that there is a place called **hell** and that Jesus loved us so much he was willing to suffer, die, and spend time in hell for **all of mankind**. He was the perfect payment for our sins. He paid the penalty for our sins so we would not have to. Jesus spent three days in the grave and hell for the punishment we deserved and then he arose from the grave bodily and returned to his Father, and now he sits at the right hand of God.

> **Ephesians 4: 8-11** [8]Wherefore he saith, When **he ascended up on high**, he led captivity captive, and **gave gifts unto men**.
>
> [9](Now that he ascended, what is it but that **he also descended first into the lower parts of the earth?**
>
> [10]**He that descended is the same also that ascended up far above all heavens**, that he might fill all things.)

Just think how much God loves us if he was willing to spend time in hell for you and me even though we are the ones deserving the punishment for our sins. We who believe in him **will not spend one second of time in hell** but go straight to the Lord to be with him forever. This is the gospel message the Bible teaches- Jesus took the punishment for sin in our place. **How about getting to know the God of the Bible who loves you so very much?**

God loves you and so do I!

The Story of Jesus Christ and His Crucifixion - As Foretold in the Old Testament

Chapter 6

It was Easter time and my wife, kids, and I were going to visit our family on both sides of the family tree. We have immediate family members who do not believe in God; or if they do, they do not honor him. I wanted to find a way this Easter to communicate our faith in Jesus Christ and why we believe to our lost loved ones. I began to look in the Bible, and it came to me I should share the Easter story found in the gospels of the New Testament with them before we had dinner. As I prepared to do just that on the Friday night before Easter, suddenly God inspired me to look at the story of the Crucifixion of our Lord and Savior **Jesus**, not from the New Testament where the eyewitnesses tell their testimony **after the fact**, but from the Old Testament that foretells the story **before it happened**. How powerful a witness it was to my own faith in Jesus that prophecy which was written about the Messiah 400 to 1,000 years or more before the event took place was completely fulfilled by Jesus when he came and lived on earth. We know these are prophecies before the facts of his crucifixion because we have unearthed ancient scrolls of the Old Testament that date back older than Jesus, such as the "Dead Sea Scrolls" found in 1947. Some of the scrolls and fragments of scripture found there date back as old as 200 B.C. No other ancient manuscripts that scholars hold as trustworthy have this type of evidence for accuracy that we have today in the Old Testament. It is still the same**. The Old Testament has not changed!**

Here is a step by step of the story of **Jesus using the prophecies of the Old Testament and how Jesus fulfilled them in the New Testament:**

1) The Messiah will be born in Bethlehem from the tribe of Judah.

> **Micah 5:2 (written approx. 700 B.C.)** [2]But thou, **Bethlehem** Ephratah (**Meaning of Ephratah is fruitful**), though thou be little among the thousands of **Judah**, yet out of thee shall he come forth unto me that is to be **ruler in Israel**; whose goings forth have been **from of old, from everlasting. (From of old and everlasting: this is not speaking of merely a man, the Messiah is much more as we will see)**
>
> **Genesis 49:10 (written approx. 1450 B.C.)** [10]The sceptre shall not depart **from Judah**, nor a lawgiver from between his feet, until **Shiloh (Shiloh is a term used in reference to Messiah.)** come; and unto him shall the gathering of the people be.

Fulfilled by Jesus: Matthew 2:1 [1]Now when **Jesus was born in Bethlehem** of Judaea in the days of Herod the king, behold, there came wise men from the east to Jerusalem,

2) The way is prepared by a messenger.

> **Isaiah 40:3 (written approx. 700 B.C.)** [3]The voice of him that crieth in the wilderness, **Prepare ye the way of the LORD**, make straight in the desert a highway for our God.

Malachi 3: 1 (written approx. 450 B.C.) [1]Behold, **I will send my messenger**, and he shall prepare the way before me:

Fulfilled by John the Baptist: Matthew 3: 1-3 [1]In those days came John the Baptist, preaching in the wilderness of Judaea,

[2]And saying, Repent ye: for the kingdom of heaven is at hand.

[3]For **this is he that was spoken of by the prophet Esaias (Isaiah)**, saying, The voice of one crying in the wilderness, Prepare ye the way of the Lord, make his paths straight.

3) Triumphant Entry into Jerusalem.

Zechariah 9: 9 (written approx. 520 B.C.) [9]Rejoice greatly, O daughter of Zion; shout, O daughter of Jerusalem: behold, **thy King cometh unto thee**: he is just, and **having salvation; lowly, and riding upon an ass**, and upon a **colt** the foal of an ass.

Fulfilled by Jesus: Luke 19: 35-37 "[35]And they brought him to Jesus: and **they cast their garments upon the colt**, and they set Jesus thereon.

[36]And as he went, they spread their clothes in the way.

[37]And when he was come nigh, even now at the descent of the mount of Olives, the whole multitude of the disciples began to rejoice and praise God with a loud voice for all the mighty works that they had seen;

And it is also confirmed in **Mark 11: 4-11** [4]And they went their way, and found the **colt** tied by the door without in a place where two ways met; and they loose him.

[5]And certain of them that stood there said unto them, What do ye, loosing the colt?

[6]And they said unto them even as Jesus had commanded: and they let them go.

[7]And they brought the colt to Jesus, and cast their garments on him; and he sat upon him.

[8]And many spread their garments in the way: and others cut down branches off the trees, and strawed them in the way.

[9]And they that went before, and they that followed, cried, saying, **Hosanna; Blessed is he that cometh in the name of the Lord:**

[10]Blessed be the kingdom of our father David, that cometh in the name of the Lord: **Hosanna in the highest. (Hosanna means "Salvation" and all of heaven and earth should shout Hooray for Salvation is here!)**

[11]And **Jesus entered into Jerusalem**, and into the temple: and when he had looked round about upon all things, and now the eventide was come, he went out unto Bethany with the twelve

4) Betrayed by a close friend.

Psalm 41: 9 (written approx. 1,000 B.C.) [9]Yea, **mine own familiar friend**, in whom I trusted, which did eat of my bread, hath lifted up his heel against me.

Also, the friend did it for thirty pieces of silver.

Zechariah 11:12 (written approx. 520 B.C.) [12]And I said unto them, If ye think good, give me my price; and if not, forbear. So they weighed for my price **thirty pieces of silver.**

Fulfilled by Judas Iscariot, a follower of Jesus- the one who betrayed him:

Matthew 26: 47-48 [47]And while he yet spake, lo, **Judas**, one of the twelve, came, and with him a great multitude with swords and staves, from the chief priests and elders of the people.

[48]**Now he that betrayed him gave them a sign, saying, Whomsoever I shall kiss,** that same is he: hold him fast.

Matthew 27: 3-4 [3]When Judas, who had betrayed him, saw that Jesus was condemned, he was seized with remorse and **returned the thirty silver coins** to the chief priests and the elders. [4]"I have sinned," he said, "for I have betrayed innocent blood."

5) Silent before his accusers.

Isaiah 53: 7 (written approx. 700 B.C.) [7]He was oppressed, and he was afflicted, yet **he opened not his mouth**: he is brought as a lamb to the slaughter, and as a sheep before her shearers is dumb, so **he openeth not his mouth.**

Fulfilled by Jesus: Matthew 27: 12–14 [12]And when he was accused of the chief priests and elders, **he answered nothing.**

[13]Then said Pilate unto him, Hearest thou not how many things they witness against thee?

[14]And **he answered him to never a word**; insomuch that the governor marvelled greatly.

And **Mark 15: 4-5** [4]And Pilate asked him again, saying, Answerest thou nothing? behold how many things they witness against thee.

[5]But **Jesus yet answered nothing**; so that Pilate marvelled.

6) Spat on and struck, hated without reason, sneered and mocked.

Psalm 22: 6-8 (written approx. 1000 B.C.) [6]But I am a worm, and no man; a reproach of men, and despised of the people.

[7]All they that see me **laugh me to scorn**: they shoot out the lip, they **shake the head**, saying,

[8]He trusted on the LORD that he would deliver him: let him deliver him, seeing he delighted in him.

Psalm 35: 15-16 [15]But at **my stumbling they rejoiced** and gathered themselves together;
The smiters whom I did not know gathered together against me,
They slandered me without ceasing.

[16]Like godless jesters at a feast,
They gnashed at me with their teeth. **(NASB)**

Isaiah 50: 6 (written approx. 700 B.C.) [6]I gave **my back** to the smiters, and **my cheeks** to them that plucked off the hair: **I hid not my face from shame and spitting.**

Fulfilled by Jesus: Matthew 26: 67-68 [67]Then they **spit in his face** and **struck him with their fists.** Others slapped him [68]and said, "Prophesy to us, Christ. Who hit you?" **(NIV)**

7) Jesus is crucified. Please read in full Isaiah 53, Psalm 22, and Zechariah 12.

> **Isaiah 53: 5** [5] But he was **pierced for our transgressions**, he was crushed for our iniquities; the punishment that brought us peace was upon him,

I want to cry when I read:

> **Psalm 22: 14-17** [14]I am poured out like water, and **all my bones are out of joint**: my heart is like wax; it is melted in the midst of my bowels.
>
> [15]My strength is dried up like a potsherd; and my tongue cleaveth to my jaws; and thou hast brought me into the dust of death.
>
> [16]For dogs have compassed me: the assembly of the wicked have inclosed me: **they pierced my hands and my feet.** [17]I may tell all my bones: **they look and stare upon me.**
>
> **Zechariah 12: 10** [10]And I will pour upon the house of David, and upon the inhabitants of Jerusalem, the spirit of grace and of supplications: and **they shall look upon me whom they have pierced,** and they shall mourn for him, as one mourneth for his only son, and shall be in bitterness for him, as one that is in bitterness for his firstborn.

The type of Roman crucifixion Jesus suffered had not yet been invented when the prophets prophesized of Jesus' crucifixion, yet it was **fulfilled by Jesus:**

> **Mark 15: 24** [24]And **when they had crucified him**, they parted his garments, casting lots upon them, what every man should take.

Matthew 27: 35 [35]And **they crucified him**, and parted his garments, casting lots: that it might be fulfilled which was spoken by the prophet, **They parted my garments among them, and upon my vesture did they cast lots.**

8) Jesus cries out!

Psalm 22:1 [1]**My God, my God, why hast thou forsaken me?** why art thou so far from helping me, and **from the words of my roaring?**

Fulfilled by Jesus: Matthew 27: 45–46 [45]Now from the sixth hour there was darkness over all the land unto the ninth hour.

[46]And about the ninth hour **Jesus cried with a loud voice**, saying, Eli, Eli, lama sabachthani? that is to say**, My God, my God, why hast thou forsaken me?**

9) They gamble for his clothing.

Psalm 22:18 [18]They part my garments among them, and **cast lots upon my vesture.**

Fulfilled: John 19: 23-24 [23]Then the soldiers**, when they had crucified Jesus**, took his garments, and made four parts, to every soldier a part; and also his coat: now the coat was without seam, woven from the top throughout.

[24]They said therefore among themselves, Let us not rend it, but **cast lots for it**, whose it shall be: **that the scripture might be fulfilled,** which saith, **They parted my raiment among them, and for my vesture they did cast lots.** These things therefore the soldiers did.

10) No bones broken, his side is pierced.

Psalm 34: 20 [20]He keepeth all his bones: **not one of them is broken.**

Zechariah 12:10 [10]And I will pour upon the house of David, and upon the inhabitants of Jerusalem, the spirit of grace and of supplications: and **they shall look upon me whom they have pierced**

Fulfilled by Jesus: John 19: 33–34 "[33]But when they came to Jesus and found that he was already dead, **they did not break his legs.** [34]Instead, one of the soldiers pierced Jesus' side with a spear, bringing a sudden flow of blood and water. [35]The man who saw it has given testimony, and his testimony is true. He knows that he tells the truth, and he testifies so that you also may believe. **[36]These things happened so that the scripture would be fulfilled: "Not one of his bones will be broken," [37]and, as another scripture says, "They will look on the one they have pierced."** (NIV)

11) Darkness shall cover the land.

Amos 8: 9 (written approx. 760 B.C.) [9]And it shall come to pass in that day, saith the Lord GOD, that **I will cause the sun to go down at noon, and I will darken the earth** in the clear day:

Fulfilled: Matthew 27: 45 [45]Now from the sixth hour **there was darkness over all the land** unto the ninth hour.

12) Buried with the rich.

Isaiah 53: 9 [9]And he made **his grave with the wicked, and with the rich in his death**; because he had done no violence, neither was any deceit in his mouth.

Fulfilled by Jesus: Matthew 27: 57–60 "57As evening approached, there came a **rich man from Arimathea, named Joseph**, who had himself become a disciple of Jesus. 58Going to Pilate, he asked for Jesus' body, and Pilate ordered that it be given to him. 59Joseph took the body, wrapped it in a clean linen cloth, 60and **placed it in his own new tomb** that he had cut out of the rock. He rolled a big stone in front of the entrance to the tomb and went away." **(NIV)**

13) To be resurrected and to ascend to God's right hand.

Psalm 16: 9-10 9Therefore my heart is glad, and my glory rejoiceth: my flesh also shall rest in hope.

10For **thou wilt not leave my soul in hell**; neither wilt thou suffer **thine Holy One to see corruption.**

Psalm 49:15 15But **God will redeem my soul from the power of the grave**: for he shall receive me.

Psalm 68:18 18You have ascended on high, You have led captive Your captives **(NASB)**

Fulfilled by Jesus: Mark 16: 19 19So then after the Lord had spoken unto them, he was received up into heaven, and **sat on the right hand of God.**

Hebrews 1: 3 3Who being the brightness of his glory, and **the express image of his person**, and upholding all things by the word of his power, **when he had by himself purged our sins**, sat down on **the right hand of the Majesty on high**:

It excites me so that we can tell the story of the birth, death, and resurrection of **my Lord Jesus Christ from the Old Testament only, written by many different writers 1450 years to 450 years**

before it happened. In the New Testament, we have eyewitness accounts from the disciples; all but one of which died horrible martyr's deaths for their faith in Jesus Christ. You must ask yourself would they be willing to die for what they knew was a lie? **Would you?**They were cowards in hiding after the crucifixion of Jesus. They were afraid that their association with Jesus could bring them the same demise as Jesus. Then something happened that all the disciples began preaching the gospel without fear. Their preaching the good news eventually brought them death. They were stoned to death, they were hanged, crucified, for what? A lie?What caused the disciples to become so brave and willing to die?The answer is that they were eyewitnesses to the resurrection of Jesus Christ. There is no other explanation that could turn such cowards around so that they became so very brave and preached the good news until death.

There are many other prophecies Jesus fulfilled in his life that reveal the truth of the Scriptures, such as being crucified with thieves (see **Isaiah 53:12** and **Matthew 27:38**) and at his betrayal money would be thrown in the temple and then given to buy a potter's field. (See **Zechariah 11:13** and **Matthew 27: 5-7**.) The mathematical odds that one person, that person being Jesus Christ could fulfill all the prophecies about the Jewish Messiah is **scientifically impossible... but He did!** The Bible is absolute truth. **God died for our sins! Thank you, Jesus!**

God loves you and so do I!

THE HISTORY OF THE WORLD – IN THE PARABLE – "THE WRETCHED TENANTS"

Chapter 7

I was reading my Bible, and God showed me something wonderful. God does this all the time for anyone who will spend time in his word. There are precious gems throughout his word. As I read this parable, "The Wretched Tenants," in **Matthew 21: 33-41**, God's Spirit opened up to me, and his truth came pouring into me like a flood. As I read this parable, God showed me a truth within this story. I saw the entire history of his relationship with mankind: past, present, and future. Let me present to you what God revealed to me in the Spirit, and I pray it will speak to you.

In my studies in the Bible, especially the Old Testament, God's dealings with his chosen people (the descendants of Abraham) is a lesson for all mankind. The chosen people's dealings with God are a microcosm of all of mankind in every generation. Looking back at Israel in the Old Testament is like looking at our front-page news. In many of the stories, I see a story within a story. I find that the failings of Israel to honor the one true God represent all people's failings; we fail to honor the one true, living God. From the beginning, since Adam and Eve first sinned in the garden, mankind has failed; and we continue to do so to this very day.

The parable starts out:

> **Matthew 21: 33** "Listen to another parable: There was a **landowner** who planted a **vineyard**. He put a **wall** around it, dug a **winepress** in it and built a **watchtower**." **(NIV)**

We know this parable is speaking of Israel. **(See Psalm 80: 8, Jeremiah 2:21, Isaiah 5 1:7.)** God planted his chosen people, the Israelites, into the Promised Land; and God was watching over them. But God was showing me a bigger picture: two stories going on at the same time. In the first story, the **wall** around the **vineyard** is the nation of Israel (preserving them as a distinct people for the Lord); and in the big picture, the second story I am seeing, the vineyard is earth and all of mankind lives in it. God wants a relationship with all his creation and wants to preserve us. The **winepress** signifies the fruit of fellowship, holiness, and love, which Israel should have produced for God; and in the big picture I see, it is all God's people who should produce good fruit. The **watchtower** is Jehovah's watchful care for his chosen people, and in the second story, it is God watching out for all of his creation.

The parable continues after he created this beautiful vineyard:

> **Matthew 21: 33** continued "Then he rented the vineyard to some **farmers** and went away on a journey." **(NIV)**

Israel is the vineyard, and the **farmers** are the people of Israel; but the Holy Spirit has taken its meaning further to me. The Holy Spirit has shown me that this vineyard is the creation story from the **book of Genesis** and that God prepared Earth and made it ready for a tenant (**mankind—we are the farmers**) to come and live in the world. He gave us everything we needed to be fruitful and fill the earth and subdue it.

> **Genesis 1:1** [1]In the beginning **God created the heaven and the earth.**

> **Genesis 1: 27** [27]**So God created man in his own image, in the image of God** created he him; **male and female** created he them.

> **Genesis 1:28** [28]And God blessed them, and God said unto them, Be fruitful, and multiply, and **replenish the earth, and subdue it:** and **have dominion** over the fish of the sea, and over the fowl of the air, and over every living thing that moveth upon the earth.

The parable continues:

> **Matthew 21: 34** "When the harvest time approached, he sent his **servants** to the tenants to collect his fruit." **(NIV)**

God is showing us that history is like the seasons. Farmers plant in the spring; the plants grow and mature in the summer, and are harvested in the autumn. In this case, Jesus was relaying to us that the **servants are God's prophets** he sent to his tenants. God throughout history has sent many prophets to bring not only the chosen people his truth, but so all of mankind would receive it. God wanted to bring us into a relationship with him and to lead us to repentance. God wanted us to love him with all of our hearts and minds as he loves us. He sent us his prophets to tell us this. **But what did his creation choose to do?**

> **Matthew 21: 35-36** "The tenants seized his **servants (prophets)** they beat one, killed another, and stoned a third. Then **he sent other servants** for them, more then the first time, and **the tenants treated them the same way....**" **(NIV)**

How sad. God is seeking to have a relationship with his people. God wants to love us. He sends us his prophets so we can get to know the owner of the vineyard, yet we reject his love. All through history God sent us his prophets; and we would not accept their words. We would kill them, beat them, and drive them away. We did not want anything to do with these prophets or the **Landowner who sent them**. How the Israelites treated the prophets is true history, and Jesus knew this when he spoke of how we treated his prophets in this parable. In the scriptures below is such an example of how mankind treated God's servants:

> **1 Kings 19: 9-10** And the word of the LORD came to him: "What are you doing here, Elijah?"
>
> 10 He replied, "I have been very zealous for the LORD God Almighty. **The Israelites have rejected your covenant**, broken down your altars, and **put your prophets to death with the sword**. I am the only one left, and now **they are trying to kill me too." (NIV)**

But this is not the saddest part. God made the greatest attempt of all to bring us into relationship with him. **God sent his Son.**

> **Matthew 21: 37-39** 37Last of all, **he sent his son** to them. **'They will respect my son,'** he said.
>
> 38"But when the tenants **saw the son**, they said to each other, 'This is the heir. Come, let's kill him and take his inheritance.' **39So they took him and threw him out of the vineyard and killed him. (NIV)**

In this parable, Jesus is telling **us we have seen the son.** Jesus is the rightful owner of the world **(vineyard)** because he created us. The apostle John makes it clear the son of God is our creator:

> **John 1: 1-5** 1In the beginning was the Word, and the Word was with God, and **the Word was God.**
>
> 2The same was in the beginning with God.
>
> **3All things were made by him**; and without him was not any thing made that was made.

[4]In him was life; and the life was the light of men.

[5]And the light shineth in darkness; and the darkness comprehended it not.

Saddest of all, we have killed God's only Son, **our Creator.** God called us into a relationship with him and what did we do? **We reject him**. We kick him out of the vineyard by killing him. We crucified him on that cross because we did not understand his light—his perfect love for his creation.

John 3:16 [16]For God so loved the world, that **he gave his only begotten Son,** that **whosoever believeth in him should not perish, but have everlasting life.**

Wow! Eternal life, for only by believing in God's son. **Eternal life**, a free gift... given to us by God. Forgiveness for our sins by only believing in God's son. So simple—it's easy to have eternal life. Then why is it so difficult for some, for many? **What is keeping you from your free gift of having eternal life with God?**

The parable does not end with our crucifying his only Son. No, there is more. And for those who do not know God's son, you should be a little **(a lot)** frightened.

Matthew 21: 40-41 [40]"Therefore, **when the owner of the vineyard comes, what will he do to those tenants?" (NIV)**

The owner of the vineyard **is coming back. Here comes the scary part...**

[41]"He will bring those **wretches to a wretched end,**" they replied, "and **he will rent the vineyard to other tenants,** who will give him his share of the crop at harvest time." **(NIV)**

The old tenets are wretched to God, and he will kick them out of the vineyard. God brings their existence to a wretched end...how horrible this is. **The new tenants are the ones who will honor God in his special way, by believing in his son, Jesus,** who he sent to **die on the cross for our sins.** There is no saving the wretched in any other way. **We are all the wretched.** We all fall short of the glory of God. All of mankind is wretched because we have not honored him. **Who can save us?** Only one – the name above all names—**Jesus!** The parable goes on to tell us that Jesus is God's way to salvation, and it is the only way. It took a perfect sacrifice only God could perform; no man is worthy to be this sacrifice: only God who is perfect can be. Jesus is God.

> **Matthew 21: 42** 42Jesus saith unto them, **Did ye never read in the scriptures,** The stone **(Jesus is the stone all scripture is built on.) which the builders rejected, (Jesus here was speaking about the leaders of Israel who rejected him, but it is also true with all of mankind throughout history that many have rejected Jesus.)** the same is become the head of the corner **(Now Jesus after his resurrection is the uppermost stone)**: this is the Lord's doing, **and it is marvellous in our eyes?**

Is Jesus marvelous in your eyes? Jesus, Lord and Savior. Do you need a Savior for your sins? May I suggest the one, true Savior: **Jesus**, the name above all names, the topmost stone of God's kingdom. I pray you won't reject the Son of God who was sent by God into our world to redeem us.

This parable, as all the parables Jesus taught, teaches such unique lessons and has true spiritual meaning. There is always a lesson to be learned from what Jesus taught. This parable does demonstrate one important lesson, and the apostle Paul says it very well below.

> **Romans 5: 8** 8But **God demonstrates his own love for us** in this: **While we were still sinners, Christ died for us.**

God loves you and so do I!

Zero in on the Right Word!

Chapter 8

I was meditating on God and happened to look down and see on the kitchen table "**Zero in on the Right Word**!" on the cover of The Merriam Webster Thesaurus. It immediately reminded me of:

> **John 1:1-5** [1]In the beginning was the **Word**, and the **Word** was with God, and the **Word was God.**
>
> [2]The same was in the beginning with God.
>
> [3]**All things were made by him**; and without him was not any thing made that was made.
>
> [4]In him was life; and the light was the light of men.
>
> [5]And **the light (Jesus)** shineth in darkness; and **the darkness (sinful man) comprehended it not.**

John was writing about Jesus in these first five versus, and he tells us he was from the beginning, he is our creator, and he is God.

Many people have trouble understanding this. John is speaking of the Second Person of the Trinity: **Jesus**, and people ask how can this be? **How can there be three persons in one God?** Or they mistakenly believe Christians are worshiping three different gods.

The inspiration for this chapter came as a result of hearing about a heated discussion between a friend of ours and some of her family members. Our friend was frustrated because she knew that she believed in the Trinity but did not know where to find and explain it through her Bible. She did not know where in Scripture to show her family the truth. Her family members remained convinced they were correct in their belief that there is no Trinity even though they could offer no evidence themselves: **this is blind faith**.

God does not ask us to have blind faith in him. There is more than enough evidence that God exists and that God teaches us he is a **Triune God and still only one God.**

Throughout all of scripture, the Holy Bible teaches us of the Triune God Christians believe in. You need to go to the Hebrew text for the Old Testament and the Greek Language for the New Testament to fully understand the meanings of the words used in the Bible for "God." God carefully chose every word because scripture is his inspired word. He wants desperately for us to know him. God knows the Hebrew and Greek languages very well, and he chose his words so we could know him intimately.

God reveals something very exciting and thrilling to me in Genesis, man is made in his image. Christianity has always taught we are made in the image and likeness of God. In Genesis, it is uniquely revealed before God even created man:

> **Genesis 1: 26** 26And **God said, Let us make man in our image, after our likeness:**

Scholars will debate and argue what this means, **"our image"** and **"our likeness."** But the word of God clarifies it very well in the very next verse:

> **Genesis 1: 27** 27So **God created man in his own image, in the image of God created he him**; male and female created he them.

The original text of the Bible was written in Hebrew and the word for God used in both verses above was **"Elohim," which is the plural**

form of a **singular God.** It allows for more than one part of God—a Trinity. I take this literally because I believe God knows Hebrew very well and wanted to reveal himself in this way. Also, God is a God of order and not of confusion- **it is man who gets confused.**

Moses, who is credited with writing Genesis, used the plural form of God instead of the Hebrew words **"El" or "Eloha"** (or Ehoah), **which are all meanings for a singular God only.** If God had used El or Eloha instead and never used Elohim in the Old Testament, **the Trinity would be an impossible teaching.** The Hebrew word "Elohim" is used 2,570 times in the Old Testament, the first time being **Genesis 1: 1** [1]In the beginning **God** created the heaven and the earth.

Elohim is used much more than El and Eloha, which are found 57 times and most often used in poetic writing- 41 times in the Book of Job.

Understanding **Genesis 1: 26-27** is very important to my faith – **God created man in his own image.** From the beginning he was explaining there is only one God, but more than one part of God "Elohim"—**the Trinity**: God the Father, God the Son, And God the Holy Spirit. **God meant what he said when he told us we were made in the image and likeness of God.** We can take this literally. You see, we **(man)** are a Tripartite (three-in-one) also. There are three parts to every person and that makes us **one complete entity; we are spirit, we are soul, and we are body.** This is revealed to us in scripture:

> **Genesis 2: 7** [7]And the LORD God formed man of the dust of the ground, and breathed into his nostrils the breath of life; and **man became a living soul.**

In the book, "The Spiritual Man" by Watchman Nee, he explains that the breath of life became **man's spirit**. Watchman explains that when the spirit was united with man's body, the end result was the soul coming into existence. He explains that is why the scriptures call man a **living soul.**

I first learned from Watchman that man is more than just soul and body. He showed me in scripture there are three parts to man, just as there are Three Persons that make up God. Scripture emphasizes the order of God—God the Father, God the Son, and God the Holy Spirit. That is why I have such faith we are made in God's image: three in one person.

Now look at what the Apostle Paul wrote:

> **1 Thessalonians 5: 23** [23]And the very God of peace sanctify you wholly; and *I pray God* your **whole spirit and soul and body** be preserved blameless unto the coming of our Lord Jesus Christ.

I learned from Watchman that scripture does not divide man into only two parts, but into three parts just as God is shown in scripture as a Trinity. God makes a distinction that separates the spirit from the soul. God places the greatest emphasis on our **spirit**, then our **soul**, and last our **body.** This order is important because just as there is an order to God with God the Father being first and then the Son, and then the Holy Spirit, **our spirit and soul are way more important than our body.** Watchman teaches so much about this. I highly recommend his books if you want to study the Bible with him.

God makes a distinction between the soul and spirit in other places of scripture.

> **Hebrews 4: 12** [12]For the word of God is quick, and powerful, and sharper than any twoedged sword, piercing even to the dividing asunder of **soul and spirit**, and of the joints and marrow, and is a discerner of the thoughts and intents of the heart.

You see, I believe the Bible is clear that we are made in the image and likeness of God **literally,** a tripartite:

1) **Spirit**—the most innermost part of our being, the holy of holies where God communicates with us and dwells within us, and where Satan has no power.

2) **Body**—the outward shell, **the only part of us** that can be seen, touched, and smelled...the body can be sensed with all of our given senses.
3) **Soul**—the combination of spirit and body, it is what makes us unique: you are you and I am me. It is our personality, our likes and dislikes; it is what makes us special and **what God sees as special in each individual.**

So, **in creation we are made in the image and likeness of God—a tripartite**. And just as Jesus is the only part of God that can be seen, it is our body only that can be seen by others. Our spirit and soul are part of us, but cannot be seen.

We are the Temple of God!

It is interesting to note, whether it is the Tabernacle in the Desert or the Temple of God's Holy City, Jerusalem, built by King Solomon, God gave instructions on how the places for worship were to be built. Both had **three major compartments that made up one temple**:

1) **The outer court**—where all persons could come and all could see and all could worship externally.
2) **The inner court or sanctuary**—becomes holy ground and only the priests are allowed to enter. They are there only to serve God but cannot come completely into his presence. There is a veil that separates them from being where God dwells.
3) **The Holy of Holies**—is where God dwells, the most holy compartment of all. No man can enter except one: the high priest and that was for only one-time each year when the high priest offered sacrifice for the sins of Israel.

Now we read **1 Corinthians 3: 16** [16]Know ye not that **ye are the temple of God**, and that **the Spirit of God dwelleth in you**?

Paul is saying to us our bodies are as the temple of God- with **three major parts that make up one body.**

1) **The body**—like the **outer court** it is the external part of us that all can see.
2) **The soul**—like the **inner court** it is our internal part others cannot see. It is where our High Priest works in our lives to change our hearts and minds to do his work, as God is our High Priest. It is what makes us special in God's eyes.
3) **The Spirit**—our **Holy of Holies.** The veil has been torn down by the sanctifying work of our High Priest, **Jesus Christ;** and God dwells in our most inner being. We now have direct access to God always, and he hears our prayers.

So God in his great wisdom has shown us that the temple is designed after his own being—**the triune God.** Mankind has been fashioned after his temple; but more importantly, in creation, God says we are made in the image and likeness of our **triune God and therefore, we are triune human beings.** This is what separates man from any other creature God ever created. Because we are a triune being, we have a spirit. God has not given any other animal this special part—**the spirit.**

Animal lovers, take heart. I do not want to get into a lengthy discussion on this, but I do believe God loves his animals and I believe they will be in heaven when we get there. They do not have a spirit as we do, but **they were given the breath of life from God,** same as us.

> **Genesis 6: 15** [15]And they went in unto Noah into the ark, two and two of **all flesh, wherein is the breath of life.**

And God speaks of animals living with us in heaven.

> **Isaiah 65: 17 and 25** [17]For, behold, **I create new heavens and a new earth**: and the former shall not be remembered, nor come into mind.

> [25]**The wolf and the lamb shall feed together**, and **the lion shall eat straw like the bullock (bull or steer)**: and **dust shall be the serpent's meat (Satan will be no more!)**. They shall not hurt nor destroy in all **my holy mountain**, saith the LORD.

One Scientific Moment: Look again at what Paul wrote above in **1 Thessalonians 5: 23**. Man was created in God's image with a spirit, soul, and body. This does contradict with secular scientists whose agenda is to push only natural ways to explain the origin of the universe. In the scientific community, **natural science** for the most part is the only way allowed to explain the origin of the universe and the origin of life. Natural science by definition does not allow for any outside Intelligent Designer (**God**) to exist. In other words, you must use natural causes to explain how we got something from nothing, how the universe created itself, how a living cell came from a non-living cell, and how an ape-like creature without a soul or spirit became man. Natural Science does not allow for a God of the Bible nor a human to have a spirit or soul because you cannot explain by natural causes how God or the human spirit and soul would have come into existence.

A scientist who takes the approach that creation literally happened as the first 11 chapters of Genesis tells us will not be in conflict with what Paul wrote. The wonderful news I have to share with you is that good science is not in conflict with the Bible and the Bible is not in conflict with good science, as we will see in some of my later chapters when **I only touch on the science that gives evidence that the Bible is true.** There is so much available for you to study, and I will give you resources to go to if you want to study science that does not conflict with the word of God.

More evidence in the scriptures for the Trinity:

God is tripartite: "**Elohim**"

1) God the Father—the one who cannot be seen, the Father God Head of the Trinity. For anyone to look upon his face would mean

instant death for us because of his honor and glory. Our own "spirit" that God created is the most holy part of our human being and like our Father God, **cannot be seen.**

> God warns Moses in **Exodus 33: 20-23** [20]And he said, Thou canst not see my face: **for there shall no man see me, and live.**
> [21]And the LORD said, Behold, there is a place by me, and thou shalt stand upon a rock:
> [22]And it shall come to pass, while my glory passeth by, that I will put thee in a clift of the rock, and will cover thee with my hand while I pass by:
> [23]And I will take away mine hand, and thou shalt see my back parts: **but my face shall not be seen.**

2) God the Son, Jesus—The part of God that can be seen and was seen many times in the Bible, not just in the New Testament, the one who is a perfect sacrifice for our sins, the bridge to life ever after with God, the one the prophecies foretold about, and God in the flesh; and that is why mankind **did see him** and did speak to him. Jesus had a body just like ours, **but he is still God**. Scripture teaches Jesus is from the beginning.

In the same chapter of Exodus above where **you cannot look upon God and live**, you see Moses having **a face-to-face meeting with God**. Only the second person of the Trinity is visible to man, and **you can look upon him** and live.

> **Exodus 33: 11** [11]And **the LORD spake unto Moses face to face, as a man speaketh unto his friend.** And he turned again into the camp: but his servant Joshua, the son of Nun, a young man, departed not out of the tabernacle.

Just think; Moses and God meet face-to-face and God speaks to Moses as if he is his friend! Taken literally, it is the second person of the Trinity, **Jesus,** who appeared in this meeting.

> **Genesis 17: 1** [1]And when Abram was ninety years old and nine, **the LORD appeared to Abram,** and said unto him, I am the **Almighty God (El Shaddai)**; walk before me, and be thou perfect.

The Hebrew word for "**Almighty**" allows for the teaching of the Trinity. "**Shaddai**" is the plural form of the root word "**Shadah.**" If God had used Shadah instead of Shaddai, just as El instead Elohim throughout the Old Testament, the Trinity teaching would be impossible to show. God tells Abraham to walk with him. They have this conversation together where God reveals the covenant he is going to make with him. If you take this literally, as I do, Jesus and Abraham are walking together and Abraham is in no danger of his life seeing and looking upon Almighty God as Moses did.

> **Genesis 18: 1** [1]**And the LORD appeared unto him (Abraham—God changed Abram's name)** in the plains of Mamre: and **he sat in the tent door in the heat of the day;**

God is described above to be sitting in the tent door, most likely in the hottest part of the day. I do take this literally, as I do all the above verses, and I see Jesus sitting with Abraham.

One more example I will give you of the second person of the Trinity in the Old Testament is when God spoke to Moses and told him he appeared to Abraham, Isaac, and Jacob.

> **Exodus 6: 2-3** [2]And God spake unto Moses, and said unto him, I am the LORD:
>
> [3]And **I appeared unto Abraham, unto Isaac, and unto Jacob, by the name of God Almighty**, but by my name **JEHOVAH (Name for God meaning "Savior" or "Deliverer")** was I not known to them.

"JEHOVAH," meaning Savior or Deliverer—**DO NOT MISS THE IMPORTANCE OF THIS.** Jesus is the savior of the world.

Below is an interesting fact; Jesus himself declared he was before Abraham. Jesus was in the temple teaching of who he was, and he claimed to be **"I am," which is a Hebrew name used for God.**

> **John 8: 56-59 [56]Your father Abraham rejoiced to see my day**: and he saw it, and was glad.
>
> [57]Then said the Jews unto him, Thou art not yet fifty years old, and **hast thou seen Abraham?**
>
> **[58]Jesus said unto them,** Verily, verily, I say unto you, **Before Abraham was, I am.**

The Jews knew what Jesus was declaring himself to be—**God,** and in their disbelief, they were so angry with Jesus for what he said; they wanted to stone him to death for blasphemy.

> **[59]Then took they up stones to cast at him: but Jesus hid himself**, and went out of the temple, going through the midst of them, and so passed by.

Listen to these Samaritans who came to faith after hearing Jesus speak, the apostle John recorded their experience. He wrote:

> **John 4: 42** [42]And said unto the woman, **Now we believe**, not because of thy saying: for **we have heard him ourselves,** and **know that this is indeed the Christ, the Saviour of the world.**

I want the special blessing that Jesus gave after his resurrection; I hope you want it too. It is given to everyone living at this very moment.

> **John 20: 29** [29]Jesus saith unto him, Thomas, because thou hast seen me, thou hast believed: **blessed are they that have not seen, and yet have believed.**

I believe Jesus is telling us above that there is a very special blessing waiting for us in heaven for believing in him even though we never saw him with our own eyes. He is going to commend us for our faith.

In the New Testament, it is crystal clear it teaches that Jesus and God are one being. Just as the Old Testament writers teach us God is Elohim, the Second Person of the Trinity is clearly revealed now in the New Testament. These scriptures below are but a sample of what you can find in the New Testament that testifies to who Jesus really is:

> **John 10: 30 [30]I and my Father are one. (Jesus spoke these words)**
>
> **Colossians 1: 15 [15]Who is the image of the invisible God,**
>
> **Hebrews 1: 3** [3]Who being the brightness of his glory, and **the express image of his person, (NIV)**
>
> **1 Timothy 3: 16** [16]And without controversy great is the mystery of godliness: **God was manifest in the flesh (visible, obvious)**, justified in the Spirit, seen of angels, preached unto the Gentiles, believed on in the world, received up into glory.
>
> **2 Corinthians 4:4** [4]In whom the god of this world **(Satan)** hath blinded the minds of them **which believe not**, lest the light of the glorious gospel of **Christ, who is the image of God**, should shine unto them.

Also, the Gospels of Matthew, Mark, Luke, and John as well as the witness of Apostle Paul, bear witness to Jesus as God. We will see many passages of scripture in future chapters testifying about Jesus.

We have seen scripture for both God the Father and God the Son. Now scripture reveals the third person of the Trinity—the **Holy Spirit**. He is mentioned numerous times in the Old Testament and fully revealed in the New Testament.

3) The Holy Spirit—God who is Spirit. He cannot be seen. (Note: **God the Son is the only part of the Trinity that can be seen.**) He is the Spirit of God **that is everywhere**, the one who convicts you of your sins, the one who leads you to belief in God being your Savior, the Counselor in the lives of believers, and the Spirit of God living in believers.

The first mentioning of the Holy Spirit came very early in scripture:

> **Genesis 1: 2** "... And the **Spirit of God (Elohim)** moved upon the face of the waters." Here is the earliest mention of the Spirit of God—the Holy Spirit—**Third Person of the Trinity.**

> **Psalm 51: 11** 11Cast me not away from thy presence; and take not thy **holy spirit** from me.

> **Isaiah 11: 2** 2And the **spirit of the LORD** shall rest upon him, **the spirit of wisdom and understanding, the spirit of counsel and might, the spirit of knowledge and of the fear of the LORD**;

The Holy Spirit has been revealed from the very beginning. He is God. He is the spirit of wisdom and understanding, counsel and might, and of knowledge and awe of God. In the New Testament, we learn we can receive him and he will dwell in us. This was frightening to me before I became a believer but I now know it is so wonderful to receive him.

In the New Testament, Jesus testifies of the Holy Spirit:

> **John 14: 16-17** 16And I **(Jesus speaking)** will pray the Father, and he shall give you **another Comforter**, that he may **abide with you for ever**; **(Be with you forever!)**

> 17Even the **Spirit of truth**; whom the **world cannot receive, because it seeth him not, neither knoweth him**:

but ye know him; for **he dwelleth with you, and shall be in you. (The Holy Spirit will dwell in the believer.)**

In the book of Matthew, the clearest evidence for the Trinity **came from Jesus himself**.

Matthew 28: 19 [19]Go ye therefore, and teach all nations, baptizing them in the name of **the Father**, and of **the Son**, and of **the Holy Ghost**:

Jesus is revealing the Three Persons of the Trinity above—all being equal, all being God, all being one God. "**Elohim**" in the Old Testament describes in the Hebrew language the wholeness, oneness, and the completeness of God.

So the Scriptures of both the Old and New Testaments allow for the Trinity and the **oneness of God**: Father, Son, and Holy Spirit. We will revisit this subject of the Trinity in Chapter 21 when I present some more evidence for the Trinity. It is important that we can find and defend what we believe in scripture, or we better start searching for the truth; and that truth only comes from God.

I have presented evidence that Jesus Christ is God using the Scriptures. We will continue in this book to look at more ways all of scripture reveals who Jesus really is—our Creator God. It is my faith that the Bible is the biography of **Jesus Christ** starting in Genesis and ending in Revelation.

Do you want to get to know my God, my Savior... my everything? He knows you, and he wants you to know him. He wants to be your Father; he wants to be your friend. God is a gentleman; he is waiting for you to invite him in.

Revelations 3: 20 [20]Behold, I stand at the door, and knock: **if any man hear my voice, and open the door**, I will come in to him, and will sup with him, and he with me.

The evidence I presented was to wet your appetite to get to know the true God:**The God of the Bible, the God that loves you**. There are over 10,000 religions out there in the world, but there is only **one**

God that teaches He took the punishment in your place for you and your sins. All God asks of you is that you repent of your sins, ask forgiveness, and believe in Jesus Christ as Lord and Savior, that he died for your sins and arose from the dead. His resurrection is our sign that **we will live forever with him** if we will ask God into our hearts.

A definition describing faith is: "A very strong belief in something in which there is no proof."

I do not necessarily agree with this definition. I believe God has shown us the evidence in the scriptures—**It is not blind proof**. The Bible says **we are without excuse.**

> **Romans 1: 20 [20]For the invisible things of him from the creation of the world are clearly seen, being understood by the things that are made**, even his eternal power and Godhead; **so that they are without excuse:**

When you look at all the scriptures written, God does not demand anything from us except one thing—**our belief in Jesus Christ and his resurrection. Salvation comes from faith, and it is by God's grace we are saved—a free gift.**

God loves us. Are you ready to love him back?

David's Song of praise to God – 2 Samuel 22

Chapter 9

Wow! **Chapter 22 in 2 Samuel** just blows me away! Written between **930 and 722 B.C.**, this passage of scripture took place approx. 1,000 years before Jesus was born. It is one of those very special passages of scripture that gives us great insight to who **Jesus Christ** is. It also foretells to us what God was feeling when mankind crucified his Son on the cross.

Old Testament scripture describes **two aspects of the Messiah.**

1) The suffering Messiah—foretelling all the pain and agony he would go through when he came into this world the first time.
2) The triumphant Messiah—this is who the Jewish people have always been looking for and they continue to do so today. They choose to ignore the prophecies of the suffering Messiah.

In this one chapter of the Bible, God shows us both aspects of the Messiah. In the first 4 verses, King David sings praises to God; he gives us messianic insight as to what he is seeing. We see him singing praises that perfectly describe who Jesus is as the **trium-**

phant Messiah. Starting in verse 5 of this chapter, David 's writing turns to the suffering Messiah.

As David opens with his praise to God, listen to his words. Knowing what Jesus claimed he did for mankind on the cross, should we not join in praises to our God most high. **Can you see him?**

> **Verses 1 - 4**: 1And David spake unto the LORD the words of this song in the day that **the LORD had delivered him out of the hand of all his enemies,** and out of the hand of Saul:

Through God resurrecting Jesus from the grave, He has delivered Jesus from his enemies. His enemies are not of this world. His true enemies are Satan and his demons.

> 2And he said, The **LORD is my rock**, and **my fortress**, and **my deliverer;**
>
> 3The God of my rock; **in him will I trust**: he is **my shield**, and the **horn of my salvation**, my high tower, and **my refuge, my saviour; thou savest me** from violence.
>
> 4I will **call on the LORD**, who is worthy to be praised: **so shall I be saved** from mine enemies.

Verses 2 through 4 above describe my **Jesus**. He is my deliverer, my refuge, and the hope of my salvation—my **Savior!** He saved me from my enemies. Scripture gives us spiritual truths that cannot be seen by our eyes but are still very true and real. Spiritually, mankind's enemy is Satan and his demons. Jesus has delivered me from his clutches. **How did Jesus save me?**He did it by what he did on the cross for my sins.

David continues, and now you can see him prophesizing about the **suffering Messiah** in the verses below. **Can you see Jesus hanging on the cross?**

> **Verses 5 - 7:** 5**When the waves of death compassed me,** the floods of ungodly men made me afraid;
>
> 6The **sorrows of hell compassed me about**; the snares of death prevented me;
>
> 7In my distress **I called upon the LORD**, and cried to my God: and he did hear my voice out of his temple, and **my cry did enter into his ears.**

My Lord and my God—how Jesus suffered on the cross! Scripture says he was afraid, and he cries out to his Father; and God hears him. We know from Matthew's and Mark's accounts in the New Testament of his death on the cross that Jesus cried out to his Father in heaven with these horrific words:

> **Matthew 27: 46** 46And about the ninth hour **Jesus cried with a loud voice**, saying, Eli, Eli, lama sabachthani? that is to say, **My God, my God, why hast thou forsaken me?**
>
> **Mark 15: 34** 34And at the ninth hour **Jesus cried with a loud voice**, saying, Eloi, Eloi, lama sabachthani? which is, being interpreted, **My God, my God, why hast thou forsaken me?**

Returning to **2 Samuel 22**, what happened next? What happened after Jesus cried out to his Father as he was dying on the cross? **God heard his son's cries,** and **God was angry!**

> **Verses 8 - 10:** 8Then the earth shook and trembled; the foundations of heaven moved and shook, **because he was wroth. (God was angry!)**
>
> 9There went up a **smoke out of his nostrils, and fire out of his mouth** devoured: coals were kindled by it.

[10]He bowed the heavens also, and came down; and **darkness was under his feet.**

Look closely now and see the further accounts from **2 Samuel and Matthew** of what God did next.

Verses 12 - 16: [11]And he rode upon a cherub, and did fly: and he was seen upon the wings of the wind.

[12]And **he made darkness pavilions round about him, dark waters, and thick clouds of the skies.**

[13]Through the brightness before him were coals of fire kindled.

[14]The LORD thundered from heaven, and the most High uttered his voice.

[15]And he sent out arrows, **and scattered them; (those who hung and watched Jesus on the cross) lightning, and discomfited them.**

[16]And the channels of the sea appeared, the foundations of the world were discovered, at the rebuking of the LORD, at the **blast of the breath of his nostrils.**

What King David is saying above is that God used the **canopy of darkness** to come and see his Son on the cross. God scattered all of the enemies of his Son, using **dark clouds, lightning.** and an **earthquake** to shake the earth.

In the New Testament account, from the **book of Matthew, we see exactly what King David was foretelling at Jesus' death.** Matthew writes:

Matthew 27: 45: [45]Now from the sixth hour **there was darkness over all the land** unto the ninth hour. **(God used the canopy of darkness to come see his son on the cross!)**

Matthew 27: 50-54: 50Jesus, when he had cried again with a loud voice, yielded up the ghost. (He died for our sins!)

51And, behold, the veil of the temple was rent in twain from the top to the bottom; and **the earth did quake**, and the rocks rent; **(The thick veil in the temple in Jerusalem tore from top to bottom from the earthquake's power)**

This thick veil was the curtain that blocked the entrance into the Holy of Holies of the temple, where God himself had his tabernacle and dwelt here on earth. This veil separated the Holy of Holies from the outer court where all could come, visit, and worship outwardly (apart from God) but could not go further. No one was allowed to enter the Holies of Holy except the High Priest and that was only once a year. Because of what Jesus did at the cross, God tore this heavy, thick veil to show us the veil is no longer required. Through Jesus Christ, our relationship with God has been restored; and we can now have direct access to God through his Son.

52And the graves were opened; and **many bodies of the saints which slept arose**,

In chapter 28, we will learn that Jesus Christ was the Firstfruits to be resurrected. We are really celebrating the Feast of Firstfruits at Easter. Jesus was the first to rise; and because of this, there will be a second to rise, and a third, and a fourth, and so on. As a sign that the resurrection really occurred, Jesus brought forth a few Firstfruits of his labor (performed on the cross). He did this by taking some saints that were dead in the grave and allowing them to rise and be seen by many after he first had risen.

53And **came out of the graves after his resurrection**, and went into the holy city, and appeared unto many.

54Now when the centurion, and they that were with him, watching Jesus, saw the earthquake, and those things that

> were done, they feared greatly, saying, **Truly this was the Son of God**.

Returning to 2 Samuel 22, after Jesus gave his life for us at the cross, we hear from Jesus after his **resurrection**. We hear how God raised him up from the grave and **saved him from his enemy, Satan**. In God's strength, Jesus was able to overcome the enemy; and we learn that he takes his rightful place, seated at the right hand of the father, his name above all names. We now see the **triumphant Messiah.**

> **Verses 17 - 20**: 17He sent from above, **he took me; he drew me out of many waters; (See this as the resurrection!).**
>
> 18He delivered me from my strong enemy **(Satan)**, and **from them that hated me: (Do you hate Jesus?)** for they were too strong for me. **(Jesus is showing us his humanity)**
>
> 19They prevented me in the day of **my calamity (the day of his crucifixion)**: **but the LORD was my stay. (Jesus always trusted in his Father.)**
>
> **20He brought me forth also into a large place (heaven)**: he delivered me, **because he delighted in me.**

Why did God find such delight in Jesus? Simple—because God the Son is the only one to have ever lived a perfect life; he kept all of God's commandments. Jesus kept all of the laws that no man could keep. Jesus was righteous before God and perfect. **This is very important to our own salvation,** as we will see.

Jesus speaking again:

> **Verses 21 - 25** 21The LORD rewarded me according to **my righteousness**: according to the cleanness of my hands hath he recompensed me.

> [22]**For I have kept the ways of the LORD**, and have not wickedly departed from my God. **(Jesus did not sin!)**

> [23]For all his judgments were before me: and **as for his statutes, I did not depart from them. (Again, Jesus did not sin—he did not depart from the law!)**

> [24]I was also upright before him, and have kept myself from mine iniquity.

I want to pause here and reflect on the scripture above. We know this is Jesus and not King David scripture is speaking of. Verses 21-23 describe the one person who kept all the ways of God and never departed from His laws—**Ten Commandments**. This is not King David described above because scripture tells us that he committed adultery and murder.

> [25]Therefore the LORD hath recompensed me according to **my righteousness**; according to my cleanness in his eye sight.

Verse 25 declares Jesus is righteous. In the verses that follow, we can know what **God requires** in order to enter his kingdom—to be saved! **Do you meet the requirements?**

> **Verses 26 - 28**: [26] "To the **faithful** you show yourself **faithful**, to the **blameless** you show yourself **blameless**,

> [27] to the **pure** you show yourself **pure,** but to the crooked you show yourself shrewd.

> [28] **You save the humble**, but your eyes are on **the haughty to bring them low. (NIV)**

Faithful, blameless, and pure—that is God's requirements to enter his kingdom. You need to be humble in order to be saved.

Today, many persons say **there is no God**. We are not afraid to use God's name in vain, we swear, we cheat, we lie...we break all of God's commandments. We do not worry about our eternal home.

> **Psalm 14: 1** [1]The fool hath said in his heart, **There is no God. They are corrupt**, they have done **abominable works**, there is none that doeth good.
>
> **Psalm 14: 3** [3]They are all gone aside, they are all together **become filthy**: **there is none that doeth good, no, not one.**

Romans 3: 10–18 attests to the truth written in **Psalm 14 that there is no one who does good.** Paul confirms there is no one that is righteous in God's eyes. We do not understand his ways and do not seek after him. We lie and we curse. Not long ago, while I was playing golf with my friends, there was a group outing of golfers on the course. I heard from the mouths of these golfers, mostly in anger but even in joy, shouting God's name in vain. It could be heard from many holes away. People don't even think when they talk this way. It has become everyday language, part of our vocabulary. We have no fear of what God will do for these actions of ours.

> Paul wrote in **Romans 3: 10–18** [10]As it is written, **There is none righteous, no, not one:**
>
> [11]There is **none that understandeth**, there is **none that seeketh after God.**
>
> [12]**They are all gone out of the way**, they are together become unprofitable; there is **none that doeth good**, no, not one.
>
> [13]Their throat is an open sepulchre; **with their tongues they have used deceit;** the poison of asps is under their lips: **(Lying is an everyday occurrence)**

> [14]**Whose mouth is full of cursing and bitterness: (Are you one that curses?)**
>
> [15]Their feet are swift to shed blood:
>
> [16]Destruction and misery are in their ways:
>
> [17]And the **way of peace (Jesus)** have they not known:
>
> [18]**There is no fear of God before their eyes.**

So where can all we sinners turn to? King David knew the answer. From **verses 29 – 37 of 2 Samuel** is the answer to **salvation!** Trust in Jesus Christ and God's holy words, and salvation is yours. Turn to the **triumphant Messiah** that is Jesus Christ. Trust in Jesus as he trusted in God when he died for our sins and then knew God would resurrect him.

> **Verses 29 - 37:** [29]For **thou art my lamp**, O LORD: and **the LORD will lighten my darkness.**
>
> [30]For by thee I have run through a **troop (horde or crowd)**: **by my God** have I leaped over a wall.
>
> [31]As for God, **his way is perfect; the word of the LORD** is tried: he is a buckler to all them **that trust in him.**
>
> [32]For who is God, save the LORD? and **who is a rock (Jesus)**, save our God?
>
> [33]God is my strength and power: and **he maketh my way perfect.**
>
> [34]He maketh my feet like hinds' feet: and **setteth me upon my high places. (Heaven!)**

[35]He teacheth my hands to war (**Jesus did our warring for us!**); so that a bow of steel is broken by mine arms.

[36]Thou hast also given me the **shield of thy salvation (God has given us Jesus!)**: and thy **gentleness hath made me great. (Through Jesus, the King of Peace, I have been made a Saint!)**

[37]Thou hast enlarged my steps under me; so **that my feet did not slip.**

The Bible, God's word, **turns darkness into light and is flawless.** His ways are perfect! He is our shield (**salvation**) for all who take **refuge in him. He gives us victory over death. How?** Jesus did it by becoming a humble servant who stooped down from his heavenly place that was with his Father, and he died on the cross for all sinners—the **suffering Messiah**. Jesus is the perfect sacrifice for all time. By doing so, he **makes us great and gives us eternal life for all who have faith.** He makes us **blameless** for all those who have **faith**. He makes us **pure** for all who have **faith** in him. The **three requirements God asks for to enter heaven are fulfilled in Jesus Christ** for those who have faith and take refuge in the blood of the Lamb

John 3: 16–17: [16]For God so loved the world, that **he gave his only begotten Son**, that whosoever believeth in him should not perish, **but have everlasting life.**

[17]For God sent not his Son into the world to condemn the world; but **that the world through him might be saved.**

The apostle Paul explains below that believing in Jesus is confessing with your mouth He is Lord and Father God truly has raised him from the dead. Do this, and you will be saved for eternity.

Romans 10: 9–13 [9]**That if thou shalt confess with thy mouth the Lord Jesus**, and shalt believe in thine heart

> that **God hath raised him from the dead, thou shalt be saved.**
>
> 10For with the heart man believeth unto righteousness; and **with the mouth confession is made unto salvation.**
>
> 11For the scripture saith, **Whosoever believeth on him shall not be ashamed.**

Paul goes on to say that it is the same for all, whether Jew or Gentile. That means he died for everyone, every tribe and every nation. Salvation is offered to anyone who calls on his name.

> 12For there is no difference between the Jew and the Greek **(We all start as unbelievers and unsaved!)**: for the same Lord over all is rich unto all **that call upon him.**
>
> **13For whosoever shall call upon the name of the Lord shall be saved.**

Scripture is all about Jesus. It did not start at the New Testament, but in **Genesis 1:1**. The plan for salvation was set before time began and fulfilled by our Messiah for the entire world. **Can you see him in 2 Samuel?** By what you know about Jesus, **can you see him?**

In Genesis, after the fall of Adam and Eve, God says to Satan, after he took the form of a serpent,

> **Genesis 3: 14-15** 14And the LORD God said unto the serpent: **(Satan)**, Because thou hast done this, **thou art cursed** above all cattle, and above every beast of the field; upon thy belly shalt thou go, and dust shalt thou eat all the days of thy life:
>
> 15And **I will put enmity between thee and the woman,** and between thy seed and **her seed (Jesus)**; it shall **bruise thy head**, and **thou shalt bruise his heel.**

Now read the of the **triumphant Messiah** in the closing verses of **2 Samuel 22** and see Jesus victory over Satan at the cross. Jesus is speaking here. **Verses 38 - 43** tell us of his victory over his enemy.

> **Verses 38-43:** 38 I have pursued **mine enemies, and destroyed them**; and turned not again until I had consumed them.
>
> 39 And I **have consumed them**, and wounded them, that they could not arise: yea, **they are fallen under my feet. (Just as Genesis 3: 15 prophesized!)**
>
> 40 For **thou hast girded me with strength to battle (God strengthened him for battle.)**: them **that rose up against me** hast thou subdued under me.
>
> 41 Thou hast also given me the necks of mine enemies, **that I might destroy them that hate me. (I pray you do not hate Jesus.)**
>
> 42 They looked, but **there was none to save (Please do not harden your heart that Christ cannot save you.)**; even unto the LORD, but he answered them not.
>
> 43 Then did **I beat them as small as the dust of the earth,** I did stamp them as the mire of the street, and did spread them abroad

Jesus has total victory! God armed Jesus for battle against Satan and his demons. The weapon was his **cross** he bore for mankind's rebellion and sins. Jesus came into the world as the **sacrificial Lamb of God**, which destroyed Satan and sin and revealed who Jesus really is—**The King for eternity**, **the Lion** that did destroy his enemies by humbly becoming the perfect Lamb sacrificed for all humanity. What Satan thought was his weakness was his strength.

Jesus was described to us in ancient times in the most ancient of texts. Jesus was there all along. I write so I can share God's great love for you! His great love for me makes me want to share it with all people, races, friend and foe alike. I pray you can see him and that you do know **he loves you**. Jesus loved all of us enough to have humbled himself that he would hang and die on the cross so that **we can have eternal life**. Please do what **2 Samuel 22** states in **verse 45**:

> [45]**Strangers shall submit themselves unto me**: as soon as they hear, they shall be obedient unto me.

I cannot close better than King David using his verse:

> **2 Samuel: 47** [47]**The LORD liveth**; and **blessed be my rock**; and exalted be the God of the **rock of my salvation.**

Please take the time to read 2 Samuel 22 for yourself in its entirety without interruption. Picture Jesus as you read. Look for him as the suffering Messiah. Look for him as the triumphant Messiah.

The Bible is uniquely written. It is not written in the western culture ways where words must describe your thoughts. Rather, it is written in the ways of the Eastern culture, where words are used to paint a picture. The Bible is written so you can see pictures, not just words. Open your mind to what God is painting. He is so wonderful.

God loves you and so do I!

Want to know what Jesus was thinking on the cross?

Chapter 10

In the last chapter, we saw evidence that King David saw not only the **triumphant Messiah**, but also the **suffering Messiah**. The Gospels of Matthew, Mark, Luke, and John are the **eyewitness accounts** of Jesus' crucifixion and the events that took place as Jesus hanged from the cross. But from these eyewitness accounts you don't get inside the head of Jesus to see the **pain and suffering** he was going through. **What was he focusing on? How hard was the pain?** What was the **physical** as well as the **mental and spiritual suffering** he was experiencing? **We don't have to leave it to our imagination!** Using the entire Bible, God tells us exactly how he suffered for my sins and yours.

The Old Testament, from this **one chapter** of the Bible, will show us Jesus clearly. This scripture was written approximately 1,000 years before the event occurred (**Jesus hanging on the cross**). At the end of this chapter, I will reveal the book and chapter I am writing from so you can read it for yourself. As you read, meditate on Jesus and the cross. Meditate that it is he speaking these words. Using your mind and your spirit, let the scriptures speak to you. I will quote the gospels from time to time during this chapter and show you the picture God revealed to me in these verses—**I see Jesus**. May you see him as you may never have seen him before and appreciate what God has done for you!

From the book in the scripture I am quoting, it begins with my Lord **Jesus Christ speaking as the suffering Messiah**:

> 1 **Save me, O God**; for the waters are come in unto my soul.
>
> 2 I sink in deep mire, **where there is no standing: I am come into deep waters, where the floods overflow me. (This is a man who is desperately in trouble, close to dying, needing God to save him.)**
>
> 3 **I am weary of my crying**: my throat is dried: **mine eyes fail while I wait for my God (This man is desperately looking for God.)**
>
> 4 Those **who hate me without reason**
> **outnumber the hairs of my head**;
> many are my enemies without cause,
> those who seek to destroy me.
> **I am forced to restore**
> **what I did not steal. (NIV) (Could this be Jesus dying on the cross?)**

I see Jesus in verse 4 above. Scripture tells us **Jesus was hated without reason**. He was a prophet. He was a miracle worker. He never did any wrong, but his enemies hated him. **He still is today**. Scripture also tells us he died on the cross for one reason: to become the sacrificial Lamb for the forgiveness of sin—the **perfect sacrifice. Jesus literally had to restore what he did not steal**. He had to restore mankind so we could be reconciled to God. Verse 4 above is a very good description of what scripture tells us about why Jesus came.

> 5 **You know my folly**, O God;
> **my guilt is not hidden from you. (NIV)**

How could this be Jesus dying on the cross when this man declares he is guilty?

Wow, Wow, And Wow! In that last verse, **Jesus talks of his guilt**; how can this be? The above scripture says he is hated without reason, he is forced to restore what he did not steal (Jesus is innocent.), and yet he says he cannot hide his guilt from God. Scripture teaches Jesus is God and perfect, never sinned; and yet he says he is guilty. **How can we reconcile this?Simple:** Jesus declares he is guilty because this is the **exact moment in time he bore all the sins of the world on the cross, yours and my sins—as his own!** Oh, how he loves humanity that he did this for us. This is confirmed in the New Testament that he bore our sins:

> **1 Peter: 2: 24** 24Who **his own self bare our sins in his own body on the tree**, that we, being dead to sins, should live unto righteousness: by **whose stripes ye were healed.**

> **Romans 5: 8** 8But **God demonstrates his own love for us** in this: **While we were still sinners, Christ died for us.**

How did Jesus feel about taking our sins as his own? Let us continue with scripture.

> 6 May **those who hope in you**
> **not be disgraced because of me,**
> O Lord, the LORD Almighty;
> **may those who seek you not be**
> **put to shame because of me,**
> O God of Israel.

> 7 For **I endure scorn for your sake,**
> **and shame covers my face.** (NIV)

I could cry reading those words. He felt scorn, rejection, and **shame for our sake** so that he could make us right with God. Our sins shamed him. Even while suffering on the cross, enduring such physical pain, he still put us first and was worried about those who hope in God. He did not want believers to be disgraced because of him. I feel so much shame for my sins.

> [8] I am become a stranger unto my brethren, and an **alien unto my mother's children.**

The above scripture is interesting for two reasons. The writer uses **mother** instead of father here. This would not be the right way to do this in that time in history or in that part of the world, even today. The father is the head of the household, not the mother. Scripture teaches that Jesus was not conceived by an earthly father, but was conceived through the Holy Spirit. Also, we know that Jesus had half brothers and sisters; and they did not believe him to be the Messiah. Scripture shows that the New Testament writers **James and Jude, Jesus' half-brothers,** testify they were not followers of Jesus until after his resurrection. The above scripture now makes sense; and remember, this is written up to 1,000 years before his crucifixion.

Returning to Verse 9:

> [9]For **the zeal of thine house hath eaten me up**; and the reproaches of them that reproached thee are fallen upon me. **(This man had zeal for God and his word)**

In **John, chapter 2**, we are told of how Jesus drove the moneychangers from the temple. With great zeal, Jesus chased them away and [17]His disciples remembered that it is written: "Zeal for your house will consume me." **(John 2: 17)**

Now we turn back to Jesus on the cross and **what is he doing?** Jesus is praying to his Father.

> [13]But as for me, **my prayer is unto thee, O LORD**, in an acceptable time: O God, in the multitude of thy mercy hear me, in the **truth of thy salvation**.
>
> **[14]Deliver me out of the mire**, and let me not sink: **let me be delivered from them that hate me**, and out of the **deep waters. (This is a very good description for Sheol or Hades.)**

> [15]Let not the waterflood overflow me, neither let the deep swallow me up, and **let not the pit shut her mouth upon me. (The pit is referring to Hades—Hell.)**

> **[16]Hear me, O LORD**; for thy lovingkindness is good: turn unto me according to the multitude of thy tender mercies.

Dying on the cross for all mankind is not inviting, not even for our Lord and Savior, but Jesus did it willingly, and he suffered physically, mentally, and spiritually for the sake of all mankind. And just as we humans must trust in God, Jesus demonstrated to all how to trust God. In his most desperate time, hanging on the cross, Jesus turned to his Father God.

Now **Jesus cries out from the cross** to God with these thoughts:

> [17]And **hide not thy face from thy servant**; for **I am in trouble**: hear me speedily.

I see Jesus; he is desperate for his Father. He is in trouble and he wants his Father to show himself. The mental anguish Jesus is suffering with is painful for me to see. He wants God to redeem him and save him from his enemies.

> [18]Draw nigh unto my soul, and **redeem it: deliver me** because of mine enemies.

> [19]Thou hast known my **reproach, and my shame, and my dishonour**: **mine adversaries are all before thee.**

Just imagine, Jesus was all alone on that cross, abandoned by all, with no one there for him. The accusations from the crowd he had to bear, and he had to bear the shame of it all. Now, Jesus breaks my heart even further as he cries out:

"Scorn has **broken my heart** and has left me helpless; I looked for **sympathy, but there was none, for comforters, but I found none."**

Can you see this is Jesus, our suffering Messiah? People scorning him have broken his heart. There was no one in the crowd who was watching him suffer that was willing to comfort him. Our rejecting him has hurt him so.

"They put gall in my food and gave me vinegar for my thirst." **(NIV)**

If we read **Matthew 27: 34, Mark 15: 23, and John 19: 28 – 30**, we will find that is exactly what happened. Jesus, even in all his pain and suffering, could think and stay on his task on why he came to earth. He stayed on task to its full completion—so that the **scriptures would be fulfilled.**

Matthew 27: 34: "[34]They gave him **vinegar to drink mingled with gall**: and when he had tasted thereof, he would not drink

Mark 15: 23: "[23]And they gave him to drink **wine mingled with myrrh**: but he received it not.

John 19: 28–30: [28]After this, **Jesus knowing** that all things were now accomplished, **that the scripture might be fulfilled**, saith, **I thirst**.

[29]Now there was set a vessel full of vinegar: and they filled **a spunge with vinegar**, and put it upon hyssop, and put it to his mouth.

[30]When Jesus therefore had received the vinegar, he said, It is finished: and he bowed his head, and **gave up the ghost. (Jesus died at this moment)**

The rest of the scripture in this secret passages deals with **Israel's guilt** for not accepting their suffering Messiah. We all must accept him, or we all will be just as guilty. The Scripture continues:

> 22Let their table become a snare before them: and **that which should have been for their welfare, let it become a trap. (The salvation message Jesus brought is now their trap)**
>
> 24Pour out thine indignation upon them, and let thy wrathful anger take hold of them.
>
> **25Let their habitation be desolate; and let none dwell in their tents.**

Verse 25 is a prophecy for Israel for not recognizing their **suffering Messiah.** This prophecy was fulfilled, as we will see.

> 26For **they persecute him whom thou hast smitten**; and they talk to the grief of those **whom thou hast wounded. (Jesus has been only wounded in death.)**

Verse 26 is very revealing. Scripture is declaring **Israel has persecuted the one who God is smitten (head over heels in love with), but it is God who has done the wounding.**

> **32Let their eyes be darkened, that they see not**; and make their loins continually to shake.

We know, if Jesus is the real Messiah (And I believe he is!), this prophecy has been fulfilled, except for a remnant: the Jews do not recognize him as their Messiah. Let us turn to the New Testament writings to see that the above scriptures were fulfilled in the New Testament:

> **In Romans 11: 7-10: (Prophecy is fulfilled—See how Israel's eyes are darkened so they cannot see.)** "7What then? **Israel**

hath not obtained that which he seeketh for; but the election hath obtained it, and the rest were blinded.

8 **(According as it is written, God hath given them the spirit of slumber, eyes that they should not see, and ears that they should not hear;)** unto this day.

9 And **David saith, Let their table be made a snare**, and a trap, and a stumblingblock, and a recompence unto them: **(Verse 22 fulfilled.)**

10 **Let their eyes be darkened, that they may not see**, and bow down their back alway. **(Verse 32 fulfilled.)**

All of the prophecies given from verse 22 through 32 above have been fulfilled in the New Testament. Jesus himself, before his crucifixion, prophesized nearly 40 years earlier the same thing in Matthew, chapters 23 and 24—see below. **In 70 A.D.**, the prophecy in **verse 25** was fulfilled. History books outside the Bible tell us that Jerusalem was completely destroyed by the Romans under the command of Titus in that year. Rome destroyed the great temple in Jerusalem and scattered the people of Israel to the four corners of the earth. Yes, there is **judgment** and **punishment** for Israel for not accepting their Messiah, as there will be for all people who **reject Jesus**, King of kings, and Lord of lords.

Jesus' prophecy of the destruction of Israel in **Matthew 23: 37–39:**

"37 O Jerusalem, Jerusalem, thou that killest the prophets, and stonest them which are **sent unto thee**, how often would **I have gathered thy children together**, even as a hen gathereth her chickens under her wings, and ye would not!

38 Behold, **your house is left unto you desolate**. **(Verse 25 was fulfilled in 70 A.D.)**

> 39For I say unto you, **Ye shall not see me henceforth, till ye shall say, Blessed is he that cometh in the name of the Lord.**

Jesus is saying he will come again and this time Israel will recognizes him as their suffering Messiah, **the one they had pierced**, and receive him as their **triumphant Messiah.**

> **Matthew 24: 1-2** 1Jesus left **the temple** and was walking away when his disciples came up to him to call his attention **to its buildings.** 2"Do you see all these things?" he asked. "I tell you the truth, **not one stone here will be left on another; every one will be thrown down." (NIV)**

Scripture and history confirms that Verse 25 was fulfilled—the temple is still destroyed to this very day.

Now, the hidden scripture continues with Israel's condemnation. But in the larger picture, this is the condemnation for all mankind, not just Israel. For rejecting the one, true savior brings judgment—**for one's own sins; there is no forgiveness without the shedding of blood**, and **that is why Jesus shed his blood, so we would not have to. Because God loves us.** Without accepting Jesus, you will be left alone to be charged for your sins, with no intercessor to defend you; and may this **NOT HAPPEN TO YOU** what occurs next!

The hidden scripture I am quoting **warns:**

> 27Add iniquity unto their iniquity: and **let them not come into thy righteousness.**

> 28Let them be **blotted out of the book of the living**, and **not be written with the righteous.**

Verse 28 above shows there are **two books your name can be written in.** The first book, the **"Book of the Living,"** has everyone's name that has ever been born (even the aborted children) in it. By your name being in this book, it shows you have existed. In this book, **your name can be blotted out;** and you face punishment that is everlasting. You will suffer because you will be separated from God, who loves you. You will have missed out on his redemption. That is total condemnation! Without faith, your name will be blotted out of the "Book of the Living." **Please don't let this happen to you!**

There is hope! Praise be to God—because there is another book your name can be written in. For those who seek him and accept his free gift of salvation, their name will be placed in this book forever. Your name **will never be blotted out**; there is no erasure for this book. The name of this second book is the **"Lamb's Book of Life."** Jesus is our lamb of God- sacrificed for our sins. **By our faith and trusting in him to make us right with God, Jesus puts our name in his book.** His proof is his resurrection from the grave.

> **Revelation 21: 27** [27]Nothing impure will ever enter it, nor will anyone who does what is shameful or deceitful, but **only those whose names are written in the Lamb's book of life.**

The "**Lambs Book of Life"** is for those **who are followers of Jesus.** The plan of salvation and restoration with God by Jesus being slain for our sins was from the very beginning. It was God's plan **that all who dwell on earth would worship Jesus**, but some will not do it. Instead, they chose to worship another (**knowingly or not**): Satan. They may not have consciously knew they were making this decision, **but they did consciously reject Jesus:**

> **Revelation 13: 8** [8]And all that dwell upon the earth shall worship him (**Mankind will worship the anti-Christ and Satan, after the believers are gone by the rapture.**), **whose names are not written in the book of life of the Lamb slain from the foundation of the world.**

For those who accept his free gift and **overcome his or her lack of faith**, they will be taken to live with him and dressed in the pure white garments of righteousness, the clothing of his Saints. **He**

will never blot names from his book of life; and, what is most awesome, he will testify about us to his Father and his angels. God loves us so very much!

> **Revelation 3: 5** [5]He that overcometh, the same **shall be clothed in white raiment**; and **I will not blot out his name** out of the book of life, but **I will confess his name before my Father, and before his angels.**

Going back to our scripture in the Old Testament—for those who are needy, Jesus will put your name in his book—are you poor? **Are you needy?** Seek God and be **glad.**

> 32 **The poor will see and be glad—you who seek God,** may your hearts live!
>
> 33 **The LORD hears the needy** and does not despise his captive people. **(NIV)**

There is hope, and there is hope for Israel! As prophesied, God will save Israel; and he already has rebuilt her cities. This occurred in 1948, when Israel became a nation after nearly 2,000 years of extinction. No other nation on earth has ever done this before. God restored Israel. In 1967, in the Six Day War, greatly outnumbered and against all odds, Israel captured Jerusalem, as foretold in scripture. **Verse 35** below prophesized it. My God lives!

> 35For **God will save Zion**, and **will build the cities of Judah**: that they may dwell there, and have it in possession

All it takes to be restored as Israel was restored is to accept **God's free gift.** Israel is restored as a nation because of the love of God, and by his power. We can be restored spiritually in the same way- by having faith in his Son, the one God sent to die on a cross, as foretold in scripture—to believe in his Son and that he is God, the perfect sacrifice only God could provide.

> As **Romans 8: 1** states, [1]There is therefore now **no condemnation to them which are in Christ Jesus**, who walk not after the flesh, but after the Spirit.

The passage of hidden scripture I wrote from closes in a happy time, when Jesus is no longer the sacrificial lamb, but King of kings-the **triumphant Messiah.** It is a time when Israel is restored, and all peoples on earth will dwell there.

> [34]Let the heaven and earth praise him**, the seas**, and every thing that moveth therein.
>
> [35]For **God will save Zion**, and will build the cities of Judah: that they may dwell there, and have it in possession.
>
> [36]The seed also of his servants shall inherit it: and **they that love his name shall dwell therein**

Those that love his name will dwell in heaven. That name is Jesus, and I am in love with him. He died on the cross for my sins. He was resurrected from the dead by God's power; and because he has risen, I have faith that I will be raised from the grave also. What a wonderful message God's word gives for those who believe. As I continue showing Jesus in scripture in this book, I pray **you will see him too.**

The scripture I used to write this chapter was **Psalm 69**, written somewhere between 1450 and 430 B.C. We are not sure who is the author of this Psalm. Various authors wrote the Psalms, so the time span was great. Most of the Psalms were written about 1000 B.C. **Can you see Jesus** and him telling you how much he paid for your **penalty of sin—the high cost he paid at the cross** to redeem you? **I pray that you do.**

> **Psalm 49: 7-9** [7] **No man can redeem the life of another** or **give to God a ransom** for him-

> **8 the ransom for a life is costly, no payment is ever enough-**
>
> **9 that he should live on forever and not see decay.**

See what Psalm 49 above is saying. No man can pay the ransom to God that would allow him to live forever! The price is too high! It took someone better than man. His name is **Jesus,** the Son of God! We cannot fool ourselves in to thinking that Jesus was only a man, a prophet, and a good person. As we look at the entire word of God, we will see him more and more and why we are to worship him. As for myself, I will never worship a man—**there is no power in a man to pay my ransom.** I put my faith in God only. **He is my Jesus!**

> **Mark 10: 45** 45For even **the Son of Man** did not come to be served, but to serve, and **to give his life as a ransom for many.**"
>
> **Hebrews 9: 15** 15For this reason **Christ is the mediator of a new covenant,** that those **who are called may receive the promised eternal inheritance**—now that **he has died as a ransom to set them free from the sins** committed under the first covenant.

The God of the Bible is the one I put my faith and trust in. He died as my ransom and has set me free from my sins. When I face God on my judgment day, He will not use my sins against me. The Blood of his Lamb has taken my sins away, as if I never sinned. This is by the grace he has given me because He loves me. **He loves you too!**

Please take the time and read Psalm 69 for yourself, in your own bible. **God loves you and so do I!**

Exodus: Chapter 15
Moses' song to the Lord

Chapter 11

It is so wondrous to me that in searching for **Jesus** in the Scriptures, **I see him** everywhere. I do not have to wait for the New Testament to find him—**He is everywhere.**

Chapter 9 was about **2 Samuel Chapter 22**, **David's song of praise to God**. The Messianic word of God I see is **Jesus on the cross, the suffering Messiah**, looking for his God his Father. As Jesus suffers and is dying on the cross, God comes down to earth in a canopy of darkness and clouds in anger and delivers his Son from his enemies **(Satan and his fallen angels).** We also see the **risen Christ—the triumphant Messiah;** and he is rewarded for his **righteousness,** and all of his adversaries bow at his feet.

In chapter 10 we read **Psalm 69**; it is showing another Messianic word of God where we can see Jesus hanging on the cross—the **suffering Messiah**. This time, Jesus tells us of what he was thinking, feeling, and praying for, fulfilling what was written and teaching us of his salvation while he is dying on the cross. You can sense his pain and suffering, his shame for our sins, which he took upon himself as his own. It is the clearest picture of what mental anguish Jesus went through for our salvation in the Bible.

Now in **Exodus 15**, in the **Song of Moses** to the Lord, the Messianic word of God has us looking at the spiritual battle Jesus went through when he came to earth. In this Old Testament scripture, you can see a **victorious Jesus—the triumphant Messiah.** He has battled **Satan and his demons** and has hurled them into depths of hell.

In Exodus 15, we are witnessing the true history of Israel. God has just defeated Egypt; Pharaoh and his armies meet their doom in the Red Sea. Moses lifts up a song of praise to the Lord for all he has done. In doing so, he gives us a Messianic prophecy of Jesus' victory over Satan. As we see Moses and the Israelites singing praises to God for victory over their adversaries, the Egyptians, **we can see believers in heaven singing praises to God for Jesus and his victory over his adversaries. This is how God has written the scriptures—in layer upon layer and painting us pictures.** Remember, we are looking at a song written between **1450 and 1400 B.C.** This is an approximately **3,400-year-old** song.

Starting with the first verse, let us see Jesus and the celebration of his victory over Satan.

> 1Then sang Moses and the children of Israel this song unto the LORD, and spake, saying, I will **sing unto the LORD**, for **he hath triumphed** gloriously: **the horse and his rider hath he thrown into the sea. (Prophetically, Satan is the rider and he has been hurled into Hell.)**

> 2The LORD is my strength and song, and **he is become my salvation: he is my God**,"

The Hebrew word for "salvation" is **"Yesuah" (the same name as Jesus). Jesus is in the Greek language. In the Hebrew language, Jesus would be pronounced** ***Yesua, which equals Joshua and means Yahweh saves!*** Jesus has become our salvation at the cross. He is our **deliverer**, our **helper**, and our **redeemer**, which are other meanings of his name.

> 3The LORD is a **man of war**: the LORD is his name.

No longer is Jesus the suffering Messiah described as the Lamb of God, but he is now reining as Lord of lords and King of kings. He is a Lion!

> **Revelation 5: 5** [5]And one of the elders saith unto me, Weep not: behold, **the Lion of the tribe of Judah, the Root of David, hath prevailed** to open the book, and to loose the seven seals thereof.

Now we will see the defeat of Satan and his destruction in hell along with his army.

> **Verse 4-5**: [4]Pharaoh's **(Satan)** chariots and his host **(his defeated army)** hath **he cast into the sea (hell)**: **his chosen captains also are drowned** in the **Red sea (hell)**.
>
> [5]**The depths have covered them**: **they sank into the bottom** as a stone.

This is the total defeat of Satan, and the last book of the Bible expresses the same thing.

> **Revelation 20: 10** [10]And **the devil**, who deceived them, **was thrown into the lake of burning sulfur,** where **the beast** and the **false prophet (The beast and false prophet are Satan's captains.)** had been thrown. **They will be tormented day and night for ever and ever.**

Jesus, by becoming the sacrificial Lamb for **all mankind,** has become the warrior who completely defeated Satan. His weapon is **"LOVE."**

Now Scripture says Jesus now sits at the **right hand** of his Father. Scripture also states that **Christ's redeeming work** was done **before the beginning of time.** Since the plan of salvation was from before time began, God foreknew mankind would sin and need a Savior; and he set the plan of redemption in place before we had even sinned.

> **2 Timothy 1: 9** [9]Who hath saved us, and called us with an holy calling, not according to our works, but according to his own purpose and grace, which **was given us in Christ Jesus before the world began,**

Now returning to **Exodus 15: 6** we read this prophecy:

> [6]**Thy right hand**, O LORD, **is become glorious in power**: **thy right hand**, O LORD, **hath dashed in pieces the enemy.**

Wow, Wow, and Wow! Foretold long before Jesus' actual death and resurrection, using the history of the Israelites who were singing praises for God's victory over Pharaoh and his army, **we can see Jesus in his glory, power, and majesty.** He totally defeated our enemy and his enemy, Satan, **at the cross for ALL MANKIND.... not just believers. Jesus is the Right Hand of God.**

Mark 16: 19 [19]So then after the Lord had spoken unto them, he was received up into heaven, and **sat on the right hand of God**.

What Jesus accomplished at the cross was total and everlasting. See what **verses 7 and 8** state:

> [7] In the greatness of your majesty you threw **down those who opposed you. (I pray you are not one who opposes God.) You unleashed your burning anger; it consumed them like stubble.**

> [8]"At the blast of Your nostrils the waters were piled up, The flowing waters stood up like a heap; The deeps were congealed in the heart of the sea. **(NIV)**

It is frightening to think of God's anger and judgment against those who oppose him. The book of Revelation again explains what being thrown down will be for those who have opposed him:

Revelation 20: 11-14 [11]Then I saw a great white throne and him who was seated on it. Earth and sky fled from his presence, and there was no place for them.

[12]And I saw the dead, great and small, standing before the throne, and books were opened. Another book was opened, which is the book of life. **The dead were judged according to what they had done as recorded in the books.**

[13]The sea gave up the dead that were in it, and death and Hades gave up the dead that were in them, and **each person was judged according to what he had done.**

[14]Then death and Hades were thrown into the lake of fire. The lake of fire is the second death. **[15]If anyone's name was not found written in the book of life, he was thrown into the lake of fire.**

The Bible is full of warnings that God's wrath will happen. He warns us because he loves us. God will not take pleasure in any of us being thrown into hell. The good news is that **we do not have to!** God has given us free choice to accept or oppose him. It is our own decision.

Now Satan believes, and he still does so to this day, that he will defeat God. He believes he can still destroy not only God**, but also mankind...but God says:**

Verse 9: [9]The enemy said**, I will pursue, I will overtake**, I will divide the spoil; **my lust shall be satisfied upon them**; I will draw my sword, **my hand shall destroy them. (Satan wants to destroy us!)**

But God had a different plan before the beginning of time; God drew up the plan of salvation so Satan could not destroy us.

1 Peter 1: 19 [19]but **with the precious blood of Christ**, a lamb without blemish or defect. **[20]He was chosen before**

the creation of the world, but was revealed in these last times **for your sake. (NIV)**

God for our sake **made this plan of salvation before the beginning of time!** Satan's plan for our destruction was **defeated before creation,** but revealed to us at the cross **through the blood of Christ.**

Satan and his demons will sink and be covered up in the "Lake of Fire," just as Pharaoh and his army was covered up.

> **Verse 10:** 10Thou didst blow with thy wind, the sea covered them: **they sank as lead in the mighty waters.**

The victory is complete. Satan's plan is defeated. **I love the words that are from verses 11-13.**

> **11Who is like unto thee, O LORD**, among the gods? **who is like thee**, glorious in **holiness**, fearful in **praises, doing wonders**?
>
> 12Thou stretchedst out thy **right hand**, the earth swallowed them.
>
> 13Thou in **thy mercy hast led forth the people which thou hast redeemed: (Jesus has redeemed us.)** thou hast guided them in thy strength unto thy **holy habitation. (Heaven!)**

Wow, Wow, and Wow! Jesus is our redeemer, and he will guide us. He will bring us to heaven at his holy dwelling. It is already done, accomplished on the cross by God for us.

> **John 3: 16** 16For God so loved the world, that he gave his only begotten Son, that **whosoever believeth in him** should not perish, but have **everlasting life.**

Exodus chapter 15 closes with one last warning. To those who do not believe there is condemnation for ones own sins, please take God's warnings to heart. Throughout scripture, Old and New, the word of God warns us to repent and have faith in the one he sent for our salvation. **Exodus 15** is no different. **Verses 14 - 16** describe the people of Palestina, Edom, Moab, and Canaan. **They symbolize unbelievers.** They are doomed.

> [14]The people shall hear, and be afraid: sorrow shall take hold on the inhabitants of **Palestina.**
>
> [15]Then the dukes of **Edom** shall be amazed; the mighty men of **Moab**, trembling shall take hold upon them; all the inhabitants of **Canaan** shall melt away.
>
> **[16]Fear and dread shall fall upon them**; by the greatness of thine arm they shall be as still as a stone;

The Bible is a book that shows God's love for you. It is also a book of warning. New Testament warnings are just as strong:

> The Apostle Luke in **the book of Acts, chapter 13 verse 40**, states: [40]"Therefore **take heed**, so that the thing spoken of in the Prophets **may not come upon you:**
>
> [41]'BEHOLD, YOU **SCOFFERS**, AND MARVEL, AND PERISH; FOR I AM ACCOMPLISHING A WORK IN YOUR DAYS, A WORK WHICH **YOU WILL NEVER BELIEVE, THOUGH SOMEONE SHOULD DESCRIBE IT TO YOU.'" (NASB)**

Jesus fulfilled the prophets' testimonies about the Messiah, the one who would come and take away the sins of the world and would be King. **Please do not be a scoffer—I am the person describing this to you through God's word. What the penalty for unbelief comes from God word and is not my own opinion.**

God is a **God of love,** but he is also **righteous.** He cannot look upon sin and have sin in his presence. As Jesus hung from the cross, he looked for his father. He cried out to him. When Jesus took all of the sins of the world upon himself, he cried out:

> **Mark 15: 34** [34]And at the ninth hour Jesus cried with a loud voice, saying, Eloi, Eloi, lama sabachthani? which is, being interpreted, **My God, my God, why hast thou forsaken me?**

God could not even look upon Jesus at that moment because the sins of the world were on him. **Are you without sin? Can God look upon you at this moment?** There is a way and only one way: the cross and the **blood** of the perfect sacrifice, **Jesus Christ.**

Once again, Luke tells us in the **book of Acts, chapter 13: 38-39:**

> [38]"Therefore, my brothers, I want you to know that **through Jesus the forgiveness of sins is proclaimed to you.** [39]**Through him everyone who believes is justified from everything** you could not be justified from by the law of Moses.

The salvation message is a beautiful love story—God's love for his creation. **He paid the price for our sins; he paid the penalty.** We were justified from sin through the death and resurrection of **Jesus.** We were **redeemed and purchased** with a price, and **Exodus 15** tells us the price was **paid in full.**

> **Verse 16**: [16]Fear and dread shall fall upon them; by the greatness of thine arm they shall be as still as a stone; **till thy people pass over**, O LORD, till the people pass over, **which thou hast purchased.**

Understand what that last verse says; **Jesus has purchased our redemption at the cross.** He paid our fine for sin so we would not have to.

> **Verse 17** [17]Thou shalt bring them in, and plant them in the mountain of thine inheritance, in the place, O LORD, which thou hast made for thee to dwell in, in the Sanctuary, O LORD, which **thy hands have established**

The above verse tells us of the historical planting of the Israelites into the **Promised Land** and that God will dwell with them in the land—in Jerusalem will be God's dwelling. **But spiritually,** it is also our inheritance in heaven **where Jesus will rule and reign.** At the end of times, we who were **bought at the cross** will be with him forever; and his footstool of heavenly throne will be Jerusalem. Look what we have to look forward to.

> **Revelation 21: 1-4** [1]**And I saw a new heaven and a new earth**: for the first heaven and the first earth were passed away; and there was **no more sea. (Sea in this case refers to "unbelievers." They will not be at the new heaven and earth.)**

> [2]And I John saw **the holy city, new Jerusalem**, coming down from God out of heaven, **prepared as a bride adorned for her husband.**

Jesus used parables while on earth to help teach many spiritual truths. It was even prophesized in the Old Testament he would do so.

> **Psalm 78: 2** [2]I will open my mouth **in a parable**: I will utter dark sayings of old:

He would use these stories because in the culture the apostles lived, they could relate to them. Our being brought up in Western civilization makes it sometimes difficult to understand. Our minds work by defining words we use and what their meanings are. Our minds do not work as well in pictures, as the Eastern culture does. The Eastern mind describes things so you can picture them in your mind without word definitions. One example of this would be the custom of marriage and how the groom would go and prepare a place for his bride and would not come back for her until the father of the groom said their dwelling was completely ready. The apostle John was doing the same thing in painting us a picture above and below in **Revelation Chapter 21**. John in verses 1 and 2 above is describing heaven, and the holy city, New Jerusalem coming out of heaven as the bride prepared for the King. It is his Tabernacle (Divine Dwelling) here on earth. He continues in the verses below to show how glorious a time this will be when all God's people will dwell with him forever:

> 3And I heard a great voice out of heaven saying, Behold, **the tabernacle of God is with men, and he will dwell with them**, and they shall be his people, and **God himself shall be with them**, and **be their God.**
>
> **4And God shall wipe away all tears from their eyes**; and there shall be **no more death, neither sorrow, nor crying, neither shall there be any more pain**: for the former things are passed away.

The Song of Moses tells us the hope we can have as believers with these inspiring words:

> **Verse 18: 18The LORD shall reign for ever and ever**.

Closing: In the last three chapters, I wanted to show the uniqueness of how the Bible is written. God speaks to us in so many ways. I see layer upon layer, written by many authors and in many books, never contradicting each other. As we read the entire word of God, he shows us that Jesus is real, and he is our Savior and Redeemer. The bible verifies this in New Testament writings. But also, from the very beginning—in the Old Testament, God has verified his word as well. You will miss out on so much of what God is showing us if you do not look for Jesus from the very beginning in Genesis.

I highly recommend you take the time to read **2 Samuel 22, Psalm 69, and Exodus 15** in your own Bibles and let the word of God speak to you without my commentary. Look for Jesus in the

Old Testament as I have. May you see that Jesus did not just pop out of the Bible from nowhere starting in Matthew. He has been there, from the very beginning.

One Note: I do not believe in Replacement Theology, which teaches Christians have replaced the Israelis as his chosen people; and God is done with them. Nowhere in the Bible do I read this. God is not done with the Jewish people, and they will be redeemed one day when the time of the Gentiles (Church Age) is completed. I do see that people living today are the same as God's chosen people in the past. We have the same faults, sins, and shortcomings in our own lives as what God has revealed in their lives. We fall short of the glory of God just as they did. When I read the Old Testament, to me it is like reading our front-page news. Man has not changed one bit in all these thousands of years. We can learn about our own society's sins by looking at the sins of our fathers in the Old Testament and how God tried to steer his people away from them.

This is another reason why the Bible is so true to my faith and me. **The Bible does not cover up any of their mistakes.** They are not perfect persons—they are flawed. Even the most important people in the Old and New Testament are shown with all their sins in full view. Moses murdered an Egyptian; King David committed adultery and murdered a man to cover up his affair. The apostle Paul persecuted the early church and had a hand in the execution of believers before he himself accepted Jesus as his Lord and Savior. There is no sin too great that God cannot forgive, except one; and that is not believing in his Son. I will continually be putting these Bible verses in my chapters so you will not miss **your free gift.**

> **John 3: 16-18** 16For God so loved the world, that he gave his only begotten Son, **that whosoever believeth in him** should not perish, but **have everlasting life.**
>
> 17For God sent not his Son into the world to condemn the world; but **that the world through him might be saved.**

> [18]**He that believeth on him is not condemned**: but he that believeth not is condemned already, because he hath not believed in the name of the only begotten Son of God.

May we as a people and as a nation learn from the lessons of the Israelis in the Old Testament. May God speak to you and create a desire in you to seek the one, true God, the one who paid a great price by dying on the cross for all mankind. I am only a humble messenger of God's love for you. He wants to give you peace and eternal life. The gift of everlasting life is free for those who ask **Jesus** into their lives. May you **search and find him.** If you are ready to meet the God of the Bible, turn to **chapter 38** now and begin your new life that will be for eternity.

God loves you and so do I!

P.S. The song of Moses will be sung again in heaven… in the future. Just before the return of Christ, the saints who overcame Satan, the beast, his image, and the number of his name (666); will be given harps by God to sing this great old song along with the song of the Lamb.

> **Revelation 15:2-3** [2]And I saw as it were a sea of glass mingled with fire: and **them that had gotten the victory** over the beast, and over his image, and over his mark, and over the number of his name, stand on the sea of glass, having the harps of God.
>
> [3]And **they sing the song of Moses** the servant of God, and the song of the Lamb, saying, Great and marvellous are thy works, Lord God Almighty; just and true are thy ways, thou King of saints.

Genesis: 22 - Abraham's willingness to sacrifice Isaac

Chapter 12

After 911, many people were shocked and amazed as to what occurred. They could see that life could end in an instant, without any warning. Many began to seek God. There were large numbers going to churches, synagogues, and mosques searching for answers. ABC, CBS, NBC, Fox News, CNN, and CNBC stations had non-stop coverage of the attack and there were several programs discussing its religious implications of the attack.

On one of his programs, CNN news station host Larry King had a panel representing the three major monotheism religions, discussing the differences in their religions and how or if they could find common ground. This program had as its guests **a Roman Catholic priest, a rabbi, a leader of the Islamic faith, and a Baptist minister.** The discussion turned to Abraham because all three religions claim him as the starting point of their faith. You can read about his life and death in the first book of the Bible**, Genesis chapters 12 through 25.**

Larry King wanted to know about Abraham and **his willingness to sacrifice Isaac**. There is a major disagreement before we even get started because Islam teaches in its Koran that it was not Isaac, but his half-brother, Ishmael, that went with Abraham to be sacrificed in this story. This totally contradicts the Bible. Even though Islam did not begin until the sixth century, they believe Christians and Jews have altered the Bible; and it is not reliable. We do not need to get into the evidence that supports the Bible has never been altered; you can find plenty of other books written that show the reliability of the Bible – both Old and New Testaments. There is more evidence for the Bibles accuracy than any other antique book ever written. But what I want to show you is that this story found in Genesis is proof in itself, as we shall see.

When Larry asked the question, it caught my interest immediately because the Jewish rabbi spoke first and stated, **"For the life of me, I do not understand why this story is in the Bible." Wow!** I was amazed, but I really should not have been. He was blind to the parallel stories found throughout the Old and New Testaments. He cannot see the prophetic word this account of Abraham and Isaac brings. Only the Baptist minister explained fully the reason for the story of Abraham and Isaac and the importance to **all humanity** this story brings.

It is interesting to note that this story has great meaning **only** if you can see God and his plan for salvation being prophesized. It makes no sense to the rabbi because he is blinded from the prophetic truth it brings about their (**and mine**) Messiah. In Islam, just as Judaism, they are blinded from the truth because they believe it is not Isaac but his half-brother, Ishmael that Abraham took to the altar to sacrifice. Because of this, the **prophetic meaning to them is lost.** To the believer in Jesus Christ, it makes a whole lot of sense as to why this story is in the Bible. Let's look into the scripture and **see Jesus** in this true story of Abraham and his son Isaac found in **Genesis chapter 22.** It begins when God seeks Abraham and tests his faith.

> **Verse 1:** [1]And it came to pass after these things, that **God did tempt Abraham,** and said unto him, Abraham: and he said, Behold, here I am.

Next is the test God gives him. Try to see God's plan for salvation completely fulfilled **approximately 2,000 years later** by Jesus Christ.

Verse 2: [2]And he said, Take now **thy son, thine only son Isaac, whom thou lovest**, and get thee into the land of **Moriah**; and **offer him there for a burnt offering** upon **one of the mountains** which I will tell thee of.

I would think the parallel testimony this has with the New Testament claim of Jesus Christ being sacrificed by his loving Father God would be eerie to a non-believer, or at least a little strange. Two very important things are revealed in verse 2 above:

1) God was asking Abraham to **sacrifice his one and only son, Isaac.** He is described as his only son because Isaac was the only son promised to Abraham. God promised him his wife Sarah would give him a son **(Genesis 18: 10).**
2) The other very important revelation is, God ordered Abraham to make the offering **on the mountain of Moriah. This is where Jerusalem was built, where the temple stood in Jesus' day and where the temple mount is still here today.**

God is showing us in scriptures two parallel stories—one that was happening in the present time with Abraham and Isaac, then another that would happen much later in history. The parallel stories are already showing us:

1) God, by asking Abraham to sacrifice his son Isaac who he loves dearly, **revealed his willingness to sacrifice his one and only son Jesus, who he loves dearly.**
2) God was asking Abraham to sacrifice his son even though **God himself found human sacrifice detestable and a great sin. Human sacrifice would bring God great anger:**

2 Kings 17: 16-17 [16] They forsook all the commands of the LORD their God and made for themselves two idols cast in the shape of calves, and an Asherah pole. They bowed down to all the starry hosts, and they worshiped Baal. [17] **They sacrificed their sons and daughters in the fire.**

> They practiced divination and sorcery and sold themselves to do **evil in the eyes of the LORD, provoking him to anger.** **(NIV)**

Over 3,000 years ago, when 2 Kings was written, worshippers of Baal were sacrificing their sons and daughters to this god. **Ask yourself:** why would God ask Abraham to do something he hated and found evil?**Who must Jesus be** if God was going to and did sacrifice him on the cross as scripture proclaims? **Answer: Jesus must be more than a man.**

3) God sends Abraham to the mountains of Moriah to offer his sacrifice. Later in history, Mount Moriah is where Jerusalem was built. Mount Moriah became the exact place where God had King Solomon build his temple. It is **exactly where the scripture and history tells us Jesus was crucified.**

I find the above facts fascinating. There is much more.

> **Verse 3:** [3]And Abraham rose up early in the morning, and saddled his ass, and took **two of his young men with him**, and **Isaac his son, and clave the wood for the burnt offering,** and rose up, and went unto the place of which God had told him.

> **Verse 6:** [6]And Abraham **took the wood of the burnt offering**, and **laid it upon Isaac his son;** and he took the fire in his hand, and **a knife**; and they went both of them together.

Look at the parallels here to the story of Jesus in the New Testament.

1) There were two servants with Isaac and Abraham; **Jesus was nailed to the cross with two prisoners (Luke 21: 32).**
2) Wood was cut for the sacrifice; **the Cross-was made out of wood for Jesus.**

3) Abraham the father had Isaac his son carry the wood to be used **for his own sacrifice; Jesus was forced to carry his own cross to be used in his own sacrifice! (John 19: 16-17)**
4) Abraham carried the **fire and the knife, the means to slay his son. Isaac's own father was** to perform the sacrifice. In the same way, **God did not allow any man** to take his own son's life**; Jesus died willingly on the cross, and therefore God himself sacrificed his only son.**

In **John 19: 11** Jesus spoke these words to Pontius Pilate,

> [11]**Jesus answered**, Thou couldest **have no power at all against me, except it were given thee from above:**

The Scripture above teaches that Jesus was willingly being obedient, even to death, of what God's plan was for his life so that what was written in the Old Testament would be fulfilled.

Now Abraham and Isaac went on together alone and this conversation takes place:

> **Verses 7- 8** [7]And Isaac spake unto Abraham his father, and said, My father: and he said, Here am I, my son. And he said, Behold the fire and the wood: but **where is the lamb for a burnt offering?**
>
> [8]And Abraham said, My son, **God will provide himself a lamb for a burnt offering:** so they went both of them together.

Imagine, here is Abraham, who waited so long, well past his prime, for a son to be born by his beloved wife Sarah—**a miraculous birth;** and now God is asking him to sacrifice his son that was promised by God to bring him heirs too numerous to count that would become a great nation **(Genesis 13: 14-17)**. What obedience and faith he has, as we will find out later.

The parallels continue in the two stories of Abraham with Isaac and God with Jesus:

1) Isaac was the only son of Abraham given to him by his wife Sarah, and scripture teaches God has an only Son. **You do not have to wait to read this in the New Testament; it is also in the Old Testament.**

> **Proverbs 30: 4 is speaking of God and his Son: [4]Who hath ascended up into heaven, or descended?** Who hath gathered the wind in his fists? who hath bound the waters in a garment? who hath established all the ends of the earth? **what is his name, and what is his son's name, if thou canst tell? (The Son's name is Jesus!)**

Do not miss what is written in scripture. The writer is asking what God's name is and the name of his son. You do not need to wait for the New Testament for God to reveal he has a Son. There is more written that tells you God has a son and that this son is God.

> **Isaiah 9: 6** [6]For unto us **a child is born**, unto us **a son is given**: and the government shall be upon his shoulder: and his name shall be called Wonderful, Counsellor, **The mighty God**, **The everlasting Father**, The **Prince of Peace.**

2) **The story of Isaac's birth is a miracle.** Both Abraham and Sarah were well past the age of bearing children yet God promised it would happen.

> **Genesis 18: 10-14** [10]And he said, I will certainly return unto thee according to the time of life; and, lo, **Sarah thy wife shall have a son**. And Sarah heard it in the tent door, which was behind him.

11**Now Abraham and Sarah were old and well stricken in age**; and it ceased to be with Sarah after the manner of women.

12**Therefore Sarah laughed within herself (Sarah did not have the faith she would bear a son in her old age; it parallels the birth that took place in the New Testament when Mary bore Jesus—but she did have faith)**, saying, After I am waxed old shall I have pleasure, my lord being old also?

13And the LORD said unto Abraham, Wherefore did Sarah laugh, saying, **Shall I of a surety bear a child, which am old?**

14**Is any thing too hard for the LORD? (Great question! Is anything too difficult for your God?)** At the time appointed I will return unto thee, according to the time of life, and **Sarah shall have a son.**

Genesis 21: 1-3 1And the LORD visited Sarah as he had said, **and the LORD did unto Sarah as he had spoken.**

2**For Sarah conceived**, and **bare Abraham a son in his old age, at the set time of which God had spoken to him.**

3And Abraham called the name of his son that was born unto him, whom Sarah bare to him, **Isaac.**

In the New Testament another **miracle birth takes place—a virgin birth according to scripture.** Scripture speaks of Jesus' birth and the miracle of his birth by a virgin named Mary. God promised us this child long before it happened. We do not have to wait until the New Testament to read about it—Old Testament Prophets knew of his birth. **Do you believe there is nothing to difficult for the Lord?**

> **Isaiah 7: 14** [14]Therefore the Lord himself shall give you a sign; Behold**, a virgin shall conceive, and bear a son, and shall call his name Immanuel. (The name Immanuel means, "with us is God!")**

Getting back to Abraham's story, he now arrives at the place where God will sacrifice his own Son 2,000 years later:

> **Verses 9-12** [9]And **they came to the place which God had told him of**; and Abraham built an altar there, and laid the wood in order, and bound Isaac his son, and laid him on the altar upon the wood.
>
> [10]And Abraham stretched forth his hand, and **took the knife to slay his son.**
>
> [11]And **the angel of the LORD** called unto him **out of heaven**, and said, Abraham, Abraham: and he said, Here am I.
>
> [12]And he said, **Lay not thine hand upon the lad**, neither do thou any thing unto him: for now I know that thou fearest God, **seeing thou hast not withheld thy son, thine only son from me.**

Who is this "angel of the Lord" who called out from **heaven** and stopped Abraham from sacrificing his son?Whenever this term, "angel of the Lord," is used in scripture, it is no one other than **Jesus Christ himself,** the Second Person of the Trinity God.

These Bible verses confirm God appearing as the "angel of the Lord" in: **Genesis 16: 7-12; Genesis 21: 17-18; Genesis 22: 11-18; Exodus 3: 2; Judges 2: 1-4; Judges 5:23; Judges 6: 11-24; Judges 13: 3-22; 2 Samuel 24: 16; Zechariah 1: 12; Zechariah 3: 1; and Zechariah 12: 8.** In several of these appearances, those who saw the angel of the Lord feared for their lives because they had "seen the Lord." Therefore, it is clear that the angel of the Lord is an appearance of God in physical form. Only the Son, the Second

Person of the Trinity, can be seen in physical form. The Angel of the Lord was worshiped in his appearances; and **only God**, not man or angels, is to be worshiped.

Jesus himself stopped the sacrifice of Isaac. Why? **God himself was teaching us he would provide the lamb for both offerings—and he did!**

> **Genesis 22: 13–14** [13]And Abraham lifted up his eyes, and looked, and behold behind him **a ram caught in a thicket by his horns**: and Abraham went and took the ram, and **offered him up for a burnt offering in the stead of his son.**
>
> [14]And Abraham **called the name** of that place **Jehovahjireh (Its meaning is 'The Lord will provide.")**: as it is said to this day, In the mount of the LORD it shall be seen.

How appropriate a name for this place that became Jerusalem, **"The Lord will provide."** Whether we look at the sacrifice made by Abraham in the Old Testament this day when the ram was caught in a thicket by his horns or the sacrifice 2,000 years later, which we read about in the New Testament, the message is the same—**God provided the lamb for both sacrifices!**

> **John 1: 36** [36]And looking upon Jesus as he walked, he saith, **Behold the Lamb of God!**

Because God stopped Abraham, he did not have to follow through with his sacrifice of his son and commit an abomination by performing **human sacrifice. But God did perform his sacrifice for us! How could God perform a blood sacrifice? Who must Jesus be? The only way God could do this sacrifice is if God was not performing a human sacrifice! Jesus must be more than human (as both Old and New Testaments testify).**

> **Isaiah 35: 10** [10]And **the ransomed of the LORD shall return**, and come to Zion with songs and **everlasting joy upon their heads**: they shall obtain joy and gladness, and sorrow and sighing shall flee away.

Jesus is coming back, and he is coming back with his saints. The saints are those who have been ransomed, and they will have everlasting joy and never again experience sorrow.

> **1 Timothy 2: 5-7** [5]For there is one God, and one mediator between God and men, **the man Christ Jesus;**
>
> [6]**Who gave himself a ransom for all**, to be testified in due time.

Scripture teaches a blood sacrifice is required for the punishment of sin. God did not really want a sacrifice given to him by man slaying animals and offering up their blood. God found no pleasure in these sacrifices for sin. **The blood of animals could never take away sin.** It only was to be a reminder to us that in our sins, we are dead already. To recover from our sins, it would take a **one-time everlasting sacrifice** not made by any human—it had to be from God. In the book of Hebrews in the New Testament, this is confirmed:

> **Hebrews 10: 3-5** [3]But in those sacrifices there is a remembrance again made of sins every year.
>
> [4]**For it is not possible** that **the blood of bulls and of goats** should **take away sins**.
>
> [5]Wherefore when **he (Jesus) cometh into the world**, he saith, Sacrifice and offering thou wouldest not, but **a body hast thou prepared me:**

Jesus came to us in human form to do God's will. Scripture below fulfills what is written in **Psalms 40: 6-8,**

> **Hebrews 10: 6-10** [6]In **burnt offerings and sacrifices for sin thou hast had no pleasure.**
>
> [7]Then said I, Lo, I come **(in the volume of the book it is written of me,) ("It is written" always refers to the Old Testament.)** to **do thy will, O God.**

Verse 7 refers to **Psalm 40: 8** and our Messiah—Jesus' willingness to do God's will.

> [8]Above when he said, Sacrifice and offering and burnt offerings and offering for sin thou wouldest not, neither hadst pleasure therein; **which are offered by the law;**
>
> [9]Then said he, Lo, I come to do thy will, O God. **He taketh away the first, that he may establish the second. (The old covenant of animal sacrifice is removed, and the new covenant of Jesus' one-time sacrifice takes its place.)**
>
> [10]By the which will **we are sanctified** through the **offering of the body of Jesus Christ once for all. (Jesus is the sacrifice for all sin once and for all.)**

Look at the scripture below and see that the apostle Peter explains to us that Jesus is our sacrificial lamb, planned before the beginning of the world. **Peter states that whoever has faith in Jesus and that he was raised from the dead has placed his faith and hope in God.**

> **1 Peter 1: 18-21** [18]Forasmuch as ye know that **ye were not redeemed** with corruptible things, as silver and gold, from your vain conversation received by tradition from your fathers;

> [19]**But with the precious blood of Christ**, as of a **lamb without blemish and without spot:**
> [20]Who verily was foreordained **before the foundation of the world**, but was manifest in these last times for you,
> **[21]Who by him do believe in God, that raised him up from the dead, and gave him glory; that your faith and hope might be in God.**

Before the **beginning of time, we were redeemed by the precious blood of Jesus Christ!** God did this so that by believing in the Son of God and that God did raise him from the dead, we would have faith and hope in Him and eternal life! **What a God we have! And since this plan was made before time began,** it is why the prophecies of Jesus are so accurate and that they are fulfilled exactly as how they are foretold.

> **Romans 3: 21-25** "[21]But now a righteousness from God, apart from law, has been made known, to which **the Law and the Prophets testify**. [22]This **righteousness from God** comes through **faith in Jesus Christ to all who believe**. There is no difference, **[23]for all have sinned and fall short** of the **glory of God**, [24]and **are justified freely by his grace through the redemption that came by Christ Jesus.** [25]God presented him as a **sacrifice of atonement**, through **faith in his blood." (NIV)**

Now we come back to Abraham. **Why was he willing to sacrifice Isaac?** Even though God commanded it of him, it is a request no man would want to perform. The only reason he was able to do it was because of **his faith! How do we know this?** Because in the New Testament in the **book of Hebrews, chapter 11,** you will find the **"Hall of Fame"** for Old Testament saints. Abraham was commended for his faith and because of it he will have eternal life.

> **Hebrews 11: 17-19** **[17]By faith Abraham**, when he was **tried (Tested by God), offered up Isaac**: and **he that had received the promises (Abraham received the promise**

> **from God that through Isaac his heirs would make him a great nation.) offered up his only begotten son,**
>
> 18Of whom it was said, That in **Isaac shall thy seed be called**:
>
> **19Accounting that God was able to raise him up, even from the dead**; from whence also he received him in a figure.

What this scripture above is telling us is that Abraham's faith was so strong that he knew God would never fail him or not keep his promises to him. He knew God promised him that through Isaac his seed (heirs) would be as numerous as the grains of sand or the stars in the sky—too numerous to count. Abraham's faith was that even **if he were to slay Isaac, God would then raise him from the dead! Scripture says, figuratively speaking, he had. Do you have such faith?** Abraham's faith is what justified him with God. **It is the same for all mankind.**

Now we can understand why this story is in the Bible that the rabbi and the cleric of Islam could not explain. The Christian faith does have an explanation that through this story in Genesis, God was prophesizing to us what he was going to do for us. God was to and did send his only son Jesus into this world to be the sacrificial lamb for the remission of sin. He did not hold back his son. **Why did God do it? Because God loves you!**

> **Romans 8: 1** 1There is therefore now **no condemnation to them** which **are in Christ Jesus**, who walk not after the flesh, but after the Spirit.
>
> **John 3: 16** 16For **God so loved the world**, that he gave **his only begotten Son**, that **whosoever believeth in him** should not perish, **but have everlasting life**

In writing this chapter, I pray that the story of Abraham and Isaac will speak to you of God's grace and love for you. I pray you can see that the plan for salvation was made before Jesus Christ came and died. Scriptures tells us that the plan was made before creation began. The word of God from the Bible is made through many writers, through many books, with many chapters—without any contradictions, uniquely testifying to this plan. You can see Jesus throughout scripture; God reveals him slowly at first throughout the Old Testament; and then Scripture is fulfilled, and all his glory is revealed in the New Testament. **I see Jesus** in this old story in Genesis: **can you?** I pray that you come to desire to know him better and see the love he has for you. May God's holy word and the Holy Spirit speak to you.

God loves you and so do I!

Broken Relationship

Chapter 13

It was Sunday morning, and it was time to get ready for church. As it is sometimes, our teenage children were having a hard time getting ready, especially our oldest child, Colin. My wife Helen gave him twenty minutes, and he was finally ready and out the door forty minutes later. This brought stress upon my wife and I; and we had words with each other. Instead of focusing on going to church to worship our Creator, we got angry at each other and fought. The drive to church was very quiet, no one speaking because of Helen and I. We were in a **broken relationship** for the moment.

Once in church, I wanted to worship God; but I could not if I remained angry with Helen. I immediately forgave Helen in my heart, and then I asked God to forgive me and my sin against my wife. His peace came over me, and I knew I had received forgiveness; and I began meditating on God.

I was filled with thoughts of broken relationships. I thought of broken relationships that are **permanent**—a break up with a girlfriend or boyfriend, lost friendships that cannot be repaired, relationships in business that sour, a marriage that ends in a bitter divorce. These are all examples of **broken relationships that are permanent**; you may never have the opportunity to mend those relationships you once enjoyed.

Getting back to my wife, the broken relationship we were experiencing was **temporary**. I knew, especially after twenty-seven years of marriage, that we would mend our relationship through **forgive-**

ness and love. The love we have for one another would endure this anger we had toward each other at this moment. As it happened, Helen had done the same thing as I did when we entered church; and she received the same peace of forgiveness that I received. During the "Greetings" part of service that we greet one another with, Helen and I both apologized to one another; and we mended our broken relationship on the spot.

I returned to my meditation, I was so thankful to God, and as I was praising him, my thoughts began to turn toward mankind's relationship with God. The thought came to me that **all of mankind is in a broken relationship with its Creator**. It began early in our relationship; in fact, it began with our very first parents, **Adam and Eve.**

> **Genesis 3: 17-19** 17And unto Adam he said, Because thou hast hearkened unto the voice of thy wife, and hast eaten of the tree, of which I commanded thee, saying, Thou shalt not eat of it: **cursed is the ground for thy sake; in sorrow shalt thou eat of it all the days of thy life;**
>
> 18Thorns also and thistles shall it bring forth to thee; and thou shalt eat the herb of the field;
>
> 19In the sweat of thy face shalt thou eat bread, till thou return unto the ground; for out of it wast thou taken: **for dust thou art, and unto dust shalt thou return.**

Talk about a broken relationship. This was not brought about by God's will, but by our own free will. Just as Adam used his free will to break the one command that God gave him to do, we today continue in our parents' steps and freely sin against God. Humans are capable of such evil! **Where does all this evil come from?**People ask, "Why is there pain and suffering in the world?" Why is there sickness and death? Why is there evil? People ask, **"Where is God?"** The answer to where God is **simple;** because of our sin, we are separated from God by the curse. God cursed all of his creation because of this **broken relationship** brought about by our sins; therefore we cannot see God. **Our sins and lack of interest** in knowing him are why we cannot see him.

For people who ask, 'Where is God?I cannot see him," little do they know that **not only did God appear to mankind in physical form** a little over 2,000 years ago, **Jesus was from the beginning because he is God.**

> **John 1: 1-2** 1In the beginning was **the Word**, and **the Word was with God**, and **the Word was God.**
>
> 2**The same** was in the beginning with God.
>
> **John 1: 10-11** 10He was in the world, and **the world was made by him**, and **the world knew him not.**
>
> 11He came unto his own, and **his own received him not.** **(Remember chapter 7, when the Landlord God sent his Son, and we received him not, but killed him instead.)**
>
> **John 1: 14** 14And the **Word was made flesh, and dwelt among us,** (and **we beheld his glory**, the glory as of the **only begotten of the Father,)** **full of grace and truth.**

Scripture clearly states the Word is Jesus, and Jesus is God; and God became flesh and dwelled among his creation. **Why did God do this?** It was his plan before creation to mend this **broken relationship** with his creation. He longs to have a personal relationship with us.

> **Ephesians 1: 4-6** 4According as he hath chosen us in him **before the foundation of the world**, that we should **be holy** and **without blame** before him **in love**:
>
> 5Having predestinated us unto **the adoption of children by Jesus Christ to himself**, according to the good pleasure of his will,

[6]To the praise of the **glory of his grace**, wherein **he hath made us accepted** in the beloved.

Scripture is telling us we can become children of God. Also, we can live forever with him. Because you are reading this book, **isn't He what you are searching for?** Isn't He what your soul is craving for? **He is God that loves you!**

2 Timothy 1: 9-10 [9]Who hath saved us, and called us with an holy calling, not according to our works, but according to his own purpose and grace, **which was given us in Christ Jesus before the world began,**

[10]But is now made manifest by the appearing of our Saviour Jesus Christ, **who hath abolished death**, and **hath brought life and immortality to light through the gospel:**

From the beginning God foreknew we would break his commandments. He foreknew we would reject him. He foreknew **we would break our relationship with him**. Therefore, he planned before time began a way to mend this broken relationship with the creation he loves.

How did God do this? Simple—first, He paid the ultimate price for our sins. He took the mocking, the sneering, the insults, the pain, and suffering that crucifixion brings. **Luke describes the event in chapter 23**.

Vs 33: [33]And when they were come to the place, which is called Calvary, **there they crucified him**, and the **malefactors (two thieves), one on the right hand, and the other on the left.**

Vs 34: [34]Then said Jesus, **Father, forgive them; for they know not what they do.**

Vs 35: [35]And the people stood beholding. And the rulers also with them derided him, saying, He saved others; **let him save himself, if he be Christ, the chosen of God.**

Vs 36: [36]And **the soldiers also mocked him**, coming to him, and offering him vinegar,

Vs 46: [46]And when Jesus had cried **with a loud voice, he said, Father**, into thy hands I commend my spirit: and having said thus, **he gave up the ghost.**

If this was all there was to the story of Jesus—his death, he would have long been forgotten by us, maybe only a footnote in the pages of history. Possibly, He would have simply been remembered as a carpenter that began a ministry at 30 years of age that lasted for only three years. He made the rulers of Rome and the Jewish elders angry, and they hung him on a tree to get rid of him. If this was the end of the story, our broken relationship with God would still be; and **we would still be cursed in our sins**. We would be on our own to face God at judgment day. Thanks be to God; **the entire Bible declares this is not the end.** Jesus wins and destroys death and brings mankind back in its relationship with God. Jesus does this through his victorious resurrection.

The resurrection is the most important event in history. Without the resurrection, there would be no hope for eternity. The eyewitness accounts are in the gospels of Matthew, Mark, Luke, and John. I have chosen the book of Luke to describe the events that took place on that special Sunday morning:

Luke 24: 1 - 8 [1]Now upon the first day of the week, very early in the morning, they came unto the **sepulcher (tomb)**, bringing the spices which they had prepared, and certain others with them.

[2]And they found the stone rolled away from the **sepulcher**.

[3]And they entered in, and **found not the body of the Lord Jesus.**

[4]And it came to pass, as they were much perplexed thereabout, behold, **two men stood by them in shining garments (angels)**:

[5]And as they were afraid, and bowed down their faces to the earth, they said unto them, **Why seek ye the living among the dead?**

[6]He is not here, but is risen: remember how he spake unto you when he was yet in Galilee,

[7]Saying, **The Son of man must be delivered into the hands of sinful men, and be crucified, and the third day rise again.**

[8]And they remembered his words,

The resurrection of Jesus is what makes Christianity different from all other religions. No other religion has such a belief. All other religions have their leader still here, in the grave, including Mohammed. Only followers in Jesus have a leader **who did not die, but lives and promises to return one day! Those who hope in him will be resurrected to everlasting glory.**

For those who believe God's word, we are invited back into the relationship with our Creator as a **free gift**—forgiveness of our sins **by what God has done on the cross**, not by our works, but by his shedding his blood for us, by becoming the Sacrificial Lamb who bore our sins.

1 Peter 2: 24 [24]Who his own self bare our sins in his own body on the tree, that we, being dead to sins, should live unto righteousness: by whose stripes ye were healed.

How can we receive this free gift? Simple!

> **John 3: 16** [16]For God so loved the world, that he gave his only begotten Son, that **whosoever believeth in him** should not perish, but have **everlasting life**.

Faith! Faith is what brings us back into a relationship with God: faith in Jesus Christ and what he did on the cross; **faith by grace and not by works.**

> **Ephesians 2: 8-9** [8]**For by grace are ye saved through faith**; and that not of yourselves: it is the gift of God:
>
> [9]**Not of works**, lest any man should boast.

For those of you who are in a **broken relationship** with God, and cannot see him or sense his presence, but want to—**Jesus is the answer.** Jesus came to earth for that purpose: to restore our relationship with God. **For those who desire him**, your broken relationship with God is only **temporary**. For **those who don't**: you are on the **road to a permanent broken relationship** with your Creator. You will never see him even though he was always there for you, offering his love.

> **Revelation 3: 20** [20]Behold, **I stand at the door, and knock (the door to your heart and soul)**: if **any man hear my voice, and open the door**, I will come in to him, and will sup with him, and he with me.

Steps to Mend your Broken Relation with God:

1) **Confess:** Confess you are a sinner. Confess you have broken God's commandments. Confess you were not seeking God in your life.

> **1 John 1: 8-9** [8]**If we say that we have no sin, we deceive ourselves, and the truth is not in us.**

[9]If we confess our sins, he is faithful and just to **forgive us our sins**, and to cleanse us from **all unrighteousness.**

2) **Repent:** God calls us into repentance. He wants us to be sorry for our sins. He wants us to turn away from our sin nature. We must want to turn away from our sins. Ask God for forgiveness for rebelling in sin.

Jeremiah 15: 19 [19] Therefore this is what the LORD says: **"If you repent, I will restore you (NIV)**

3) **Invite: Ask Jesus to come into your life.** Let the broken relationship with your Creator be healed. Begin a relationship with him that will **last forever!** Seek the kingdom of God.

Matthew 7: 7-9 [7]Ask, and it shall be given you; seek, and ye shall find; knock, and it shall be opened unto you:

[8]For every one that asketh receiveth; and he that seeketh findeth; and to him that knocketh it shall be opened. [9]Or what man is there of you, whom **if his son ask bread, will he give him a stone?**

I once was in a **broken relationship with my Creator** just like you may be right now. I was 23 years old before I came to Christ; I am now fifty-one. After I heard and believed the gospel, I spent a few years struggling before asking Jesus into my life because I was scared that I would miss out on this earth's pleasures. I liked to golf. I was single, and I liked to go to bars and meet women and party. I was scared that a commitment to Christ would take the fun out of living. **It is Satan's lie.** I have found true joy in life with Jesus as my Lord and Savior. I have been restored in my relationship with God. I found that God accepted me just the way I was, and He changed me a little bit at a time by changing my heart.

It took the hurt of my father being diagnosed with cancer and being given a death sentence by the doctors to make my commitment to Jesus. Praise God; because my father made that same commitment when he became ill, I know where he is spending eternity **right now,** and it gives me great joy and peace that I will see him again. We may not all get that same chance. Only God knows how many days our lives on earth will be. There is no guarantee we will be here tomorrow.

How can I know this assurance that my sins are forgiven?It is written in the scriptures:

> **Hebrews 10: 14:** [14]because by one sacrifice **he has made perfect forever** those **who are being made holy**.
>
> "Then God adds in **Hebrews 10: 17-18** [17]**And their sins and iniquities will I remember no more.**
>
> [18]Now where remission of these is, **there is no more offering for sin**.

Jesus was and is our everlasting sacrifice for sin. There is no longer any other sacrifice for sin. There is no way to earn or pay God for his love—**it is a gift.**

> **Revelation 22: 17** [17]The Spirit and the bride say, "Come!" And let him who hears say, "Come!" **Whoever is thirsty, let him come**; and whoever wishes, **let him take the free gift of the water of life. (NIV)**

It is my prayer that I have given you enough of God's holy word that you will seek the truth for yourself. The decision is yours. I do know that if you will truly seek God, he will reveal himself to you. I pray you will find his love for you overwhelming and that you will want to spend eternity with him **right now**, before it is too late.

God loves you and so do I!

Job: Only God is God and I am man!

Chapter 14

The book of Job in the Old Testament is one of my favorite books in the Bible. From this book alone, you can learn and receive all of the **great glory** of God. Lessons on how to handle life's hardships can be learned from the life of Job, who goes from riches to rags, health to illness, and joy and peace to great suffering and agony. Through his perseverance, in the end, God restored him back to wealth, health, and joy; blessed by God who doubled all that Job possessed. A believer will receive this and more in heaven.

There is more to this book than it's telling Job's life history. Sandwiched around his life story are the messages of **creation, wisdom of God, sin and accountability, judgment for the unbeliever, redemption; Jesus, the cross, salvation and resurrection; God's answer to evolutionists; and even dinosaurs.** In this one old book written well before the birth of our Lord Jesus Christ, Job trusted in him—he saw him as **his Intercessor**. He had faith in God and knew that he would **redeem him**. Job foresaw things only a man of faith could know of God. Many scholars place the book of Job as possibly the oldest book in the Bible.

The book of Job is written poetically; what great truth it bears about our Creator God. May this chapter be a blessing to you and tweak a desire to know him better.

The Wisdom and Greatness of God

Compared to God's greatness and wisdom, humans can only bow in awe. Man's knowledge has increased with unbelievable advancements, especially in the past 100 years. This does not compared to God's wisdom; we can only see a very small part **of his greatness and wisdom. It is unreachable to fully understand his greatness.** Food for thought of his greatness is found throughout the Book of Job.

> **Job 4: 17** [17]Shall mortal man be more just than God? **shall a man be more pure than his maker?**
>
> **Job 9: 4** [4]**He is wise in heart**, and mighty in strength:
>
> **Verse 5** [5]Which removeth the mountains, and **they know not**: which overturneth them in his anger
>
> **Verse 6** [6]Which **shaketh the earth out of her place**, and the pillars thereof tremble
>
> **Verse 8** [8]Which **alone spreadeth out the heavens (A very scientific statement)**
>
> **Verse 9 & 10** [9]Which maketh **Arcturus**, **Orion**, and **Pleiades**, and the chambers of the south.
>
> [10]Which doeth great things past finding out; yea, and **wonders without number.**
>
> **Job 11: 7- 8** [7]"**Can you discover the depths of God?** Can you discover the limits of the Almighty?
>
> [8]"They are high as the heavens, what can you do? Deeper than Sheol, what can you know? **(NASB)**
>
> **Job 12: 10** [10]In whose hand is the soul of every living thing, and **the breath of all mankind.**

Job 12: 13 [13]**With him is wisdom and strength**, he hath counsel and understanding.

Job 21: 22 [22]**Shall any teach God knowledge? (I am afraid that in his arrogance, man is attempting to teach God today.)** seeing he judgeth those that are high.

Job 28: 12 [12]But where shall **wisdom be found?** and **where is the place of understanding? (My faith and understanding is in God and not man)**

Verses 23 & 24 [23]**God understandeth** the way thereof, and **he knoweth the place thereof.**

[24]For he looketh to the ends of the earth, and **seeth under the whole heaven; (God sees everything—is your God this mighty?)**

Job 36: 22-23 [22]"Behold, God is exalted in **His power**; **Who is a teacher like Him? (Really ask yourself this question)**

[23]"**Who has appointed Him His way**, And who has said, You have done wrong'? **(NASB)**

Job 36: 26 [26]How great is God—**beyond our understanding!** The number of his years is past finding out. **(NIV)**

This is the God I serve and it is only a part of his picture—**I am in awe of him**. As the words Steven Curtis Chapman put in song: "God is God, and I am man; I can only see a part of the picture he's painting...For **only God is God!"**

Science: Creation Versus Evolution

In Job and in many other books, you will see that God paints more to the picture given to us in Genesis about the wonderful universe he created. Although the book of Job is written poetically it is still very scientific as well. Many say the Bible is not scientific; **I beg to differ**. God gives us enough information to know **he is the Creator who spoke the universe into existence.** He molded man from the earth to bring us into existence as well. This is obvious; for when we die, we eventually return to dust, the dirt of the earth. God does not ask us to accept this evidence with blinders on. Read below and see the science in the book of Job. Job could only have attained this knowledge through God.

> **Job 9: 8** [8]Which alone **spreadeth out the heavens,**

This is a very good description of what the universe looks like to scientists. **Scientists call it the "Big Bang."** The Bible has been saying, what the scientist observe, all along; it just the timetable that man disagrees with God. God said he created the universe in six days, and man wants to debate this with him and say to him, "No you didn't." My God is mighty enough to do it in six days, just as he said he did.

> **Job 11: 12** [12]"An idiot will become intelligent
> When the **foal of a wild donkey is born a man**. **(NASB)**
> **(I think evolution would have us believe something close to this is possible.)**

Chapter 26 is one of God's most scientific chapters in the Bible. Starting with **verse 7** it reads:

> **[7]He stretcheth out the north over the empty place**

This is exactly what science tells us is seen above earth using the Hubble Space telescope. In space over our Northern Hemisphere, stars and planets are less numerous—it is like a hole in the universe. Scientists tell us that earth is in a unique place in the universe. We are in a special place where there is a hole in the universe so we can observe it. If we were anywhere else in our galaxy, we would be blinded by the closeness of the stars, unable to observe what God has created. How could the writer of Job know this when this hole cannot be seen by the naked eye and has only been discovered recently?

"and **hangeth the earth upon nothing." (Poetically, this is a very good way to describe earth's orbit around the sun and gravitational pulling to keep it in place.)**

> **Verse 8: [8]He bindeth up the waters in his thick clouds;**
> and the cloud is not rent under them.

> **Verse 14** [14] And these are but the outer fringe of his works;
> how faint the whisper we hear of him!
> **Who then can understand the thunder of his power?" (NIV)**

Chapter 36 starting with verse 22 and **chapters 37, 38, and 39** describe God's wondrous work in nature too numerous to describe in this chapter. God is given all of the credit for how nature works in these chapters. I urge you to read these chapters and see God's marvelous creation.

I would like to see the evolutionists' answer the questions God asks Job in **chapters 38 and 39**. They are done in poetry, but they are very enlightening.

The start of chapter 38 is what I call God's answer to evolutionists:

> **Verse 2:** [2]Who is this that darkeneth counsel **by words without knowledge? (God is challenging us; who do you believe, man or God?This is why I trust God and not what man says, man is fallible but not God!)**

> **Verse 4: [4]Where wast thou when I laid the foundations of the earth? (Ask yourself, where was man that we can give God the answers how he did it?)** declare, if thou hast understanding.

> **Verse 5:** [5]Who hath laid the measures thereof, if thou knowest? or who hath stretched the line upon it? **(Ask yourself, was man there when God created the earth?)**
>
> **Verse 6:** **[6]Whereupon are the foundations thereof fastened?** or who laid the corner stone thereof;

God is asking man, as Ken Ham, the founder of Answers in Genesis puts it so well, **"Were you there?"** Was man there when God created the universe and formed the earth?Why do we believe man over God? Do we have superior wisdom and knowledge that we can be wiser than our Creator?God is asking all of mankind these questions in the book of Job.

Other poetic questions God asks man in Job 38:

> [8]"Or **who enclosed the sea** with doors
> When, bursting forth, it went out from the womb;
> [9]When I made a cloud its garment
> And thick darkness its swaddling band,
> [10]And **I placed boundaries on it**
> And set a bolt and doors,
> [11]And I said, **'Thus far you shall come, but no farther;**
> **And here shall your proud waves stop'? (NASB)**

For the most part, this is a very true and scientific statement, except during natural disasters such as floods, hurricanes, and tsunamis.

God's mighty power is revealed in the book of Job! God has a very good understanding of science and nature. The Bible **does not contradict good science anywhere in its revelation.** Remember, Job contains poetic writings; but it brings great truth, as we will continue to see.

> [12]"Have you ever in your life **commanded the morning**,
> And caused **the dawn to know its place, (NASB)**

[14] **The earth takes shape like clay under a seal;**
its features stand out like those of a garment. **(NIV)**

[16]Hast thou entered into the **springs of the sea?** or hast **thou walked in the search of the depth? (Man still cannot do this today!)**

[18]**"Have you understood the expanse of the earth?**
Tell Me, if you know all this. **(NASB)**

Just think what God was asking Job! Here is a man who lived approximately 4,000 years ago or longer. He could not possibly have known the size of the earth, and yet he declares it through God's questioning! The questions are beyond my comprehension—that this could be written so long ago unless God is the author and I believe he is.

The questioning continues:

[29]Out of whose womb **came the ice?** and the hoary frost of heaven, who hath gendered it?

[30]The waters are hid as with a stone, and **the face of the deep is frozen.**

How could Job, a man living in the Middle East all of his life, possibly know on his own that it could get cold enough that **water could turn hard as stone?** He could never have witnessed it where he lived. How did this get written in the Bible if man was ignorant of these things when this book was written?

God continues to ask questions:

[33]Knowest thou the ordinances of heaven? canst thou set the dominion thereof in the earth?

> [34]Canst thou lift up thy voice to the clouds, that abundance of waters may cover thee?
>
> [35]**Canst thou send lightnings**, that they may go and say unto thee, Here we are? **(Man is being bold enough in this day and age to think he can control his own destination and do it alone without God!)**
>
> [36]Who hath put **wisdom in the inward parts?** or **who hath given understanding to the heart? (Evolution cannot explain how our minds could develop and acquire knowledge. Why are we not like any other animal?)**
>
> [37]**Who can number the clouds** in wisdom? or who can stay the bottles of heaven,

God is asking tough questions to a bold and fallible mankind. There is much man does not understand. Only God has the explanation to his creation and nature **because He was there and we were not. I have learned to trust God over what man thinks he knows.** I go to the Bible first when I have questions and check all of man's wisdom with God's word. I pray you will trust in God in this same way.

I want to add three more scientific facts from other books of the Bible to show the scientific evidence of scripture **before we look at dinosaurs**. Two are taken from the Old Testament; the first is found in the **book of Isaiah,** and the second is found in the **book of Psalms.** The last one we will look at is from the New Testament in the **book of Acts**. There are many more examples I can give from other books that show the Bible is true to science and is not flawed, but these three will demonstrate it for you nicely.

It is said that **the church had preached that the earth is flat**, just as it taught **the earth was the center of the universe** and the sun orbits it. It is a fact that man held onto this belief for centuries and so did the church, **but the Bible NEVER taught either. It is a lie and false teaching that it came from the bible—IT DID NOT!**

It was man's fallibility that interpreted it incorrectly. God had it right from the beginning.

We have already seen in **Job 26: 7** that God describes poetically the **earth is in orbit;** and now in Isaiah, **God teaches the earth is round** and that he stretched out the heavens (**universe**) as if it were a tent to dwell in. This is very scientific and correct. The Bible has been right all along, and it is man who has gotten it wrong—because **we are fallible.**

> **Isaiah 40: 22** [22]It is **he (God!)** that sitteth **upon the circle of the earth**, and the inhabitants thereof are as grasshoppers; **that stretcheth out the heavens** as a curtain, and spreadeth them out **as a tent to dwell in:**

Again we have to ask ourselves, how could merely a man named Isaiah living approximately 2,750 years ago, without the benefit of a telescope, know this scientific fact that the earth is round?How would he know the universe is stretched out like a tent for us to live in?**Simple**—my answer is that the Bible is the inspired word of God.

In the **book of Psalms**, the writer testifies to a worldwide flood—that the waters stood above the mountains and then retreated. It confirms the deep of the oceans had earthquakes that would cause the ocean basins to sink, and the mountains to rise.

> **Psalm 104: 5-9** [5]**Who laid the foundations of the earth,** that it should not be removed for ever.
>
> [6]Thou coveredst it with the deep as with a garment: **the waters stood above the mountains.**
>
> [7]**At thy rebuke they fled**; at the voice of thy thunder they hasted away.
>
> [8]**They go up by the mountains; they go down by the valleys unto the place which thou hast founded for them.**

> [9]Thou hast set a bound that they may not pass over; **that they turn not again to cover the earth.**

Again, the Psalm above is poetic in nature, but is very scientific in truth. It would be exactly what creation model scientists would expect to have happened during a catastrophic event, such as the worldwide flood described in **Genesis 6-9; and there is much evidence for it.**

One example I will give you comes from Creation Magazine, volume 24, March 2002, and the article is about **giant oyster fossils**. These giant oyster fossils measure 12 feet in width and weigh about 650 pounds each; and there are roughly 500 of them scattered high in the Andes Mountains 13,000 feet above sea level. Fossilized oysters have been found across the globe including the mountains in Switzerland. **How in the world did these dead sea creatures get deposited high in the mountains all over the world?** Secular scientists will give you an answer using the evolution model that will totally contradict the creation model. It is up to us all to choose which model makes more sense. We will learn more about these two models used for origin of life in chapters 24 and 25.

In Acts, the author, Luke, was inspired to write these words:

> **Acts 17: 26** [26]And hath made of **one blood all nations of men** for to dwell on all the face of the earth, and hath determined the times before appointed, and the bounds of their habitation;

Scripture above is saying that from **one blood came all the nations of the world.** This would verify what scripture says in Genesis that Adam and Eve are the first humans, and all mankind can be traced back to these first two parents. Because of the advancements in the field of microbiology, scientists have proven that mankind does have a common ancestor. There is no doubt all of mankind is related. All the races of the world have come from the first parents, Adam and Eve. It proves that microevolution (changes within species) does occur. **God loves variety**. Ken Ham has written a book called **"One Blood"** and explains scientifically how all the races of the world could come from our first parents. There are also many articles on the Answers in Genesis web site, about this topic. Remember this, good science does not contradict the Bible and the Bible does not contradict good science.

Could the Bible possibly speak of Dinosaurs?

God continues with science in chapters 40 and 41 in the book of Job; **God gives mankind a biology lesson. Chapters 40 and 41** are what I call the "**dinosaur chapters.**"

The word 'dinosaur' was not invented until 1841, by Sir Richard Owen, thousands of years after the book of Job was written. In **Chapter 40,** starting with **verse 15,** you will see a creature name "**Behemoth**" described. **What animal is God painting in this description?**

> 15 Behold now **behemoth, which I made with thee**; he eateth grass as an ox.
>
> 16 Lo now, his strength is in his loins, and **his force is in the navel of his belly.**
>
> 17 He moveth **his tail like a cedar**: **(A cedar tree of Lebanon where the cedar tree can grow 40 feet high and 12 feet in diameter. This is no elephant or hippo tail being described.)** the sinews of his stones are wrapped together.
>
> **18 His bones are as strong pieces of brass; his bones are like bars of iron.**
>
> 19 He is the chief of the ways of God: **(God says he is the greatest in size of all his creatures.)**
>
> 23 **When the river rages**, he is not alarmed;
> he is secure, though the Jordan should surge against his mouth. **(NIV)**

The river Jordan at flood stage is over 40 feet high, and yet the waters at flood stage cannot budge this creature! You may turn and read commentaries or footnotes in your Bible and man interprets scripture here might be describing an elephant or a hippo. **Hogwash!** With a tail that might be 40 feet long and with a girth of 12 feet? Both the elephant's and the hippo's tail would be best described as a rope, **never a tree**. God's Behemoth could stand in flood stage waters of 40 feet high and not be moved. I assure you, the elephant and the hippo would be swimming for their lives and not just standing there. It looks to me that man is interpreting and getting it wrong again instead of taking the Bible literally where he should.

Man has a great imagination. In fact, the dinosaurs depicted in documentaries and in motion pictures such as the Jurassic Park series are just that, figments of some ones imagination. Scientists, because they have bought into the eons of years for evolution, have come up with this neat little story of God's greatest sized creatures without one shred of evidence. We will see in chapters 24 and 25 that evolution is a belief system, the same as creation is a belief system. It all depends on your starting point.

Without having a photograph of Behemoth, this creature fits the description of the dinosaur that has a long neck and a long tail-*perhaps a Brachiosaurus or Apatosaurus* (**Brontosaurus**). It was the largest of God's creatures, ate grass, had strong legs and bones, had a large belly, and a **tail like a cedar.** If you have Internet access, type in the search word "**brontosaurus**," and you will see artists' pictures of such an animal on some sites. **See how this animal described by God to Job fits well with that picture.**

In chapter 41 you will see another creature described as **"Leviathan." Again, Bible footnotes or commentaries will say it might possibly be a crocodile. This is, once again, man telling God what this animal is without ever being there to see it.** The book of Job describes Leviathan having the ability to shoot fire from its mouth and pour smoke from its nostrils. Poetically as Job is, this animal should be taken literally with having some sort of defense mechanism that was like fire and smoke. Today, we have electric eels in the ocean that have the ability to shoot electricity at high voltage for defense. Octopus can spray its ink to cover its trail and make its escape from predators. The Bible does use a Hebrew word for leviathan that was translated much later into English as **dragon(s).** What Job is telling us is this, once we had an animal that would be described as a **dragon** in the past, as a **dinosaur** today, and in **Job chapter 41—Leviathan.**

We can argue this point, but I believe dinosaurs were here on earth at the exact same time as man. There is so much evidence **that man has seen dinosaurs** in the past **with his own eyes**, before he dug them up as fossils. Archeologists have found ancient stone carvings done on rocks, and there are paintings in caves that are thousands of years old that depict dinosaurs. You can surf the Internet and see much evidence that **man and dinosaurs co-existed**. Again, I highly recommend the Answers in Genesis web site.

What happened to dinosaurs?Simple: they became extinct like animals continue to do so today. I believe most became extinct right after Noah's flood and during the ice age that would have occurred after the worldwide flood. Yes, the creation model believes there was an ice age (but only one) just as the evolutionary model believes in ice ages (more than one).

Scientific Moment: A recent discovery that *Creation Magazine* first reported on in 1997 shows scientists discovered a fossilized bone of a T-Rex that had not completely fossilized. The leg bone of this T-Rex was dug up in the United States in 1990. Deep inside the long bone of the leg, scientists found traces of red blood cells. Now in 2005, it has further been reported that soft tissue and complete blood vessels have been found within the bone. The tissue has been found to be still flexible and resilient. This has to make one wonder how traces of blood and soft tissue from the T-Rex **could have lasted 65 million years** and remain flexible. This evidence speaks volumes for a Biblical account with a more recent creation than secular scientists would have us believe. You can check this discovery out from secular sources also. If you have access to the Internet, search, "soft tissue found in T-Rex bone," and also go the Answers in Genesis web site and type in the same search and see how scientists who believe in creation explain this find.

A good book written by a scientist who took an analytical look at Genesis and Noah's Flood is ***The Genesis Record- A scientific***

and devotional commentary on the book of beginnings, written by Henry M Morris, Ph.D. His field of science is hydrology, which, simply put, is the study of the origins and processes of water.

Books like above, videos, scientific information, and more are available for your study at the web site www.**AnswersInGenesis.org.** If the creation-evolution debate is keeping you from trusting the Bible, I strongly urge you to investigate what scientists who take Genesis literally can teach you. They can more than defend their belief in creation. They have scientists who are experts in their field of study—in every field of science.

I know now through my studies that the Bible does not contradict good science and that **good science does not contradict the Bible**. We will expand more on this in chapters 24 and 25 when I will present the only **two models** for the origin of life and the evidence science has developed that both models look at. **Only the conclusions are different**.

Sin and Our Accounting for It, Judgment for the Unsaved (We All Start Here!)

The Bible is continually warning us to look inward at ourselves and see the sin that is in us. The book of Job is no different. There is an important reason for it. Unless you can see the sin(s) you have committed against God, you will never realize how much you need him; and you will never feel the need to repent. That is the whole purpose of the Ten Commandments. If you do not see yourself as a sinner, you will never rely on him as heavily as he wants you to. You will never experience him as the loving Father who desperately loves you.

In Genesis, **the foundational book of the entire Bible**, we learn where sin comes from as well as disease and death: Adam and Eve **(I take this literally in Genesis that they are real people—mankind's first parents).** Adam brought sin into our world by disobeying our Creator God. We, as Adam and Eve's offspring, **are born into sin**. It is the reason why I have no problem understanding and seeing the evil in the world and why people are capable of doing such evil to one another. Mankind enjoys many of the sins he performs—**we**

love to sin. The Bible teaches **we all have sinned and fallen short of God's glory.** Because of our sins**, we are all under the curse of sin.** In the book of Job, you get great insight into what God teaches and what the **wages or our earnings are for sinning against God.**

> **Job 4: 9** [9]By the blast of God **they perish**, and by the breath of his nostrils are they consumed.
>
> **Job 8: 13-15** [13]So are the paths of **all that forget God**; and the hypocrite's hope **shall perish**:
>
> [14]**Whose hope shall be cut off**, and whose trust shall be a spider's web.
>
> [15]He shall lean upon his house, but it shall not stand: he shall hold it fast, but **it shall not endure**.

What are you relying on other than God that will bring you into eternity.... what are you hoping for after death? Look at scriptures highlighted words above. They perish—**all that forget God** shall perish; and their hope shall be cut off... it shall not endure.

> **Job 9: 20** [20]If I justify myself, **mine own mouth shall condemn me**: if I say, I am perfect, **it shall also prove me perverse**.

Job above is admitting he has sinned. If he were to deny it, his own mouth would condemn him. All have sinned; we can say we are innocent, but deep down we all know we have sinned. We have all not forgiven a wrong, spoken badly of someone, wanted our neighbors goods, lusted after something immoral, and loved something more than **He who created us. Our mouths may be pleading our innocence, but it will not hold up in God's court ...for we all know our guilt!**

> **Job 10: 14-15** [14] **If I sinned**, you would be watching me and **would not let my offense go unpunished.**

[15] If I am guilty—woe to me!
Even if I am innocent, I cannot lift my head,
for I am full of shame
and drowned in my affliction. **(NIV)**

Are you guilty of sin in God's eyes? Are you ashamed for the sins you have committed? **I admit I am.** Do you understand that a perfect and just God must punish the offenses we commit? God in this book of Job is teaching us that sin will not go unpunished. There are consequences for our actions.

Hell (It Is a Real Place!)

As we discussed in chapters 4 and 5, no one wants to speak about hell. Many choose to believe there is no hell and hope that there is a heaven. Where do we get this belief that there is no hell? Is it from God's teaching, or is it man's teaching? Is it only hope and a means for us to justify our lives for the way we choose to live them? **According to scripture, hell is a real place.** In Job we can learn what it is like. From all being guilty of sin and admitting to it, we learn what we all have earned, (I include myself, for I am guilty.)
At the end of chapter **10 verses 20-22**, you get a small picture of what hell is like.

[20] Are not my few days almost over?
Turn away from me so I can have a moment's joy
(That is what a lot of us are telling God to do!)

[21] before **I go to the place of no return (hell)**,
to the land of **gloom and deep shadow**,

[22] to the land of **deepest night**,
of deep **shadow** and **disorder**,
where even the light is like darkness."

How scary is this description? Look at the key words—a place of no return, gloom and deep shadows, deepest night, shadow and disorder, and **where even the light is like darkness**. Job is seeing a place after death that no one in his or her right mind would want to go. Look at this as more than a warning. Look at this as God's love for you that he does not want anyone to perish and that he does warn us.

Again in **chapter 18**, there is some more insight of what hell will be like. Please read the entire chapter in your Bible. It warns that unbelievers are on the wrong path, and there are traps ready to seize them. When the trap does finally snare one at his or hers death, terrors will make him or her afraid from every side and Satan, "the firstborn of death," will be there to devour the unbeliever.

> **Verse 5**: [5]Yea, the **light of the wicked (All have fallen short of the glory of God and therefore are wicked.)** and the spark of his fire shall not shine.
>
> **Verse 8**: [8]For he is cast into a net by his own feet, and he walketh upon a snare.
>
> **Verse 9**: [9]The **gin (trap)** shall take him by the heel, and the **robber (Satan—he is a robber of our joy.)** shall prevail against him.
>
> **Verse 10**: [10] **A noose is hidden for him on the ground**;
> a trap lies in his path.
>
> **Verse 11**: **[11]Terrors shall make him afraid on every side,** and shall drive him to his feet.
>
> **Verse 13**: [13]It shall devour the strength of his skin:
> even **the firstborn of death (Satan)** shall devour his strength.
>
> **Verse 14** [14]His confidence shall be rooted out of his tabernacle, **(What are you confident in that you are relying on? I pray it is God.)** and it shall bring him to the **king of terrors. (Satan is waiting.)**

Verse 17: [17] The memory of him **perishes from the earth;** he has no name in the land. **(God says to me the land is heaven and unbelief will make us miss out on our destiny.)**

Verse 18: [18]He shall be driven from light **(God is the light.) into darkness (hell)**, and chased out of the world. **(The sinner is going to be banished from heaven.)**

Verse 21 [21]Surely such are the **dwellings of the wicked, (I cannot stress enough all have fallen short of God's glory, and therefore all are evil.)** and this is the place of him **that knoweth not God. (Do you know God? I pray you do!)**

Chapter 18 is a very frightening description to me of what is going to happen to unbelievers in Jesus Christ. I am being very bold here. Using all of scripture, we know this is the fate for those who will not accept **God's free gift** of salvation. If the word of God showed another way to be saved, I promise I would tell you about it. I cannot find it.

Fate of All Sinners (Mankind)- We All Start Here

The fate of all **sinners (Everyone who ever lived or will live starts here.)** is described in **chapter 20**. I do not want to be counted with the unrighteous sinners, and I pray that **you** will not want to be either. **There is a way out; and God prepared it for us, as you will see later. Please read chapter 20.**

Chapter 20: Verse 5: [5]That the **triumphing of the wicked is short**, and **the joy of the hypocrite but for a moment**?

Above, God is telling us the joys of the earth last for only the time you are alive and at death, they cease. This is a simple truth. **Sin can be very pleasurable**; it is not always painful, **but its time is short.** There is so much more God has planned for those who become his children!

Verse 7: [7]Yet he shall perish for ever like his own dung: they which have seen him shall say, **Where is he? (Unforgiven sinners will perish forever and we will ask where they are.)**

Verse 10: "His own hands **must give back his wealth." (NIV) (We only have our wealth while on this earth. At death we must all give up what God has given us.)**

Verse 11: **[11]His bones are full of the sin of his youth,** which shall lie down with him **in the dust. (The unbelievers' sins remain with them forever. The wages for sin is death—we all die...why? It all began in Genesis chapter 3.)**

Verse 17: [17]He shall not see the rivers, the floods, the **brooks of honey and butter. (A good description of missing out on heaven—Heaven is God's desire for us.)**

Verse 18: [18]That which he laboured for shall he restore, and **shall not swallow it down:** according to his substance shall the restitution be, and **he shall not rejoice therein. (We cannot take our property with us at death. What does a man profit if he loses his own soul? There will be no rejoicing.)**

Verse 20-21: [20]Surely he shall not feel quietness in his belly, **he shall not save of that which he desired.**

[21]There shall none of his meat be left; therefore shall no man look for his goods **(Verses 20 and 21 state we cannot buy our way into heaven; our wealth will not get us there, nor will it last...Can man save himself?)**

Verse 27: [27]The heaven shall **reveal his iniquity**; **(God will expose our guilt, and we will know we are unrighteous; for we all fall short of the glory of God.)**

> **Verse 29**: 29This is the **portion of a wicked man from God**, and the heritage appointed unto him by God. **(The fate of the wicked will be judgment for their sins.)**

Again, chapter 20 clearly warns of the fate of all who are unrighteous in God's eyes. **How can one be counted amongst the righteous? God does have a plan, as we will see.**

Now that we have seen through Job how God deals with sin and also that there is a real place of eternal punishment called hell, the book of Job deals with the judgment of God.

Judgment

In **Job chapter 22**, it speaks of a time when God did pass judgment on wicked men already. It was a time when God regretted ever creating human beings because of their wickedness. Thank goodness God found one worthy man and his family among the wicked. Job reveals that God sent a flood –**a great flood, Noah's flood**, which you can read about in **Genesis Chapters 6-9**.

God asks everyone this question.

> **Job 22: 15** 15Hast thou marked the old way **which wicked men have trodden? (Job is speaking of the ancient days and how evil men were in Noah's days.)**

The consequences for the wickedness of men in Noah's day was this:

> **Job 22: 16**: 16Which were cut down out of time, **whose foundation was overflown with a flood: (Noah's great flood—it is judgment: total destruction because of their evil ways.)**

The reason for God's action was this:

> **Job 22: 17**: 17Which said unto God, **Depart from us**: and what can the Almighty do for them? **(Are you one that is**

asking God to leave you alone? God wants to have a relationship with you!)

Chapter 24 is an important chapter for the sinner to see what God sees. No one escapes his eyes. His eyes are on man's ways; and sees man's heart. This is another chapter I urge you to read in its entirety.

> **Job 24: 13**: 13They are of those that **rebel against the light; (God himself) they know not the ways thereof**, nor abide **in the paths** thereof. **(His word is the Bible, and it is the road map to life.)**

Unless you come into the light of God's word, you will never know his ways. You will never be able to stay on the path that leads to eternity with him if you continue to rebel and stay in your self-destructing lifestyle.

> **Job 24: 15-16** 15 The eye of the adulterer watches for dusk;
> he thinks, **'No eye will see me (God can see you!)**,'
> and he keeps his face concealed.
>
> 16 In the dark, men break into houses,
> but by day they shut themselves in;
> **they want nothing to do with the light. (NIV)**

God is the light and the word of God is the Bible. Someday God will bring sinners out of the darkness and into the light where their sins will shine.

> **Job 24: 22-24** 22He draweth also the **mighty with his power**: he riseth up, and **no man is sure of life**.

We do not live forever on this earth. No man is sure how long he has. God could take him when he least expects it. He has to be ready.

> [23]Though it be given him to be in safety, whereon he resteth; yet his eyes are upon their ways.

We may think we are in a safe place and God has blessed us that we are living in a good place without strife, but God sees our ways and how we are living our lives.

> [24]They are exalted for a little while, but are gone and brought low; they are taken out of the way as all other, and cut off as the tops of the ears of corn.

Ungodly people may seem to get away with it and go unpunished, but God sees their ways; and they will be brought into judgment in God's court.

> **Job 34: 21- 22** [21]For **his eyes are upon the ways of man**, and he seeth all his goings.
>
> **[22]There is no darkness, nor shadow of death, where the workers of iniquity may hide themselves.**

Job is showing us we are all evildoers in God's eyes for all have sinned; we are all guilty—**we all start here!** We cannot hide our sins from him whose eyes see everything. **Can we save ourselves? Who can save us?**

Can Man Save Himself?

The Bible teaches that **man cannot save himself**. God is a righteous God and cannot look upon sin. Therefore, since we all have sinned and fallen short of the glory God, **it is impossible for us to save ourselves. The book of Job attests to this.**

In **chapter 25** you learn:

> **Verse 2**: [2] "Dominion and awe **belong to God**;
> he establishes order in the heights of heaven. **(NIV)**

Verse 4: [4]**How then can man be justified with God?** or how can he be clean that is born of a woman?

Verse 5-6: [5]Behold even to the moon, and it shineth not; yea, **the stars are not pure in his sight.**

[6]**How much less man**, that is a worm? and the son of man, which is a worm?

I hope this has not hurt your ego. In God's need for righteousness and because we all have sinned, it is impossible to be pure in God's eyes. Even the lights of the stars are not pure to God. It is hopeless!

In **chapter 40** you find:

Verse 9: [9]Hast thou an arm like God? or canst thou thunder with a voice like him? **(Verse 9 is asking, "Are you like God?")**

Verse 10: [10]Deck thyself now with majesty and excellency; and array thyself with glory and beauty.

According to verse 9, you must be like God to save yourself; and then in verse 10, God dares you to dress yourself like a god, as if you are like him. **Are you a god that can save yourself?**

Scripture is telling us we are sinners and are not like God. What can merely a man do to save himself?The good news of the Bible is that **he does not have to!**

Redemption: Jesus, the Cross, Salvation, and Resurrection

In the book of Job, you will see part of the picture God is painting in the rest of His word, the Bible. In the book of Job, you can see God's plan for salvation and that we have a **redeemer in God's court of justice who is defending us for our sins right now—he is**

Jesus. Through him we will be resurrected; and with our own eyes, **we will see our redeemer.**

In **Job chapter 5**, Eliphaz, Job's friend, advises him he should appeal to God. He sees Job as a fool taking root **without a defender**.

> **Verse 4**: ".... crushed in court without a defender." **(NIV)** **(When I read this, I wrote in my Bible: Jesus is our defender in God's Court—It's true!)**

Verses 14-16 are interesting passages of scripture, I found Jesus and what he did for us on the cross—**Can you see him?**

> **Verse 14**: 14They meet with darkness in the day time, and grope in the **noonday as in the night**. **(Scripture reveals, that as Jesus hung from the cross, it became as night at midday.)**

Get ready to see Jesus in **verses15-16.**

> **Verses 15-16** 15But **he saveth** the poor from the sword, from their mouth, **(The poor are you and me and the sword in our mouth is the tongue that condemns us.)** and from the hand of the mighty. **16So the poor hath hope, (The poor are you and I. We have hope in the one who saves—Jesus!)**

In **chapter 7**, Job raises an interesting question to God.

> **Verse 21**: 21 **Why do you not pardon my offenses**
> **and forgive my sins?**
> For I will soon lie down in the dust;
> you will search for me, **but I will be no more."**

Do you ever ask this question?Do you ever feel like your sins are not forgiven and cannot be forgiven?Do you ever feel like you are unworthy of God's forgiveness? Job is at a low time in his life and does not sense God's love for him. He is so low; he desires death over his suffering. We will soon see through Job that God does forgive our sins and we are worthy because of his love.

In **chapter 9**, Job sees that it is impossible for a mortal to be righteous before God. He states:

> **Verse 15**: ".... I could only plead with my judge for mercy" **(NIV) (That is exactly what we must do. We must examine ourselves and ask for forgiveness and repent for our sins.)**

Shortness of Life?

Chapter 14 is one of my favorite chapters of Job. In the beginning, as many of us do, Job sees life as hopeless because life is short; we live here on earth for a short time and then we are gone. But life goes on so much longer. Job puts it this way:

> **Verse 5**: [5]Seeing **his days are determined, the number of his months are with thee**, thou hast appointed his bounds **that he cannot pass;**

> **Verse 7**: [7]For **there is hope of a tree**, if it be cut down, that **it will sprout again,** and that the tender branch thereof **will not cease.**

> **Verse 10**: **[10]But man dieth, and wasteth away**: yea, **man giveth up the ghost**, and **where is he?**

Do you ever think of your own mortality?Job realizes that life on earth is short. You only have so many trips around the sun. A tree has more hope than us because it can sprout again even if it is cut down.

Verse 13 is awesome. Job sees much more than what he says in **verses 5, 7, and 10**. He doesn't fully realize yet the truth in what he is saying.

> [13]O that thou wouldest **hide me in the grave**, that thou wouldest keep me secret, **until thy wrath be past**, that **thou wouldest appoint me a set time, and remember me!**

God does remember—those who believe in him—even the ones who do not. Job is slowly revealing what he sees.

Salvation and Resurrection—We Have A Defender, An Intercessor!

Verses 14 - 17 is the meat of what **God did for all of mankind. Believe this and you will be saved!** This is the gospel message of Jesus Christ that is fully revealed in the New Testament. **This is the salvation message foreseen by Job.**

> **Job 14: 14 - 17** [14]If a man die, **shall he live again? all the days of my appointed time will I wait, till my change come. (Job is saying he will wait for his resurrection!)**
>
> [15]**Thou shalt call, and I will answer thee**: thou wilt have a desire to the work of thine hands. **(Job is saying God will want to see him again after he is dead and gone!)**
>
> [16]For now thou numberest my steps: dost thou not watch over my sin?
>
> [17]**My transgression is sealed up in a bag, and thou sewest up mine iniquity.**

Job believes his sins will be gone forever, sealed up in a bag, never to be opened. God will never use his sins against him—**this is the same good news taught in the New Testament.**

God did this for us! He not only covered up our sins, he took them away—**as if we had never sinned,** and therefore made us righteous in his eyes. He took away our sins with his blood at the cross—he was a perfect sacrifice for our sins **because Jesus is God! Believe and be saved—It is a free gift.**

Chapter 16: Jesus is our defender and our friend. He is our intercessor, pleading to God the Father in our behalf. We know this is true when we read the entire Bible and see God's other authors verifying it. The next 3 verses give you great insight as to what God is doing for you and me!

> **Job 16: 19- 21** [19] Even now my **witness (Jesus)** is in heaven; my **advocate** is on high. [20] **My intercessor (Jesus) is my friend** as my eyes pour out tears to God; [21] **on behalf of a man he pleads with God as a man pleads for his friend. (NIV)**

Just think about what Job is telling us! Jesus is our **witness** to our Father in heaven. He is our **advocate**, our **intercessor**. Jesus pleads with God for our salvation as our **friend.**

In **Chapter 19,** Job speaks of his redeemer; and you know using the entire Bible that his **redeemer is Jesus! The verses below match so perfectly with what is taught in the New Testament.** This is the **resurrection** of our bodies! **What faith Job has.** How could he describe so perfectly maybe 1,000 years or more before Christ's birth that he would have a Redeemer?

> **Job 19: 25-27** [25]For **I know that my redeemer liveth**, and that he shall stand at the latter day upon the earth:
>
> [26]**And though after my skin worms destroy this body, yet in my flesh shall I see God:**
>
> [27]Whom **I shall see for myself**, and **mine eyes shall behold**, and not another;

Job doesn't guess, Job knows he has a redeemer who lives! He knows this redeemer will stand on earth in the end of days. Even though Job's flesh is no more, **he knows he will see him in his flesh with his own eyes. Job is speaking of his own resurrection!** Job is yearning for God—**so am I**. It is my prayer you are too!

Chapter 33 is full of God's wisdom, love, salvation, and redemption.

Job 33: 4 [4]The spirit of **God hath made me**, and the **breath of the Almighty** hath given me life.

God created you and I! I love how scripture put it—**God's own breath has given me life!** How fantastic is that?

Job 33: 24- 25 [24]Then he is gracious unto him, and saith, **Deliver him from going down to the pit: I have found a ransom.**

Jesus is our ransom, and he paid the price in full for us at the cross! He alone can deliver us from hell! Think about what Job is saying here.

[25]His flesh shall be fresher than a child's: **he shall return to the days of his youth**

When we get our heavenly bodies, we will return to the days of our youth forever more. This is not a fairy tale. This is God's promise to us.

Believe in what God did at the cross for you, admit you are a sinner, and you will be delivered from going into the pit of hell. Job foresaw the truth before it happened:

Job 33: 26-30 [26]He shall pray unto God, and **he will be favourable unto him:** and **he shall see his face with joy**: for he will render unto man his righteousness.

[27]He looketh upon men, and **if any say, I have sinned**, and perverted that which was right, and it profited me not;

[28]He will deliver his soul from going into the pit (hell), and **his life shall see the light.**

[29]Lo, all these things worketh God oftentimes with man,

> **[30]To bring back his soul from the pit, to be enlightened with the light of the living.**

Wow! Reread 26- 30 to see what God has done for you! In using verse 28 and the rest of what scripture teaches—Old and New, those who confess they have sinned and believe in Jesus do not get what they deserve. God will find favor in you, and you will live in the light of God forever. You will know the truth because God is the light of all truth. **Truth from scripture:** This is what Jesus did for us; he paid the price in our behalf and took God's punishment for sin in place of us. This is the good news of the Bible from beginning to end.

Conclusion: In Job, I see a picture of God painted before it happened. Job is one of the oldest books in the Bible and yet Job reveals truth about God before it happened in history. He foresaw a redeemer who would rescue him and resurrect him from the dead. Can you see Jesus through Job? How trustworthy do you find God's word?

What happened to Job long ago is the same that is happening today in our own lives. **We want answers!** All the questions concerning pain, suffering, death, afterlife, evil, heaven, hell, etc. were asked long ago in the book of Job. Yet through all Job's suffering, he knew his **redeemer** would rescue him, and long after death, he would see him with his own eyes.

> Repeating **Job 19: 25 - 27** [25]For **I know that my redeemer liveth**, and that he shall stand at the latter day upon the earth:
>
> **[26]And though after my skin worms destroy this body, yet in my flesh shall I see God:**
>
> [27]Whom **I shall see for myself**, and mine eyes shall behold, and not another;

That redeemer is Jesus! And what he did at the cross is a free gift to **all mankind...not just Christians; but for Buddhists, Moslems,**

and Atheists... and Germans, Swedes, Indians, Chinese, blacks and whites, etc... for all mankind!

> **John 3: 16** [16]**For God so loved the world**, that he gave his only begotten Son, **that whosoever believeth in him** should not perish, but **have everlasting life.**

What do you need to do to receive this free gift God has given us?

1) Have **faith** in the one he sent, his only begotten Son, and **believe** he died on the cross for your sins and that he arose from the grave and will redeem us at God's chosen time. **Faith.**
2) **Admit** you are a sinner and that there is no way to save yourself. Jesus is your free gift and your free ticket into heaven and **you must accept** this free gift.
3) **Repent** of your sins and **confess them to God** and **ask for his forgiveness**! Have faith that all past, present, and future sins are covered and wiped away by the blood of Jesus that he shed for you and for me at the cross.

I pray you now know Jesus as your Lord and Savior and that you will sense his **love** for you because you are so special to him!

God loves you and so do!

The Book of Hebrews: The Fulfillment of Scripture

Chapter 15

The book of Hebrews to me is like the book of Job in the Old Testament. Both books are among my most favorite books of the Bible. The book of Job is one of my favorites because it tells us about the great glory of God and all his wisdom. It tells of his creation. It shows us sin and the cost we will have to pay for it. From the vantage point Job was peering into the future from, the book of Job prophesizes of the redemptive work of Jesus Christ, his work to bring us to salvation, and the resurrection of our body after death to see God in one's own flesh. I love the book of Hebrews in a similar fashion because it is **the full summary of the entire Old Testament scripture—showing how the Son of God, Jesus, fulfills all that is written.** The book of Hebrews testifies that the bible is the **biography of Jesus Christ!**

May **you see** the full glory of God, his plan for salvation, our Redeemer Jesus Christ, the Holy Spirit, creation, and **hope for the resurrection of your own being.**

Full Revelation: God, His Son, and the Holy Spirit-The Trinity of God

Make no mistake about it; the writer of this book testifies about the Trinity of God—God in three persons. It was what all the writers of the Bible were revealing. God used from the beginning the Hebrew word **Elohim to reveal who he was.** In Old Testament scripture, it is the plural form of God, first used in Genesis chapter one. Now this writer declares Jesus is the Son of God—**not an angel.**

Hebrews Chapter 1 declares who Jesus is:

> **Verses 2 – 3:** [2]Hath in these last days spoken unto us **by his Son**, whom **he hath appointed heir of all things**, by whom also **he made the worlds; (God is declaring Jesus is our Creator.)**
>
> [3]Who **being the brightness of his glory**, and **the express image of his person, (God declares Jesus is just like him; the Bible teaches there is only one God—Jesus is God!)** and upholding all things by the word of his power, when he had by himself purged our sins, **sat down on the right hand of the Majesty on high:**

The Hebrew writer declares Jesus is God—**the exact image of his being.** Further, **he is not an angel.**

> **Verses 4-6:** [4]Being made **so much better than the angels**, as he hath by inheritance obtained a more excellent name than they.
>
> [5]For unto which of the angels said he at any time, **Thou art my Son**, this day have I begotten thee? **(God is declaring there is no angel he has called "my son.")** And again, I will be to him a Father, and he shall be to me a Son?
>
> [6]And again, when he bringeth in the firstbegotten into the world, **he saith, And let all the angels of God worship him.**

Look at verse 6. Only God is to be worshiped (the first commandment), not man, nor angels, nor idols, nor money, nor pleasure...**only God**. The writer declares to us that the **Son is to be**

worshiped. Therefore Jesus, God's Son, must be God; or we would be breaking the first commandment of God. **The second person of the Trinity** in scripture is fully realized as God. Father God himself declares **Jesus is to be worshiped**.

The writer continues by revealing what **God says about Jesus:**

> **Chapter 1 Verses 8–13:** [8]**But unto the Son he saith, Thy throne, O God**, **(God is calling his Son God, and there is only one God the scriptures declare.)** is **for ever** and ever: a sceptre of righteousness is the sceptre of thy kingdom.
>
> [9]Thou hast loved righteousness, and hated iniquity; **therefore God (God is calling his Son Jesus God again.), even thy God**, hath anointed thee with the oil of gladness above thy fellows.
>
> [10]And, Thou, Lord, **in the beginning hast laid the foundation of the earth; and the heavens are the works of thine hands: (God is declaring Jesus is our Creator—we are the work oh his hands!)**
>
> [11]They shall perish **(mankind is mortal.)**; but thou remainest **(Jesus is forever!)**; and they all shall wax old as doth a garment;
>
> [12]And as a vesture shalt thou fold them up, and they shall be changed: but **thou art the same (God never changes; He remains the same always.)**, and thy years shall not fail.
>
> [13]**But to which of the angels (God again says Jesus is not an angel!) said he at any time, Sit on my right hand, until I make thine enemies thy footstool?**

In all the verses above, Father God is declaring **Jesus is God. Look at verse 8 above.** Father God is saying my Son is God, and his throne awaits him and he is righteous. In verse 9, Father God declares his Son created the universe. God is painting the full revelation who Jesus is—**He is God!**

The book of Hebrews goes on to reveal Jesus has always existed, and he is the same past, present, and forever.

> **Chapter 13: 8:** [8]Jesus Christ the same yesterday, and to day, and **for ever.**

The Book of Hebrews Testifies of the Holy Spirit—The Third Person of the Trinity

To the **Holy Spirit**, the third person of the Trinity, God testifies; and He speaks about the gifts of the Holy Spirit:

> **Hebrews 2: 4**: [4]**God also bearing them witness**, both with signs and wonders, and with divers miracles, and gifts of **the Holy Ghost**, according to his own will?

The scriptures testify it is **the Holy Spirit** who woos, convicts, instructs, and leads one to Jesus Christ as savior. It is the same message, whether you read about the Holy Spirit in the New Testament, or in the Old Testament. If you are searching for him right now, **do not harden your heart**.

> **Hebrews 3: 7-8:** [7]Wherefore (as **the Holy Ghost** saith, To day **if ye will hear his voice,** [8]**Harden not your hearts**

The Hebrew writer confirms above what David was speaking of in **Psalm 95**.

> **Psalm 95: 7-8** [7]For **he is our God**; and we are the people of his pasture, and the sheep of his hand. To day **if ye will hear his voice,**
>
> [8]**Harden not your heart**

God has fully revealed to us in the book of Hebrews that the Psalmist, King David, was speaking of God, but it is God **the Holy Spirit** who is everywhere. This is again confirmed in Hebrews chapter 4.

> **Chapter 4: 7:** [7]Again, he limiteth a certain day, **saying in David**, To day, after so long a time; as it is said, To day if ye will hear **his voice (Holy Spirit), harden not your hearts.**

The Hebrew author again testifies the existence of the Holy Spirit in chapter 9.

> **Chapter 9: 8:** **[8]The Holy Ghost** this signifying, that the way into the holiest of all was not yet made manifest, while as the first tabernacle was yet standing

The writer of this book clearly understands there are three parts to God—**Father, Son, and Holy Spirit**, all one God, just as Genesis told us from the beginning **(Elohim)** and that we are made in the image and likeness of God. This has special meaning to me because I have come to realize I am made in God's image **literally. I have a body, I have a soul, and I have a spirit** (three in one form)**...the same as God.**

> **1 Thessalonians 5: 23**, Paul writes, [23]And the very God of peace sanctify you **wholly**; and *I pray God* your **whole spirit** and **soul** and **body** be preserved blameless unto the coming of our Lord Jesus Christ.

Clearly, there are three parts that makeup **my being**. There is only one part of me others can see, my **body**. **My spirit** and **soul** are not visible. It is the same with God. Jesus is the only part of God we can see physically. God the Father and God the Holy Spirit that is everywhere is not visible. I take the Bible literally when it says we are made in the image and likeness of God as the scriptures record.

Full Revelation: Who Our Creator Is

Throughout scripture, starting with **Genesis 1:1**, the Bible claims we have a creator God. **John 1:1-5** claims the Word **(Jesus)** is God and through him all things were made:

The Word (Jesus) Became Flesh

> [1]In the beginning was the **Word**, and the **Word was with God**, and **the Word was God**.

Look at verse 1. From the very beginning, the Word was with God and **the Word was God**. The Bible also teaches there is only **ONE GOD!** I believe this with all my heart. Who must Jesus be then, according to scripture?

> [2]The same was in the beginning with God.

> **[3]All things were made by him**; and **without him was not any thing made that was made.**

The apostle John testifies that the **Word,** who he reveals as being **Jesus, is our CREATOR. Genesis 1: 1** states, [1] In the beginning **God (Elohim)** created the heavens and the earth. **Who then must Jesus be? Simple**—He is God.

> [4]In him was life; and the life was the light of men.

> [5]And the light shineth in darkness; and **the darkness comprehended it not.**

John is revealing Jesus is life and he gave it to us. Because of sin, we are in the darkness; and for those who remain in the darkness, they cannot understand his light. His light is shining, right now and always, to bring you into it.

The writer of the **book of Hebrews** attests to what John has written about Jesus. This was not fully revealed in the Old Testament, whose ancient writings ended 400 years before the birth of Christ. It is now fully revealed in the New Testament. You need the entire Bible to see God. The below verses confirm the Son of God made the universe.

> **Hebrews 1: 2:** 2Hath in these last days **spoken unto us by his Son**, whom he hath appointed heir of all things, **by whom also he made the worlds;**

In **verse 10**, God says about his Son:

> 10And, **Thou, Lord, in the beginning hast laid the foundation of the earth; and the heavens are the works of thine hands:**

There is no question throughout scripture, starting in Genesis, God was revealing himself as our Creator and that he appointed the Second Person of the Trinity, **His Son**, to make all creation in the universe through him. The Book of Hebrews attests to it.

God Warns Us for Our Disbelief

Just as in the last chapter when we looked at the book of Job, Hebrews warns the sinner **(Everyone starts here.)** there is no escaping those ignoring the Lord's salvation.

> **Hebrews 4: 12-13:** 12For **the word of God is living and active**. Sharper than any double-edged sword, it penetrates even to dividing **soul** and **spirit**, joints and marrow; it judges the thoughts and attitudes of the heart. **13Nothing in all creation is hidden from God's sight. Everything is uncovered and laid bare before the eyes of him to whom we must give account. (NIV)**

The word of God is sharper than a double-edged sword. This is why I have put so much scripture in this book. God says so much more than what I can humanly say. I want you to see God's word and not mine so you can believe—**have faith!**

> **Hebrews 2: 2-3: "...**every violation and disobedience received its just punishment, [3]**how shall we escape if we ignore such a great salvation?** This salvation, which was first announced by the Lord, was confirmed to us by those who heard him." **(NIV)**

Please do not ignore the salvation message found throughout the entire Bible. I cannot put into words the importance of what God has done for us!

> **Hebrews 4: 1-3** [1]**Let us therefore fear**, lest, a promise being left us of entering into his rest, **any of you should seem to come short of it.**
>
> [2]**For unto us was the gospel preached**, as well as unto them: but **the word preached did not profit them, not being mixed with faith** in them that heard it.

Hearing the gospel message is not good enough. **You must mix it with faith once you have heard it.**

> [3]For **we which have believed do enter into rest**, as he said, As I have sworn in my wrath, if they shall enter into my rest: although the works were finished **from the foundation of the world.**

There is rest for those who believe in Christ. There is still time. But God has made an **oath** in his righteous anger over **our disbelief** that we will not be able to enter Jesus' rest. Our disbelief is what angers him; it is faith that pleases God, **as you will see!** Remember this when we study chapter 11 of Hebrews in a little bit.

> **Hebrews 6: 16-17** [16]For **men verily swear by the greater (This is why we place our hand on a Bible when making an**

> **oath or we swear to God—be careful doing this.**): and **an oath** for confirmation is to them an end of all strife.
>
> [17]Wherein **God,** willing more abundantly to shew unto the heirs of promise the immutability of his counsel, **confirmed it by an oath**:

God himself has made an oath. Since they're in no one or nothing greater than He, He swore it upon himself. An oath is a promise God will not break, and **it is impossible for God to lie:**

> [18]That by two immutable things, in which **it was impossible for God to lie,** we might have a strong consolation, who have fled for refuge to lay hold upon the hope set before us:
>
> **[19]Which hope we have as an anchor of the soul, both sure and stedfast,** and which entereth into that within the veil;

The above scripture is telling us **it is impossible for God to lie.** God has confirmed it by an oath that is sworn onto himself. **There is no one higher than he! Whatever God says, your soul can be sure of.** I put this scripture in so you will heed his warnings. I put it in so you will know **we can trust his promises.**

Warning Against Unbelief: In Chapter 3 verses 18 and 19 below, it is God who is making this oath: you will never be able to enter into his rest in unbelief. **Unbelief is the same as being disobedient to God.**

> **Hebrews 3: 18-19** [18]And to whom **sware he** that **they should not enter into his rest**, but **to them that believed not**?
>
> [19]So we see that **they could not enter in because of unbelief.**

The prophets of God have warned us, the disciples of Jesus have warned us, and now the Holy Spirit is warning us. God has sworn you cannot enter rest in disbelief. Jesus while on the earth warned us. He continues to warn from heaven.

> **Hebrews 12: 25** [25]**See that ye refuse not him that speaketh**. For if they escaped not **who refused him that spake on earth**, much more shall not we escape, **if we turn away from him that speaketh from heaven:**

In summary, we have seen God's warning for us. He tells us not to refuse what he has spoken. Unbelief is the same as disobedience. **God loves us**, and he wants us to heed his warnings so we can accept his free gift of redemption.

Full Revelation—Jesus Is Our Redeemer

Ancient Job could not fully understand God's plan for salvation. From his vantage point, he only knew that someday after he was gone and buried, in the future, he would see his Maker face-to face.

> **Job 19: 25-27:** [25]For I know that **my redeemer liveth**, and that he shall stand **at the latter day upon the earth**:
>
> [26]And though **after my skin worms destroy this body, yet in my flesh shall I see God:**
>
> [27]Whom **I shall see for myself**, and **mine eyes** shall behold, and **not another;**

Throughout scripture more and more is revealed about God and his plans; the book of Hebrews summarizes it completely. The book of Hebrews **fully reveals** Jesus is our **redeemer and he is God's plan of salvation**. He is not only the sacrifice who takes away the sins of the world; **he is our High Priest forever.**

Hebrews 4: 14-16 [14]Seeing then that **we have a great high priest**, that is passed into the heavens, **Jesus the Son of God**, let us hold fast our profession.

[15]For we have not an high priest which cannot be touched with the feeling of our infirmities; but **was in all points tempted** like as we are, **yet without sin. (Jesus came to earth in human form and was tempted in every way—just as we are—and yet he did not sin!)**

[16]Let us therefore **come boldly unto the throne of grace, that we may obtain mercy**, and **find grace** to help in time of need.

Jesus is the sacrifice that makes us right with God. By his own blood, we are now able to come into eternal life. Jesus, the Son of God, was tempted just as we are today—yet did not sin, becoming our perfect sacrifice; and **through him we can receive mercy and grace.**

Hebrews 9: 11-14 The Blood of Christ saves: [11]But Christ being come an high priest of good things to come, by a greater and more perfect tabernacle, not made with hands, that is to say, not of this building;

[12]Neither by the blood of goats and calves, but **by his own blood he entered in once into the holy place, having obtained eternal redemption for us. (Scripture is saying by Jesus' own blood, he entered where God the Father is and obtained eternal redemption for us!)**

[13]For if the blood of bulls and of goats, and the ashes of an heifer sprinkling the unclean, sanctifieth to the purifying of the flesh:

[14]How much more shall **the blood of Christ, who through the eternal Spirit offered himself without spot**

> **to God;** purge your conscience from dead works to serve the living God?

Jesus, without spot (sin), became the one-time offering for sin so all of our sins can be forgiven. We no longer need to feel guilty for our sins; we have been forgiven, and now we can serve the living God!

God offers us a New Covenant. One that is better than the Old Covenant.

> **Hebrews 9: 15** [15]And for this cause **he is the mediator of the new testament,** that **by means of death, for the redemption** of the transgressions that were under the first testament, they which are called might receive **the promise of eternal inheritance.**

Under the old covenant, God gave us his laws to keep. All of mankind could not keep his laws. God gave us his commandments so we would see how utterly hopeless it is for us not to sin. We cannot be righteous enough by ourselves not to break them. Jesus came into the world to give us a new covenant—through his death we can receive eternal life.

Jesus Christ is the perfect sacrifice once and for all. We are made right with God through him!

> **Hebrews 10: 5-10** [5]Wherefore **when he cometh into the world**, he saith, Sacrifice and offering thou wouldest not, **but a body hast thou prepared me: (God prepared a body for his Son.)**
>
> [6]In **burnt offerings and sacrifices for sin thou hast had no pleasure. (God had no pleasure in offering of animals for sin.)**

[7]Then said I, Lo, I come (**in the volume of the book it is written of me, (The volume of the book is The Old Testament! It writes of Jesus.**) to do thy will, O God.

[8]Above when he said, Sacrifice and offering and burnt offerings and offering for sin thou wouldest not, neither hadst pleasure therein; which are offered by the law; **(Again, scripture is saying God took no pleasure in offering of animals for sin.)**

[9]Then said he, Lo, I come to do thy will, O God. He taketh away the first, that he may establish the second. **(God took away animal sacrifice so that the sacrifice of Jesus would become the one-time sacrifice for sin.)**

[10]By the which will **we are sanctified through the offering of the body of Jesus Christ once for all.**

Hebrews testifies that Jesus was written about in the volumes of the Old Testament. God was painting us his picture of his blood sacrifice he would offer up for sin in the Old Testament; and then he came and completely fulfilled the prophecies in the New Testament. Now Hebrews testifies the Holy Spirit is a witness to us. For those who know the Holy Spirit, he has written God's laws in our hearts and minds, no longer wanting to break them as we had done when we did not know Jesus.

Hebrews 10: 15-18 [15]Whereof **the Holy Ghost** also is a witness to us: for after that he had said before,

[16]This is the covenant that I will make with them after those days, saith the Lord, **I will put my laws into their hearts**, and **in their minds** will I write them;

We are filled with the Holy Spirit when we accept the sacrifice of Christ! We will then want to keep his laws because we have them in our hearts and minds. We will have a new nature, and we will want to please God. This does not happen all at once. Our new nature grows as the Holy Spirit grows in us.

Verse 17 of Hebrews is God's promise to us:

> [17]**And their sins and iniquities will I remember no more. (Fantastic!)**
>
> [18]Now where remission of these is, there is **no more offering for sin.**

The above scripture fully revealed that Jesus Christ's saving work is finished! God will remember our sins no more for those that believe in him and confess that they are sinners. There is nothing we can do, no offering we can make for our own sins. It is finished.

> **Hebrews 10: 11-14** [11]And every priest standeth daily ministering and offering oftentimes the same sacrifices, **which can never take away sins: (The old covenant sacrifice could not take away sin. To cover their sins, they had to make sacrifices each year.)**
>
> [12]**But this man, after he had offered one sacrifice for sins for ever, sat down on the right hand of God; (Jesus' work is done, a one-time sacrifice for sin that lasts forever.)**
>
> [13]From henceforth expecting till **his enemies be made his footstool (Just as what was written from the beginning in Genesis 3: 15)**.
>
> [14]**For by one offering he hath perfected for ever them that are sanctified. (We have been made right with God forever—those that are sanctified by his blood. We are sanctified by faith.)**

In summary, we now have a High Priest, Jesus Christ, in heaven whose work is finished forever. We cannot make our own sacrifices for our sins; they can never take them away. We cannot be good enough and earn our way to heaven—**It is a free gift**! Earlier in this chapter, we saw how God warned that it is **our unbelief that condemns us. I told you to keep in mind it is our faith that truly pleases God when we review Chapter 11. So here we go.** God's plan for salvation before creation was always one thing: **FAITH!**

I urge you to read **Hebrews 11**, the entire chapter. The very first verse is the **perfect definition of what faith is.** Every Old Testament person was justified by his or her faith. Chapter 11 is the **"Hall of Fame of Old Testament Believers."**

Some excerpts:

> **Hebrews 11: 1 Fully Reveals What Faith Is! It Is the Perfect Definition**
>
> [1]Now faith is **being sure of what we hope for and certain of what we do not see.** [2]This is what the ancients were commended for. **(NIV)**

I just love this definition of faith above. **To be certain** (sure, convinced, positive, confident, firm, definite, assured) **in what we do not see! Wow! I want to have faith like that.** It is exactly that kind of faith God commended the ancient patriarchs of believers:

> **Verse 3 (for those who might think evolution is true): [3]By faith** we understand that **the universe was formed at God's command**, so that what is seen was not made out of what was visible. **(NIV)**
>
> **Verse 4: [4]By faith Abel** offered unto God **a more excellent sacrifice** than Cain, by which **he obtained witness that he was righteous**, God testifying of his gifts: and by it he being dead yet speaketh.

> **Verse 5 – 6 [5]By faith Enoch was translated that he should not see death; and was not found**, because God had translated him: for before his translation he had this testimony, that **he pleased God.**

Oh, to have faith like Enoch. He pleased God so much by his faith that he never experienced death but was taken up to heaven. This is an example of the rapture of God's people, prophesized in **the Old and New Testaments** (not just the Book of Revelation) in a very small scale. The faith of the believer today will be enough to please God that when the time comes for his return, he will do the same for us as he did for Enoch. We will look at the rapture of the church when we study the Feasts of Israel in later chapters.

The scripture below is so very important.

> **[6]But without faith it is impossible to please him**: for he that cometh to God **must believe that he is**, and that **he is a rewarder of them that diligently seek him.**

Verse 6 confirms that without faith there is no pleasing God. That is the most important message in the verses above. He awards those who diligently seek him. Faith is what saves us, and it is our faith that pleases God.

> Verse **7 (for our evolutionary friends again): [7]By faith Noah,** being warned of God of things not seen as yet, moved with fear, **prepared an ark** to the saving of his house; by the which **he condemned the world**, and became heir of the **righteousness which is by faith.**

The bible does teach there was a worldwide flood and by faith Noah acted so mankind would have a chance to be made right with God. Noah acted on his faith to build the ark as God commanded him. You see, before this flood came, the world would have been very different. It had never seen rain because earth did not need it for its moisture. The temperature of the earth would have been relatively the same everywhere. The humidity of the earth would produce dew at nighttime, which would be enough to sustain plant and animal life. It took tremendous faith by Noah to build such a huge ocean liner for something that never before occurred: **rain.** For the first time in history, it would rain and it would be only a part of the reason for a worldwide flood. We will se in chapter 24 that Noah's flood would be the cause for where most of the fossil record came from when this flood would have deposited billions of dead things all over the world. Just think, a flood of this magnitude never happened again, or ever will—**It was a one-time event, just as God promised.**

It seems like today it takes tremendous faith to understand that this was a true historical event. Many, including those who are leaders in the church, are trying to explain this and other Bible stories away as if they never occurred. My faith will never allow this to happen to me. Not only that, science using the "**creation model**" fits very well with what we observe in nature, as we will see in chapters 24 and 25.

The book of Hebrews continues with the hall of fame:

> **Verse 8–10 (Father Abraham): [8]By faith** Abraham, when he was called to go out into a place which he should after receive for an inheritance, **obeyed**; and he went out, not knowing whither he went.
>
> **[9]By faith** he sojourned in the land of promise, as in a strange country, dwelling in tabernacles with Isaac and Jacob, the heirs with him of the same promise:
>
> [10]For he looked for a city which hath foundations, **whose builder and maker is God.**

Now read verse 13 below. They all died in faith for **promises** they have not received as yet.

> **Verses 13 [13]These all died in faith**, not having received the promises, but **having seen them afar off**, and were

> **persuaded** of them, and **embraced them**, and **confessed** that they were strangers and pilgrims **on the earth**.

These people of faith did **what we must do today**. We must be **persuaded** that the word of God is true and Jesus is his Son. We must **embrace** the good news of salvation he brings. We must **confess** that we are sinners and Jesus is Lord of the universe. We must do all this if we believe what the Bible is saying.

By faith, these believers were looking for a better place—**heaven. Because of their faith,** God is preparing such a place for them and all who have faith in Jesus.

> [16]But now **they desire a better country**, that is, an **heavenly:** wherefore **God is not ashamed to be called their God**: for **he hath prepared for them a city.**

Jesus is preparing a fantastic place for believers—heaven. This is confirmed in the New Testament:

> **John 14: 1-3** [1]Let not your heart be troubled: ye believe in God, believe also in me.
>
> [2]**In my Father's house are many mansions**: if it were not so, I would have told you. **I go to prepare a place for you.**
>
> [3]And if I go and prepare a place for you, **I will come again**, and receive you unto myself; that **where I am, there ye may be also.**

I love the verses below, because before it ever occurred, God was showing us his love and what he was willing to do for us—**sacrifice his Son for the forgiveness of sin**, as we already studied in Chapter 12 of this book. Once again we see that Abraham's faith was so strong that he knew God would have resurrected Isaac if he had put him to death. Abraham believed God's promises. **Should we not also?**

> **Verses 17-19:** [17]**By faith** Abraham, when God tested him, **offered Isaac as a sacrifice.** He who had received the promises was about to sacrifice his one and only son, [18]even though God had said to him, "It is through Isaac that your offspring will be reckoned." [19]**Abraham reasoned that God could raise the dead, and figuratively speaking, he did receive Isaac back from death.** (NIV)

God commended Old Testament patriarchs for their faith. It is their faith that pleased him and will earn them a place in heaven—**not their works! It is the same for us.**

> **Ephesians 2: 8-9** [8]For **by grace are ye saved through faith**; and that not of yourselves: it is the gift of God:
>
> [9]**Not of works**, lest any man should boast

Job was looking for the time when he would meet his redeemer face to face. He was prepared. The writer of Hebrews shows us the way—**It is by faith**. I pray that you are ready—do not delay; you never know when you will take your last breath. Then it will be to late.

I want you to know God loves you very much just the way you are—with all your flaws. It is faith in him that saves you, and is his work in your life that changes the heart and mind to allow you do good works. He just asks you to come to him just the way you are and start a new relationship with him, and let him be your counselor, your friend, and your God so that you can depend on him and **stop relying on yourself**. He wants to be your Father, a better Father than any earthly father could ever be. I pray you will let him be your Father.

If you do not know God the way the Old Testament patriarchs do and you are ready to have a personal relationship with him, I invite you to turn to **chapter 38** now and begin your eternity with him!

God loves you and so do!

Hope! Where do you put yours? 1 Corinthians chapter 15

Chapter 16

I call **1 Corinthians chapter 15** my Bible chapter. It is where **all my hope** lies in scripture. Someone who is very dear to me, someone I love very much, inspired me to write on this great chapter of the Bible.

This special person has no hope. She sees no **light** at the end of the tunnel. The end is dark and empty. There are **no tomorrow** at the end of the **tunnel of life.** The end is six feet under. That is where the end of life leads for my special some one. No more dreams, no more happiness, no more being with your loving family and friends. No eternity, **no God!**

My loved one is an agnostic. Since she cannot see God and cannot touch him, and since there is no evidence that is satisfactory to this person I love—there is **no hope!** As the years pass, I think of her more and more as the end of the tunnel draws nearer and nearer.

What can I say to her that I haven't said already to convince her that there is a God and he **loves** his created child very much? I do not understand the ability of looking at life as if we are here on earth for naught. The Bible says about 70 years is a good life. **Is that all there is?** Is that all we should **hope** for? That is all that my loved one is seeing. I worry for my special someone who is already past the 70 years God calls a good life. She is on what you can call borrowed time. Oh, how I hated to admit that.

Today, my son Colin was at his friend Jacob's house across the street; and my wife and I were on our way to our friend's retirement party. We had to stop there to give our son instructions for what to do while we were away. As we drove up, my wife informed me our son's friend and his family was getting ready to leave town for the weekend. When Jacob's mother saw us drive up, she came running out of the house to explain that she would not be home Monday to drive car pool for our kid's school. She explained that their 19-year-old nephew was killed in an auto accident and they would be gone for his funeral. I hate to say this—**six feet under. Was that all there was for this young man to had hoped for?** If we exist for only the time that we live in our physical bodies, whether it is seventy plus years or only nineteen years—**life is too short.** There has to be more than what these earthly bodies can give us. Praise God; his word says there is!

Do you need to be the eternal optimist to **want more** than what these earthly bodies gives us to believe in God? Must one be naive? Must one be blind? **What is the key that opens the door to faith? To me, it is HOPE!**

The more I thought about this situation, the more God inspired me to write about his wondrous glory and the **hope He brings**. God gives **hope** where there is none.

Where do I put my hope? 1 Corinthians chapter 15 best describes where my hope is grounded, and I place all of my hope in **Jesus Christ and his resurrection**. This one chapter of God's word inspires me to sing praises to him—to worship him! To put my hope for eternal life with God, my hope is **in Him and Him alone!**

The words of Paul the apostle, **I Corinthians 15: 1-8**

> 1 Moreover, brethren, **I declare unto you the gospel** which I preached unto you, which also ye have received, and wherein ye stand;
>
> **2 By which also ye are saved, if ye keep in memory what I preached** unto you, unless ye have believed in vain.

> 3For I delivered unto you first of all that which I also received, how **that Christ died for our sins according to the scriptures**;
>
> 4And that he was buried, and that **he rose again the third day according to the scriptures:**

According to the scriptures—this is important! Paul was not talking about New Testament writings—he was talking about **Old Testament scriptures** written hundreds to thousands of years before Jesus Christ came into this world, prophecies about the Messiah—the chosen one. The New Testament writings were not part of the Bible in Paul's lifetime, and so he was referring to the Bible of the Jews—the Old Testament. Read **Psalm 22** or **Isaiah 53** for just two examples of prophecy of the cross and the resurrection in the ancient scriptures that Jesus Christ fulfilled.

Starting in verse 5, Paul tells us of the witnesses who literally saw Jesus alive after his death and burial:

> 5And that he was seen of **Cephas (the Apostle Peter)**, then of the twelve:
>
> 6After that, **he was seen of above five hundred brethren at once**; of whom the greater part remain unto this present, but some are fallen asleep.
>
> 7After that, **he was seen of James; then of all the apostles**.
>
> 8And last of all **he was seen of me also**, as of one born out of due time.

Look at the above verses. **Look at all the eyewitnesses that saw the risen Lord.** Paul says Jesus first appeared to Peter and then to the rest of the apostles. What is amazing is he appeared to over **five hundred persons** all at the same time. Afterward he appeared to James, and lastly to Paul himself, who testifies to what he saw. **Why would so many witnesses want to lie?**In a court of law, it would be declared Jesus has risen positively with having so many witnesses—**the proof is overwhelming.**

Paul is such a great witness for my hope in eternal life because of what he was before he became a believer in Jesus Christ. He writes these words we read:

> **I Corinthians 15: 9- 10** [9]For **I am the least of the apostles,** that am not meet to be called an apostle, **because I persecuted the church of God**.
>
> [10]**But by the grace of God I am what I am**: and his grace which was bestowed upon me was not in vain; but I laboured more abundantly than they all: yet not I, but **the grace of God which was with me.**

Paul was a devout Jew. He knew the laws of his faith as good as anyone practicing Judaism, and he tried to follow the laws to the letter. He was zealous to earn his favor with God and the eyes of all the religious leaders of the Jews. This zeal for his faith led him to hunt down Christians and seek their punishment; even their execution; and he had many executed. **Only the Lord Jesus Christ appearing to him** well after Jesus was put to death on the cross could change such a man as he was. It was God's **grace (the same grace that is offered to all to this day**) that made him the greatest Gentile Apostle of all time who has affected all generations of believers and still does to this day. He also died a martyr's death for his faith in Jesus Christ. **Why would anyone die a martyr's death for a lie?**

How the apostles are said to have died according to early church teachings:

1) **Peter** died by Crucifixion. It is said he felt unworthy to die the same death as Jesus and requested to be **crucified upside down** on an x-shaped cross.

2) It is believed that **Matthew** died a martyr in Ethiopia, killed by a **sword wound.**
3) **James, the half-brother of Jesus** who did not have faith in Jesus until after his resurrection, was **thrown over** one hundred feet down from the southeast pinnacle of the temple when he refused to deny his faith in Christ. When they discovered that he survived the fall, his enemies **beat James to death** with a fuller's club.
4) **James,** son of Zebedee, was a fisherman by trade when Jesus called him to a lifetime of ministry. James was **beheaded** at Jerusalem. Interestingly, at his trial before his execution, the Roman guard assigned to him was so amazed at James testimony about Jesus that he knelt beside James to accept the same punishment.
5) **Bartholomew** was a missionary to Asia. He witnessed about Jesus in present-day Turkey. Bartholomew was martyred when he was **flayed to death** by a **whip.**
6) **Andrew** was **crucified on an x-shaped cross** in Patras, Greece. It took him two days to expire and he preached about Jesus during that time from his cross.
7) **Matthias** was the apostle chosen to replace the traitor Judas Iscariot. He was **stoned** and then **beheaded.**
8) **Thomas, the one who doubted,** was **stabbed with a spear** in India during one of his missionary trips.
9) **John** faced martyrdom when he was **boiled** in a huge basin of boiling oil during a wave of persecution in Rome. However, he was miraculously delivered from death. John was then sentenced to the mines on the island of Patmos where He wrote his prophetic book of Revelation. John was the only apostle to have lived out his days.
10) **Paul, the great Gentile apostle,** was **tortured** and then **beheaded** by the evil Emperor Nero at Rome in 67A.D.

All these men suffered and ultimately died—for what? A Lie? Who in his right mind would do this? They would be the most evil of men if they were making false statements about Jesus in order to fool us. This would make no sense. These men had to have believed Jesus was literally raised from the dead.

The Absolute Necessity of Christ's Resurrection

My hope and belief in Jesus Christ's resurrection is imperative as it is for all who **hope** for eternal life. **It is so important to my hope.** I cannot put it into words better than Paul.

> **I Corinthians 15: 13-18 13But if there be no resurrection of the dead, then is Christ not risen:**
>
> 14And **if Christ be not risen**, then is our preaching vain, and **your faith is also vain.**
>
> 15Yea, and we are found false witnesses of God; **because we have testified of God that he raised up Christ:** whom he raised not up, if so be that the dead rise not.
>
> **16For if the dead rise not, then is not Christ raised:**
>
> **17And if Christ be not raised, your faith is vain; ye are yet in your sins.**
>
> **18Then they also which are fallen asleep in Christ are perished.**

Wow! According to the teachings of Paul, my entire hope for eternal life with God hinges on the fact that Jesus Christ was resurrected from the dead, **or my faith is futile;** and Jesus had no power to forgive my sins. He died on the cross for no reason if his blood was spilled on the cross for naught, and if God did not truly raise his Son from the dead. **Paul declares if the resurrection never happened, those who have died believing in Jesus have perished forever.**

Paul goes on to state what a pitiful people believers would be if the resurrection of Jesus Christ is not true. It is a **strong statement on how important it is to have hope in a risen Christ!**

I Corinthians 15: 19 [19]**If in this life only** we have hope in Christ, **we are of all men most miserable.**

Below is the truth of scripture and where **I have my hope**—In Jesus Christ! Paul declares:

1 Corinthians 15: 20 - 22 and 26 [20]**But now is Christ risen from the dead**, and become the **firstfruits** of them that slept.

Firstfruits is the resurrection. We will learn more about this in the chapters covering the feasts of Israel later in this book. For now, Jesus is the first to have risen, and because there is a first, there will be a second, and a third, and a fourth, and so on.

[21]For since by **man (Adam)** came death, by **man (Jesus—being both human and God)** came also the **resurrection of the dead.**

[22]**For as in Adam all die, even so in Christ shall all be made alive.**

[26]**The last enemy that shall be destroyed is death.**

There it is! In these four verses is where all my hope lies. Without the resurrection of Jesus, I am to be pitied more than any other man in this world. But Paul as an eyewitness to Jesus Christ declares, **He is raised! His Resurrection now destroys death.**

Paul goes on to say that **if the resurrection is not true, then:**

Verse 32: "...if the dead rise not? **let us eat and drink; for to morrow we die."**

Paul is saying we might as well eat, drink, and be merry if the dead are not raised because someday we will die and be no more. We might as well get our fun and have a little heaven on earth while we can. Unfortunately, that is exactly how many are living their lives with no concern for their own eternity.

Returning to scripture, Jesus Christ offers us this great hope for everlasting life when Paul writes:

> **1 Corinthians 15: 44-45, 47 and 49** [44]It is sown a **natural body; it is raised a spiritual body. There is a natural body, and there is a spiritual body.**
>
> [45]And so **it is written (Paul is referring to the Old Testament.)**, The first man Adam was made a living soul; the **last Adam (Jesus Christ is the last Adam.)** was made a quickening spirit.
>
> [47]**The first man is of the earth, earthy**; the **second man is the Lord (God in the flesh, the Second Person of the Trinity, my Jesus!) from heaven.**
>
> [49]And as we have borne the image of the earthy, **we shall also bear the image of the heavenly. (As we have been born with an earthly body, we too will be raised and given a heavenly body!)**

In **Verses 55-57**, Paul gives us this final testimony to **what we can hope for**:

> [55]**O death, where is thy sting? O grave, where is thy victory?**

How can we have victory over death? How can we take the sting out of death?

> [56]The **sting of death is sin**; and the **strength of sin is the law**.

> 57 But thanks be to God, which **giveth us the victory through our Lord Jesus Christ.**

Sin brought death into the world but it is **only a sting**. Victory is given to us through Jesus Christ. There it is—my faith... **my hope**! I pray it will be yours too.

God gives us our victory over sin and ultimately death through the power of Jesus Christ and his resurrection from the dead. It is **my hope—my only hope! My hope** is that he truly is the Son of God, and he truly died **for me and my sins** on the cross. **My hope** is that he truly rose from the dead as the scriptures say and because of this, I will be raised from the grave too! It is **my hope** because scripture teaches Jesus Christ was the perfect sacrifice for sins; because of this, my sins will not be counted against me. **My entire hope hinges upon Jesus Christ! My faith is that God loves me that much.**

There has to be more to life than this earthly natural body. There has to be more than the 70 plus years God gives us in this natural body. There has to be more than the 19 years my neighbor's nephew had in life. My faith says there is, and there is no other God I would rather serve, than the **living God of the Bible! There is no other god like Him!** He is God who will judge us for what we have done on earth...

> **Romans 3: 23** 23 For all have sinned, and come short of the glory of God;

I am glad it is God and not man that will judge. The prophet Jeremiah tells us God delights in loving kindness, but also in justice and righteousness. He will judge Jews and Gentiles alike, and there will be punishment for sin.

> **Jeremiah 9: 24-25** 24 But let him that glorieth glory in this, that he **understandeth and knoweth me**, that **I am the LORD** which exercise **lovingkindness, judgment, and righteousness, in the earth**: for in these things I delight, saith the LORD.

> [25]Behold, the days come, saith the LORD, **that I will punish all them which are circumcised (Jews) with the uncircumcised (Gentiles);**

So everyone deserves judgment and all deserve punishment for sin. **But thanks be to God**, He is also the God of love and died on the cross for our sins! For those who put their **hope** in Jesus Christ, he and he alone justifies us and makes us right with God, **just as if we never had sinned. Wow! That's why I love him so much** and pray you too will put your **hope** in **him**!

In the book of Romans, Paul puts it very well what Jesus Christ has done for all sinners. We are justified by his love and grace, and we will avoid the wrath of God when he comes to judge the world.

> **Romans 8: 1** [1]There is therefore now **no condemnation to them which are in Christ Jesus**

> **Romans 3: 24** [24]and are **justified freely by his grace** through the redemption that came **by Christ Jesus.**

> **Romans 5: 8-10** [8]But **God demonstrates his own love for us** in this: **While we were still sinners, Christ died for us.**

> [9]Since **we have now been justified by his blood**, how much more shall we be saved **from God's wrath** through him! [10]For if, **when we were God's enemies, we were reconciled to him through the death of his Son**, how much more, having been reconciled, shall we be saved through his life!

Closing:

1 Corinthians 15 is my Bible chapter. I place all my hope in life eternal because of Jesus Christ, the Son of God. Scripture shows God loves us, even as sinners. Please do not make excuses for yourself that God is not like the Bible teaches because of all the terrible things happening on earth, both natural disasters (floods, hurricanes, earthquakes, disease, death, etc.) and that caused by man (murder, rape, robbery, hatred, war, etc). Let God, who delights in loving kindness, justice, and righteousness, deal with all that. Please deal with what you can control—what is in your heart. Hope for eternity; he has placed it into your heart to want to live forever. Trust the word of God and ask Jesus to come into your life—**he will**. If you do not know him and are ready to meet him, please turn to chapter 38 now. He is always ready and waiting for you! **God loves you and so do I!**

Bring thy Children up in the ways of the Lord

Chapter 17

I was reading the newspaper today and read in the local section, "Community seeks teen drug use solutions." Later in the day, I was standing in line at the post office, waiting to be served; and this young lady with two small boys and a third child on the way was in front of me. She was holding the youngest child, and he was looking at me so I made some funny faces and got him to laugh. This allowed his mommy and I to strike up a conversation; and I started by saying to her, "I remember when my children were that age."

I proceeded to tell her I have a 14-year-old boy and an 11-year-old girl. I also stated that I have two good children, and my wife and I are not having any problems yet as they enter their teenage years. She said to me, smiling back, "They're not quite at the age yet." I agreed and restated that they are good children, and I do not expect too severe of problems, as they grow older. (Colin is now seventeen and Courtney is fourteen—**I can still say this is true**). I decided to be bold with her in hopes of planting a seed with her in raising her own young family. I responded back, "The reason I have faith in my children is that they have been brought up in a Christian home and are 'Born Again' Christians and are **learning** the teachings of the Bible."

She smiled sheepishly at me and did not respond to my statement. She was taken back and probably was glad the line moved ahead so she could end our conversation.

How are these two stories related?

1) The newspaper article on teen drug use.
2) The mother with two children and a third on the way.

I believe they both show the sad shape of our culture and society as a whole. You see, the **thought of going to the scriptures of the Bible to teach our young how to live a moral and fulfilling life is not even considered for answers**. It is not politically or socially acceptable to mention ones faith in Jesus Christ in public. Taking a strong stand in having faith in Jesus Christ makes people feel uncomfortable. Many people feel faith is a private matter, and we should not challenge or talk to people about it—leaving each to his or her own conscience and values. It will probably get worse in the future, for our children and children's children, as our multicultural society continue to diversify. But when you feel that the Bible speaks the truth for all people as I do and are convinced that what you decide about Jesus Christ has **eternal ramifications**, you must find a way to share Jesus with others.

In quoting the newspaper, "Substance abuse among students isn't a school problem, it's a community problem." **(I agree with this).** The community held a brainstorming meeting to find preventative options, and these are the ideas that were presented:

1) The community needs some type of youth recreational facility or teen center. Teens frequently complain of having nothing to do and having nowhere in town to hang out.
2) Let teens that have recovered from substance abuse speak to students on their own level. One teen states that, " programs like D.A.R.E., which is geared to fifth graders, come at a time when students are too young to relate to its message."
3) Group members suggested implementing a hotline for students to call for help and information or parents to use to report parties **where alcohol is served to underage drinkers**.
4) A web site offering contacts and information was also proposed.
5) Pledge cards for students to sign vowing they will remain sober and drug-free.

Thc above points are all valid ideas. All of the suggestions above were given to help our teenagers combat drugs. There is, however, one idea that I see they missed; and it is too often missed in our society and culture today: the article made no mention of what **God can do** and **his written word, the Bible.**

In today's society, we take advise from parenting experts, psychologists, new age teachers.... anyone we can. But how many ever open their Bibles to the word of God and seek his wisdom and understanding. **How many parents are teaching God's wisdom to their children?If you do want your children to learn spiritual things, how many of you are relying on someone else—a minister, priest, or a Sunday school teacher—to teach your children the ways of God?**

Too many parents do not lead by example. They want their children to have faith in God, but they leave it up to some one else to educate them or worse—they will say their children can decide for themselves when they are old enough to leave the house if they want to believe in God or what kind of god they want to worship. This is free choice to the ultimate degree. **This totally contradicts the teachings of the Bible!** Scripture states parents are given a commission by God to teach their children in the ways of the Lord.

> In **Deuteronomy 4: 9** 9 Only **be careful**, and watch yourselves closely so that **you do not forget** the things your eyes have seen or **let them slip from your heart as long as you live. Teach them to your children and to their children after them. (NIV)**
>
> In **Chapter 6: 6-7** of the same Book of **Deuteronomy** we read: " 6And these words, which **I command thee this day**, shall be in thine heart:
>
> 7And thou **shalt teach them diligently unto thy children**, and shalt **talk of them** when thou **sittest** in thine house, and when thou **walkest** by the way, and when thou **liest** down, and when thou **risest** up.

Scripture tells us to teach our children God's ten commandments. We have those in our society like the ACLU and Americans United for Separation of Church and State trying to keep God's laws out public limelight—**as though they are harmful to our children.**

> Again in **Chapter 11: 19** [19]And **ye shall teach them your children**, speaking of them when thou **sittest in thine house**, and when thou **walkest** by the way, when thou **liest** down, and when thou **risest** up.

You can see by these verses that God wants us to be teachers of our children. He wants us to teach them his commandments, and also to teach them his wisdom. God does not ask us to, but commands us to teach them to our children. We should teach them when we are sitting down with them, when we are walking with them, when we lie down at night, and when we get up in the morning. In other words, we should be continually taking time and talking to our children about God. God does not want us to forget his ways and let them slip away...but to remember and teach our children. He does not want us to leave it up to others. Teach, by example. If you have children, **can they see Christ in the way you lead your life?**

The greatest gift we can give our children is the knowledge of God. King Solomon, who the Bible claims is the wisest man who ever lived, spoke these words:

> **Proverbs 22: 6 [6]Train up a child in the way he should go: and when he is old, he will not depart from it.**

My hope is that because my children have been taught and are continually being taught the word of God, they will not stray.

Important: I am not advocating that you pound it into your children like a drill sergeant or by giving ultimatums, "the you do what I say or else" type of teaching. **This will not teach their hearts**. Do it in love and respect for your children. I remember as a teenager just out of high school this girl who worked with my best friend and I at a large department store. Eventually, she became engaged to my friend.

This girl was raised in a very strict Christian home with many rules (She could not keep them, just as we have never been able to keep God's ten commandments). Even after being engaged, my friend had to have her in by 10:00 P.M. Growing up, she was not allowed to listen to music, dance, wear make-up, and who knows what. When she got a little freedom from these rigid sets of rules, she completely rebelled. This sweet girl when I first met her started partying with the people we worked with. She began to drink and do drugs, and this is not the worst of it. Even though she was engaged to my friend, she began to sleep with many of the guys at work and later, was having an affair with the assistant manager of the store who was married. She was able to keep this from my friend for a long time. I knew about it, but I did not know how to break it to him. I eventually was forced to when she made a move for me. Fearing I would tell, she accused me to my friend of propositioning her. I told him the truth and to no avail because he chose to believe her. A few months later, the truth came out; and my friend apologized for not believing me.

That incident in my life had a lasting affect on me. I saw this beautiful girl, both inside and out, with a wonderful personality turn into something very different. I do not know what has become of her. I pray she has returned to the faith of her youth. I believe her rebellion was so strong because her parents, who only wanted the best for her, tried to make sure she followed the word of God by being **"the enforcers." You cannot force morality on people**—it must come from the heart. You must love God in your heart enough that you will not want to break his laws and sin. God's laws must be written in our hearts and minds. I believe that is what happens when we accept Jesus into our heart. It puts his commandments in our heart and we do not find pleasure in sin any longer because we love God.

> **Ephesians 3: 17: 17That Christ may dwell in your hearts by faith**; that ye, being rooted and **grounded in love,**

This is what I am teaching my children. Problems and temptations in the world come to all of us and someday my children must be able to face them on their own. **God is arming** them to face them head on because they are learning the Bible and what it teaches, and they know that God is the **absolute authority and holder of all wisdom**, and where all **understanding** comes from.

> **Psalm 111: 10** [10]**The fear of the LORD (having awe and reverence for God!) is the beginning of wisdom**: a good understanding have all they that **do his commandments**: his praise endureth for ever.

> **2 Timothy 3: 16** [16]**All Scripture is God-breathed** and is useful for **teaching**, rebuking, **correcting** and **training** in righteousness, **(NIV)**

They also know that **God is LOVE!**

> **Romans 8: 39** [39]Nor height, nor depth, nor any other creature, **shall be able to separate us from the love of God, which is in Christ Jesus our Lord.**

My children are being trained in God's ways and understanding. It starts with the fear of the Lord, **knowing God is God and he is all powerful with all wisdom and all strength and he alone is to be worshiped**—and it ends with **God's great love, and compassion, and forgiveness** for our sins. Yes, our children are being taught they are sinners; but they are forgiven sinners and know that God loves them. Both my children understand:

> **Romans 3: 23** [23]**For all have sinned**, and come short of the glory of God;

> **John 3: 16-17** [16]For God so loved the world, that he gave his only begotten Son, that **whosoever believeth in him** should not perish, but **have everlasting life**.

> [17]For God sent not his Son into the world to condemn the world; but **that the world through him might be saved.**

The greatest gift I have given my children is bringing them up in the ways of the Lord, and the **greatest gift God has given all of us is his Son, Jesus Christ,** and the promise of eternal life for all who believe.

That is why I have confidence in my children. That is why, if they stray for a time, they will return to their faith. My confidence comes from **God and his written word.** And that is why I have taken responsibility to train my children from their earliest childhood.

Sometimes, I would talk to them about the Lord when we awoke in the morning. Sometimes, I talked to them as we drove down the street. My daughter Courtney at her youngest age would love to talk about God. I would ask her when we were alone in the car, "What do you want to talk about?" and she would answer, **"Let's talk about God."** So we would talk and I would teach her about God. We had such fun together this way.

I learned what faith really was through my daughter. I would be so amazed at her faith as I shared the great stories found in the Bible. I would say to myself, "If I had faith like hers, I could move mountains."

> **1 Corinthians 13: 2** [2]If I have the gift of prophecy, and know all mysteries and all knowledge; and if **I have all faith, so as to remove mountains, but do not have love, I am nothing. (NASB)**

It takes us to become as children to have faith as this. Through faith, we can learn to love.

> **Matthew 18: 1-5** [1]At the same time came the disciples unto Jesus, saying, **Who is the greatest in the kingdom of heaven?**
>
> [2]And **Jesus called a little child unto him**, and set him in the midst of them,

3 And said, Verily I say unto you, **Except ye be converted, and become as little children, ye shall not enter into the kingdom of heaven.**

4 **Whosoever therefore shall humble himself as this little child**, the same is greatest in the kingdom of heaven.

5 And whoso shall receive one such little child in my name receiveth me.

I want to have the same faith as my daughter at four years-of-age displayed. I want to believe every story written in the Bible as she did. I want to love others as Jesus taught us to love.

We sometimes had to teach them tough love that also had the element of grace with it when they did wrong. One particular time, our son Colin at the age of twelve did something very wrong. My wife and I did not come down on him without explanation. It gave us the opportunity to show him the love, grace, and mercy of God by giving him love, grace, and yes, mercy for what he had done. It gave me an opportunity to explain to him how I too had failed **(sinned)** when I was his age and to also explain, unfortunately, I still do sin. Colin learned I disappointed my parents many times growing up, and I had to ask my parents for forgiveness; but more importantly, **God's forgiveness**. I was able to explain to him when we break God's commandments; we disappoint God, and need to ask for his forgiveness. When we do this then, our relationship with God is again restored. I explained to my son that because Jesus died on the cross for our sins, our sins are forgiven.

We talked as a family about God whenever we saw an opportunity to teach our children. If we saw something on television and a lesson could be learned about what God teaches in the Bible, we would begin a discussion with them. For example, if a program condoned having sex before you were married, I would ask them, "What does God teach about this?" Anything else taught other than what is in the Bible is only man's opinion. Our opinions have no bearing to what God teaches, we cannot sway his thought to be like ours, although many in society as well as the church is trying to do just that.

The Bible teaches God is the absolute truth; **not man**. Our opinions are only just that—opinions. I tell my children, when it comes to what a person believes, **test it with what God says in his word before assuming anything man says is true (including what your own Dad says).** I built the foundation with my children that God is our authority, and the Bible is his word to us.

As they were growing up, we talked about God at nighttime, daytime, and anytime they or I needed to share God with one another. We have our children in a very good Christian school, we attend church, and my children are involved in their youth groups; but we take full responsibility in their education about God and the word of God has final say. I am in the Bible learning about God, so I can teach my children and not leave it up to others to do it for me. **Psalm 78** says it best, "Teach the children the deeds of the Lord."

Look at **Psalm 78 verses 1 - 8** and see what **God says:**

1 O my people, **hear my teaching**;
listen to the words of my mouth.

2 I will open my mouth in **parables (Jesus taught this way—this is prophecy fulfilled.), I will utter hidden things, things from of old-**

3 **what we have heard and known,**
what our fathers have told us.

4 **We will not hide them from their children;**
we will tell the next generation
the praiseworthy deeds of the LORD,
his power, and the wonders he has done.

5 **He decreed statutes** for Jacob
and **established the law** in Israel,
which **he commanded our forefathers**
to **teach their children,**

6 so the next generation would know them,
even the children yet to be born,
and they in turn would tell their children.

7 Then they would put their trust in God
and would not forget his deeds
but would keep his commands.

8 They would not be like their forefathers—
a stubborn and rebellious generation,
whose hearts were not loyal to God,
whose spirits were not faithful to him. **(NIV)**

Is this not what we all want for our children—to have our children know the great deeds our Lord has done? God has given parents the commission to do so. It is our responsibility. I believe the Bible holds the answers to all problems. Obedience to God, reverence to him, love to our Father in heaven—this is what I teach my children.

Teaching my children is no guarantee that they will not stray. In many Christian homes, children have rebelled against their parents, and ultimately God. But not teaching them anything or leaving it up to them when they leave the house is not the answer.

Statistics I have heard state it becomes very difficult to make a commitment to Jesus if you have not done so by the time you are twenty-one years of age. Thank God I beat the statistic because I was twenty-three. My parents did bring my four brothers and I up in faith in God and Jesus Christ, but they had to leave it up to others to teach us because they were not trained to do the teaching themselves. They were not trained because the teachings of their church taught you left it up to them to instruct.

I, on the other hand, was blessed because God changed my life in time for my own children; and I began studying his word earnestly. God's word taught me, and I became the spiritual leader of our household while my children were still young enough, so I could do as the Bible commands fathers to do. God's word taught me to trust him completely in all things. I have become a teacher to my children, and the book we study is the Bible—the word that is God breathed.

As parents, should we not be concerned with the eternity of our children?Should we not give them the best opportunity to seek and worship the one true God? I wrote to each of my children in their baby books, "I want you to spend eternity with me—there is no greater gift I can give you as your earthly father than to tell you about Jesus Christ."

I pray you will bring up your children up in the way of the Lord. Do it in love and respect—the Holy Spirit will grow in their hearts and minds.

God loves you and so do I!

Is God Pro-Choice?

Chapter 18

I watch the show "Faith Under Fire" on PAX Television, hosted by author and former atheist Lee Strobel on Saturday nights. What Lee does is take a hot issue and invite both sides of the issue to come in and discuss/debate what they believe and why they believe it. One of the discussions on this night's program was on the topic of abortion and whether God is pro-choice or pro-life.

It is so important to know the word of God and not take someone's word for it. People can twist and find whatever they want by how they interpret the word of God. People (including ministers, priest, theologians, etc.) are sometimes very willing to misrepresent the word of God to make their point.

> **1 Timothy 6: 3-4 [3]If anyone teaches false doctrines** and does not agree to **the sound instruction of our Lord Jesus Christ** and to godly teaching, **[4]he is conceited and understands nothing.**

I include myself in this list because I am only a man, and I am capable of being wrong. If I am not capable in pointing to scriptures that testify to what I believe, then I am only giving you my opinion. In order for someone to not misrepresent God's word, he must be able to back up what he says using scripture throughout the Bible—**not just in one verse.** Truth that comes from God is **absolute**. Truth that comes from man can be **flawed.** By looking at and interpreting only one verse from one book of scripture and not following the entire Bible, you can be deceived. It is important to look at the **entire** word of God.

Tonight's debate on whether God is pro-choice or pro-life is a prime example. The woman who took the position that God is pro-choice in this debate quoted scripture to state her belief that the Bible teaches that the woman's body is more important than the unborn life in her womb. She used only one example from scripture to make her point. Her whole defense was taken from the book of **Exodus, chapter 21.** Her claim was that God places more value on life after birth than before birth. She uses **Exodus 21: 22-25** to make this claim.

> 22 "If men who are fighting **hit a pregnant woman** and she gives **birth prematurely** but there is no serious injury, the offender must be fined whatever the woman's husband demands and the court allows. 23 **But if there is serious injury, you are to take life for life,** 24 eye for eye, tooth for tooth, hand for hand, foot for foot, 25 burn for burn, wound for wound, bruise for bruise. **(NIV)**

If I had just taken her word for it, never looking at the verses myself, never applying the rest of the Bible to see if what she said is true, she could have deceived me into believing what she was saying was true. But, because I wanted the truth and only the truth of the Bible, I looked up the above scripture myself.

Her argument has a few flaws:

1) Where in this scripture above does God say that the unborn infant is **less important?**
2) Where does it say **only the woman** is protected from being struck and **not the unborn?**
3) Could it be these verses protect **both the woman and the unborn from wrongful injury or death?**I believe it does.

I believe that human life is so precious to God that he indeed protects both the mother and the unborn infant in these verses. How can we know this for sure?**Simple**—because we have many, many more Bible verses that claim our Father in heaven loves us forever and before creation began. Let's look at just some of scripture that points to God's love **for us.**

Many of these Bible verses I chose came after viewing "The Father's Love Letter." Please visit their web site (www.**father-sloveletter**.com) for a special time, and see for yourself God's love for you.

> **Ephesians 1: 4-5** [4]According as he hath **chosen (foreknew) us** in him **before the foundation of the world,** that we should be holy and without blame before him **in love**:
>
> [5]Having predestinated us unto **the adoption of children by Jesus Christ to himself**, according to the good pleasure of his will,

Through the love of Jesus Christ, we can become the adopted children of God; and it gives God great pleasure to do this for us.

God loves us so much and knows us intimately. He knows when we are standing or sitting. He knows our inner thoughts. He knows everything about us. He knows us better that anyone else could possibly know.

> **Psalm 139: 1-3** [1]O lord, thou hast searched me, **and known me**.
>
> [2]Thou **knowest my downsitting** and **mine uprising, thou understandest my thought** afar off.
>
> [3]Thou compassest my path and my lying down, and **art acquainted with all my ways.**

God foreknew us before we were even born:

> **Jeremiah 1: 5** [5]**Before I formed thee in the belly I knew thee**; and **before thou camest forth out of the womb** I sanctified thee

> **Psalm 139: 13-14** [13] For you created my inmost being;
> **you knit me together in my mother's womb.**
>
> [14] I praise you because **I am fearfully and wonderfully made**;
> your works are wonderful,
> I know that full well. **(NIV)**

Just think what Paul's letter to the Ephesians, Jeremiah, and the Psalm writer are telling us! God knew us **before we were in** our mother's wombs and **before we came out** of their wombs. God put us together **while we were in the wombs of our mothers**. We are **fearfully (awesomely)** and **wonderfully** made. **Ask yourself**—how could God who loves you and put you together himself ever be pro-choice?God has an everlasting love for you! **God is love!**

> **1 John 4: 16** [16]And we have known and believed **the love that God hath to us. God is love**; and he that dwelleth in love dwelleth in God, and God in him.

God created mankind in his own image:

> **Genesis 1: 27** [27]So **God created man in his own image**, in the image of God created he him; **male and female** created he them.

God knows us intimately—he knows everything about us!

> **Matthew 10: 30** [30]But **the very hairs of your head are all numbered. God's love for us knows no bounds!**

Jeremiah 31: 3 [3]The LORD hath appeared of old unto me, saying, Yea, **I have loved thee with an everlasting love:** therefore with lovingkindness have I drawn thee.

We should all be praising our Lord continually for our existence—just think of what the alternative is: **to never have existed!**

Psalm 71: 6 [6]By thee have I been holden up **from the womb**: thou art **he that took me out of my mother's bowels**: my praise shall be continually of thee.

When we accept Jesus, we are called "CHILDREN" of God!

1 John 3: 1 [1] Behold **what manner of love the Father** has bestowed on us, that **we should be called children of God**! Therefore the world does not know us, **because it did not know Him**.

We become God's own offspring!

Acts 17: 28 [28]For in him we live, and move, and have our being; as certain also of your own poets have said, **For we are also his offspring**.

This one in Psalms blows me away!

Psalm 139: 15-16 [15] **My frame was not hidden from You,**
When I was made in secret,
And skillfully wrought in the lowest parts of the earth.

[16] **Your eyes saw my substance, being yet unformed.**
And in Your book they all were written,
The days fashioned for me,
When *as yet there were* none of them.

God has a book with your life story written in it. God foreknew you and wrote it before you were even formed, before you lived even one day. It had in it when you would be born, where you would be born, who your parents would be, and what country you would live in. God knows you very well.

Below are scriptures to get excited about. We can become **children of God**, not just created beings. Being children of God, we will be joint-heirs with Jesus Christ. He will be the greatest Father you can ever have if you will ask him to be.

> **John 1: 12** [12] But as many as **received Him (Jesus Christ)**, to them He gave the right to **become children of God**, to those **who believe in His name: (NIV)**

> **Romans 8: 7** [17]And **if children, then heirs; heirs of God, and joint-heirs with Christ**; if so be that we suffer with him, that we may be also glorified together.

When Jesus returns and sets up his eternal kingdom, look at what he promises those who believe!

> **Revelations 21: 4** [4]And **God shall wipe away all tears from their eyes**; and there shall be **no more death, neither sorrow, nor crying, neither shall there be any more pain**: for the former things are passed away.

Because of these Bible passages and more**, I believe God is pro-life.** God loved us before time began, he knit us in our mother's womb, he saw us as an unborn human in our mother's womb, he knows every hair on our heads; we are children of God. **He loves me—he loves you too!**

Do you really think it would have been all right with God if your mother had aborted you before you were born? Would it have been all right with you?

Open up your Bibles. Dig into God's word and ask the Holy Spirit to lead you and teach you. It is the word of God and not man where all truth comes from. We learn truth by studying his word and asking God to reveal truth to us. I believe it is time we stop telling God what is moral and immoral based on our own desires and pray to him, "My Father in heaven, **You set the rules and not me!** I am ready to listen to you and your teachings. I am ready to seek the truth so please help me to find the truth. Teach me your ways."

Trusting God first, even when we do not understand his ways, is very pleasing to him. It shows we have faith. The next chapter will deal more with the subject of trusting God's word even when we disagree or do not understand his ways.

God loves you and so do I!

Did God really mean that?

Chapter 19

It was wintertime and I was down in Saginaw visiting the family. I was on the way to the golf dome to hit some balls with my brother Greg when we started discussing the truth of the Bible. I believe the Bible is **absolute truth,** and there are no errant words in it. The word is **God-breathed and inspired, not written by man**. I lead my life by this simple quote I heard Ken Ham from Answers in Genesis ministry say: "If you can believe the first 11 chapters of Genesis, you will not have any difficulty believing the rest of the Bible and the good news of Jesus Christ's resurrection."

Greg agreed with me on the authority of God's word but disagreed with me on one point, saying he believes that there are human opinions in the Bible and pointing to teachings of the apostle Paul. He pointed out the teachings of women not being able to speak in church or take an active roll in ministry. Greg is referring to scripture passage:

> **1 Corinthians 14: 33-35 33For God is not the author of confusion, but of peace,** as in all churches of the saints.
>
> **34Let your women keep silence in the churches**: for it is not permitted unto them to speak; but they are commanded to be under obedience as also saith the law.

[35]And if they will learn any thing, let them ask their husbands at home: for **it is a shame for women to speak in the church.**

That is male chauvinism at its highest. The apostle Paul also wrote:

1 Corinthians chapter 11: 3-5 [3]But I would have you know, that **the head of every man is Christ**; and **the head of the woman is the man**; and **the head of Christ is God**.

I do try to lead my life with Jesus as my head. I want to trust him in everything I do and let him lead my thoughts.

[4]Every man praying or prophesying, having his head covered, dishonoureth his head.

[5]But **every woman that prayeth or prophesieth with her head uncovered dishonoureth her head:** for that is even all one as if she were shaven.

Now Paul doesn't leave us hanging why this is written.

Verses 7 - 10: [7]For a man indeed ought not to cover his head, forasmuch as **he is the image and glory of God**: but **the woman is the glory of the man.**

[8]For the man is not of the woman: but the woman of the man. (For our evolutionary friends, who came first?)

[9]Neither was the man created for the woman; but the woman for the man.

[10]For this cause ought the woman to have power on her head because of the angels.

Paul explains this is God's order to things. How do we explain these writings in today's world? **Did God really mean it?** Did

Paul write this to give us his opinion or God's? Should we obey these teachings?

I tried to explain it to Greg the way my minister explained it to me when I questioned these same passages of scripture. I explained to Greg that God knows the nature of man, and that left to our own, we would let **women do all the work** in the church. **(Unfortunately, this is what we see in churches today.)** I explained God wanted to make sure men would take leadership roles and not sit back and let the women do all the work. It was also the culture in Paul's day for women to be submissive to their husbands.

My brother shot back, "That's just an attempt to justify these scripture passages." To Greg, this makes his point that the Bible has human opinions. Now, Greg loves the Lord and has great understanding of the Bible. He has studied, especially Paul's teachings. I did not have an answer to why this is in the Bible, other than what I said earlier, so I left it at that. Beside, we had reached the golf dome; and it was time to hit some golf balls.

But I could not get this out of my mind. My faith in God and his word being absolute truth made me want to answer this challenge to why Paul wrote this **if it is not God inspired**. For Paul also wrote in other passages:

> **1 Corinthians 11: 1-2 and 12:** [1]Be ye followers of me, even as I also am of Christ. **(Paul is saying follow his example as he has followed Christ's example.)**
>
> [2]Now I praise you, brethren, **that ye remember me in all things, and keep the ordinances, as I delivered them to you. (Paul is urging us to keep to the teachings he has given us.)**
>
> **Verse 12:** [12]For **as the woman is of the man**, even so is **the man also by the woman**; **but all things of God**.

What Verse 12 above is saying is that the first woman, Eve, came from the first man Adam. Since that time, all children, male and female, have been born of women. But even so, **all things come from God.**

> And in, **1 Corinthians 14: 36-38:** [36]What? came the word of God out from you? or came it unto you only?
>
> **[37]If any man think himself to be a prophet, or spiritual, let him acknowledge that the things that I write unto you are the commandments of the Lord.**

Look at verse 37 above. Paul speaks with such authority and writes just as if God himself has commanded it. Paul knows the Holy Spirit inspires him by what he writes.

> [38]But if any man be ignorant, let him be ignorant.

Paul is challenging us if we dare to prove him wrong. Paul is speaking with great authority, **one who is not representing himself, but representing God and God's word**. How then can I reconcile these scripture teachings of Paul with today's world?

I found a way. The key words are **submission** and **obedience**. I recognize I don't know everything, but I trust that God does. I submit myself to the greater authority, and that is Jesus Christ. **I submit myself to God's authority and say he sets the rules and not man.**

I have not always done this in my life. I have justified so many things as to why I did them, even most of the time knowing there was no way my thinking was lining up with scripture. **Why did I do it?Simple—I wanted to justify what I was doing.** Justifying things can clear the conscience. I wanted it my way; I wanted to have fun. I did not want to do his way. In other word, I was being selfish. I loved to play golf and still do. In the past, I would play as much as possible, including Sundays by skipping church, even after I came to Christ. I justified it in my mind that I could worship the Lord while chasing after that little white ball knowing full well I was worshiping that little white ball I was chasing after. I have done a lot of compromising of God's rules—justifying in my mind, regardless what the scriptures said.

Today we see many in the church challenging, "**Did God really say that?" "Did God really mean that?" "Do we have to follow what the apostle Paul taught?"** I did not mean for this book to have any controversial subject matter, but when you speak boldly using the truth of scripture, you will not always make everyone happy. Please forgive me if I offend you, but I am only trusting the word of God. Some Church leaders today deny the sin of homosexuality, saying Jesus never spoke out against it—he only spoke of love and forgiveness. That is a great truth, but not completely accurate. They forget the authority Jesus placed on all scripture and that he obeyed every word written in scripture. Jesus did not come to abolish the law; he came to fulfill it. Jesus himself warns and strongly rebukes anyone who teaches otherwise:

> **Matthew 5: 17-19** [17]**"Do not think that I have come to abolish the Law** or the Prophets; I have not come to abolish them **but to fulfill them**.
>
> [18]**I tell you the truth, until heaven and earth disappear**, not the smallest letter, not the least stroke of a pen, **will by any means disappear from the Law** until everything is accomplished.
>
> [19]Anyone who breaks one of the least of these commandments and **teaches others to do the same will be called least in the kingdom of heaven**, but whoever practices and teaches these commands will be called great in the kingdom of heaven.

Unfortunately, that is what I see happening in many of our churches today. To deny what is written against sexual immorality is denying the authority of scripture, **all of it**. I heard Reverend James D. Kennedy on television in one of his sermons say this about the sin of homosexuality, "If God did not speak against the sin of homosexuality, **then God owes Sodom and Gomorrah a huge apology**."

I want to state here and now that I do not look down on or dislike the homosexual person. We are all brothers and sisters in Christ.

Jesus himself would be the first to be anyone's friend, no matter the circumstances. God loves everyone. But **I do let God set the rules. I submit myself to his higher authority.** I cannot put myself into their shoes and know what it is like. I do know the sins and iniquities that I have in my own life and how I have to deal with and try to overcome them with God's help. The sins I struggle with—many so-called experts in secular fields of study would say that they are not sins at all. But am I going to believe what man says without the support of the word of God, which contradicts the word of God, and apply that to my life. That would deny the authority of scripture, and I just cannot do that.

I know many today will not agree with my opinion. But if you disagree, where does your opinion come from?**Does it come from the word of God or by what you feel?**Our feelings of right and wrong can deceive us, but God's word cannot. Ask God to reveal the truth to you. I know one thing, God asks us to love our neighbor as well as our enemy, and God teaches that we have all sinned and fallen short of His glory. So I will leave what God teaches for you to seek out for yourself, and I will never sit in judgment of anyone—**that is God's job**. But also, I can never deny the word of God where I receive my truth.

Maybe, as believers, we have compromised what is Biblical teaching with what we want to believe. We compromise the word of God to justify our behavior. I have known Christians who will live with a companion (maybe who is not a believer) out of wedlock and justify having sex with him or her. They will claim because they love him or her it is not sin even though the entire Bible teaches it is. They have made justification for it in their own minds against what is written in scripture.

We have done this with so much of the Bible. We have more faith in scientists, most who are atheists or at least agnostics that support evolution; and we reject the word of God and how he said he created the universe in Genesis. Church leaders are reading between the lines and have added billions of years to the creation story when God said he literally did it in **six days**! We will discuss this further in my chapters on creation.

I see so many compromises based on feelings and not based on evidence and the word of God. I hear people say, "I feel God would not mean that, God would not do that, or Jesus never said that." You ask them why, and they will say, " Oh, I just feel that way, it's my personal belief." By doing so, our perception of God is what we want him to be and **not what scripture says he is.** By doing so, if we are wrong in our assumptions, it could have consequences we did not intend—even eternal ramifications.

Getting back to what Paul wrote, maybe we are doing the same thing with these scriptures. Maybe we are justifying by saying God did not really mean this, just as we have done with so many other passages we don't understand or agree with. **Scriptures says God is unchanging. Can we say the same for man?**

Scripture says God set this way to his order: woman submitting to man, and man to Jesus, and Jesus to God as a test to see how obedient we will be to submit ourselves to his ways. God wants us to trust his words; to do his will in our lives and not pursue our own selfish ways.

> **Ephesians 5: 20-24** 20Giving thanks always for all things unto God and the Father in the name of our Lord Jesus Christ;
>
> 21**Submitting yourselves one to another** in the fear of God.
>
> 22**Wives, submit yourselves unto your own husbands, as unto the Lord.**
>
> 23For the husband is the head of the wife, even as Christ is the head of the church: and he is the saviour of the body.
>
> 24Therefore **as the church is subject unto Christ**, so **let the wives be to their own husbands in every thing.**

I have reconciled myself that all scriptures are true and that my understanding of them is sometimes flawed, **not the word of God**.

It shows that his ways are not the same as our ways and we cannot always know the **why of God**.

As it is written, **Isaiah 55: 8-9:** [8]For **my thoughts are not your thoughts, neither are your ways my ways**, saith the LORD.

> [9]For as the heavens are higher than the earth, so are **my ways higher than your ways, and my thoughts than your thoughts.**

All of scripture, including the New Testament writings, is the inspired word of God. Verse 16 below verifies all scripture is God breathed:

> **2 Timothy 3: 14-16:** [14]But continue thou in the things which thou hast learned and hast been assured of, knowing of whom thou hast learned them;
>
> [15]And that from a child thou hast known **the holy scriptures, which are able to make thee wise unto salvation through faith** which is in Christ Jesus.
>
> [16]All Scripture is **God-breathed** and is useful for **teaching**, **rebuking**, **correcting** and **training** in righteousness, **(NIV)**

The above scripture is saying **God inspires all scripture. All scripture is good for teaching, rebuking, correcting, and training.** I cannot deny the **absolute truth** of God's word. I may not understand all of it, but I trust it. I may not be able to obey everything written in scripture, but I will not deny the authority of it. I may be blind to why it is God's way to have these passages on woman's submission in scripture, but I will not deny the authority from which it came—**God breathed**.

> **Acts 17: 11-12** [11]Now the **Bereans (Body of believers who placed great emphasis on Scripture)** were of more noble character than the Thessalonians, for they received

> the message with great eagerness and **examined the Scriptures every day to see if what Paul said was true.**
>
> [12]Many of the Jews believed, as did also a number of prominent Greek women and many Greek men. **(NIV)**

As believers, we should be as the Bereans, who Paul commended for their examining the scriptures every day to see if what Paul was saying was true. We should base our opinions on the greater truth that is found in the Bible and not by man, whose thinking can be flawed.

> **1 Thessalonians 2: 13** [13]For this cause also thank we God without ceasing, because, when **ye received the word of God which ye heard of us**, ye received it **not as the word of men, but as it is in truth, the word of God**, which effectually worketh also in you that believe.

Paul is saying we are to take the teachings of the New Testament as the word of God, **as the truth.** When it comes to one's personal beliefs, I will believe it as truth when it lines up with the teachings of the Bible. God has given me every reason to believe him. The God of the Bible is the only one that **gives us a guarantee of living for eternity in heaven. It comes by faith.** No other world religion offers such a guarantee. Islam has no such guarantee. Judaism has no such guarantee. You can know right now where you will spend eternity. **Below is your "GUARANTEE":**

> **John 3: 16** [16]For God so loved the world, that he gave his only begotten Son, that **whosoever believeth in him should not perish, but have everlasting life.**

Take heart; if you choose to follow the word of God from the Bible, Jesus gave us the greatest example of submission ever given. He submitted to God's will to die and suffer on the cross for the sins of the world.

Husbands, as our wives are to submit to us as **Ephesians 5: 20-24** states, God does not let us off the hook—**we are to love our wives as much as Christ loves us**.

> **Ephesians 5: 25: [25]Husbands, love your wives**, even **as Christ also loved the church, and gave himself for it;**

Closing: I do love my wife this way. I hold my wife in high regard; I respect and honor her. I am so thankful God has given me such a wonderful lifetime partner as she. Husbands, treat your wives with love and respect. Abuse of the spouse is running rampant in our society, and its time we stop this and love one another as God intended. God hates divorce; it is bad for the children—it is bad for everyone. It is time we live our lives for others and not our selfish ways. **Keep God in your marriage** and grow together in your love for him. And watch your marriage blossom—**united as one.** It won't always be wonderful, but you will be able to work things out by staying together, forgiving one another, and loving each other.

God loves you and so do I!

Pray for the Sick!

Chapter 20

Recently I went with my mother to her Catholic church for Sunday service. During prayer, the priest asked us to pray for those we know who are sick and to bring them before the Lord. As I lifted up prayer, I thought of Alma, who became a friend through my wife's sister Becky. She is like a second mother to Becky and has become dear to our family as well.

Alma is in her later 80's; and this dear woman is in the later stages of lung cancer and has a short time left on this earth, unless God intercedes and heals her. Becky has taken a leave from her normal job to take care of Alma until the end comes.

As I lifted Alma in prayer, I began to meditate on sickness—how severe it can be, taking our loved ones away from us. As I thought of Alma, I thought of my own father who succumbed to cancer himself at the age of 58. I thought of how painful it is to lose some one you love dearly. My meditating turned to thoughts on **how short life is.**

> **Psalm 39: 4-5** 4 "Show me, O LORD, my life's end
> and the number of my days;
> **let me know how fleeting is my life.**
>
> 5 You have made my days a mere handbreadth;
> the span of my years is as nothing before you.
> **Each man's life is but a breath. (NIV)**

James 4: 13-14 [13]Go to now, ye that say, To day or to morrow we will go into such a city, and continue there a year, and buy and sell, and get gain:

[14]Whereas ye know not what shall be on the morrow. **For what is your life? It is even a vapour, that appeareth for a little time, and then vanisheth away.**

Scripture is saying our life is but a **breath**. Our life is but a **vapor** and then we are gone—vanished. When compared to eternity, **life is so very short.**

In the book of Job, God warns how short life is.

Job 14: 5 [5]Seeing his days are determined, the number of his months are with thee, thou hast appointed **his bounds that he cannot pass**;

Job 14: 10 [10]But **man dieth, and wasteth away**: yea, man giveth up the ghost, and **where is he?**

Job 27: 8 [8]"For **what is the hope of the godless** when he is cut off,
When God requires his life? (NASB)

We all have a date when our days on this earth are finished. **Job 27: 8** is true; **when you are godless**, what hope is there? A godless person will reach the end of his or her days and say what? My life is finished. Six feet under and....what? **How sad!**

As I continued meditating on this, God's words came to me in floods. God has great promises of everlasting life. He puts eternity in our hearts so that we all want it. As long as I can remember, well back into my childhood, I wanted to live forever. I wanted to go to heaven. **Do you?**

Ecclesiastes 3: 11 "He has made everything beautiful in its time. He has also **set eternity in the hearts of men;** yet they cannot phantom what **God has done from beginning to end." (NIV)**

God gives us a desire to live forever; God also gives us great warnings that all will live forever; **there is no death**. There will be either **great health** or great **sickness that lasts for eternity**. The word of God teaches **there are two ways to go.** There is eternal life with God for the righteous, and there is a **sickness that is so severe for the ungodly it will last forever.**

> **Daniel 12: 2** [2]And many of them that sleep in the dust of the earth shall awake, some to **everlasting life**, and some to **shame** and **everlasting contempt.**

> **Matthew 25: 46** [46]And these shall go away into **everlasting punishment**: but **the righteous into life eternal**.

This **sickness** is the **curse for our sins,** and it leads to **everlasting punishment;** and it is ultimately the only disease that matters. The name of this disease is "**Spiritual death.**" We were all infected with this disease **through sin**. Maybe if we all were to look deep inside we would see the truth of what the Bible says about our **own sins**.

> **Ezra 9: 6** [6]And said, O my God, **I am ashamed and blush to lift up my face to thee**, my God: for our **iniquities are increased over our head**, and **our trespass is grown up unto the heavens. (Can you see the sin in yourself? Do you feel shame? Do you realize someday you will have to face God?)**

> **2 Kings 14: 6** "but **every man** shall be put to **death for his own sin**."

> **1 John 1: 8-10** [8]**If we say that we have no sin, we deceive ourselves**, and the **truth is not in us**.

> [9]**If we confess our sins, he is faithful and just to forgive us our sins**, and to cleanse us from all unrighteousness.
>
> [10]**If we say that we have not sinned, we make him a liar, and his word is not in us.**

When we cannot admit that we are sinners, the disease remains in us. If we physically die in our sins, spiritual death happens. It is a death that causes everlasting pain and suffering.

Warning:

> **Ezekiel 18: 4** [4]"Behold, all souls are Mine; the soul of the father as well as the soul of the son is Mine **The soul who sins will die. (NASB)**
>
> **Romans 3: 23** [23]**For all have sinned**, and come short of the glory of God;
>
> **Mark 9: 47** [47]And if thine eye offend thee, pluck it out: **it is better for thee to enter into the kingdom of God with one eye, than having two eyes to be cast into hell fire: (Jesus does not want you to do this literally, he wants you to turn from your sins and repent.)**
>
> **Matthew 25: 41** [41]Then shall **he say also unto them on the left hand**, Depart from me, **ye cursed, into everlasting fire, prepared for the devil and his angels:**
>
> **Revelations 20: 14** [14]And death and hell were cast into the lake of fire. **This is the second death.**

(Important: do not miss the warning below)

> **Romans 1: 20** [20]For **since the creation** of the world **God's invisible qualities**—his eternal power and divine nature—

> **have been clearly seen,** being understood from what has been made, **so that men are without excuse. (NIV)**

So God warns us that we are in peril throughout his word, that we are all in danger from the disease caused by sin. There is **no one who is without excuse**. One way or another, **God has shown himself clearly to you.**

God does not want to leave us in sickness. **God offers us the cure** freely, **a gift we cannot repay. (Please remember this to the end of this chapter.)**

Job endured long-suffering and knew God would cure him of his afflictions. Job longed for that time when God would cure him of sin and what it brings.

> **Job 14: 14-17** [14]If a man die, **shall he live again?** all the days of my appointed time **will I wait, till my change come.**
>
> **[15]Thou shalt call, and I will answer thee: thou wilt have a desire to the work of thine hands.**
>
> [16]For now thou numberest my steps: dost thou not watch over my sin?
>
> **[17]My transgression is sealed up in a bag,** and thou sewest up mine iniquity.

The ancient Job foresaw his own resurrection and would see God. He also knew that all of his sins would be forgiven, sealed up in a bag, never to be used against him. This is part of the great news of the entire Bible.

The writer of **Psalm 86** saw the day of his deliverance.

> **Verses 11- 13** [11]Teach me thy way, O LORD; **I will walk in thy truth**: unite my heart to fear thy name.

[12]I will praise thee, O Lord my God, with all my heart: and **I will glorify thy name for evermore.**

[13]For great is thy mercy toward me: and **thou hast delivered my soul from the lowest hell.**

The writer of this Psalm was giving all the credit to God that he will be delivered from hell. He takes no credit for himself, as if he could earn it for himself.

In the book of **Isaiah, chapter 25** promises:

Verse 8 [8]**He will swallow up death in victory**; and **the Lord GOD will wipe away tears from off all faces**; and the rebuke of his people shall he take away from off all the earth: **for the LORD hath spoken it.**

The promises of God's miracle cure are found throughout the Bible.

Psalm 32: **1-2** [1] Blessed is he
whose transgressions are forgiven,
whose sins are covered.
[2] Blessed is the man
whose sin the LORD does not count against him
and in whose **spirit** is no deceit. **(NIV)**

Our sins can be forgiven; they will not be counted against us! We can all be blessed this way. In the most holy place of our being, **our spirit**, we can be free of sin and know the truth.

Psalm 103: 3-4 [3]**Who forgiveth all thine iniquities**; **who healeth all thy diseases;**

[4]**Who redeemeth thy life from destruction**; who crowneth thee with lovingkindness and tender mercies;

Sin is the disease, and it is God's forgiveness and love given to us by the one who redeems us, his son Jesus, who is the **miracle cure**. We are forgiven not because of what we have done, but what Jesus has done for us. Sins are covered over only one way, by the blood of Jesus Christ. **Please read these promises from God below**—don't miss your cure!

> **Luke 15: 7** [7]"I tell you that in the same way, **there will be more joy in heaven over one sinner who repents** than over ninety-nine righteous persons who need no repentance. **(NASB)**

> **Romans 5: 8** [8]But God commendeth his love toward us, in that, **while we were yet sinners, Christ died for us.**

In **Philippians, chapter 2**, Paul writes of Jesus:

> **Verses 6-11** [6]Who, **being in the form of God (Jesus!)**, thought it not robbery to be **equal with God**:

> [7]**But made himself of no reputation**, and **took upon him the form of a servant**, and was made in the **likeness of men**:

Note: Paul, using the limitations of human language, describes Jesus in scripture as being equal to God; and there is only one God. He being God took the form of man and came humbly as a servant, with no great reputation. As I have shown in past chapters, when we use the entire Bible, there is no doubt scripture is teaching us Jesus is God and is not a created being, as some religions and people that do not know the Bible will proclaim.

> [8]And being found in fashion as a man, **he humbled himself**, and **became obedient unto death, even the death of the cross.**

9Wherefore God also hath highly exalted him, and **given him a name which is above every name:**

10That **at the name of Jesus every knee should bow**, of things in heaven, and things in earth, and things under the earth;

11And that **every tongue should confess that Jesus Christ is Lord**, to the glory of God the Father.

Jesus humbly came to earth and took the form of a servant with one purpose for his life: to be obedient to God and die on the cross—**to die for our sins**. His glory now is that his name is above all other names, and we all will someday bow down and confess Jesus Christ is Lord.

1 Timothy 1: 15 15This is a faithful saying, and worthy of all acceptation, **that Christ Jesus came into the world to save sinners; of whom I am chief. (Count me with the sinners and I trust Jesus to save me!)**

The writer of **Hebrews in chapter 10** shares that Jesus offered the ultimate sacrifice.

Verse 10: 10By the which will **we are sanctified through the offering of the body of Jesus Christ once for all.**

Verse 12: 12But this man, **after he had offered one sacrifice for sins for ever, sat down on the right hand of God;**

Old Testament priests had to annually offer blood sacrifice to cover the sins of the chosen people. That is what the Old Testament was showing us when there was sacrificing lambs, offering them up for the sins the people of Israel had committed the previous year. These sacrifices prophesized that Jesus, being God, would become the perfect sacrifice so that our sins would be covered over, sealed in a bag, **not counted against us forever**. Once Jesus came to earth as a man, he sacrificed himself as the blood sacrifice that would last for eternity. His work was done, and now Jesus sits at the Right Hand of his Father.

In Book of **John, chapter 3, the whole hope of Christianity is found.** A good friend of mine said once to me his whole faith stands on this one simple truth.

> **John 3: 16** [16]For God so loved the world, that he gave his only begotten Son, that **whosoever believeth in him should not perish, but have everlasting life.**

What a great message! But it does not stop here. God continues this beautiful message with another warning so we won't miss what he is offering us. I cannot stress this warning and the love of God that saves us enough!

> **John 3: 17 & 18-21** [17]For God sent not his Son into the world to condemn the world; but that **the world through him might be saved.**
>
> [18]He that believeth on him is not condemned: **but he that believeth not is condemned already, because he hath not believed in the name of the only begotten Son of God.**
>
> [19]And **this is the condemnation**, that **light (Jesus is the light; he is the Word of God, the truth.) is come into the world**, and **men loved darkness (Darkness is our sins, untruth, not believing the word of God.) rather than light**, because their deeds were evil.

Important: understand verse 19 above and verse 20 below. The condemnation is when you do not come to Jesus, you continue in your ways and you stay in your sins. One who does evil (we all have sinned) and rejects Jesus will remain in the darkness by his or her choosing. They will not accept the fact that they are sinners.

> [20]For **every one that doeth evil hateth the light**, neither cometh to the light, lest his deeds should be **reproved.** **(Sinners do not want to be found at fault or criticized.)**

Verse 21 follows: I remember my own struggle with the fear of coming into the light before I came to faith. I feared the thought of needing to change my life. I feared the thought that I would not be able to do the things I was doing any longer that were enjoyable to me, but sinful in God's eyes. I feared the thought of changing my belief system. Satan wants to put the fear in you. He does not want you to come to see the light of God. He will use every means against you. Remember this; the bible says Satan exists. His greatest deception he uses against us is to have us think he does not exist. You can defeat him through Jesus Christ. Once you have faith in him, you will come into the light and it is wonderful. You will have God's guarantee that you live forever in eternity in heaven with everlasting health.

> [21]But he that doeth truth **cometh to the light**, that his deeds may be made manifest, that they are **wrought (meaning formed, created)** in God.

I remember when I had to humbled myself and admit I was a sinner, and asking the light—Jesus to come into my life. It was truly wonderful to know God loved me just the way I was and he accepts me. When I came to Jesus, I saw the sins I had committed and I saw by only trusting God, could I be saved.

Whether we believe in eternity or not, **it will not change the truth**. My own faith tells me I will spend eternity somewhere. Because I have **confessed** I am a sinner, **repented** of my sins, and I **humbled** myself and **asked Jesus into my heart**, I take God's promise of eternity with love and joy with me to my grave. I fully hope and expect to rise again in the presence of my Maker, not because of what I have done or did not do—but what God did for me. **He did it for you too!**

Please check your heart. Check to see if the scripture lines up to what you know is true. Will God let sin go unpunished?Do you believe there are two ways to go in your eternal life?Can anyone be worthy enough to escape the damnation of his or her own sins?Can anyone in himself or herself earn heaven?Why would you want to?Take the first step. **Humble yourself** and **admit to God** you are a sinner and **ask God** for **forgiveness.** Ask Jesus to be your Redeemer and Intercessor by **asking him into your life.** Ask God to fill you with his **Holy Spirit** so you may be born again and become a child of God. **Jesus is the cure for our infliction and disease.**

Jesus himself warns us in his own words there is one sin that is unpardonable. It is the sin of blasphemy against the Holy Spirit. **What does that mean?**

> **Matthew 12: 31-32** [31]Wherefore I say unto you, All manner of sin and blasphemy shall be forgiven unto men: but **the blasphemy against the Holy Ghost shall not be forgiven unto men.**
>
> [32]And whosoever speaketh a word against the Son of man, it shall be forgiven him: but **whosoever speaketh against the Holy Ghost, it shall not be forgiven him**, neither in this world, neither in the world to come.

Jesus is telling us that all sin can be forgiven, even words used against him. But if you speak against the Holy Spirit, you will never be forgiven in this world or the next. When Jesus spoke these words, he was speaking to the Pharisees (the religious leaders of Israel) who rejected Jesus and the miracles he performed. They were saying his miracles were not of God but of the devil, Satan. In effect, they were denying where Jesus received his power and therefore **rejecting him.**

> **John 3: 18** [18]He that believeth on him is not condemned: **but he that believeth not is condemned already**, because **he hath not believed in the name of the only begotten Son of God.**

> **John 3: 36 [36]Whoever believes in the Son has eternal life, but whoever rejects the Son will not see life**, for God's wrath remains on him."

What scripture is telling us is that the unforgivable sin clearly is **permanently rejecting** Jesus Christ. So, speaking against the Holy Spirit is equivalent to **rejecting Christ with such finality that no future repentance is possible.**

The Holy Spirit is always wooing us, convicting us of our sins; and he enables us to accept Jesus Christ as Lord. But man resists his wooing:

> **Acts 7: 51** [51]Ye stiffnecked and uncircumcised in heart and ears, **ye do always resist the Holy Ghost:** as your fathers did, **so do ye**.

To the person who rejects the Holy Spirit, the words of God seem foolish.

> **1 Corinthians 2: 12-14** [12]Now **we have received**, not the spirit of the world, but **the spirit which is of God**; that we might **know the things that are freely given to us of God.**
>
> [13]Which things also we speak, not in the words which man's wisdom teacheth, **but which the Holy Ghost teacheth**; comparing spiritual things with spiritual.
>
> [14]But **the natural man (unbelievers) receiveth not** the things of the **Spirit of God**: for **they are foolishness unto him**: neither can he know them, because they are spiritually **discerned (separated).**

Only by receiving the Holy Spirit into our hearts and minds, the one who teaches us the truth about God and spiritual truths, can we know and receive the free gift of Jesus Christ and eternal life.

The deliberate refusal of this grace of God is the one sin that is irreversible at judgment day—it is the **unpardonable sin.**

The Holy Spirit knocks at everyone's door to his or her heart. If you let him in, he will enter. There is no excuse to not receive him. **He is knocking right now! This is not a coincidence you are reading this book right now.**

> **Revelation 3: 20** [20]Behold, **I stand at the door, and knock**: if any man hear my voice, and open the door, **I will come in to him**, and will sup with him, and he with me.

The word of God has been the same since the beginning of time. He knew we would sin before he created the world. He put a plan into motion immediately so he could pardon us for our sins. It was a free gift, **one we could not pay for. Remember early in this chapter I asked you to keep this in mind to the end. God has an invitation for you.** The free gift was being offered from the beginning of scripture and was fully revealed in the New Testament. The prophet **Isaiah** foresaw it and he wrote about it in **chapter 55** of his book. Let's look at God's free gift that **we cannot pay for described in the Old Testament.** It is the same message as given in the New Testament.

> **Isaiah 55: 1** [1] **"Come, all you who are thirsty,**
> come to the waters;
> and **you who have no money,**
> **come, buy and eat!**
> Come, buy **wine** and milk
> **without money and without cost. (NIV)**

God is telling us that he will quench our thirst. He will feed us. Jesus is the Bread of Life who poured out his blood like wine as a sacrifice for our sins. He will take care of us, and he will not charge us for it. Your money is no good; there is **no cost you can pay.**

> **Verse 2:** [2] Why spend money on what is not bread,
> and your labor on what does not satisfy?
> **Listen, listen to me**, and **eat what is good,**
> and **your soul will delight** in the **richest of fare** (**Fare is your "entrance fee"—which is free!). (NIV)**

God is saying do not work and spend your time on what cannot satisfy or give eternal life. Do not spend your time in sin. Take in his love and eat of it, and your soul will delight in the riches of God. .

> **Verse 3:** [3]**Incline your ear**, and **come unto me: hear, and your soul shall live**; and **I will make an everlasting covenant with you**, even the sure mercies of David.

Listen to God. Accept his invitation, and he will make a covenant **(oath made by God)** with you that will last forever. God's oath is not like man's that can be broken; it is impossible for God to break his promises.

> **Verse 6 & 7:** [6]**Seek ye the LORD while he may be found, call ye upon him while he is near:**

Because you are reading this book, you are seeking; and God is near right now. You can find him.

> [7]**Let the wicked forsake his way**, and the unrighteous man his thoughts: and let him **return unto the LORD**, and **he will have mercy** upon him; and to our God, for **he will abundantly pardon.**

God has a pardon with your name on it. His invitation is to return to him, and he will show you mercy and pardon you. This pardon is clearly revealed in the book of John.

> **John 3: 16** [16]For God so loved the world, that he gave his only begotten Son, that **whosoever believeth in him** should not perish, but **have everlasting life.**

Poetically, Isaiah closes chapter 55 with a picture of heaven where pain and suffering will pass away; and it will be replaced with joy, peace, and happiness.

> **Verse 12 and 13:** [12]For ye shall go out **with joy**, and be led forth **with peace**: the mountains and the hills shall break forth before you **into singing**, and all the trees of the field **shall clap** their hands. [13]Instead of the thorn shall come up the **fir tree**, and instead of the brier shall come up the **myrtle tree**: and it shall be to **the LORD** for a name, for an **everlasting sign that shall not be cut off.**

God is near right now. Go to **chapter 38** if you have not already begun a personal relationship with Jesus and would like to get started doing so right now.

God loves you and so do I!

P.S. Since I have written this chapter, Alma has lost her battle with cancer; and now she is in the hands of her Maker. I pray she had the cure.

"Hear, O Israel: The LORD our God is one LORD"

Chapter 21

In chapter 8, we first discussed the Bible's teaching of the Trinity. I showed evidence that the Bible teaches the Three Persons of the Trinity in both the Old and New Testaments. Now I want to focus on the Old Testament. I will rehash some of the evidence I already have shown and add new evidence using the Old Testament only. This chapter was inspired by what I saw on television. May it speak to you.

Tonight, I watched Lee Strobel's show on PAX, "Faith under Fire." The Trinity was the topic of discussion, and the debate was between a believing Christian and a non-believing Jewish rabbi. **The rabbi won the debate on all counts.** You see, the rabbi kept quoting the Old Testament scripture passage taken from **Deuteronomy 6: 4** (the title of this chapter), and the believing Christian only spoke using New Testament scripture, which has no meaning for the rabbi and Judaism- it is not part of the Torah or their Bible (Old Testament). As Christians, we must be able to defend and explain the Trinity and why we believe so strongly the Bible testifies to it. It is not by blind faith that we accept this teaching of the Bible—Old and New Testaments both testify to it. Depending on our audience, we should be able to witness to the Trinity using either or both the Old and New Testaments.

If I were to have written a letter to Lee explaining why the Christian believer lost the debate to the rabbi, it would have gone something like this:

Dear Lee,

In watching the debate about the Trinity, your guest who defended its teachings lost the debate from the onset. He lost because he did not quote the Old Testament once; he only spoke using the New Testament. People of the Jewish faith—or for that matter, add the Islamic faith also—will never be convinced of the Trinity using the New Testament scriptures—they both think the New Testament is not scriptural. Islam teaches the New Testament has been altered from its original texts and therefore is corrupted.

To combat this, you should have had as your guest an expert on the Old Testament and the Hebrew language, a Messianic Jewish believer, who understands where Judaism is coming from. I learned important lessons on the Hebrew language and how each word has unique meanings from such a believer—**Meno Kalisher**, a believer in Jesus Christ and a minister living in Israel. Meno was born and raised in Israel by Christian parents. He had to learn to defend and answer tough questions about his faith being a Jew who believed in **Yeshua** (Jesus Christ). In order to be a witness to his fellow Jews of his faith in Jesus, he learned to do so using the **Old Testament only**. As Meno states, "Jesus just didn't pop out of a cake in Matthew and say, **'Here I am!'.**"

Meno explains one of the most important scriptures in the Jewish religion is **Deuteronomy 6: 4-5**. It is embedded in the door-post of every home and business of a practicing Jew. Judaism refers to **Deuteronomy 6: 4-9** as the "**Shema**." It means to heed, listen, and obey. Adult Jewish males recite the Shema twice daily to affirm their faith. Meno states this is why it is so important to understand Hebrew and be able to go to Old Testament text to share your faith in Jesus. **Jesus is in the Shema scripture below!**

> **Deuteronomy 6: 4-9** 4 Hear, O Israel: **The LORD our God is one LORD**:

> 5And **thou shalt love the LORD thy God** with all thine heart, and with all thy soul, and with all thy might.
>
> 6And these words, which I command thee this day, **shall be in thine heart:**
>
> 7And **thou shalt teach them diligently unto thy children**, and shalt talk of them when thou sittest in thine house, and when thou walkest by the way, and when thou liest down, and when thou risest up.
>
> 8And thou shalt bind them for a sign upon thine hand, and they shall be as frontlets between thine eyes.
>
> **9And thou shalt write them upon the posts of thy house, and on thy gates.**

The first line of the Shema of Judaism, **Deuteronomy 6: 4**, is the most important scripture in Judaism, and it clearly states that **there is only one God**! Then how can I say Jesus is in this verse? How can I ever defend the Trinity using this verse?Are Christians deceived when they believe Jesus is God?Is the Bible full of contradictions?By understanding the Hebrew language, the "Trinity" is clearly in the Shema.

It is important to understand the Hebrew language many times has two words with the same meaning. In the scripture text above, the Hebrew word used for **"one"** is **"echad."** It allows for the **plurality of one, yet it is one**. It's meaning is completeness, **bringing harmony to many things** and **making them whole—one unit**. To eliminate and close the door to the Trinity, God would have used the Hebrew word for **"one"** as " **Yachid**," which is the **singular form for one**. **Yachid** would not have allowed doctrine for the Trinity to ever be taught.

Other examples in the Bible of the word for **"one"** used in plural form (**echad**) are:

> **Genesis 1: 5** [5]And God called the light Day, and the darkness he called Night. And the evening and the morning were **the first day (Two parts, evening and morning, making one day)**.
>
> **Genesis 2: 24** [24]Therefore shall a man leave his father and his mother, and shall cleave unto his wife: and they shall be **one flesh. (A man and his wife are considered as one by God.)**
>
> **Ezra 2:64** [64]The **whole congregation** together was forty and two thousand three hundred and threescore, **(In other Bible versions, congregation is translated as army. The army of 42,360 is called one army.)**
>
> **Ezekiel 37: 17** [17]And **join them one to another** into **one stick**; and they shall **become one** in thine hand. **(I cannot help but think of the cross—two pieces of wood joined together to form it.)**
>
> **Numbers 13: 23** describe a cluster of grapes as "**one**" (**echad**). [23]And they came unto the brook of Eshcol, and cut down from thence a branch with **one cluster of grapes**,

More importantly, in **Deuteronomy chapter 6** and many other chapters in the Old Testament, the Hebrew word for God used is "**Elohim.**" It is the most common (used 2,570 times) original name for God used in the Old Testament, giving him respect and holding him up in awe. It allows for the Trinity because it is the **plural form of El or Eloha** (which are singular name words for God). The usage in the Old Testament for El and Eloha is comparatively rare. These singular forms for God were used in poetry and late prose. The book of Job is where it is found most often (41 times). It is very important to understand that "**Elohim**," **even though it is plural in form**, is commonly used **with a singular verb or adjective**.

Scripture would have completely knocked out any chance for the Trinity if the Hebrew word for God used had been **El** or **Eloha only, especially if it had been used in Deuteronomy 6: 4. But God chose Elohim instead.** Meno states, "God knows Hebrew very well." God intended to reveal himself as **Elohim**—allowing for the Trinity, all being equal, all being **one** God."

Further evidence from the teachings of Judaism reveals: When Old Testament reveals the Holy Spirit; He is called the **"Spirit of YHWH"** or "**Spirit of Elohim." He is called "Holy Spirit"** in the Jewish interpretative teachings of the Talmud and Midrash, which are second only to the Torah in importance.

The Holy Spirit is written about from the very beginning:

> **Genesis 1: 2** [2]And the earth was without form, and void; and darkness was upon the face of the deep. And **the Spirit of God (Elohim)** moved upon the face of the waters.

The Hebrew word for Spirit describes God as like being the wind, the breath—**God that cannot be seen**.

God spoke words to Moses that revealed the Father head of God in **Exodus 33: 20**. To look upon him would cause immediate death because of his glory.

> [20]And he said, **Thou canst not see my face: for there shall no man see me, and live.**

Again, God cannot be seen, or you will die. The Apostle John verifies this that **no man** has ever looked upon or seen God the Father, **except one—and he sits at the Father's side.**

> **John 1:18:** [18] **No one has ever seen God,** but **God the One and Only, who is at the Father's side,** has made him known. **(NIV)**

But early in the same chapter, Moses and Joshua saw God face-to-face and lived:

> [11]And **the LORD spake unto Moses face to face,** as **a man speaketh unto his friend.** And he turned again into the camp: but his servant **Joshua**, the son of Nun, a young man, departed not out of the tabernacle.

God appeared to Abraham several times, the one that could be looked upon and live:

> **Genesis 17: 1 & 3** [1]And when **Abram (God later changed his name to Abraham.)** was ninety years old and nine, **the LORD appeared to Abram**, and said unto him, I am the Almighty God; walk before me, and be thou perfect.
>
> [3]And **Abram** fell on his face: and **God (Elohim) talked with him**, saying,
>
> In **Genesis 18:1** the Lord appeared to Abraham again, [1]And the LORD appeared unto him in the plains of Mamre: and **he sat (God is sitting) in the tent door in the heat of the day;**
>
> And in **Exodus 6: 2-3** [2]And **God (Elohim) spake unto Moses**, and said unto him, I am the LORD:
>
> [3]And **I appeared** unto Abraham, unto Isaac, and unto Jacob, **by the name of God ("El") Almighty ("Sadday")**, but by my name **JEHOVAH (meaning is "Savior" or "Deliverer")** was I not known to them.

In all the Old Testament scriptures above, separate names for God are used—some that are singular along with Elohim that is plural. But in the scriptures, **God appeared and could be seen and looked upon without dying**. What is interesting in the last verse above is that God reveals himself to Moses by a **new name, "Jehovah," and**

the name for God means "SAVIOR" or "DELIVERER." What a perfect name for this newest revelation about God. This is God in the Second Person in the Old Testament—**this is my Jesus**!

We can see through all of scripture that God was teaching us of the Trinity. The First Person of the Trinity is **God the Father**, who could not be looked upon without dying. We are taught the Third Person of the Trinity; the **Holy Spirit** that is everywhere and again cannot be seen. Then we see Old Testament scripture that shows us God that **can be looked upon without dying**, who could sit and speak to you face to face. Using further revelation from scripture and the entire Bible, this is Jesus, our Messiah—**God the Son**. This makes up the Trinity of God.

We know God has a Son by using Old Testament scriptures. In the Book of Proverbs, Agur foresaw this in his writing, but could not see the full revelation of it from his vantage point. He asks, "What is the name of God's Son?"

> **Proverbs 30: 3-4** [3]I neither learned wisdom, **nor have the knowledge of the holy. (I love the humbleness of Agur—he admits he is only a man, and lacks knowledge.)**

In verse 4 below, Agur now see the Messiah who has both come down to earth and ascended into heaven. He asks who our creator is and the **name of his Son!**

> [4]Who hath ascended up into heaven, or descended? who hath gathered the wind in his fists? who hath bound the waters in a garment? **who hath established all the ends of the earth? what is his name, and what is his son's name, if thou canst tell?**

The writer of Psalm 45 foresaw the **Messiah God** being placed above all other humans by God the Father.

> In **Psalm 45: 6-7** [6]Thy throne, **O God**, is **for ever and ever**: the sceptre of thy kingdom is a right sceptre.

The Father God has set **God the Son** above all. [7]Thou lovest righteousness, and hatest wickedness: **therefore God, thy God**, hath anointed thee with the oil of gladness above thy fellows.

He is saying to God the Son; your God has anointed you. Using the entire Bible, we can know, the Messiah is both man and God, and he is Jesus Christ, as we will see by the prophet Isaiah.

The Old Testament foretells of the Messiah. He is described as **God in the flesh. He is born in human form, and yet he is still God.** The prophet Isaiah describes him this way:

> **Isaiah 9: 6** [6]For unto us **a child is born**, unto us **a son is given**: and the government shall be upon his shoulder: and his name shall be called Wonderful, Counsellor, **The mighty God, The everlasting Father, The Prince of Peace.**

Isaiah could see the Messiah before he was born and knew he was **mighty God** (El Sadday), our **Father**, and the **Prince of Peace (used to describe Jesus in the New Testament).**

Jeremiah 23 describes a future Messiah coming from the line of David. This heir of David will be a righteous branch, a King who will reign wisely, and in his day Judah (the tribe that David comes from) will be saved. **This king**, an heir of David, **is born** into this world, and thus **he is a man. But he is also God**. Meno asks how can this be that he can be in the line of David, a man, yet it can also be said in scripture **he is God (YHWH).** This is the most used name for God in the Old Testament, occurring 6,823 times.

> **Jeremiah 23: 5-6** [5]Behold, the days come, saith the LORD, **that I will raise unto David a righteous Branch (Scripture is saying he will be a man—an heir of King David.)**, and **a King shall reign and prosper**, and shall execute judgment and justice in the earth.
>
> [6]In his days Judah shall be saved, and Israel shall dwell safely: and **this is his name** whereby he shall be called, **THE LORD (*YHWH*) OUR RIGHTEOUSNESS. (This**

> **heir of King David, a man, will be called "YHWH," a name used for God)**

YHWH is another word in the Hebrew language **for God**. It means, "**God is Lord.**" As you can see from scripture above, prophecy tells us God will come into this world in the flesh, as a man—and still be God **(YHWH).** From these scriptures and many more, God reveals to us the Second Person of the Trinity. Using the Old Testament only, we can see Jesus coming into full view, especially when we see he completely fulfilled all of the prophecies concerning the Messiah, both the suffering and triumphant descriptions the Old Testament gives.

Isaiah 53 and **Psalm 22** are the most famous chapters that describe the **suffering Messiah;** Jesus came the first time to redeem us. I urge you to read these chapters for yourself. Some excerpts from these chapters:

> **Isaiah 53: 1** 1Who hath believed our report? and to whom is the arm of the LORD revealed? **(The arm is the Messiah who sits at the right hand of God!)**

> **Isaiah 53: 3** 3**He is despised and rejected of men**; a man of sorrows, and acquainted with grief: and we hid as it were our faces from him; **he was despised**, and **we esteemed him not.**

> **Isaiah 53: 5** 5But **he was wounded for our transgressions**, he was bruised for our iniquities: the chastisement of our peace was upon him; and **with his stripes we are healed. (Other versions of the Bible use "pierced" instead of wounded.)**

> **Psalm 22: 1** 1**My God, my God, why hast thou forsaken me?** why art thou so far from helping me, and from the words of my roaring?

> **Psalm 22: 16** [16]For dogs have compassed me: the assembly of the wicked have inclosed me: **they pierced my hands and my feet.**

Why does Judaism miss the scriptures of the suffering Messiah? **Simple**—because they choose to ignore these prophesies. They choose to dwell on the prophesies of the **triumphant Messiah** only, such as what we read in **Jeremiah 23** above. They long for the **triumphant Messiah** as we believers in Christ do also. They await for their Messiah who will come in the future to reign forever. For the believer, this will be **the second coming of Christ**. As a Christian, I believe Jesus is the Messiah **both Jews and Christians** are looking for. When Christ returns, the remnant of Jews will recognize him this time.

The book of Isaiah chapter 11 is a beautiful prophecy of the **triumphant Messiah.** It will be a time when the wolf will lay down with the lamb. It will be a time when there is full knowledge of the Lord. Jesus, being in the line of David, who is from the line of Jesse, will have returned to earth. Jews and Gentiles alike will seek the rest of the Lord, and it will be glorious. Scripture says in **verse 11 it will be the second time** he has set his hand to recover the remnant of his people. This prophecy will be fulfilled at Jesus Christ's second coming.

> [10]And in that day there shall be a root of Jesse, which shall stand for an ensign of the people; to it **shall the Gentiles seek**: and **his rest shall be glorious.**

> [11]And it shall come to pass in that day, that **the Lord shall set his hand again the second time to recover the remnant of his people**

Closing: Christians have the foundation for the Trinity in the original Hebrew text and the complete revelation of who God is from **Genesis chapter 1 verse 1** to the end in **Revelation 22 verse 21**—God the Father, God the Son, God the Holy Spirit, an **echad or Trinity** that makes a **one** complete whole God: **Elohim.**

I see Jesus everywhere in Scripture—Old and New. Jesus did not just pop out of the New Testament out of thin air. Jesus was there in the beginning. According to **Genesis 1: 1 and John 1: 1– 4**, Jesus is our Creator. **Genesis 3: 15**- prophesized Jesus would crush the serpent's **(Satan)** head, and Satan would strike his heal (**This happened at the Cross.**) What Satan thought would destroy our Savior Jesus when he was put to death and was buried was only a wound. Jesus triumphed over Satan by rising from the dead. Jesus is our redeemer from the very beginning.

Whereas we could not see God in the Father head and the Holy Spirit form, God was totally revealed in the flesh in Jesus Christ (**Isaiah 9: 6, Hebrews 1: 8 - 9**).

The words in **Psalm 45: 7** of the Old Testament is totally revealed here in **Hebrews 1: 8-9**: (the exact same words in scripture in verse 9 of Hebrews are what is read in Psalm 45 verse 7.)

> 8But **unto the Son he (God) saith, Thy throne, O God**, is for ever and ever: a sceptre of righteousness is the sceptre of thy kingdom.
>
> 9Thou hast loved righteousness, and hated iniquity; **therefore God, even thy God**, hath anointed thee with the oil of gladness above thy fellows.

By using all of scripture, Christians can be witnesses in their belief to others of the Trinity and that Jesus is the Messiah God to the Jewish people. We can defend our position of a triune God to those of the Islamic faith. It is not a blind faith that we have our belief in the Trinity. It is based on sound Scriptural interpretation from the original text and in the original language it was first written, and given to mankind—Hebrew. It was from the vantage point the prophets were seeing the Messiah born and crucified and resurrected 500 – 1,500 years ahead of time.

May I leave you with this blessing that Paul wrote. Genesis speaks of our being made in God's image because it is true—we are made with a spirit, we have a soul, and we have a body.

1 Thessalonians 5: 23 [23]And the very God of peace sanctify you wholly; and *I pray God* your whole **spirit** and **soul** and **body** be preserved **blameless** unto the coming of our Lord Jesus Christ.

God loves you and so do I!

The Dream Giver-God Speaks In Dreams

Chapter 22

I like the name "dream giver." I read Bruce Wilkinson's book titled "The Dream Giver," and our God can send us dreams to communicate with us.

> **Acts 16: 9** [9]**And a vision appeared to Paul in the night**; There stood a man of Macedonia, and prayed him, saying, Come over into Macedonia, and help us.

God had spoken to me in the past through a dream some 28 years ago, before I accepted Jesus as my Savior. In that vision, I saw Jesus triumphant return at his second coming. I wrote about that dream in the first chapter, "I see him, I see him!" printed in this book. How magnificent that dream was. What an important message God spoke to me in that dream. In that dream, God warned me of my eternal fate if I remained lukewarm in my love for Jesus.

> **Revelation 3: 16** [16]So then **because thou art lukewarm**, and neither cold nor hot, **I will spue ("spit") thee out of my mouth.**

In the last several years, I longed for God to speak to me in a dream again. I wanted God to give me new and wondrous revelation, new insight that would figuratively **knock my socks off.** Whenever I would think about it at bedtime, I would I pray for it to happen.

Over the past year, I kept having this same recurring dream. I dismissed it as meaningless since I saw no purpose in having it. Little did I know God was trying to communicate with me using this dream. It's a boring dream, so bear with me of my retelling of it to you. The dream goes like this:

My family (my wife Helen, son Colin, and daughter Courtney) and I get in line to enter a parlor in the mall that not only shows movies, but also they have snow cones as their main attraction. You must pay first, and then you get in line at the refreshment counter. There are three machines that make snow cones that are spaced out along a long glass counter that turns a corner and continues on so many customers can be served at once. Today though, only one machine is in operation because it is the beginning of the day, and the customer line is still short.

As my family and I wait with only a couple of customers ahead of us, the snow cone machine stops functioning. The workers are calmly trying to get it working again. As they work, the customer line gets a little longer. We continue to wait, and they continue to work on the machine to no avail. My family decides that I can wait in line while they do some shopping, and they leave. The customer line continues to grow.

Time keeps marching on, and they just cannot get that machine to work. I know there are two other machines to make snow cones and wonder why they don't get one of those up and running and forget about this broken machine. The lines keep getting longer, and my patience is running a little bit thin. I am beginning to feel a little anger building.

The waiting game continues. The line is getting long. Some of the customers start to leave. They will come back later, hoping that the problem will be fixed when they return. I am a diehard and remain in line with only a few customers ahead of me. Even though people are dropping out of the line, it continues to get longer.

I now notice the workers appear to have given up trying to fixing the snow cone machine and are readying the machine farthest from the line, around the corner from us. It will take some time to be readied. The line is getting longer even though more and more people keep dropping out. The long wait is getting my temper boiling. I must bite my tongue out of fear of what might come out of my mouth.

Finally the few people who were ahead of me drop out, no longer willing to continue to wait; and **I am first in line**. By now I am steaming inside. The waiting has really gotten the best of me.

This is where my recurring dream would always end. I would be angry inside and wanting to cry out in pain, **"WOE IS ME"** and then I would wake up. Never in my wildest dreams was I thinking God was trying to communicate to me in this dream. And why was it always ending at the same place in my dream?I really did not give it much thought until I was finally revealed the ending last night. I finally saw the ending, and just like the first time God spoke to me in a dream many years ago where he revealed to me about being lukewarm for him the message for me was clear. It was not what I was praying for, great revelation of his word or prophecy; but it was exactly what I needed. I am embarrassed to continue because it reveals a great deal about who I am.

To finish the dream:

I continued waiting for my snow cone and because the people in front of me dropped out, I am now first in line with many, many people waiting behind me. I am fuming angry at all the waiting. They are close to being up and running using the machine they have prepared, and I am spouting out words of anger and letting everyone around me know **I am angry**. The people waiting in line are uncomfortable with seeing a grown man having a tantrum, blasting out words of anger, and so are the workers doing their best to ignore me.

All I can think about is that when they do open the new line, all these people behind me will jump out ahead of me and will get served first, **ahead of me;** and it's not fair. I am letting everyone know it isn't fair. I have been **waiting the longest, and I want to be served first. Oh, the anger I feel—and I DON'T CARE WHO KNOWS!**

The workers are ready to open the new line now. By my actions, I have made it clear to everyone how angry I am and they better not try and get ahead of me. The workers made sure of it. One came out from behind the counter, grabbed me by the arm, and escorted me to the machine, **first in line.** The workers remembered that I came with my family, and the one that is escorting me knows something that she cannot wait to tell me. She tells me my wife and kids are back and have been informed of how badly I behaved while they were away, and this lady also wants me to know what is in store for me when I leave this establishment.

Somehow I could see Helen even though she was not with me as the worker was talking with me. I could see her disappointment in me. I could see I have hurt her once again. I have embarrassed her once again. I am still so very angry, and I did not care how Helen felt.

In my anger, I let this worker know, "I don't care what my wife says to me. I am right and everyone else is at fault **and I don't care who sees me behaving this way."**

This is when I awaken from my dream. I am wide awake and still burning up inside. This dream has actually made me angry enough inside to remain mad after I have awakened. As I am laying there thinking of what just occurred, God spoke to me in a quiet soft voice, **"Don't you care if I see you this way?"**

I immediately could see how evil my anger is—**how dark, how horrible, how dirty my sin is.** I became very ashamed and began praying to God and asking for his forgiveness. I also realized that I do care how I behave, and that I want Jesus to shine through me. I also knew then that God had answered my prayer. For some time now, God was trying to communicate to me through this dream; but it was not getting through until now. It was being blocked. I found out a little later how it finally got through.

God communicated by this dream; He wanted me to get a hold of my anger. He is hurt by my sins. He cares that I do these things. I must admit that since my earliest childhood, I have had to deal with anger. When I am angry, just as in my dream, I want the world to know it; and I take it out on people I love so that they can know the hurt I feel. I have always known it was wrong and sinful, but my short fuse and emotions I could never control. I am an emotional person who shows emotion easily. People have never had a problem knowing my feelings—good or bad.

I got up at this point, started my coffee, and got the morning newspaper, content on making changes in my life to get control of my anger; **but I wasn't going to tell anyone...this was too embarrassing.** But I could not get over my dream. I felt God had really spoken to me; and so when my wife Helen got up, I could not resist sharing my dream with her. I have never been one to keep things from her, so I told her.

Here is where more information is needed. You see, two days earlier, after church on Sunday, while still in the parking lot, our family was trying to decide what to do for lunch. None of us were in agreement; and we all began to dig in our heels, but no one can dig in his heels as strongly or loudly as I can. I dug in my heels and shouted down all the competition my kids were giving me, and the car got quiet. I had done it again. I had made everyone in the family scared to speak. I won the shouting match, as usual. I felt bad, so I gave in and we went and got pizzas to take home and eat (what the children wanted) with me resenting it all the way. After we got home, I knew Helen was upset; and she retreated to our travel trailer to be alone.

After I told her my dream and the message God showed me, Helen shared something with me also—that her prayers have been answered too. She shared that when she went to the trailer on Sunday, she prayed for our family, but especially for me, that God would communicate how horrible my anger is. She prayed for me again on Monday for the same thing, for God to reveal to me how my anger affects those I love.

Once again, **God has surprised me**. He answered prayer in a way I did not expect, and he did not do it through my prayers alone, but with Helen and I praying for two different things. **God did answer both our prayers, using my dream as his catalyst. It was a revelation that could change me.** I wanted a dream of prophetic proportions, but God gave me something I needed more badly. I need to give my anger up for my family, friends, and most importantly, **for God**.

I believe it was Helen's prayer for God to speak to me that I was finally able to see the ending to this recurring dream. The message is clear. I must let God take control of my life and my anger. I must leave my anger at the cross for good.

If you are reading this paper and you have an anger problem as I do, I hope these Bible verses below will help you conquer your anger. I will be working on mine.

Proverbs 29: 11 [11] A fool gives **full vent to his anger**, but a wise man keeps himself under control. **(NIV)**

Proverbs 22: 24-25 [24]**Make no friendship with an angry man**; and with a furious man thou shalt not go:

[25]Lest thou learn his ways, and get a snare to thy soul.

James 1: 19–22 "My dear Brothers, take note of this: Everyone should be quick to listen, slow to speak, and **slow to become angry' for man's anger does not bring about righteous life that God desires.** Therefore, get rid of all moral filth and the evil that is so prevalent and humbly accept **the word planted in you, which can save you.** Do not merely listen to **the word**, and so deceive yourselves. **Do what it says.**" **(NIV)**

I highlighted **"word"** above because it is used to describe who Jesus is in scripture. The apostle John tells us Jesus is the Word and is God. **Let us listen to the Word.**

John 1: 1 [1]In the beginning was **the Word (Jesus)**, and **the Word was with God, and the Word was God.**

Scripture reveals that we should show the fruit of the Spirit as believers in Jesus Christ. With faith comes the fruit, and the fruit is:

Galatians 5: [22]But the fruit of the Spirit is **love, joy, peace, longsuffering, gentleness, goodness, faith,**

Peter writes that to our faith we should add virtue, knowledge, **temperance**, **patience**, godliness, **brotherly kindness**, and **charity**.

2 Peter 1: 5-7 [5]And beside this, giving all diligence, **add to your faith virtue; and to virtue knowledge;**

> [6]And **to knowledge temperance; and to temperance patience; and to patience godliness;**
>
> **[7]And to godliness brotherly kindness; and to brotherly kindness charity.**

God does not want us to live our lives in anger. What kind of example am I to my children if I get angry when things do not go my way?What kind of witness can I be to friends who see my anger?

To make this change that God asks me to do, I must rely on him. There is no good in my flesh to make the kind of change that is needed. It will take a changed heart, mind, and spirit, and that comes from God. I love to lean on God. I have heard people without faith say Christians are weak minded. I say it is being humble and being a child of God. It is what pleases our Maker.

> **Matthew 18: 3** [3]And he said: "I tell you the truth, **unless you change and become like little children, you will never enter** the kingdom of heaven. **(NIV)**

Anger is only one sin that we may struggle with. The world is full of many kinds of sin. What is the sin in your life that you struggle the most with?Give it to God and ask him to help you to be delivered from its temptation. God changes most persons slowly, a little bit at a time. It takes faith and reliance on him. As you trust God more and more with everything you have and do, the fruit of the Spirit that you read about in Galatians above will become more and more evident in your life. I pray that you will seek God in your life and enjoy the Fruit that it brings.

God loves you and so do I!

I'm afraid! I don't know his Son!

By: Ken & Helen Kreh

Chapter 23

The book of Proverbs was written between 1,000 and 700 B.C., mainly by King Solomon, but also by others. The scripture below is by Agur, son of Jakeh.

> **Proverbs 30: 3-5:** 3 I neither learned wisdom, nor have the **knowledge of the holy.**
>
> 4 Who hath ascended up into heaven, or descended? who hath gathered the wind in his fists? who hath bound the waters in a garment? who hath established all the ends of the earth? **what is his name, and what is his son's name, if thou canst tell?**
>
> **5 Every word of God is pure**: he is a shield unto them that put their trust in him.

Yesterday, we went to a funeral and memorial for a very dear friend, an elderly lady of 88 years young, when she passed on from this earth. God showed himself to my dear wife Helen and I in her passing, and we are both going to share what took place from our own perspective.

Ken's Perspective

It was the first time we went to a funeral where there was no minister, no one to mention the name of God at this time of passing of a sweet soul. The funeral director, who we know personally, afterwards spoke to us and stated he knew beforehand there would be no mentioning of God or scripture. You see, Gerry was an agnostic all of her life, as was her departed husband who passed away long before her, and her two children who loved their mother very much. **God, however, had other plans;** and he revealed to us how the Holy Spirit moves and works in us for his great plan. I will never forget this glorious day. Indeed, we serve a most loving Father and wondrous Son—**his name is Jesus!**

The Holy Spirit began working for Gerry's redemption many years earlier. After the death of her husband John, she moved to Traverse City. Unbeknown to Gerry, God had surrounded her with many Christian families. When our family moved in, it did not take long for everyone to become friends. Over the years, she became like a mother and grandmother to many in our subdivision and was dearly loved. Over the years, Helen would tell me there was a softening of Gerry's heart towards things of God, but by no means did she know who he was.

In the early 90's, she had a very serious car accident. This very active woman who never acted her age began to slow down. Eventually, her son John and daughter Nancy persuaded her to sell her home and move into a condo where there would be less upkeep. The girls of the sub would keep in touch with Gerry, and she would always say, "You girls are the highlight of my day."

Gerry continued to slow down as all do with age and sadly suffered a stroke in 2002 that severely affected her walking and speech for a time. We continued our close friendship with Gerry and would drop in on her to see how she was doing. **God, however, was never a subject of conversation.**

Our visits became less frequent with the busyness of life and children, but I know Gerry would be on Helen's mind quite often. Gerry's family would call once in a while and report how Gerry was doing.

In the fall of 2003, Helen received a call from Gerry's daughter-in-law Mary and she told her that Gerry was not doing well. This prompted Helen, her good friend Ruth, and our daughter Courtney to drop in and visit Gerry, who was now in a home for assisted living.

How close it was for their meeting to not have taken place. **But God had other plans.** When the girls arrived, Gerry was out with her daughter Nancy and her husband Tom. If it hadn't been for Ruth and Courtney needing to use the restroom, they would have missed each other. This delayed the girls long enough for Gerry to return home. Gerry came up to them using her walker. It took quite a long time, as it was work for her to walk now.

Gerry was now suffering with dementia, could not make full sentences, and often spoke in gibberish. A blank and non-understanding look was on her face. It was very sad for my wife to see Gerry deteriorating in this way.

As Nancy and Gerry approached, she noticed and became excited; and Helen made out her say, "You came," and looked at Courtney and said, "Pretty." Helen reached out to Gerry, hugged and greeted her. Gerry began trying to speak, but it was all gibberish coming from her lips. Helen was now closest to Gerry and Nancy: Ruth and Courtney were together speaking to one another.

Suddenly, Gerry looked at Helen and spoke clearly, **"I'm afraid."** Helen, confused and unsure of what she just heard, repeated back to her, "What? Gerry...You're afraid?" She responded and Helen heard these words from Gerry, **"I don't know his son.**" Helen was taken back and trying to comprehend what she spoke when again Gerry said, **"I don't know his son."** Before Helen could respond, Gerry grabbed herself, indicating the urgent need to go to the bathroom. The visit ended here, but Helen could not get over Gerry's words, **"I don't know his son."**

When Helen returned home and told me what occurred, and although she was uncertain now, at the time it seemed plain as day this is what she heard Gerry say, **"I'm afraid"** and **"I don't know his son."** I told Helen, "Even if those weren't the words Jerry spoke, **they were the words God wanted you to hear."** We both came to the same conclusion—we had to go back and **share the gospel with her.** We planned to go the very next day. Helen recruited Ruth to go with us. The three of us were determined to share the good news of Jesus Christ with Gerry.

With Bible in hand, we dropped in at the home and waited as Gerry was brought to us by her attendant because she was just finishing lunch in the dining room. Gerry was put in her chair, and Ruth, Helen, and I gathered in chairs around her. Gerry was confused, and I could tell she no longer recognized me. I was a complete stranger to her. I began by asking Gerry if I could read from the Bible to her. She replied, "Yes." It was amazing what took place the rest of the time, Gerry replied clearly. There was no gibberish.

I read from the **Psalms**; I read **John 3:16** to her. **I read verses in Genesis to explain God was her Creator.** I read verses from both the Old and New Testaments **that would show God's great love for her and how she could have eternal life.** After reading scripture, I asked Gerry, "Do you want to live forever with Jesus in Heaven?" She replied, "Yes." I asked her, "Would you like to pray the **sinner's prayer** for the forgiveness of your sins and **to ask Jesus into your heart."** Again, she replied, "Yes." So we all prayed with and for Gerry and led her to accept Jesus as her Lord and Savior. After we completed praying I told Gerry, **"You are going to live forever now. You will be in heaven with Jesus forever."** She was smiling and appeared so happy. I will admit I did not know if what we shared with her penetrated to her heart. But I did have enough faith at the time that I had thoughts God could penetrate that clouded mind. I left it in God's hands, hoping what occurred was real to Gerry, knowing only God knows for sure.

Over the months, I shared with other Christian friends this story, deep down wondering if it was too late for Gerry. Did she wait too long to get to know the Son? Could God get through the fog of her mind? Did we wait too long? **I had no assurance, only hope.**

A week ago, Helen was out: and I received word of Gerry's passing. Peggy, another Christian friend placed in Gerry's life, called with the news. I shared with her how we had led Gerry through the sinner's prayer last fall and how it gave me hope that she is in heaven. Peggy was so relieved and joyful to hear this. Peggy told me what the family planned for Gerry's memorial. There was to be an open microphone where one could share a story about Gerry and his or herself. Peggy and I both were determined to share something with the friends and family of Gerry about Jesus and I wanted in particular to share my last visit with Gerry at the microphone so that last moment I spent with her could be used for God's glory. I prayed for guidance from the Holy Spirit.

The day arrived. **What a blessed day!** In the morning, I played golf in a tournament scramble for the members and was placed on a team not of my choosing. On the second hole, while we were waiting, my partner Dick who I have known for years noticed the bracelet I had on and have been wearing for some time now. It has the letters **"G.O.L.F.,"** and he asked me what the letters stood for. I told him it stands for, **"God offers love and forgiveness."** We began talking about Jesus and how we both believe in him. What a thrill it is to me when you meet a fellow believer and he has the same hopes as you. At the end of playing golf, in the parking lot, I shared my story about Gerry with him. He was so excited that Gerry, an agnostic, gave her life to Jesus. He told me I had won one for God's kingdom. I was weak in faith at that moment and told him of her many ailments and how I wondered if God did penetrate her heart, or if it was it too late. As Christians, we want all persons to **know the Son**. Dick assured me God could speak to Gerry in her condition. I told him thanks and left for home.

It was now time to go the funeral home. Peggy, Ruth, Helen, and I went to the memorial together. I was nervous about sharing my last visit with Gerry because I felt there would be many agnostics there, and I was afraid I would offend some of them, but I wanted to share with them so they might search for Jesus. I did not want to come out like I was condemning Gerry or anyone, but I wanted to tell the truth about Jesus. I prayed for the Holy Spirit to guide me.

When we arrived, the funeral home was full of friends and family of Gerry's. It was an open casket, and Gerry looked peaceful. As the time neared for the proceedings to start, Peggy lost her nerve—there were too many people. Helen told me she would not be going up to the microphone. Now, I had a dilemma. I did not know how I was going to start my last experience with Gerry. **Only God knows how close it came for me losing my own nerve and not going up. But God had other plans.**

At the last moment, Helen leaned over to me and stated that she, Ruth, Peggy, and now Joanne were going to all go up together and say a word as a group. They were all part of the "Stitch and Bitch" club that met on Monday nights that Gerry fondly named. The girls in the subdivision would meet and take turns at each other homes; Gerry loved being part of this girls social club.

When they went up to the microphone, I was so energized and excited. I went up right behind them and sat in a seat off to the side and behind them to make sure I would be next at the microphone. I knew exactly what I wanted to say. I was excited to go up there, and I knew it was the Holy Spirit leading the way.

After the girls all spoke, I went up and spoke. To the best of my memory I stated:

"The reason I am up here is because of the girls who just spoke. God placed Christian friends all around Gerry; and because of this, I want to share my last visit with her with you. Last fall Helen, Ruth, and my daughter Courtney went to visit Gerry. When Gerry saw Helen, she said to her, **"I don't know his son."** The next day Ruth, Helen, and I went to her, and we shared from the Bible. We shared the gospel message with her that because of what Jesus did, we can all have everlasting life. In **1 Corinthians, chapter 15** Paul tell us we all can have hope for **eternal life because of the resurrection of Jesus.** I invite you all to read this chapter, 1 Corinthians chapter 15, and see the hope we all have in Jesus Christ. Because of this hope, I plan to see Gerry in heaven some day."

I was the last to speak and the memorial ended. We were all invited to dinner at the Park Place Hotel afterward. As we dismissed, several friends of Gerry's came up and thanked me for sharing. **The biggest blessing came at the dinner**.

We found a table to sit at and as I sat, a dear friend of Gerry's, Judy, whom I vaguely remembered meeting long ago, approached. I did not know what to expect, and I thought I might get an earful for what I just said at the open microphone.

Judy grabbed me gently by the arm and began saying, "Thank you for sharing with us. I am a Christian and have been Gerry's close friend for over 20 years. We met when Gerry's husband became ill and needed attendance. I was a nurse and I took care of Gerry's husband and we became good friends. Over the years, I tried to share with Gerry, but she would not accept Jesus. On my way up today (I am 4 hours away.) I was praying and seeking answers to where Gerry will spend eternity. **I was asking God for the answer.** In my spirit I heard his voice say, **"I will give you your answer today."** Judy finished by saying to me, **"You gave me my answer!"**

It gave me chills when she shared this with me. The Holy Spirit used me as a messenger to give Judy her answer. My answer to Judy was that Gerry would be in heaven. The Holy Spirit used Judy to give me my answer. **Yes, it was enough. Gerry did receive the message of eternity and did receive Jesus as Lord and Savior.** God is able to penetrate a cloudy mind and enter into a loved one's heart in that condition. It is never too late as long as one still has breath.

It also taught me how much God loves us, **how little he asks of us. God wants us to have faith in his Son, Jesus, and that He resurrected him from the grave. It is all God asks of us.** Here is a woman, all of her life an agnostic, not teaching her children in the way of the Lord, not living for God; and yet, late in life, she comes to God and receives **full forgiveness of her sins.** God loved Gerry very much! **He loves you very much!**

Come to God! **Read 1 Corinthians, chapter 15. Read John 3:16. See how much God loves you.** Ask Jesus into your life and ask for forgiveness. He will give it to you. Have faith.

I will never forget this day.

God loves you and so do I!

Helen's Perspective

The Power of Prayer

I was reminded today about the power of prayer and the way God uses each of us to carry out his plan. I'm in awe when he gives me a glimpse of the bigger picture and how some of the pieces fit together so beautifully that it can only be a "God thing." This happened today at the funeral of my friend, Gerry.

We were told of her passing in her sleep on April 17th of 2004, she was 88 years old. From the world's perspective (which included pretty much all of Gerry's family) she had led a good and full life. An after-life wasn't reflected upon except to say that if anyone deserved Heaven (if there was such a place) it would have been Gerry. However, from my Christian perspective I had to wonder where she was spending eternity. I wondered if the prayers of myself and the other Christian ladies that God had surrounded Gerry with had been answered. The prayers we offered up to God for her salvation. We could see a "softening" in Gerry over the years but the opportunity to lead her to Christ had not been there for us until September 2003…I had received a phone call from her daughter-in-law, Mary, letting me know that Gerry was in failing health. She was on oxygen all the time now and it didn't look good.

One afternoon, a Sunday, while out to eat with my friend Ruth and daughter Courtney we decided to drop in and visit Gerry. When we arrived, she wasn't there. She had been taken out for a drive on the peninsula with her daughter Nancy and son-in-law Tom. Well, another time then I thought to myself. Courtney and Ruth both needed to use the restroom so we were delayed in leaving. Just when we were walking out the door to leave- they pulled up to the sidewalk to bring Gerry back.

We approached their vehicle to say hello. Gerry lit up when she saw us and said, "You came!" She also looked at Courtney and said, "Pretty!" After that what she spoke had a lot of gibberish mixed in and it was hard to understand what she was trying to say. Her stroke two years earlier left her unable to speak for a while and then eventually some understandable words here and there. Nancy explained it was worse when she was really tired and that they had her out for hours. We accompanied Gerry, with her walker, back to her building.

When we got inside the door, Ruth, Courtney, and Nancy were in a conversation and I was standing next to Gerry. She looked at me and said, "I'm afraid!" I repeated back to her, "What? Gerry, you're afraid?" and she responded, "I don't know his son." I was questioning what I just had heard her say, I was confused by her statement. But, again I heard her say, "I don't know his son." I heard it plain as day.

The impact of her statement didn't even have time to sink in when she suddenly grabbed herself, indicating the urgent need to get to the bathroom. He was ushered away before I could respond. We said our good-byes to Tom and Nancy and we left.

Later, at home, as I was reflecting on this, I shared it with my husband Ken. It was undeniable we had to return and talk to Gerry about Jesus. I called Ruth and we planned to go there the next day.

It was a nice visit; Gerry was alert and sitting in her chair. We prayed with her and Ken read the Bible to her and led her in the Sinner's Prayer. When he asked her if she wanted to accept Jesus and live with him in Heaven she said yes (clear as a bell). Still, we left there wondering in the state she was in, did she really understand?Was this a true acceptance and conversion?How were we to know until we get to Heaven?I always felt that God had placed Gerry in my life for a reason and I had begun to feel guilty that I let him down in that area. I knew I hadn't done enough to win her to the Kingdom.

Gerry's funeral was different than most. There weren't any hymns, no preacher speaking of God or Heaven. Rather it was family and friends sharing fun or touching stories about her life. We knew there would be an opportunity to speak and Ken was prepared to share about our last visit with Gerry and her praying the Sinners Prayer. What I didn't know was that he was losing his nerve to get up in front of all those people and share it with them. My friend Peggy was planning to go up as well and share but felt she no longer could. To give her support, Ruth told her she and I would go as well. We included our friend Joann in this. So, as a group (formerly known as the Monday night "Stitch and Bitch" club- so named by Gerry) we all went up and Ken regained his courage to walk forward with us, taking a seat behind us at the front to wait his turn.

We all spoke of our friendship with Gerry and our get togethers. We then sat down. When we got back to our seats, Peg said, Oh no, we abandoned Ken!" He was fine.

He told the group about our last visit and Gerry's prayer and he invited everyone to checkout 1 Corinthians 15, then he sat down as well. He was the last one to speak and we were invited to join the family for dinner at the Park Place Hotel in Traverse City. On the way to the funeral home, we decided we would leave promptly after and not attend the dinner, but we did. Some how, we found ourselves headed to the Park Place.

Several people approached Ken, thanking him for sharing. We discovered Gerry had more Christians in her life than we realized and some had indicated they didn't really speak to her about spiritual things. Her friend Judy was the exception.

She came over and shared with us of how she witnessed to Gerry over the 20 years she had known her and in fact, on her 4 hour drive up to Traverse City she had been praying to God to reveal to her where Gerry was spending eternity and the Holy Spirit told her she would have an answer today! She wasn't sure how this was going to happen but when she heard Ken speak, she knew. She had received her answer and when she shared this with us we in turn received ours. Praise God. We can rejoice that God did answer our prayers and Gerry did accept the free gift of salvation.

I was blessed today with a beautiful lesson from God. He has a plan for each of us and he will work out the details of the plan. No "one" person needs to think they have to do it all- He has many workers in the field and together there is a beautiful harvest! I will no longer consider my role in someone's life without meaning or purpose. It's one link in a chain, alone it doesn't amount to much but added to others it's strong and makes a difference.

Summary:

The gospel of Luke puts it in words that expresses what Helen and I wanted to share...we are rejoicing that our friend Gerry will be in Heaven. **How about you!**

> **Luke 15: 6-7 "Rejoice with me; I have found my lost sheep.'** [7]I tell you that in the same way there will be **more rejoicing in heaven over one sinner who repents** than over ninety-nine righteous persons who do not need to repent." **(NIV)**

God loves you and so do I!

Evidence For Creation- Week One

Chapter 24

I lead a **two-week** class on evidence for creation and taught this subject in Sunday school. May this scientific and Biblical evidence give you faith that the Bible is unique from all other books ever written. The Bible is full of knowledge and wisdom. This is only the tip of the iceberg of all the information that is available for you to study creation as God has revealed it to us in scripture. The Bible is never in conflict with good science, and good science is never in conflict with the Bible.

Scientific Evidence for Creation—Week One
Bible Verses:

> **Genesis 1:1** [1]In the beginning **God created the heaven and the earth.**
>
> **Genesis 1: 12-13** [12]And the earth brought forth grass, and herb yielding seed **after his kind**, and the tree yielding fruit, whose seed was in itself, **after his kind**: and God saw that **it was good.**
>
> [13]And the evening and the morning were the third **day.**

The Hebrew word for **"day"** used above is **"Yom."** In almost all instances in the Bible, its meaning is a **literal 24-hour day**. In chapter one of Genesis, using "evening" and "morning" as it does, it can be taken literally God was referring to a real 24-hour day. This is what God was trying to communicate with us. **God knows Hebrew very well.**

1) Welcome

1) I am not claiming to be an expert or a scientist. I do claim I spent a full year studying Genesis and creation exclusively and have continued to study creation over the past four years.
2) I take **Genesis literally**. Creation, to me, took place in literal 24-hour day periods over a one-week time as **Genesis 1 and 2** describes. I follow Bible-believing scientists and teachers who have given me the evidence that **we can take the first 11 chapters of Genesis literally.**
3) Ken Ham, the founder of **'Answers In Genesis',** states, "If you can believe in the first 11 chapters of Genesis literally, you will have no problem believing the rest of the entire Bible." I found this to be true in my own life and experience.
   Web site: **AnswersInGenesis.org**

2) Purpose of this Class

1) To present that there are two models for the origin of the universe and life, the **Creation Model** and the **Evolutionary Model**.
2) To present evidence that the Evolution Model is a **belief system** and is **not science**—it as much a belief system as the Creation Model, which is accused of not being scientific.
3) To present evidence that the **Creation Model** of the Bible uses better science looking at the evidence for the origins of the universe and life than the Evolutionary Model.
4) To **arm you with the truth**. There is **no reason** to believe that evolution ever occurred. It is a fact that scientists **cannot prove** evolution ever happened. It is an attempt to take God

out of the beginning of the universe and have all things in it form by natural causes.

5) That you can trust the Bible to be the absolute truth and God's revelation to man. From the first verse in **Genesis**, "In the beginning **God created** the heaven and the earth," to the last verse in **Revelation.**
6) To give you **sources** to go that are the **science experts**; sources where the evidence for creation is given in what we observe in the universe, nature, and life. There are scientists and teachers, who look at the evidence through the creation model and believe it—and trust the word of God over what man proclaim, yet understand the evolutionary model.

3) My Personal Testimony

1) I became a born again Christian in Feb. 1977 at the age of twenty-three. It was a 2-year process, and it took my father's illness and death of cancer to accept Jesus as my Lord and Savior.
2) As the years went on, I stayed in my faith; but I remained a babe in Christ for a long time. I did not actively try to grow my faith, satisfied that getting to heaven was enough.
3) Over the years I had two major barriers (I did not want to acknowledge them.) to my continued growth in faith—1) I was a heavy smoker, so I did not always want fellowship with other Christians because I was convicted it was wrong **for me** to smoke, and 2) I was in love with golf—it was my god that consumed my thoughts almost always, much more than my thoughts of God.

"My Miracle"

1) November 1, 1997, twenty years after coming to Christ- God freed me from my two pack-a-day smoking habit. I had no intention of quitting. I lied to my children and my wife (my wife for probably over the one hundredth time) that I would quit. I promised my wife and children this would be my last

night of smoking—this was a Friday night. Come Monday however, I had every attention of going to the gas station to buy a carton of cigarettes and coffee and smoke my brains out. I would smoke in hiding until my wife caught me again as she always did, and then I would smoke freely in front of the family as I always had. **God had other plans for me.** On Monday morning, I woke up, and the physical need for smoking was completely gone; and I knew this was from God.

2) I quit smoking because **God freed me without my asking**. I loved smoking and yet, in a moment, I did not need cigarettes anymore. What is interesting afterward, at my wife's request, I took a complete physical. The doctor examined and tested my lungs. After the results came back, he stated my lungs were exactly where they should be for a man my age. I asked him how this could be because of my heavy smoking habit. He said I was very lucky. **At that moment** I claimed a healing by the Lord for my lungs. Not only did God free me of smoking, but he healed me also on the inside, as if I never had even smoked. **I cannot prove it, but I have faith.**

God Begins the Growing in Me!

1) Changes in me began, slowly at first.
2) I discovered contemporary Christian music. It became my favorite music to listen to.
3) Church and fellowship with other believers became important to me.
4) Golf became less and less important; it no longer consumes my thoughts.
5) Our family began camping. I rediscovered the enjoyment of reading while camping, when I started reading the 'Left Behind' series on one of our trips.
6) Even though I was not very good at it, I begin to share my faith with some of my friends. I truly want others to know the love God has for everyone.

Ken Ham of Answers in Genesis Comes to Traverse City

1) For the first time ever, I am given facts about evolution no secular sources are giving us. I am given truth that there is **no need** to compromise the teachings of the Bible in the creation story of Genesis or mix into Genesis, evolutionary ideas. I bought $260.00 worth of books and tapes on **creation** and subscribed to **Creation Magazine, a fantastic source for scientific evidence for creation.** Scientists in every field of science, including studying fossils and the fossil record, write articles in this magazine; and the colored pictures showing God's great creation are beautiful.
2) My faith explodes with the **absolute truth** of the Bible. That night, I put on the **full armor of God's** truth and know that he is the authority and author of creation, **not man**. I became hungry to study Genesis, and God had me spend one solid year in Genesis and nothing else.
3) God in my spirit led me in my studies. When I was armed enough with his truth, God moved me to new studies. I also knew God armed me this way not to debate or to war with others over whether he used evolution to create life. He wanted me to trust him. God taught me that **no man, including the scientist**, is equal to God' wisdom. God is greater than anything man can come up with, and as it says in **Job 38: 4 [4]Where wast thou when I laid the foundations of the earth?** declare, **if thou hast understanding.**
4) The most important reason God had me studying Genesis was so I could arm my two children with the absolute truth of the Bible. I do not want biased teachers in public schools, filling my children with **only** evolutionary ideas that could affect their faith. Also, I know today that many, many people loose their faith because they believe their teachers that Darwin has proven the Bible is fallible. The example below can happen to children in our society today.

Quoting from a newsletter I receive from Coral Ridge Ministries and Dr. D. James Kennedy:

"Tom DeRosa, founder and president of the Creation Studies Institute and author of *Evidence for Creation: Intelligent Answers for Open Minds*, was one such person. Raised Catholic, in high school he spent it in Catholic seminary, he was voted as Best Seminarian. In 1964, instead of taking vows to enter the priesthood, **he became an atheist**. His encounter with Darwin in **college** led to that decision. It lasted 13 years and by that time was an established public school **science teacher.** DeRosa **is not alone** in having had his faith derailed by Darwin. Many believe science has proven God had nothing to do with how life came into existence. The Big Bang, random chance, life evolving from a simple cell, over billions of years formed the universe and all that is in it-they believe there is no need for a Creator God."

"By the grace of God he encountered Christ after he learned that grace was a free gift of God. Not just his theology but also his science underwent a complete change. He saw the lies and misinformation that evolution teaches." **(Story taken from Coral Ridge Ministries-August 2003).**

4) How I look at Origin of Life Now

1) I look at science through the **Creation Model,** not the Evolutionary Model. The two models **are always** in conflict, and you must choose **(yes choose)** which model you are going to trust. We should not compromise the word of God, and there is no reason to ever need to, once you understand where each models starting point is.
2) Programs concerning Dinosaurs and ape-to-man shows, such as on the Discovery Channel and PBS-TV no longer are enjoyable for me because I see the fallacy that these programs propagate. I do not panic when the newspaper reports they found the latest missing link from ape to man.
3) Even watching golf on TV, I found reason to challenge the evolutionary ideas they proclaimed. While I was watching golf on the television, during the Australian Open telecast, the announcers spoke of The Great Coral Reef as being

millions of years old. And at the Hawaiian Open later that year, the announcers spoke how it took millions of years to form the islands through volcanic activity. I did not have the answers then, but I knew where to go for answers. I went to **www.AnswersinGenesis.org** to see what creation scientists had to say on these subjects. In regards to the age of islands, I searched the words "Hawaiian Islands," and I found my answer in the **"Island of Surtsey."**

The Lesson of Surtsey by Edgar Andrews, as he wrote in Creation Magazine, we learn, ".... We may refer to the volcanic island of Surtsey, off Iceland, which was **produced** during an eruption covering the period **November 1963 to June 1967. Within a period of months** this sterile, virgin rock was transformed into a **'mature'** island with beaches, pebbles, sand, vegetation and many other features which would superficially suggest **great geological age**." There are many secular websites you can go to and visit this island with pictures, history, and scientific information about the island—it is large compared to other islands in the area. What evolution teaches takes millions of years to form; **Surtsey came into existence in less than four years.**

4) PBS-TV in September of 2001 aired a 7-part episode on evolution, in an attempt to convince the public that evolution is positively true and is science. I watched the entire series and I thank God for Answers in Genesis. For each episode, Jonathan Sarfati, Ph.D. responded to what the series was trying to state as fact but was in actuality misleading and misrepresenting evidence. By using the creation model, the evidence would come out totally different. Both models use assumptions that cannot be proven to make their case—you must choose which model makes more sense.

Now I understand that **the results to the evidence depend on whose eyeglasses you are wearing and looking through.** You can look though the **eyeglasses of long age** and random chance, or you can look through the **eyeglass that start with the Bible** and has faith in a Creator God. **I choose God and his word—the Bible.**

5) The Two Sets of Glasses Scientists Use For the Origin of Life

Which set of glasses you put on to look at the evidence will determine the conclusions you decide to be true. Both type of scientists have the same evidence to study; only their conclusions differ.

1) The Evolutionary Model

1) Glasses of long age: Evolution's **starting point is time and lots of it.**
2) Natural causes by random chance for the universe to form (the Big Bang). It is the origin of life **without** a designer (**God**).
3) Billions of years for it to take place. (Reason: evolutionists as well as creationists know that for **macroevolution** to ever have happened, it would take **eons of years** to occur, or it could never have happened.)
4) With enough time, anything is possible **without a Creator** God.
5) Evolution is a **belief in a miracle without a miracle maker**—the miracle of life happening without God, a miracle of life by random chance only.
6) Evolution is not science; it is a **Belief System, same as creation model.**

2) The Creation Model

1) Unlike the evolutionary model, which starts with lots of time, the **creation model starts with the word of God—the Bible.**
2) **Observes the exact same evidence for origins of life** as evolution model does, but because its starting point is the Bible, this model comes up with totally different answers.

3) Model starts with creation as God states in Genesis and teaches a great flood occurred (**Noah's Flood**) that altered the world we live in and where most of the fossil record comes from.
4) The creation model believes **in a miracle with a miracle maker**, the God of the Bible.
5) Creation is not science; it is a **Belief System, same as evolution model.**

Definition of Science

The definition for "scientific method" is: through **observation**, **experimentation**, and **testing** and following principled guidelines, you can collect data for the pursuit of knowledge.

Ken Ham explains since the origin of the Universe **happened in the past** and **no one was there to observe** how it happened, it requires **faith to believe in how life and the universe began.** Nor can we in a lab produce an **experiment** that will replicate the start of it all. It was a **one-time event in history**. **It was not observable.** Therefore, evolution is as much of a belief system as creation is. Neither can be scientifically proven—they both **require faith.**

Definition of Evolution: Two Kinds

1) Microevolution

Allows for changes **within a species** through copying changes in the DNA. These changes occur within a species when there is **a loss of information, not a gain in information**. Microevolution **is not** molecules to man. Microevolution is an **observable fact** in nature.

Problem for Evolution: Never has it been observed in science or nature a mutation that was caused **by a gain of information** in the DNA. That is why a dog remains a dog, a cat a cat, a butterfly a butterfly. The changes **add no new information and are not changes that improve the species... changes at the molecular level are bad usually.**

The creation model also allows for the changes we see at this level. It has no problems with **changes within the species** because of the **Second Law of Thermodynamics** (I will explain later) is being observed here and **is totally compatible with creation model.** The variety we see in species comes from changes in the DNA, but that does not add new information—the information was already there in the parents and was passed on through the genes to the offspring.

2) Macroevolution

This is the **theory** of molecules to man**.** The theory allows for changes in the DNA where more and new information is passed on to the cell than its original parent cell. The changes cause an **upward movement** of information in the DNA, so you can jump from one species to a new species.

Problem for Evolution: Never has Macroevolution been observed in nature or in a scientific lab. It is **unobservable**. No experiment can be designed to enable us to observe macroevolution. Therefore, it **requires faith** to believe in macroevolution; it is **not** science. Macroevolution requires **faith** in **time—lots of time**, millions upon millions of years. The evolutionary model **cannot** work without eons of time. That will always be the evolutionist's argument. They will say it takes **10's of thousands or even millions of years** for a change in the DNA to occur, so of course you cannot observe it. They accuse the creation model of bad science. This is **blind faith**. Evolution must believe in something you cannot prove.

The creation model **does not** allow for this change from one species to a new species or molecules to man—macroevolution. Creation is not in conflict with what is observable in nature—species reproducing after its own kind..

6) Law of Uniformitarianism (Used in Evolutionary Model Only)—Not a Law But a Theory

This law (only a theory) states that all processes in the universe are occurring at relatively the same rates as we observe in the present. It teaches there has never been any large difference in the rate or character processes possible today. The present is the key to yesterday. **This theory is not provable** and **does not allow for a worldwide catastrophe** that could make huge changes in the past. It does not allow for a worldwide flood—**Noah's Flood,** as recorded in the book of **Genesis, chapters 6-9.**

Keep this theory of Uniformitarianism in mind when looking at the next sets of evidence.

7) Evidence Both Models Can Observe

1) Fossil Record

The evolutionary model observes fossils as dead things, in the **present**, and believes that over a long period of time they became buried in sediment. **With a little bit of water** and **lots of time**, the animals were buried; they absorbed minerals from the sediment and became rock.

The creation model also observes fossils as dead things, in the **present**, but believes they were buried quickly in sediment (before predators and natural decomposition had a chance to eliminate their carcass) by **lots of water over a little bit of time**. In **Genesis chapters 6-9**, you can read about where all the water came from.

The evolutionary model suggests the layers of fossils found in the fossil record is proof that macroevolution occurred. Their theory would have us **believe in billions of years. They believe** in macroevolution, therefore, life forms began simple and over time, kept evolving into more complex forms. It is **their belief** in why the more complex forms of life are buried in rock layers above the simpler life forms, as in a hierarchy. This is their conclusion at looking at the fossil record.

Problem for Evolution: this is **not provable because fossils are buried in the present** and no human was there to observe their burial.

Creation Model sees the same Fossil record, **but comes up with a totally different conclusion.** Creation model has a great flood **(Noah's Flood)** that buried billions of dead things all over the earth rapidly. Nothing escaped this great flood. This model **believes** the simplest forms of life, **which are the least mobile** and would not had been to escape the flood, would be buried first while the more mobile creatures could escape, until they too succumbed to the flood, and were buried in water and sediment as the flood waters engulfed them. Just as what you would expect from a **world wide catastrophic flood**, we can observe least mobile to more mobile creatures buried in rock layers all over the world. This fits well with Genesis chapters 6-9.

Is There Any Proof That Fossils Could Have Formed rapidly in a Catastrophic Event?

In Museums around the globe, there is evidence for quick burial. In the Creation Magazine, volumes 23 No.1 from December 200-February 2001 edition are such examples. On page 11 of that issue, is a fossil of an animal giving birth at the exact time she and her offspring are fossilized together. You can see all but the tip of the offspring's head coming out of the birth canal. On that same page, is a fish making lunch of another fish. Half of the smaller fish is in the larger fishes mouth when they too became fossilized together. Both examples show how quickly being buried in sediment can occur. Neither animal had time to finish what they were doing and get out of the way so they would not be buried.

Questions to ask Yourself (Remember the Law of Uniformitarianism evolution uses when asking.)

1) What happens to creatures today when they die and lay on the ground for any length of **time**? What is left of them in a week? Month? Year?This past summer, I observed a dead squirrel in my yard and I purposely left it to see what would happen. In a very short time, all that was left was the hide and its fur.
2) What happens to the **largest** animal in the world today (the whale) when it dies in the ocean? Why, if evolution is true, within 2 to 3 years, there is nothing left of the dead whale, **including its bones?**
3) Why are not fossils still being formed today?

Let us examine the fossil record scientists make such a big deal about. **The Fossil Record we observe today** *from the book, "The Young Earth," by John D. Morris*

1) **95%** of all fossils are marine invertebrates-particularly shellfish.
2) Of the remaining **5%**, Algae and plant fossils make up **4.75% of the 5%.**
3) **95%** of the remaining **.25%** are other invertebrates, including insects **(0.235%)**
4) The remaining **.0125% includes all vertebrates- mostly fish. 95%** of the few land vertebrates consist of less than one bone. **95% of mammal fossils were deposited during the Ice Age.** (Note: The Creation Model allows for an Ice Age, which would have happened shortly after Noah's Flood.)

Both models are looking at the same set of evidence for fossils, but **come up with totally different conclusions.**

8) Methods for Dating Fossils *taken from the book "The Young Earth"*

All Dating Methods use **assumptions not possible** to prove or observe (not scientific). So before they can date fossils, they are making assumptions without any scientific proof.

1) The Kinds of Rocks the Fossil is found in, Dates the Age

Evolutionary scientists use the rock the fossil is found in to date its age. The Rock is dated by the **Index fossil** that is found in the rock. Evolution dates the fossil by using the **Geologic Time Scale.** In other words, the fossil dates the rock and the rock dates the fossil.

Assumption used: The earth is very old. Where is the proof?

2) Carbon 14 dating

Don't be fooled. This dating method cannot be used on rock or even fossils, since they too are rock. Carbon 14 dating can only be used on organic material.

3) Radioactive Isotopes Dating

Without going into detail, there are three assumptions that this dating method cannot scientifically prove.

1) Constant decay rate.
2) No loss or gain of parent or daughter.
3) Known amounts of daughter present at start. This method cannot date fossils because sedimentary rock, where fossils are found, cannot accurately be dated by this method.

9) Law of Uniformitarianism: Problems Evolutionary Model faces because of this Law

The Evolutionary Model relies on this law (**theory**) to support its theory. Without it, it just will not work because evolution holds that the key to yesterday is what is observable in the present. We cannot observe **Macroevolution** in the present—thus, evolution requires vast amounts of time at a constant rate of change for its model to hold up to scrutiny. The **Creation Model** does not need this **theory**.

Without going into detail, the following problems below are not answerable using the Evolutionary model, but these problems do **have answers** using the Creation model. *Taken from "The Young Earth."*

1) The decay and reversal of earth's magnetic field

The largest problem for the evolutionary model is that the magnetic field in the past, based on today's rate of decay, would be far too strong. It would mean in the past, our magnetic field was much stronger—to the point that life on earth would have been **impossible only some 20,000 years ago** because of the amount of heat produced by the strength of the magnetic field. **100,000 years ago**, using this law of Uniformitarianism, the magnetic field would be so strong; earth would be compared to a **Neutron Star.**

The creation model: has no problem with the magnetic field since we have a great flood in our history that would have totally affected the magnetic field of the earth. The earth's magnetic field being less than 20,000 years is what Genesis teaches, when Genesis is taken literally.

2) The Amount of Helium in our Atmosphere

Helium is produced beneath the earth's surface by radioactive decay. We can measure the amount of Helium in our atmosphere, and project the age of the earth's atmosphere using this Law. Problem for Evolutionary model is, using this law, the earth's atmosphere can be no older than 2 million years old, **way less than the evolutionary model requires.**

The creation model: no problem. Noah's Flood would have had a huge effect on helium in our atmosphere. The earth's age can be much younger than projected by the Law of Uniformitarianism because of Noah's Flood. It would have caused more helium to escape into our atmosphere, at a much faster rate, than the evolutionary model.

3) Salt in the Oceans

To put it simply, the problem for evolutionary model is the oceans **are not** salty enough. Our oceans, using the law, can be no older than 32 million years. Again, there is not enough time for evolution to happen in.

The creation model: no problem. Noah's Flood would cause huge effects on the saltiness of our oceans. Much more salt in our oceans, at a faster rate, due to Noah's Flood.

4) Rocks on the Earth Surface and (5) Erosion of earth's Continents

We can measure erosion of the continents at its present rate. To put it simply, **all continents** would be at sea level in 4 million years. Evolutionists believe they are already many times that old already. At current rate of erosion, **we should have no sedimentary rock left on this earth**, yet we do all over the earth.

The creation model: no problem. Noah's flood would have had huge effect on earth's continents and sedimentary rock would be very young.

6) Sediment in Oceans

27.5 billion tons per year go into our oceans, 410 million billion tons are on the ocean bottom. Problem for evolutionary model, **using the law**, it would make our oceans no more than 15 million years old. If the oceans are as old as evolutionists believe, we should be able to walk the entire earth because the oceans **ought to be completely full of sediment.**

The creation model: no problem. Creation Model does not need eons of time. The earth is young, created by God in human time according to the Bible approx. 6,000 or so years ago (This is my belief, I have no problem with creation as God gave it to man in his word—the Bible.) **There is much evidence for a young earth we can observe today.**

7) Geological evidence for a Young Earth

1) Surface features
2) Deficiency of bioturbation
3) Lack of Soil Layers
4) Undisturbed Bedding Planes
5) **Polystrate Fossils**
6) Soft-sediment deformation
7) Limited extent of unconformities

You can research all of these sets of evidence above for yourself, but I will go over Polystrate Fossils to give you one example how the creation model fits well with the evidence for a young earth. All above information is *taken from "The Young Earth."* This book deals with all subject matter above in great detail and is a great read.

Polystrate fossils are fossils that go through **many layers of rock**. There are fossilized trees throughout the world that stand tall and are spanning many layers of rock. This happened when a tree was in water and became water log and stood straight up and down, bobbing from the floor of the ocean to above—like a yo-yo. Since sediment accumulates at about one millimeter every 1,000 years, it would have taken millions of years to have deep burial of the tree trunk.

Question: How long would it take for that dead tree trunk to rot and fall over? Could it remain upright for millions or even hundreds of years—while the mud slowly accumulated around it?**Obviously not**. We can conclude that the length of time for accumulation of sediment was less than the time it takes for wood to decay—trees will decay in only a few decades at most.

Because of the volcanic eruption of Mount. St. Helens in 1980, we **were able to observe** how **polystrate fossils could be formed quickly**. Trees were buried quickly in sediment when Spirit Lake was filled with forests of trees, that became water logged and stood up, and then were buried by sediment from the eruption.

Other things scientist were able to observe from Mt. St Helen's eruption are:

1) Geological structures being formed quickly- **strata (rock layers), canyons, and log deposits, etc.**
2) How catastrophic events can cause things to happen **quickly.** Scientists were able to observe rock strata being formed in hours that they state takes millions of years. And a miniature **Grand Canyon, about a ¼ of a mile long,** was formed in **one day** by the eruption.

During Noah's Flood, it was much more than rain coming down. The **fountains** of the oceans were exploding, and volcanoes, earthquakes, tsunamis, tornados, and hurricanes would have been breaking out everywhere, upon the entire earth. It was the **most catastrophic event** in the history of the world. So much so, God promised he would never send such a judgment again, and he gave us the rainbow as his sign. Before the flood, there never was a rainbow.

> **Genesis 7: 11–12** [11]In the six hundredth year of Noah's life, in the second month, the seventeenth day of the month, the same day **were all the fountains of the great deep broken up**, and the windows of heaven were opened.

> [12]And the **rain was upon the earth forty days** and forty nights.

According to Scripture, not only did rainfall, but also **the fountains in the oceans burst open** causing a worldwide flood that covered all of the land, including the mountains. The fountains bursting are describing **earthquakes** in the ocean, and these earthquakes would have caused **tsunamis**. We all saw the devastation the Indian Ocean Earthquake caused at the end of 2004. Think of what would have occurred during Noah's flood, when maybe hundreds or more occurred in a short time. Also, **hurricanes** would be happening during Noah's flood, the worse the world would ever know. Think of the destruction. Think of Hurricane Katrina of 2005 happening all over the world at the same time. This was what was occurring during the catastrophic event called Noah's Flood.

> **Genesis 7: 21-24** [21]And **all flesh died that moved upon the earth**, both of fowl, and of cattle, and of beast, and of every creeping thing that creepeth upon the earth, and every man:
>
> [22]All in whose nostrils was the breath of life, of **all that was in the dry land, died.**
>
> [23]And every living substance was destroyed which was upon the face of the ground, both man, and cattle, and the creeping things, and the fowl of the heaven; and they were destroyed from the earth: and **Noah only remained alive, and they that were with him in the ark.**
>
> [24]And the waters prevailed upon the earth an hundred and fifty days.

According to Scripture, all life that needed dry land and air to breath perished during the flood, except those who were in the ark with Noah. It is funny, scientists believe that Mars, which has no liquid water left on it once was completely covered by water, yet, they cannot believe in a worldwide flood on earth, which is largely covered by water.

Scientific Moment: Do you know the bible teaches from the very beginning that he placed water in outer space?**It is true!** He divided the water in space from the water of earth's atmosphere on the second day.

> **Genesis 1: 6-8** [6]And God said, Let there be a **firmament (expanse of the heavens)** in the midst of the waters, and **let it divide the waters from the waters.**
>
> [7]And **God made the firmament**, and **divided the waters which were under the firmament from the waters which were above the firmament**: and it was so.
>
> [8]And **God called the firmament Heaven.** And the evening and the morning were **the second day**.

Do you see what verses 7 and 8 are telling us scientifically?The firmament is the dividing line of earth's atmosphere with Outer Space, or expanse of the heavens. Verse 7 declares outer space had and does have **water in it.** Today we have comets, which are nothing more than dirty large snowballs, traveling in outer space at tremendous speed. On the second day of creation, God took the water that was below the firmament and divided it from the water **that was above the firmament. What did God call the firmament?** Heaven! This is more than just our earth's atmosphere where our clouds are. **God was right all along.** The bible taught from the beginning there is water in outer space, and there still is evidence for it—every time you see another dirty snowball go by in outer space.

Unlike scientists who do not believe in a catastrophic worldwide flood, I believe that Noah's flood is real and that there is a record for it—**the Fossil Record.**

> **Genesis 9: 11-13** [11] I establish my covenant with you: **Never again will all life be cut off by the waters of a**

> **flood; never again will there be a flood to destroy the earth."** [12] And God said, "This is the sign of the covenant I am making between me and you and every living creature with you, a covenant for all generations to come: [13] **I have set my rainbow in the clouds, and it will be the sign of the covenant between me and the earth.** (NIV)

According to Scripture, God promised he would never again send such a flood. We have had many, many floods all over the world and do so today. Local floods are a fact. Therefore, Noah's Flood, had to be more than a local flood or **God is a liar,** and we have already learned it is impossible for God to lie.

> **Hebrews 6: 18** [18]That by two immutable things, in which **it was impossible for God to lie**

If you are a Christian reading this book, you must know God's word is **absolute truth!** We can trust his word from the first verse in Genesis to the end verse in Revelation. If it is not so, then how can we trust that the gospel message of Jesus Christ is true?How can we trust that any of the Bible is true?How can we trust that our salvation is secure if there are any inaccuracies in the Bible? How can we trust when the apostle John wrote that Jesus is our Creator?

> **John 1: 1-3** [1]In the beginning was the Word, and **the Word was with God**, and **the Word was God**. [2]The same was in the beginning with God.
>
> [3]**All things were made by him; and without him was not any thing made that was made.**

I no longer take what the evolutionary scientists tell us and try to fit it with what the Bible says. Instead, I take what the Bible says first, and then see what Bible believing scientists, who take the teachings of Genesis literally, and then look at the evidence. In doing so, science fits very nicely with what I observe today; such as species reproducing species after its own kind—just as what the book of Genesis said about 6,000 years or so ago.

> **Genesis 1: 11-12** [11]And God said, Let the earth bring forth grass, the herb yielding seed, and the fruit tree yielding fruit **after his kind**, whose seed is in itself, upon the earth: **and it was so.**
>
> [12]And the earth brought forth grass, and herb yielding seed **after his kind**, and the tree yielding fruit, whose seed was in itself, **after his kind**: and **God saw that it was good.**
>
> **Genesis 1: 20-21** [20]And God said, Let the waters bring forth abundantly the moving creature that hath life, and fowl that may fly above the earth in the open firmament of heaven.
>
> [21]And God created great whales, and every living creature that moveth, which the waters brought forth abundantly, **after their kind,** and every winged fowl **after his kind**: and **God saw that it was good.**
>
> **Genesis 1: 24-25** [24]And God said, Let the earth bring forth the living creature **after his kind**, cattle, and creeping thing, and beast of the earth **after his kind**: and it was so.
>
> [25]And God made the beast of the earth **after his kind**, and cattle **after their kind**, and every thing that creepeth upon the earth **after his kind**: and **God saw that it was good.**

Everything I have shown in this chapter points to the fact that the bible is true. There are many scientific claims in the Bible that are compatible with what we observe in science and nature. The Bible has no conflict with good science that is observable. All species we observe in nature produce after their own kind. There is great evidence for it. Even dinosaurs produced after their own kind and God spoke of these magnificent animals in the Book of Job, chapters

40 and 41. Reread my chapter 14 on dinosaurs, and know that man did observe them in the past, as recorded in scripture, and recorded in ancient cave paintings and stone carvings. I have seen these art treasures on Answers in Genesis videos, and they date back thousands of years. With desire, an open mind, and a little bit of work, you can do as I have, and see what secular scientists do not want you to know.

The next chapter is more evidence for creation as recorded in the Bible. The evidence in the molecular science field is pointing towards creation and not evolution. Keep your mind open to God's possibilities.

God loves you and so do I!

Scientific Evidence for Creation- Week Two

Chapter 25

Bible Verses:

Genesis 1: 26 [26]And God said, **Let us make man in our image**, after **our likeness**: **(God is speaking here of the Trinity. The Hebrew word for God used here is "Elohim." It is the plural form of "El" which is a singular word for God. This allows for the Trinity. God was never lonely.)**

Isaiah 2: 22 [22] **Stop trusting in man**, who has but a breath in his nostrils. **Of what account is he? (NIV) (God is asking you this question! Start trusting God for answers!)**

Hebrews 11: 3 [3]**By faith** we understand **that the universe was formed at God's command,** so that what is seen was not made out of what was visible. **(NIV) (Do you have this kind of faith?Or is your faith in what man says?)**

In week one we touched on scientific evidence that disputes evolution and was taken from materials I purchased from Ken Ham the night I heard him speak in Traverse City. Week one only touched on what is available to you at Answers in Genesis Ministries. If you have a hearts desire for creation as I do, I know you will thoroughly enjoy all it has to offer.

Today, I am entirely going with notes I took from a tape series called, "*The Origin of life: Equipping Course*" by Dr. Bob Compton & Mike Riddle, Masters Degree in Education. This tape is worth reviewing and is available on their web site at **www.train2equip.com.**

We are going to look at **major problems** the **evolutionary model** has with the **laws of science.** Evolution is in major conflict with the **laws and what we observe** in science. We will also see the creation model **is not in conflict** with the laws of science.

I pray this will arm you with the full truth of Creation in the Biblically account of Genesis.

More Problems Evolution Cannot Answer

Problem 1 - Evolution Breaks the First Two Laws of Thermodynamics

Law 1: Matter and energy **cannot be created** or destroyed. Matter and energy **cannot create themselves.** In other words, you **cannot** get something from nothing

Problem for Evolution: Evolution **cannot** get past this law. Evolution cannot explain where life or anything else in the universe comes from. Evolution relies on a **miracle** to get started, **with no miracle maker.** Evolution requires that the universe **create itself,** which **is impossible based on this first law.**

Law 2: The Law of Entropy—decaying, wearing down. This law states that matter and energy **starts complex and gets less complex over time**, and we are losing **energy to do work**. It is the law of **increasing entropy**, less energy to do work.

Problem for Evolution: It is obvious that this law is the **exact opposite** of what evolution requires and teaches. Evolution **cannot** get passed this law.

Creation Model: God provided the matter and energy in the universe. The Bible also is exactly in line with the second law, since

God **cursed** all of **creation** after Adam and Eve sinned (**Genesis chapter 3**) and the creation that was very good up until this time, began to rundown, decay, and lose energy. Death and disease in **all living things** were also part of the curse.

Science states: Three Types of Systems- Open, Closed, and Isolated

1) Open System—matter and energy can come in and out.
2) Closed System—matter cannot come in or out, but energy can come in and out.
3) **Isolated System**—no matter or energy can **get in or out.**

The universe is an **Isolated System**. It is wearing out and winding down, getting less complex—the opposite of what evolution requires.

Evolution will tell you we live in an Open System, and the Second Law only speaks of Isolated Systems; and will use **bad science** by using the following two examples:

1) Seed or acorn growing into a tree.
2) Embryo grows into a baby and into a human being.

Both examples are not true because the **DNA** in both the seed or acorn, and the embryo, already has all the information in it to tell them what to become. The DNA tells them what they are. In other words, the information to become a tree, or a human being is programmed into the cell **from the beginning**.

It is a lie to say an Open System is not under Second Law of Thermodynamics. It is, just like the Isolated System. It is also **untrue** that we live in an Open System. The universe is an Isolated System where no matter or energy can get in or get out. Everything in the universe remains in the universe.

Ice Crystals is a bogus argument used by evolutionists to say it is an Open System. Ice Crystals have **no useful information** and is a **loss of energy** from its liquid form **(entropy).** Proteins require energy input from the outside, and **Ice Crystals are giving off energy. They are the opposite process needed to become more complex.**

Problem 2 - Four (4) Mechanisms to Create More Complex Life

1) Must have an Open System
2) Source from energy (example—the Sun)

Note: 3 and 4 are left out in Evolutionary Model

3) A mechanism is required to **capture energy**
4) A mechanism is required to **convert energy** to do useful work.

Problems for Evolution: **using #3 & #4**—example: Your Home Computer, take all of the insides out: floppy discs, hard drive, memory, etc. and begin typing on keyboard, and see if anything is imputed on the screen. You **must** be able to **capture** the input from the keyboard in order to be useful.

To put it another way, you **cannot build matter** until you **capture energy** and until you **have matter** you **cannot capture energy.** You **need both at the exact same time** in order to do useful work. How impossible without having a Creator is this? **Refutes Evolution**. Evolution cannot explain the **mechanisms that create life or where they came from**—It is a belief system.

Creation Model: Since we have an architect in **Creator God**, #3 and #4 is not a problem. God provided the mechanisms to capture and convert energy during **creation.**

Problem 3 - Evolution cannot explain the Life's Origin through Science

1) **DNA**- where did it come from? All this information and evolution cannot explain it.
2) No explanation for why **Life** contains only **Left-handed amino acids.**
3) No explanation for how **Life** could start with or without **oxygen** in the atmosphere.
4) No explanation how **Life** could start in the **oceans** because **Hydrolysis does not allow Molecules to form, it decomposes them.**
5) **No explanation for the Origin of Information—vast amounts of information in every cell of a living thing.**

What is evolution? **It is a belief system.**

Second Law of Thermodynamics & Creation Model

Evolutionists will use the second Law against creation and ask: **Where did God come from?** Instead of answering their question, **have them answer** these two questions?

1) **Can something create itself?** Can a car? Can a building? Can yourself?
2) **Can nothing create something?**

That is God! Self-Existing, Eternal Being—revealed to us through the Bible. **No beginning, no end!**

Evolution says, matter and universe is self-existing. **Wrong!** The Second Law expressly states that matter and energy **cannot be eternal (entropy)**. Everything is decaying and losing energy. This is observable in our universe. Some day our sun is going to loose all of its energy and die—there is no stopping this.

Problem 4 - Life is Complex—Evolution: Micro (Observable) & Macro (No Evidence)

Life is complex - DNA & RNA, Life is a Complex Information Processing System! Life is much more than chemical reactions as Darwin theorized.

DNA = Deoxyribonucleic Acid. Two strands neatly aligned with one another—**Master Genetic Code.** Stores all information essential for all cell activity.

1) Contains a sugar.
2) Nucleic- associated with nucleus of the cell.
3) Contains an acid.

RNA = Ribonucleic Acid. RNA is a single strand. It is responsible to take Genetic information from DNA and **put it to use to build proteins.** It has vast amount of information.

1) Contains a sugar.
2) In Nucleus of cell.
3) Contains an acid.

RNA is a single strand, short term and decays fast, while DNA has two strands, more stable and long term.

DNA, passes information to RNA—to make Protein!

Problem For Evolution: It cannot explain **where all this information came from in DNA and RNA for it to happen from random chance over time.**

Note: One cell division lasts 20 minutes to 80 minutes; during this time the entire **Molecular Library** equivalent to **1,000 books with 1,000 pages is copied correctly. Wow!** This is happening continually all throughout our bodies. **We have billions of living cells that make up our bodies.**

Creation Model: It knows where all the **information** comes from—**our Creator God.** It is not random chance; it was planned and wonderfully made by the God of the Bible.

Problem 5 - How does DNA do this?

It needs help. From a **protein** called **DNA Polymerase**, made up exclusively of Left-handed **Amino acids.**

Problem for Evolution: DNA requires a **protein** that already exists **beforehand to replicate itself. DNA would be useless without a Protein that already exists. This would mean that DNA and DNA Polymerase would have to evolve at the same time, which is scientifically impossible!** Evolution cannot explain this.

Creation Model: Again, this is no problem, since God created DNA, RNA and DNA Polymerase all at **same time.**

Problem 6 - Mechanism is in place to Prevent Copying Changes

DNA Polymerase is genetically made to **copy DNA correctly**. Information to create DNA Polymerase comes from DNA. This means DNA has an Information Code in it **to ensure an exact copy is made of the original DNA.**

Problem for Evolution: **Why would the evolution process develop a mechanism that prevents copy changes?**

Creation Model: God created each species after its **own kind. Exactly what we see in nature and the Bible teaches.**

Genesis 1: 21 21 And **God created great whales**, and every living creature that moveth, which the waters brought forth abundantly, **after their kind**, and every winged fowl **after his kind**: and **God saw that it was good.**

Problem 7: Common question in Evolutionary books—which came first?

Which came first? DNA? RNA? Or Proteins? **Note:** Not a valid question because they all **need each other to work! They must all be present at the same time or you have nothing.**

Most evolutionists says RNA because:

1) DNA is **too complex** to have chemicals evolve from random chance.
2) DNA needs **proteins to duplicate itself,** but proteins need **information from DNA** to do their work.
3) Evolutionists say since RNA carries Genetic information, and, unlike DNA, it is a single-strand molecule, and therefore, it came first.

Problem for Evolution with this science:

1) RNA **must** be able to **replicate** itself. It **cannot** without DNA Polymerase.
2) RNA must be able to act as a **catalyst** (speed up chemical reactions.) Proteins in our bodies called **enzymes** speed up chemical reactions. Our bodies **without** these proteins would **slow down** so much so **we would die. We need Proteins for Life!**
3) RNA is very unstable. Half-life in temperatures above 100 degrees Celsius is just minutes. This shoots down Hydro Thermo Theories. Half-life is too short.
4) RNA is **not a simple molecule**. It is vastly complex and full of information.
5) RNA has been shown scientifically that it does have some enzyme properties, but science **cannot** show that RNA can copy itself.

Evolution's answer to this: Time! Given enough time the impossible becomes possible. **Time is the evolutionary miracle!** Time makes the impossible happen.

What is evolution? It is truly a **belief system.**

More Problems with Time for Evolution: Given more time, it scientifically shows **more decay only!** This is observable in the universe, nature, and **man**. Time only **proves** the Second Law of Thermodynamics is **true,** and so is God's holy word—the **Bible.**

More Problems in RNA to have ever evolved:

1) RNA must be able to copy itself. RNA must have a way to develop, a mechanism, and a template to do so.
2) RNA must develop a mechanism to check for errors, it does not have this.
3) There must be a location, call it a **soup mix,** that contains all of the ingredients; and four mechanisms to put the soup mix all together.
4) How could the first RNA molecule, with all the vast information in it, **spontaneously originate?**
5) Where did all the information originate that is **encoded** in RNA.

Probability Math: Not enough time for RNA to evolve in **20 billion years**.

Dual Problems skipped over in Evolutionary Textbooks:

1) Proper parts need to be properly arranged.

1) Selecting the proper composition (parts)
2) Problem of coding or **arranging parts in proper sequence.**

To help explain the above, look at the examples below:

Example 1: You **cannot just** throw letters using your keyboard, at your computer, and have **useful information. It must be arranged properly in words and sentences also!**

Example 2: We have five colors (red, blue, green, yellow, and purple) in a box. We randomly pull out colors. Our objective is to pull out the 5 colors in the **proper sequence.** How many tries mathematically could it take, **to get it right?**

Answer: 1 color = 1 way; 2 colors= 2 ways (2 x 1); 3 colors = 6 ways (3 x 2 x 1) 4 colors = 24 ways (4 x 3 x 2 x 1); **5 colors = 120 ways** (5 x 4 x 3 x 2 x 1)

It could take up to 120 attempts for as something as simple as 5 colors to be arranged in proper sequence.

How about something a little more Complex?

Example 3: We take only **200 colors** (compared to RNA, this is very simple). How many different sequences are there?

200 colors to get in proper sequence = 200 factorial ways = **10 to the 375th power**. (That is 10 with **375 zero's** after it!).

Mathematicians say it is mathematically impossible to have ever occurred at 10 to the 50th power.

RNA= Billions of parts, required to be put into proper sequence. No amount of time will make this mathematically possible. 20 billion years is not enough!

2) Second Law of Thermodynamics

Law works against RNA ever evolving. More time, equals more decay, and less energy to do the work; to **make molecules become more complex.**

Is there **anything** in the Laws of Physics that suggests **how coded information,** which are equivalent to **one million words in length, arise spontaneously by any known naturalistic process? WE DO NOT!!!**

3) Big Problem for Evolution: Protein and Life

Protein and Life have **all Left-handed Amino Acids (100%). Non-living matter has both-Left and Right.** It is **Mathematically impossible** to get all Left-handed amino acids **by chance.**

Compound this problem for evolution is this:

All Ribose Sugars in DNA and RNA are Right-Handed!

All Amino Acids and Proteins in **Life** are Left-Handed and all Sugars in **Life** are Right-Handed. Double trouble—mathematically impossible.

Evolution Model is M + E + Time = Life

Creation Model is M + E + Time + God = Life

Creation Model is the only model for origins we have been able to observe!

Example: Ocean is our Soup. It has everything in it. Take DNA completely apart and put it in the ocean. **Will DNA assemble itself over time? No. It takes an Intelligent Designer—a Creator God to do so!**

Fact—We are Fearfully and Wonderfully Made!

> **Psalm 139: 14** [14]I will praise thee; for **I am fearfully and wonderfully made:** marvellous are thy works;

1) There is **125 billion miles of DNA** in a Human Body, **100 trillion cells. Your personal DNA would wrap around the earth 5 million times!**
2) Your veins and blood arteries would stretch **around the earth 3 times!**
3) One molecule of Hemoglobin (blood) has **2,378 atoms—It is the most complex molecule in the universe!**
4) The Human body makes **140 million of those atoms in minutes!**
5) **Who has the better Scientific Model for the Origin of Life?Evolution** that does not keep the laws of science, or **Creation, as told in the Bible,** that breaks no laws of science?

<u>Conclusion</u>

I have presented evidence these past two weeks that is not being made **public** in secular writings, and scientific publications; evidence for creation that evolutionists would like to keep in the closet. This information is only the tip of the iceberg that is available for us to research. I wanted to wet your appetite about creation science. **I also wanted to present to you the "Creation Model" for the origin of life,** and show how it fits very well with all the areas in science—Astronomy, Biology, Physics, Chemistry, Microbiology, etc., and the **holy word of God**. There is no conflict with the Bible and good science.

My Personal Belief!

I have studied, not only the scientific evidence for Creation, but also the Biblical. I have come to the conclusion that the Creator God, of the book of Genesis, is fully revealed as **Jesus,** in the book of John chapter one. The Bible is the **absolute truth, and I can rely**

on every word and sentence God inspired. It is God, and not man, who does have absolute wisdom and truth. It is God, and not **matter and energy, in a "Big Bang" Theory,** who knows, and has revealed in **Genesis** how he did it—**God spoke the universe into existence and molded man out of the dirt of the earth!**

> **Hebrews 11: 3** [3]**By faith** we understand **that the universe was formed at God's command,** so that what is seen was not made out of what was visible. **(NIV)**

I have studied**; the word "day" in Genesis,** the Hebrew word used is " **Yom."** In the context of how the word is used, most Hebrew scholars agree the word means a literal 24-hour day period.

Man compromises what God says in the Bible, to fit his own thinking instead of conforming his thinking to what God says. We see people of faith, compromising the teachings of the Bible, and say that God could have used lots of time for creation. They justify this by saying time has no meaning to God and will quote:

> **2 Peter 3: 8** [8]But, beloved, be not ignorant of this one thing, that **one day is with the Lord as a thousand years**, and **a thousand years as one day.**

This is a misuse of this verse when using it in this way. You must look at Bible Prophecy when God uses "a day is like 1000 years and 1000 years is like a day."

One of my favorites scripture passages is this prophecy about Israel:

> **Hosea 6: 1-2** [1]Come, and **let us (Israel) return unto the LORD:** for **he hath torn**, and he will heal us; **he hath smitten,** and he will bind us up.
>
> [2]**After two days will he revive us**

This is where we use **2 Peter 3: 8**. The two days in verse 2 above is **2,000 years** (**one day equaling 1,000 years). This prophecy has**

been fulfilled in our lifetime! In 70 A.D., the Romans destroyed Israel and the temple in Jerusalem, and scattered the chosen people to the four corners of the earth. Israel was torn apart. Nearly 2,000 years (two days in prophecy) later it happened—In 1948, **Israel was reborn!**

> in **the third day** he will raise us up, **and we shall live in his sight**. **(The Millennial reign of Jesus Christ, Israel will recognize him—this could happen in our lifetime!)**

This fits very well with the Genesis account of creation, and the history and timetable of the Bible. The first and second day **(2,000 years)** lasted from Creation to Abraham. The third and fourth day **(next 2,000 years)** is the history between Abraham and the birth of Jesus. The fifth and sixth day, **the Age of Grace,** is the time we now are living in. It has lasted **almost 2,000 years (two days). The Seventh day has not yet come (the end day of the week). It will be a day** (1,000 year reign of Jesus Christ) **of rest, of jubilee!**

More examples found in the Bible to support this are: **Genesis Chapter 1 and 2**, when God created the universe **in 6 days** and He rested for **one day, the last day of the creation week.**

In **Leviticus chapter 25,** you read of the "Sabbath year" **and the "year of Jubilee"** and then we read in **Exodus 20: 8–11:**

> 8Remember the **sabbath day**, to keep it holy.
>
> **9Six days shalt thou labour, and do all thy work:**
>
> 10But **the seventh day is the sabbath of the LORD thy God**: in it **thou shalt not do any work**, thou, nor thy son, nor thy daughter, thy manservant, nor thy maidservant, nor thy cattle, nor thy stranger that is within thy gates:
>
> **11For in six days the LORD made heaven and earth, the sea, and all that in them is,** and **rested the seventh**

day: wherefore the LORD blessed the sabbath day, and hallowed it.

Did God mean we should labor 6,000 years and rest for 1,000 years or did he mean a literal 24-hour day? Did God literally mean he created in six literal 24-hour days and rested on the seventh day?It is my personal belief God did, and so I do not have to compromise the word of God in order for my belief to reconcile itself with science. I do not have to add, subtract, or read between the lines of my Bible.

Other Reasons Why I Believe the Bible as being Six Literal Days!

1) If life has existed for millions upon millions of years, as the evolution model professes, that means **disease, suffering, death etc.—all detestable things we see in the world today, were always here, and had nothing to do with man falling away from God,** as Adam and Eve is professed to have done in God's holy word—the Bible. Survival of the fittest, molecules to man, fighting for superiority, pain and suffering—It would mean our **SIN AGAINST GOD** had nothing to do with the reason for suffering and death. The salvation message gets lost. It would mean Adam's sin did not bring death—because in the evolutionary model, **suffering and death was already here.**
2) In Genesis, we have a beautiful revelation of how God created the heavens and the earth and all that is in it. After each day's work, God called what he had done "**very good." The evolutionary model does not allow for a description of "very good"** in its model, unless you feel what is described above in #1 as **"very good.**" You cannot reconcile this model with what is described in Genesis one and two.
3) I believe in a catastrophic worldwide flood—**Noah's Flood**, as described in **Genesis Chapters 6 - 9.** I believe this is where the fossil record came from, including the **Dinosaur's.** Job Chapters 40 and 41 describe such creatures (See chapter 14 of this book.)

4) I believe the word of God, that man sinned against him, exactly and as simple as Genesis describes. It explains to me why there is pain and suffering, death, why the world is so imperfect, **and most of all—why our relationship was broken with God** and why we only see a part of what God is painting. **I see why Jesus Christ had to die for my sins, and yours.**
5) Just as Ken Ham said it would be, "If you can believe the first 11 chapters of Genesis, you will have no problem believing the rest of the Bible."—It did so for me. **The Salvation Message is not lost because we have the reason God died on the cross, in Genesis chapter three.**
6) Believing the Bible and the Creation Model together makes sense to me for what is happening in the world today. The pain and suffering, world turmoil, disasters this earth is experiencing, all point to prophecy that is yet to be fulfilled. Bible prophecy becomes more real and absolute.
7) I put God's **word and his light** above men. I have more **faith** in what God says about the origin of life than what man thinks he knows, including our evolutionary scientists. Whenever I read in the newspaper scientists found the missing link to man...I do not panic. I wait and see the evidence explained by scientists who follow the Creation Model. It has never failed because the glasses for evolution are long age, and the eyeglass of creation, is the **Bible! Creation makes better sense and better science to me.**
8) **Most Importantly:** Jesus himself told us that Noah's flood was real, **He believed in the great flood!** The gospel writers speak of Jesus, telling his disciples, that at his second coming, it will be like the days of Noah.

Luke 17: 26-27 [26]And **as it was in the days of Noe**, so shall it be also in the days of the Son of man.

[27]They did eat, they drank, they married wives, they were given in marriage, **until the day that Noah entered into the ark, and the flood came, and destroyed them all.**

Mathew 24: 37-39 [37]But **as the days of Noah were**, so shall also the coming of the Son of man be.

[38]For as in the days that were before the flood they were eating and drinking, marrying and giving in marriage, **until the day that Noe entered into the ark,**

[39]And knew not until the flood came, and took them all away; so shall also the coming of the Son of man be.

My prayer for you is that you too will be fired up for what the Lord has done...in **Creation.** I pray that your faith will grow and be strong. I pray you will stand on **God's word, not man's word.** I pray that you will know that the Bible means what it says and you can count on it. I pray that you find peace in the scriptures and the knowledge that Jesus Christ is where all hope lies!

If the question of evolution is keeping you from a relationship with Jesus Christ, I urge you to see what creation science is all about. At the back of this book, are suggested readings and sources you might want to investigate and do your own research with. Do not let evolution hold you back from spending eternity with our creator—Jesus Christ.

To finish up our chapters on creation, please take the quiz in Chapter 26 to see how much you have learned from this Creation/ Evolution study.

God loves you and so do I!

Questionnaire for:
Two Models of the "Origin of Life"

Chapter 26

The Two Origins: 1) Evolutionary Model and (2) Creation Model

(X) Mark the answer you feel best fits your beliefs. Answers to questions are at end of test.

1) What is the Evolutionary Model?

___A) Science explaining how life & universe came into existence.

___B) Belief System explaining how life & universe came into existence.

2) What is the Creation Model?

___A) Science explaining how life & universe came into existence.

___B) Belief System explaining how life & universe came into existence.

3) What is the foundation that the Evolutionary Model is based on? What is its starting point?

___ A) Time and lots of it. ___ B) Bible- Genesis chapters 1 - 11.

4) What is the foundation that the Creation Model is based on? What is its starting point?

___ A) Time and lots of it. ___ B) Bible- Genesis chapters 1 - 11.

5) Which Model claims that there is evidence for a Catastrophic Worldwide Flood? Noah's Flood- Genesis chapters 6 - 9?

___ A) Evolutionary Model ___ B) Creation Model

There are two types of evolution taught: (1) Micro Evolution- Changes within a species where a dog remains a dog, a cat a cat, etc. and **(2) Macro Evolution**- This is molecules to man, causes an upward movement of information so that you can jump from one species to the next.

6) Which type of changes can the Creation Model and Evolutionary Model both agree on?

___ A) Micro ___ B) Macro

7) Which type of changes do they disagree on?

___ A) Micro ___ B) Macro

8) How does the Evolutionary Model explain where fossils come from?

___ A) a little bit of water and lots of time.

___ B) Lots of water and a little bit of time.

9) How does the Creation Model explain where fossils come from?

___ A) a little bit of water and lots of time.

___ B) Lots of water and a little bit of time.

10) In the dating of the Fossil Record, do Dating Methods use pure science or do they use assumptions not possible to prove or observe (which is the basis of science)?

___ A) Pure science- provable.

___ B) Science tainted with assumptions- that are not provable.

11) In nature, is it possible to observe fossils ready to be formed today or did fossils happen only in the past?

___ A) Fossils are being formed in the present.

___ B) Fossils happened in the past and are being found today.

12) Is there evidence that dinosaurs lived on earth at the same time as man? Are there living fossils being found today?

___Yes- there is evidence. ___No- there is no evidence.

13) Is there scientific evidence the earth is much younger than what the worldview is teaching?

___Yes- there is evidence. ___No- there is no evidence.

14) How long does it take for changes in nature to occur? A volcanic island or coral reef to form? How long for a Grand Canyon to form?

___ A) Eons of time.

___ B) Can happen relatively quickly with the right circumstances.

15) Which Model uses better science for explaining the Origin of Life?

___ A) Evolutionary Model ___ B) Creation Model

16) Many Christian leaders believe there is an agenda in the secular world to push the Evolutionary Model to get God out of our society, therefore truth is relative and there are no absolutes- so man can set the rules and not God. Is the Bible absolute truth or is it relative?

___ A) The Bible is **absolute truth**- inspired word of God.

___ B) Truth is relative- Man decides.

Answers: 1) B, (2) B, (3) A, (4) B, (5) B, (6) A, (7) B, (8) A, (9) B, (10) B, (11) B, (12) Yes, (13) Yes, (14) B, (15) B, and (16) A.

God loves you and so do I!

The Seven Feasts of Israel-Appointed by God

Chapter 27

This was an eight-week Sunday school class I taught at church in the fall of 2005. I used a video series led by Zola Levitt, a Jewish believer in Yeshua (Jesus). **I hope you can see Jesus in this study.**

Introduction

This is a fascinating study! Through Bible verses and discussion we see the picture these Old Testament Feasts are revealing.

We find all seven of the Feasts God appointed Israel to keep in **Leviticus chapter 23**. In these seven feasts, **we see Jesus** revealed and how they tell the "Christian Love Story."

Chapters 27 through 34 will inform you what each festival foretells in these prophetic feasts given to Moses 1,500 years before Christ:

1) **The Passover** and **the Feast of Unleavened Bread** symbolize the crucifixion and burial of Jesus.
2) **The Feast of Firstfruits** is the Resurrection of Jesus.
3) **Feast of Weeks** symbolizes Pentecost, when the Holy Spirit came.
4) **The Feast of Trumpets** is the Rapture.

5) **Day of Atonement** is celebrating salvation and redemption for the Jews.
6) **The Feast of Tabernacles** is the final Kingdom when Jesus returns.
7) The **added Festivals of Chanukah and Purim** are festivals of joy.
8) The Miracle of Passover—Zola Levitt calls it **"The Crown Jewel"** of the biblical feasts. The Messiah appears in every moment of this supper. This last chapter on the feasts is a presentation of what takes place this night and will shed clear light on the mysteries of the Lord's Supper.

The goal of this study on the feasts is to:

1) **Strengthen your faith**. We will see Jesus prophesized about in these 3,500-year-old festivals. Jesus, through these festivals, is revealed in the Old Testament and he fulfills them all in the New Testament.
2) To know that the **Bible is the inspired word of God** and we can trust what it says.
3) To better equip us so **we can share with others**, unsaved family and friends, **why we believe in Jesus.**

Thank you for studying these chapters. It is my hope you will enjoy what is presented using God's word.

God loves you and so do I!

Feast(s) One and Two - Passover/ Unleavened Bread Overview - Leviticus 23: 4-8

The Messiah is clearly presented in this **3,500-year-old** crown jewel of the Biblical festivals. The Passover Feast is the most glorious of Bible stories. In Week 8 of this class, we will revisit Passover and see the amazing "**Christian love story**" in detail.

Important information about this feast and related scripture:

The Jewish faith has combined Passover and Unleavened Bread into one eight day festival. It is celebrated each year on the first full moon of spring.

During Passover, every food that is not of Passover must be cleaned out of the house. Even pets must follow the law and eat Passover food only, or you cannot feed your animals.

It is interesting that the Jews know far better the Passover meal and what Jesus was saying at the Last Supper because of their traditions, customs, and other writings—and how Jesus, being a Jew, must have followed the regulations perfectly. We will see in chapter 34, exactly what Jesus was saying to his disciples at the "Last Supper."

Exodus chapters 11, 12 and 13 give us the Passover story and regulations. In Leviticus chapter 23, all seven feasts, all appointed by God for the Jews to keep, are summarized. All seven feasts symbolize what God is going to do, at his chosen time, for mankind.

The Jewish people are still waiting for the prophet Elijah to return. Elijah is one of two men who never died but **were taken**

to heaven without dying, giving us hope for the rapture of the church in the future.

1) The first is **Enoch (Genesis 5: 24)** [24]And Enoch walked with God: and he was not; **for God took him.**

It is confirmed in **Hebrews 11: 5, that Enoch never experienced death:** [5]By faith Enoch was translated that **he should not see death;**

2) **Elijah** was the second **(2 Kings 2: 11)** "[11]And it came to pass, as they still went on, and talked, that, behold, there appeared a chariot of fire, and horses of fire, and parted them both asunder; and **Elijah went up by a whirlwind into heaven.**

There are four questions the youngest child asks on each Passover—it will be fully shown in chapter 34 when we walk through the entire meal. It is very interesting what these questions are and how they pertain to Jesus.

Unleavened bread is made without yeast. **Yeast symbolizes sin.** There can be no yeast in the house during Passover. **Jesus' body** is symbolized in the unleavened bread because scripture declares Jesus is without sin.

> **Hebrews 4: 15** 15For **we do not have a high priest (Jesus)** who is unable to sympathize with our weaknesses, but **we have one who has been tempted in every way**, just as we are—**yet was without sin.**

The communion Christians partake of today in church came from Jesus following the Passover regulations. At the Last Supper, Jesus and his disciples were celebrating the Passover meal. The sharing of unleavened bread and wine is one part of that meal. **The Last Supper is Passover.**

The Bible states the best ever Passover was celebrated by King Josiah **(2 Kings 23:22).** It is the half-way point from the first Passover described in Exodus to the time when Jesus celebrated it at the Last Supper and what we read about in the four gospels of the New Testament.

The Passover meal begins with a woman lighting the candles at the table. A woman has only one function at the Passover meal, and that is to bring light to the celebration. Just as a woman brings light to the Passover meal, **the woman, Mary** brought the Messiah into the world. Jesus is the light of the world.

> **John 8: 12:** [12]Then **spake Jesus again unto them, saying, I am the light of the world:** he that followeth me shall not walk in darkness, but shall have the light of life.
>
> **He was born of a virgin**: **Isaiah 7: 14** [14]Therefore the Lord himself shall give you a sign; Behold, **a virgin shall conceive, and bear a son,** and shall call his name Immanuel (**meaning is "God with us!**).
>
> **Isaiah 9: 6 declares he is God!** [6]For unto us a child is born, unto us a son is given: and the government shall be upon his shoulder: and his name shall be called Wonderful, Counsellor, **The mighty God**, **The everlasting Father,** The Prince of Peace.

This is confirmed in the gospels:

> **Luke 1: 30-35:** [30]And the angel said unto her, Fear not, Mary: for thou hast found favour with God.
>
> [31]And, behold, thou shalt conceive in thy womb, and bring forth a son, and **shalt call his name JESUS.**
>
> [32]He shall be great, and shall be called **the Son of the Highest:** and the Lord God shall give unto him the throne of his father David:
>
> [33]And he shall reign over the house of Jacob for ever; and of **his kingdom there shall be no end.**

> 34Then said Mary unto the angel, **How shall this be, seeing I know not a man? (Scripture declares Mary is a virgin.)**
>
> 35And the angel answered and said unto her, **The Holy Ghost shall come upon thee,** and the power of the Highest shall overshadow thee: therefore also **that holy thing** which shall be born of thee **shall be called the Son of God.**

Scripture declares Mary conceived a child by the power of the Holy Spirit, and not by man, and that is why we know he is God and is known as the Son of God. Jesus is God!

In the meal, bitter herbs signify us before our salvation, our walk on earth when we were outside the light. The wine symbolizes the blood shed for us **(Matthew 26: 27-28).** The wine is Jesus' proposal to us to accept his salvation and be covered by the Lamb of God who takes the sins of the world away. (Wait until you see this in chapter 34.)

> **John 1: 29** 29The next day John saw Jesus coming toward him and said, **"Look, the Lamb of God, who takes away the sin of the world!**

The water in the meal signifies baptism. Jesus fulfilled his own baptism by allowing John the Baptist this great honor, again fulfilling prophecy:

> **Isaiah 40:3** 3The voice of him that crieth in the wilderness, Prepare ye the way of the LORD, make straight in the desert a highway **for our God.**
>
> **Matthew 3: 3** 3**For this is he that was spoken of by the prophet Esaias, (Isaiah)** saying, The voice of one crying in the wilderness, Prepare ye the way of the Lord, make his paths straight.

Isaiah 11: 2 [2]**And the spirit of the LORD shall rest upon him, the spirit of wisdom and understanding, the spirit of counsel and might, the spirit of knowledge** and of the fear of the LORD;

Matthew 3: 16 [16]And **Jesus, when he was baptized**, went up straightway out of the water: and, lo, the heavens were opened unto him, and **he saw the Spirit of God descending like a dove, and lighting upon him:**

Look at the unleavened bread. It has **burn marks** that look like bruises and scars. It also **has holes** you can see through. At the time of Jesus' trial and crucifixion, his body was **whipped and deeply bruised and scarred**. The crown of thorns **punctured** his head. His hands and feet were **pierced** as he hung on the cross. A spear to make sure he was dead **pierced** his chest. The unleavened bread is the perfect picture of our Lord 's own body at his crucifixion. See these scriptures to see how the Messiah, our Jesus, was going to be **beaten, to suffer, to be pierced, and ultimately die for our sins:**

Isaiah 52: 14 [14]As many were astonied at thee; his visage was so **marred more than any man, and his form more than the sons of men:**

The prophet Isaiah above foresaw the whipping and beating Jesus would suffer. He was marred from this cruel beating more than any other man that ever lived.

Psalm 22: 16 [16]For dogs have compassed me: the assembly of the wicked have inclosed me: **they pierced my hands and my feet.**

Isaiah 53: 5 [5]But **he was wounded for our transgressions**, he was bruised for our iniquities: the chastisement of our peace was upon him; and **with his stripes we are healed.**

Psalm 34: 20 [20]He keepeth all his bones: **not one of them is broken.**

Just think what Jesus went through for our sins as he hung on that tree. Because he was willing, he stood accursed by God the Father, for the sins we committed, and not him.

Deuteronomy 21: 22-23 [22]And if a man have committed a sin worthy of death, and **he be to be put to death, and thou hang him on a tree:**

[23]**His body shall not remain all night upon the tree**, but thou shalt in any **wise bury him that day**; (for **he that is hanged is accursed of God**;) that thy land be not defiled, which the LORD thy God giveth thee for an inheritance.

We can see the crucifixion of Jesus clearly in the Old Testament written up to over 1,000 years before it happened. Oh, how **our Lord suffered for us**. It was fully revealed in the New Testament given to us by his disciples, who are the eyewitnesses to what occurred. Below are only some of the verses that describe what Jesus went through:

Galatians 3: 13 [13]**Christ hath redeemed us from the curse of the law, being made a curse for us**: for it is written, **Cursed is every one that hangeth on a tree:**

John 19: 1 [1]Then Pilate therefore took Jesus, and **scourged him**.

Mark 14: 65 [65]And some began to **spit on him**, and to cover his face, and **to buffet (beat, pound) him**, and to say unto him, Prophesy: and the servants did **strike him with the palms of their hands.**

Mark 15: 17 [17]And they clothed him with purple, and platted a **crown of thorns, and put it about his head,**

Mark 15: 24 [24]And when **they had crucified him**, they parted his garments, casting lots upon them, what every man should take.

John 19: 33-34 [33]But when they came to Jesus, and saw that **he was dead** already, **they brake not his legs**:

[34]But one of the soldiers **with a spear pierced his side,** and forthwith came there out blood and water.

In the first Passover, the Lamb's shed blood was placed on the sides and top of the doorframe. It is the perfect picture of Jesus' shed blood for our own Passover:

Hebrews 9: 22 states, [22]And almost all things are by the law purged with blood; and **without shedding of blood is no remission. (Sins will not be forgiven without blood being spilt. Jesus shed his blood for us.)**

The Passover Lamb had to be without blemish or defect (**Exodus 12: 5**). **It took the very best.** It is the perfect picture of our Savior**, Jesus Christ, without any defect (sin),** whose sacrifice would be pleasing enough for God to accept and would take our sins away forever. You can just read the highlighted words to see what Jesus has done for us.

Hebrews 9: 11-15 [11]But **Christ** being come an high priest of good things to come, by a greater and more perfect tabernacle, not made with hands, that is to say, not of this building;

[12]Neither by the blood of goats and calves, but **by his own blood** he entered in once into the holy place, **having obtained eternal redemption for us.**

13For if the blood of bulls and of goats, and the ashes of an heifer sprinkling the unclean, sanctifieth to the purifying of the flesh:

14How much more shall the blood of Christ, who through the eternal Spirit offered himself **without spot** (sin) **to God,** purge your conscience from dead works to serve the living God?

15And for this cause **he is the mediator of the new testament,** that **by means of death, for the redemption of the transgressions** that were under the first testament, **they which are called might receive the promise of eternal inheritance.**

And **Hebrews 9: 22- 28** 22And **according to the Law**, one may almost say, all things are cleansed with blood, and **without shedding of blood there is no forgiveness.**

23Therefore it was necessary for the copies of the things in the heavens to be cleansed with these, but the heavenly things themselves with better sacrifices than these.

24For Christ did not enter a holy place made with hands, a mere copy of the true one, but into heaven itself, **now to appear in the presence of God for us**;

25nor was it that He would offer Himself often, as the high priest enters the holy place year by year with blood that is not his own.

26Otherwise, He would have needed to suffer often since the foundation of the world; **but now once** at the consummation of the ages **He has been manifested to put away sin by the sacrifice of Himself.**

> [27]And inasmuch as it is appointed for men to die once and after this comes judgment,
>
> [28]**so Christ** also, **having been offered once to bear the sins of many**, will appear a second time for salvation without reference to sin, **to those who eagerly await Him. (NASB)**

Christ's perfect sacrifice is described in **Hebrews chapter 10**. I urge you to take the time and read it for yourself in your own Bible. We will learn more of this in chapter 34 about the Passover and the symbolism it has of the shedding of Jesus' blood when we fully see the festival of Passover being presented.

God loves you and so do I!

Feast 3 - The Feast of Firstfruits (Easter) - Leviticus 23: 9-14

Chapter 28

The true and elegant origin and meaning of Easter is given to us in this feast. Jesus is our "**Firstfruits,**" the first to be raised from the grave.

> **1 Corinthians 15: 20-22:** 20But now is **Christ risen from the dead**, and **become the firstfruits** of them that slept.
>
> 21For since by man came death, **by man (Jesus is both man and God.) came also the resurrection of the dead.**
>
> 22For as in Adam all die, even so **in Christ shall all be made alive.**

Important information about this feast and scripture study:

It is celebrated on the first **Sunday after Passover.** An appropriate time for it, since our Savior Jesus Christ is the **Firstfruits.** He is the first to be resurrected, and it was on this first Sunday after Passover when Jesus was crucified—on the day the Jews celebrated the Feast of Firstfruits, **Jesus arose from the grave**. This is why Christians celebrate worship on Sunday and not the Sabbath day as the Jews do, that is the last day of the week: Saturday **(Leviticus 23: 3)**. Interesting Note: Islam's holy day is Friday.

This Feast was given by God for his chosen people to pray for the fertility of the land. On the very first Feast of Firstfruits, over 400 years had passed since famine and infertility of the land **(the story of Joseph)** caused Jacob and his sons to leave Canaan **(Genesis 46)**. During that time, they became slaves to Egypt and suffered. God heard their cries and delivered them using **Moses as an intercessor**. Now they were being led to the Promised Land. This paints a beautiful picture of Jesus, **our intercessor in heaven that is prophesized in the Old Testament and fulfilled in the New Testament:**

> **Job 16: 19–21:** [19] Even now
> **my witness is in heaven**;
> my advocate is on high.
>
> [20] **My intercessor is my friend**
> as my eyes pour out tears to God;
>
> [21] on behalf of a man he pleads with God
> as a man pleads for his friend. **(NIV)**
>
> **Isaiah 53: 12** [12] Therefore I will give him a portion among the great,
> and he will divide the spoils with the strong,
> because **he poured out his life unto death,**
> and **was numbered with the transgressors.**
> **For he bore the sin of many,**
> **and made intercession for the transgressors.** **(NIV)**

The intercessor spoken of by Job and Isaiah is fully revealed in Hebrews of the New Testament:

> **Hebrews 7: 23-25** [23]Now there have been many of those priests, since death prevented them from continuing in office; [24]but **because Jesus lives forever**, he has a

> permanent priesthood. 25Therefore **he is able to save completely** those who come to God through him, **because he always lives to intercede for them. (NIV)**

We who believe in him will enter into heaven, our Promised Land, through what he did for us at the cross.

Firstfruits is much more than fertility. It is better described as **"Resurrection."** Our term "Easter" does not do it justice. In fact, it has pagan roots. The Easter bunny and egg hunts also have pagan roots. They both symbolize fertility and wanting to become pregnant. The name "Easter" comes from the Babylonian goddess "Ishtar" who was the "goddess of fertility." The goddess has taken many names and is still in many ways worshiped throughout the world today. If you have Internet access, do a search on the word "Ishtar"; and you will see the history behind her and how our Feast of Firstfruits has taken on her name. At Easter time, we are really celebrating Firstfruits, a much better description for the resurrection of Jesus Christ.

> **1 Corinthians 15: 22 & 23:** 22For as in Adam all die, even so in Christ shall all be made alive.
>
> 23But every man in his own order: **Christ the firstfruits**; afterward they that are Christ's at his coming.

The Jewish people do not celebrate the Feast of Firstfruits any longer. I find this fascinating. Here is one of seven feasts appointed by God for the Jewish people to keep and they do not follow it any longer. I believe it is because it **points to the Resurrection.**

Resurrection is in the Old Testament: We are not talking about God being resurrected in these scriptures below, but man being resurrected from the grave. These men below never saw or heard of it happening before, yet they had great faith in God and he being able to resurrect when the time came.

1.) Abraham was willing to sacrifice Isaac, yet Abraham was sure his son would be resurrected. **Genesis 22: 4- 5 [4]Then on the third day** Abraham lifted up his eyes, and saw the place afar off.

> [5]And Abraham said unto his young men, Abide ye here with the ass; and **I and the lad will go yonder and worship, and come again to you.**
>
> Abraham had such faith in God's promises to him that he told the two men who were with him that both he and Isaac would return after they worship God. It is confirmed in the book of Hebrews that Abraham had such faith that if God would have him sacrifice Isaac, God would raise him from the grave.
>
> **Hebrews 11: 17–19 [17]By faith** Abraham, **when he was tried, offered up Isaac:** and he that had received the promises offered up his only begotten son,
>
> [18]Of whom it was said, That in Isaac shall thy seed be called:
>
> **[19]Accounting that God was able to raise him up, even from the dead**; from whence also he received him in a figure.

2.) Job was certain he would see his Creator with his own eyes after he died.

> **Job 14: 13-15** [13]O that **thou wouldest hide me in the grave,** that thou wouldest keep me secret, until thy wrath be past, **that thou wouldest appoint me a set time, and remember me!**
>
> **[14]If a man die, shall he live again?** all the days **of my appointed time will I wait, till my change come. (The change Job is waiting for is his resurrection!)**

[15]Thou shalt call, and **I will answer thee**: thou wilt have a desire to the work of thine hands

And Job 19: 25-27 [25]For **I know that my redeemer liveth**, and that he shall stand at the latter day upon the earth:

[26]And though after my skin worms destroy this body, **yet in my flesh shall I see God**:

[27]Whom **I shall see for myself, and mine eyes shall behold, and not another**; though my reins be consumed within me.

Resurrection in the New Testament: Jesus himself is promising he is going to prepare a place for believers; and when he returns, he will receive us.

John 14: 1-3 [1]Let not your heart be troubled: **ye believe in God, believe also in me.**

[2]In my Father's house are many mansions: if it were not so, I would have told you. **I go to prepare a place for you.**

[3]And if I go and prepare a place for you, **I will come again, and receive you unto myself**; that where I am, there ye may be also.

When Jesus ascended into heaven, it was a sign that the resurrection of the body is true.

Acts 1: 9 [9]And when he had spoken these things, while they beheld, **he was taken up; and a cloud received him out of their sight.**

Jesus is coming back for his followers:

> **1 Thessalonians 4: 16** [16]For the Lord himself shall descend from heaven with a shout, with the voice of the archangel, and with the trump of God: **and the dead in Christ shall rise first:**

Jesus is the Firstfruits of those who will be resurrected to everlasting life. Since Jesus is the first, there will be a second, and a third, and a fourth, and so on:

> **1 Corinthians 15: 20-21** [20]But now is **Christ risen from the dead, and become the firstfruits of them that slept.**
>
> [21]For since by man came death, by man came also the resurrection of the dead.
>
> Now scripture states not all believers will experience death; and when Jesus does come back, all living believers will go to be with him in heaven:
>
> **1 Corinthians 15: 50-55** [50]Now this I say, brethren, that flesh and blood cannot inherit the kingdom of God; neither doth corruption inherit incorruption.
>
> [51]Behold, I shew you a mystery; **We shall not all sleep (not all believers will die.), but we shall all be changed,**
>
> [52]In a moment, in the twinkling of an eye, **at the last trump: for the trumpet shall sound, and the dead shall be raised incorruptible, and we shall be changed.**
>
> [53]For this corruptible must put on incorruption, **and this mortal must put on immortality.**
>
> [54]So when this corruptible shall have put on incorruption, and **this mortal shall have put on immortality,** then

shall be brought to pass the saying that is written, **Death is swallowed up in victory.**

[55]**O death, where is thy sting?** O grave, where is thy victory?

Zola Levitt puts it beautifully, "A true believer CANNOT BE PERMANENTLY BURIED." Jesus is coming back for us.

The Old Testament speaks throughout about **eternal salvation and eternal life:**

Isaiah 45: 17: [17]Israel has been saved by the LORD
With an everlasting salvation;
You will not be put to shame or humiliated
To all eternity. **(NASB)**

Ecclesiastes 3: 11-14 [11]He has made everything appropriate in its time **He has also set eternity in their heart**, yet so that man will not find out the work which **God has done from the beginning even to the end.**

[12]I know that there is nothing better for them than to rejoice and to do good in one's lifetime;
moreover, that every man who eats and drinks sees good in all his labor—**it is the gift of God.**

[14]**I know that everything God does will remain forever; there is nothing to add to it and there is nothing to take from it**, for God has so worked that men should fear Him. **(NASB)**

Psalm 145: 1 [1]I will extol thee, my God, O king; and **I will bless thy name for ever and ever.**

Psalm 139: 24 [24]And see if there be any wicked way in me, and **lead me in the way everlasting.**

I love the scripture below given to us by the prophet Isaiah. God promises the ransomed of the Lord shall return and have everlasting joy. The "ransomed" are the sinners who have turned to the Lord Jesus Christ and the cross where he suffered and died for us. This is fully revealed as we use all of scripture and see prophecy fulfilled by Jesus.

> **Isaiah 35: 10** [10]**And the ransomed of the LORD shall return,** and come to Zion with songs and **everlasting joy upon their heads: they shall obtain joy and gladness, and sorrow and sighing shall flee away.**
>
> **Psalm 23: 6** [6]Surely goodness and mercy shall follow me all the days of my life: and **I will dwell in the house of the LORD for ever.**
>
> **Psalm 86: 12** [12]I will praise thee, O Lord my God, with all my heart: and **I will glorify thy name for evermore**.
>
> **Psalm 92: 8** [8]But thou, LORD, art most high **for evermore.**

All of the scripture above promises life that is everlasting. This is for everyone who trusts the Lord. In fact, life everlasting is for everyone—there are two ways to go:

> **Daniel 12: 1-3** describe the resurrection of both saints and unbelievers. [1]And at that time shall Michael stand up, the great prince which standeth for the children of thy people: and there shall be a time of trouble, such as never was since there was a nation even to that same time: and at that time **thy people shall be delivered, every one that shall be found written in the book**.
>
> [2]And many of them that sleep in the dust of the earth shall awake, **some to everlasting life**, and **some to shame and everlasting contempt.**

[3]And they that be wise shall shine as the brightness of the firmament; and they that turn many to righteousness as the stars **for ever and ever.**

Everlasting life or everlasting contempt is the only two ways the Bible speaks of. By far, more is written in the Bible of warnings of everlasting punishment than what is written about heaven:

Psalm 25:3 [3] No one whose hope is in you
will ever be put to shame,
but they will be put to shame
who are treacherous without excuse. (NIV)

Psalm 14: 1 [1]The fool hath said in his heart, **There is no God. They are corrupt,** they have done abominable works, **there is none that doeth good.**

Psalm 34: 22 [22]**The LORD redeemeth the soul of his servants**: and none of them that trust in him shall be desolate.

A very strong warning in 2 Thessalonians 1: 8-9 [8]In flaming fire taking vengeance **on them that know not God, and that obey not the gospel of our Lord Jesus Christ:**

[9]Who shall be **punished with everlasting destruction** from the presence of the Lord, and from the glory of his power;

Matthew 23: 33 [33]Ye serpents, ye generation of vipers, **how can ye escape the damnation of hell?**

Matthew 25: 41 [41]Then shall he say also unto them on the left hand, **Depart from me, ye cursed, into everlasting fire,** prepared for the devil and his angels:

Matthew 25: 46 [46]And **these shall go away into everlasting punishment**: but the righteous into life eternal.

John 3: 18–19 [18]He that believeth on him is not condemned: **but he that believeth not is condemned already,** because **he hath not believed in the name of the only begotten Son of God.**

[19]And **this is the condemnation**, that light is come into the world, and men loved darkness rather than light, **because their deeds were evil**.

Jude, the half-brother of Jesus, warns us that if we remain in our sins we will end up like the ancient cities of Sodom and Gomorrah and suffer the same fate:

Jude 1: 7 [7]Even as Sodom and Gomorrha, and the cities about them in like manner, **giving themselves over to fornication**, and going after strange flesh, are set forth for an example, **suffering the vengeance of eternal fire.**

The Great White Throne Judgment- Revelation 20: 11–14

This last judgment foresaw by the apostle John is for everyone who did not accept God's free gift of salvation. Islam teaches **everyone** will go through such a judgment; **that is not true!** Those **who accepted Jesus as Lord and Savior** will not be going through this judgment. **I do not want anyone to go through this judgment.** Just read the **bold print** in scripture to see how horrible it will be:

[11]And I saw a **great white throne**, and **him that sat on it**, from whose face the earth and the heaven fled away; and there was found no place for them.

[12]And **I saw the dead**, small and great, **stand before God**; and **the books were opened**: and **another book was opened, which is the book of life**: and **the dead**

> **were judged** out of those things which were written in the books, **according to their works.**
>
> [13]And the sea gave up **the dead** which were in it; and death and hell delivered up the dead which were in them: and **they were judged every man according to their works.**
>
> **[14]And death and hell were cast into the lake of fire. This is the second death.** [15]And **whosoever was not found written in the book of life was cast into the lake of fire.**

Let us be ready to share the good news of everlasting life to those who are perishing. We do not like to think about hell. People say we should not talk about it. I beg to differ. If you love people, you should warn them of the everlasting punishment; for whoever does not take the free gift of salvation that God wants to give to all his creation, will be cast in the lake of fire and we should love people enough to warn them what awaits for those who disbelieve.

Let the scriptures do their work; let the Holy Spirit do his work. Let those who are perishing see God's word, so they can be convicted of their sins (as I was and am of mine), so they have a chance to repent of them before it is too late. Let the words of God convince them they need a Redeemer, his name being Jesus Christ, the Son of the Living God. Let the Old and the New Testaments, the entire Bible, convict them of the truth:

> **John 3: 16** [16]For **God so loved** the world, that he gave his only begotten Son**, that whosoever believeth in him should not perish, but have everlasting life.**

Jesus is our Firstfruits. He is the first to have been resurrected. Let us prepare ourselves to be ready for our own resurrection and follow him into eternal life and glory. It is a free gift from the Father who loves us.

God loves you and so do I!

Feast 4 - Pentecost (Shavuot)- Feast of Weeks- We receive the Holy Spirit- Leviticus 23: 15-22

Chapter 29

In chapter 27 we saw how Passover foretold of the Lamb of God—Jesus Christ and his shed blood for our sins. Also, Unleavened Bread is bread without leaven (yeast), which symbolizes sin. Jesus is the **Bread of Life** and the **sacrificial Lamb without blemish** (sin), whose body was beaten, whipped, and hung on the cross for our sins.

In chapter 28, we studied the Feast of Firstfruits and how Jesus is the Firstfruits, being the one who was the first resurrected. We can all look forward to our own resurrection because of the Son of God and his resurrection.

The Old Testament foreshadows of our Lord Jesus Christ. You can find him everywhere when you open your mind in the picture the word of God presents us. It is the way God had his authors write his words. In telling you truths in the physical world, God presents Jesus in his unique way.

In **Leviticus chapter 14** you will see the regulations for lepers. I want to take the first seven verses of that scripture to show the hidden meaning God is showing us. Our God's holy word is written in layer upon layer of understanding, and the Holy Spirit can peel away the layers so **we can see Jesus!**

Leviticus 14: 1-7 [1]And the LORD spake unto Moses, saying,

[2]**This shall be the law of the leper in the day of his cleansing:** He shall be brought unto the priest:

[3]And the priest shall go forth out of the camp; and the priest shall look, and, behold, **if the plague of leprosy be healed in the leper**;

[4]Then shall the priest command to take for him that is to be **cleansed two birds alive and clean**, and **cedar wood**, and **scarlet**, and **hyssop**:

[5]And the priest shall command that **one of the birds be killed** in an earthen vessel over **running water**:

[6]As for the **living bird, he shall take it**, and the **cedar wood**, and the **scarlet**, and the **hyssop**, and shall **dip them** and **the living bird in the blood of the bird that was killed over the running water:**

[7]And he shall sprinkle **upon him that is to be cleansed from the leprosy seven times**, and shall **pronounce him clean,** and shall let the **living bird loose** into the open field.

God is showing us Jesus Christ in his unique way in the scripture above. Many reading it would think it only being ritualistic. There are many symbols presented in these verses that foreshadow the story of Jesus Christ. God shows us that **Jesus is our High Priest**; the **leper** is **humanity** (you and I) **in its sins**. Sin is the disease Jesus Christ came into the world to cure us from. Leprosy is a horrible disease that leaves large sores and open wounds that are easy to see. God can see all of our sins so easily; they are not hidden from him.

Why two birds? (Verse 4) The **slain bird** is Jesus Christ **crucified**; **the live bird** is Christ **Resurrected. Cedar wood** symbolizes the **cross**, **scarlet yarn** is Christ's **suffering**, **Hyssop** symbolizes **faith that heals us** from our sins. **Why running water?** Running water symbolizes **the Holy Spirit**. The priest must take the blood of the dead bird and sprinkle it onto the person to be cleansed **seven times. Why seven times?** Because our Lord **Jesus Christ shed his blood seven times** for us!

1) His body was whipped beyond recognition.
2) The crown of thorns pierced his head.
3) His left hand was pierced.
4) His right hand was pierced.
5) His left foot was pierced.
6) His right foot was pierced.
7) A spear was plunged into his side to make sure he was dead.

After all this, the priest then releases the **live bird** into the open fields—**This is the resurrection**!

In the same way, the seven Feasts of Israel in **Leviticus chapter 23** point us to Jesus. Jesus died and was buried during the feasts of Passover and Unleavened Bread. He was resurrected on the feast of Firstfruits. And now on the **Feast of Weeks** (Pentecost), God again shows us how special and true his word is.

The first Pentecost **(Feast of Weeks)** celebrated was when Moses received the laws from God. It is called the Feast of Weeks, also known as the Festival of Harvest, because it is celebrated at the end of harvest time for the barley crop and the beginning of the wheat harvest. It is celebrated **seven weeks and one day from Passover**; this is where it gets its name. Pentecost is the Greek name for "fiftieth." The Hebrew name for Pentecost is "Shavuot" (pronounced sha-voo-ote). Counting the days from the second day of Passover to Pentecost is called the "Counting of Omer." The cutting of the omer of the new barley marked the beginning of the counting period. On the fiftieth day, Pentecost is observed.

What we received on the first Pentecost is the Law or **Ten Commandments**. What we received on the first Pentecost after the resurrection of Jesus was **the Holy Spirit**—the Third Person of the Trinity:

First Pentecost with Moses	Pentecost after Chris Resurrection
God gives us his Commandments	God gives us **The Holy Spirit**
50 days from the crossing of the Red Sea	50 days from the resurrection
Law of Yahweh written in Stone	Law of Yahweh written in our **Hearts**
Three Thousand slain	Three Thousand receive salvation
The letter of the Law	The Spirit of the Law

Pentecost- Holy Spirit Prophesized in the Old Testament and Fulfilled in Acts Chapter 2

Pentecost was clearly **God's chosen time** for Jesus' followers to receive **the Holy Spirit.**

These first followers were the first of millions upon millions to be touched by the Spirit of God (Elohim). Luke's account in **Acts chapter 2** fulfills the prophecies of his coming.

> **Acts 2: 1-4** 1And when **the day of Pentecost was fully come**, they were all with one accord in one place.
>
> 2And suddenly there came **a sound from heaven** as of a rushing **mighty wind**, and **it filled all the house** where they were sitting.
>
> **3And there appeared unto them cloven tongues like as of fire, and it sat upon each of them.**
>
> 4And **they were all filled with the Holy Ghost**, and began to speak with other tongues, as the Spirit gave them utterance.

The coming of the Holy Spirit fulfilled the prophecies given to us from the prophets Joel and Isaiah. Joel means **"Jehovah is God."** The book of Joel was written approx. 800 years before the birth of

Christ. Isaiah, written between 745 and 680 B.C., means **"Jehovah is Salvation."** Both prophets speak of the Holy Spirit:

> **Joel 2: 28** [28]And it shall come to pass afterward, **that I will pour out my spirit upon all flesh;**
>
> **Joel 2: 32** [32]And it shall come to pass, that **whosoever shall call on the name of the LORD shall be delivered:**
>
> **Isaiah 44: 3** [3]For I will pour water upon him that is thirsty, and floods upon the dry ground: **I will pour my spirit upon thy seed (Believers are the seed.)**, and my blessing upon thine offspring **(Believers are also his offspring.)**:

At the celebration of Pentecost, two loaves of fine bread (**made with leaven**) are waved.

The two loaves symbolizes **mankind**. God only recognizes two races of peoples—the **Jewish people** and the **Gentiles** who make up the rest of mankind. God's word is for both the Jew and the Gentile, and that is the reason for two loaves—one symbolizing the Jewish people and the other symbolizing the Gentiles. The loaves are made with leaven because leaven symbolizes **"sin,"** and as scripture says [23]For all have sinned, and come short of the glory of God; **(Romans 3:23)**.

Doves are used in celebrating Pentecost. The dove is the symbol for the **Holy Spirit.** When Jesus was baptized, the Holy Spirit descended upon him in the form of a dove.

> **Luke 3:21-22** [21]Now when all the people were baptized, it came to pass, **that Jesus also being baptized**, and praying, the heaven was opened,
>
> **[22]And the Holy Ghost descended in a bodily shape like a dove** upon him, and a voice came from heaven, which said, **Thou art my beloved Son; in thee I am well pleased.**

Interesting notes:

1) It was prophesized in the Old Testament the Jewish people would reject their Messiah and Paul confirms it is so in **Romans chapter 9**; he is grieved for their unbelief. He would gladly take their place in order that they might be saved.

> **Romans 9: 1-3** [1]I say the truth in Christ, I lie not, my conscience also bearing me witness in the Holy Ghost,
>
> [2]That **I have great heaviness and continual sorrow in my heart**.
>
> [3]**For I could wish that myself were accursed from Christ for my brethren**, my kinsmen according to the flesh:

2) From the first Pentecost after Jesus' resurrection- the **"Church Age"** began. It is time for the harvesting of the Gentiles, and it is a long time period. It is nearly 2,000 years since Christ Resurrection and when the Holy Spirit first came. It will last until it is completely fulfilled, in the end times.

> **Luke 21: 24** 24And they shall fall by the edge of the sword, and shall be led away captive into all nations: and **Jerusalem shall be trodden down of the Gentiles, until the times of the Gentiles be fulfilled**.

3) We, as believers, are to do what we can to harvest in the crop—to lead people to Christ.

> **John 4: 34-35** [34]**Jesus saith** unto them, My meat is to do the will of him that sent me, and to finish his work.
>
> [35]Say not ye, There are yet four months, and then cometh harvest? behold, **I say unto you, Lift up your eyes, and look on the fields; for they are white already to harvest.**

4) Peter had to use the Old Testament at Pentecost to teach about the Holy Spirit.

> **Acts 2: 14-16** [14]But **Peter**, standing up with the eleven, lifted up his voice, and said unto them, Ye men of Judaea, and all ye that dwell at Jerusalem, be this known unto you, and hearken to my words:
>
> [15]For these are not drunken, as ye suppose, seeing it is but the third hour of the day.
>
> [16]**But this is that which was spoken by the prophet Joel; (Joel 2: 28)**

5) A remnant of Jewish believers will always be present, and that is confirmed in **Romans chapter 11.**

> [1]I say then, **Hath God cast away his people? God forbid.** For I also am an Israelite, of the seed of Abraham, of the tribe of Benjamin.
>
> [2]**God hath not cast away his people which he foreknew.** Wot ye not what the scripture saith of Elias **(Isaiah)?** how he maketh **intercession to God against Israel saying,**
>
> [3]Lord, **they have killed thy prophets**, and digged down thine altars; and I am left alone, and they seek my life.
>
> [4]But what saith the answer of God unto him? **I have reserved to myself seven thousand men, who have not bowed the knee to the image of Baal.**
>
> [5]Even so then **at this present time also there is a remnant according to the election of grace...** [25]For I would not, brethren, that ye should be ignorant of this mystery, lest ye should be wise in your own conceits; **that blindness**

in part is happened to Israel, until the fulness of the Gentiles be come in.

Paul is telling us that until the time the of Gentiles is fulfilled and given grace by the work Jesus has done on the cross, there will always be a remnant of Jews who will have faith in Jesus Christ. It is sad that the vast majority of Jews chose to reject him going on 2,000 years now. But there is hope in the later days when Christ returns. Those Jews who are remaining at his return will be saved!

> 26And so **all Israel shall be saved**: **as it is written**, There shall come out of Sion the Deliverer, and shall turn away ungodliness from Jacob:
>
> **27For this is my covenant unto them, when I shall take away their sins.**
>
> 28As concerning the gospel, they are enemies for your sakes: but as touching the election, **they are beloved for the father's sakes.**

God says there will always be a remnant of Jewish believers. The word of God goes to the Jews first and then to the Gentiles.

More facts from scripture:

> 6) God is a good bookkeeper. As 3,000 were slain at the time Moses gave us the Laws, **(Exodus 32: 28)** 28And the children of Levi did according to the word of Moses: and **there fell of the people that day about three thousand men.** 3,000 receive the Holy Spirit at the first Pentecost after Christ's resurrection as Peter led them to Christ (**Acts 2: 41**) 41Then they that gladly received his word were baptized: and the same day **there were added unto them about three thousand souls.**

7) The Feast of Pentecost was already 1,500 years old when the Holy Spirit first came as a pouring out to all believers in 33 A.D.

God's word is so uniquely written. Hidden in scripture, revealed in layer upon layer, and completely fulfilled in the New Testament so we will not miss our chance at salvation through the redemptive work of Jesus Christ. So we will trust God, who sent his Son to redeem the world!

God's timetable is being fulfilled with the Feasts:

1) **Feast of Passover and**
2) **Unleavened Bread** symbolizes the death and burial of Jesus Christ.
3) **Feast of FirstFruits** is the resurrection of Jesus Christ.
4) **Feast of Weeks**—The Holy Spirit comes and is poured out on all who believe.

Do you see where we are on God's timetable?Jesus' death, resurrection, and the coming of the Holy Spirit have fulfilled the first four feasts described in Leviticus chapter 23. The above feasts are all spring, early summer feasts. The next three feasts are all "**fall celebrations**." God's prophetic timetable will continue to be fulfilled with the next feast celebrated. We are in the prophetic time between feasts—**the Church age**. Our Lord will hit perfectly in his own time the next feast, and it will usher in the return of our Lord Jesus Christ. **Are you ready to see the return of Jesus Christ?**It will happen at the sound of the trumpet when Jesus will come for his bride—his **church**! The next feast to be fulfilled is appropriately called **"The Feast of Trumpets."**

God loves you and so do I!

Feast 5 – Feast of Trumpets (Rosh Hashanah) - The Rapture of the Church- Leviticus 23: 23-25

Chapter 30

God loves trumpets. Rosh Hashanah is the start of Jewish New Year. This year, it will begin at night on **October 3, 2005**. This festival is as important to the Jewish people as Easter (Firstfruits) is to the Christian believer.

In our study so far we have found:

1) Passover and
2) Unleavened Bread foreshadow the death and burial of Jesus.
3) Firstfruits is the foreshadowing of Jesus' resurrection.
4) Pentecost brings us the Holy Spirit.

The above **four festivals** of Israel given by God to his chosen people are all spring and early summer festivals. **Jesus has fulfilled** the first three festivals, and the **Holy Spirit** has come on the fourth. Just as God has fulfilled the first four festivals on his exact timetable, we wait for the next three festivals to be fulfilled, starting with the **Feast of Trumpets**, the **first** fall feast.

Important information about this feast:

To the Jewish people, Rosh Hashanah is a time for respect for the **Torah** (God's word), praying for peace for their enemies, and to go over all their sins to be ready for **Yom Kippur** (Day of Atonement). For the Christian, we should also respect God's word, **pray for unbelievers**, and be ready for Christ's return.

The Feast of Trumpets is prophetic in that we are presently in the church age, and **we are working at this time for the harvest of souls.** We wait for the harvest to be completed and the trumpet sounded. In the fields of the earth, are believers and unbelievers together. When the trumpet sounds, **the believers will go and worship the Lord;** and the unbelievers will remain here on earth. This is exactly what happened during the Jewish history of the Festival of Trumpets. As it was when Jesus lived on earth, when the Rams Horn or **shofar (trumpet)** sounded **from the temple**, the Jews would stop what they were doing and go to the temple to worship the Lord and celebrate **Rosh Hashanah;** while the Gentiles (unbelievers) would remain in the field and continue working. Jesus was using the same kind of example to explain his **second coming** to his disciples, so they could understand what to expect at his return in the final days. His story paralleled the customs and practices of the Jews during the Feast of Trumpet. Because of this, the apostles, being Jews themselves, could relate to his story:

> **Matthew 24: 39-41** That is how it will be **at the coming of the Son of Man**. 40Two men will be in the field; **one will be taken** and the other left. 41Two women will be grinding with a hand mill; **one will be taken** and the other left.

Jesus in his great wisdom was telling us that **at the rapture**, he would bring the believers to him to worship in heaven forever while the unbelievers would remain on earth. Jesus was telling his disciples that the first man and the first woman in the above scripture represented believers, while the second man and second woman represented unbelievers. At the rapture, it will happen with a great shout from the Lord; and then the Trumpet of God will sound, as you will see.

The Rams Horn (**shofar**) began with the sacrifice of Isaac, when God provided the ram that was caught in the thicket by his horn. The ram's horn became an instrument to be used as a **trumpet.**

The story of Jericho found in the book of Joshua is another parallel story that symbolizes God's people (believers) entering the Promised Land (heaven)! In the true, historical description of the Jews entering Jericho, it is the beginning of the Jewish people's triumphant entry into their **Promised Land**. Jericho to this day is a desert oasis and is beautiful. **Jericho symbolizes heaven.** The Israelites were able to enter Jericho **by the blast of their trumpets (shofar) and a shout.** It will be the same for believers when Christ returns and meets his believers in the air, **as we will see:**

> **Joshua 6: 3: 5** [3]And ye shall compass the city, all ye men of war, and go round about the city once. **Thus shalt thou do six days.**
>
> [4]And seven priests shall bear before the ark seven trumpets of rams' horns: and **the seventh day** ye shall compass the city seven times, **and the priests shall blow with the trumpets.**
>
> [5]And it shall come to pass, that when they make a long blast with the ram's horn, and **when ye hear the sound of the trumpet, all the people shall shout with a great shout**; and the wall of the city shall fall down flat, and **the people shall ascend up every man** straight before him.

Wow! I see something very prophetic here. Remember in my earlier chapters I explained that time to God is like a day being a thousand years and a thousand years as a day, and that God uses this formula for **prophecy**. By understanding and believing that the history of the world began with Adam and Eve approximately 6,000 years ago, **see what God is showing us prophetically:**

1) **Jericho,** Zola Levitt points out, **symbolizes heaven**! We all long to enter this Promised Land.
2) It took **six days** of preparation for the chosen people to enter Jericho. **What happens on the seventh day for the Israelites?**The chosen people hear the trumpet blast, and they shout a great shout and **ascend into Jericho.** This fits well with God's timetable. We have had nearly 6 full days (6,000 years) in the history of man. Here is the math: from Adam and Eve to Abraham is 2,000 years or **2 days**. From Abraham to Jesus is another 2,000 years or **2 days**. From The Death of Jesus to present is almost another 2,000 years or **2 days**. This is almost 6,000 years of history or **six days**. **What is going to happen for the believer on the seventh day?**When the trumpet sounds, Jesus will give a great shout; and we that are in Christ will **ascend** and meet him in the air to go with him into the kingdom of God—heaven! I believe the time is near when we will hear God's trumpet blast.
3) Notice that the Ark of the Covenant where God dwells with his people is with them at Jericho. God is with us right now where he dwells—in our spirit, the holy of holies of our being.

Again, God is using true history of the chosen people to give us prophetic insight. When you trust the word of God, you can see the layer upon layer God builds his words on so we can know he is the one, true God. So many times there is a story within a story, and it shows man does not have the wisdom and understanding to write as God does. I believe it shows that everything in the Bible is there for God's purpose.

Is the Rapture Real?

Believers in Jesus will not agree on this subject. **That is okay!** It **should not** be something that will cause division and strife among believers. It is not critical to your salvation which way you believe.

As for me, it is my hope. I do look forward to a **pre-tribulation rapture.**

Let us look at some key scripture **where my hope in the pre-tribulation rapture** is found.

1) As mentioned earlier, two men of the Bible never experienced death – Enoch **(Genesis 5: 24—Hebrews 11: 5 confirms this is true.)** and Elijah **(2 Kings 2: 11).** My God is powerful enough to do this for all believers, and all at once.
2) Noah's ark (**Genesis, chapters 6- 9**). When the whole world was utterly destroyed, God protected Noah and his family from the destruction. God provided a way out of the destruction for these believers.
3) Daniel's three friends are saved from the blazing furnace **(Daniel 3: 16-28).**
4) Daniel was thrown into the lions' den and God protected him **(Daniel 6: 16-23).**
5) God provided a great fish for Jonah, who would have drowned **(Jonah 1:17).**
6) God provided Lot a way out before he destroyed Sodom and Gomorrah **(Genesis chapter 19).**
7) God provided a way out for his chosen people when the tenth plague struck Egypt by the blood of the sacrificial lamb **(Exodus chapters 11 and 12).**
8) God parted the Red Sea for Moses and the Israelites to escape their destruction by Pharaoh and his army **(Exodus chapter 14). It is estimate the number of Israelites grew to over 3 million people before their exodus out of Egypt.**

In all cases above, **God provided a way out for his believers. Two never experienced death, and the others would have perished if God hadn't provided.** This, all by itself, does not prove anything. We need to look at more scripture in God's word to see the picture he is painting.

I see in the next two scripture readings a prophetic time when believers will vanish, and all that remain is the unbelievers. If you believe the rapture must take place before the tribulation, it is possible to picture a terrible time in history where evil reigns. Scripture describes a time when it will cost you your life to be righteous. Because of the way scripture is written with many layers of truth, this will not be the only interpretation that can be seen. As I meditated on God's word, I saw these visions of truth.

1) Please read Psalm 12 fully in your own Bible. I am only going to pull excerpts that God used to paint me this picture.

> 1 Help, LORD, **for the godly are no more;**
> **the faithful have vanished from among men. (NIV**
> **(Faithful Godly people have vanished—could this be speaking of the rapture?)**
>
> **2 Everyone lies to his neighbor;**
> their flattering lips speak with deception. **(NIV)**
> **(It appears there is no one left who speaks the truth.)**
>
> 3The LORD shall cut off all flattering lips, and the tongue that speaketh proud things:
>
> 4Who have said, With our tongue will we prevail; our lips are our own: **who is lord over us? (Do you have a Lord, or are you setting your own rules?)**
>
> 5For the oppression of the poor, for the sighing of the needy, **now will I arise, saith the LORD; I will set him in safety** from him that puffeth at him. **(The Lord is the protector of the needy (I am needy.), and He will set us in safety!)**

Look at verse 5. It says the Lord will set the poor and the needy (believers) in safety from the one who puffeth at him. The one who puffeth wants to destroy the believers, he is the Anti-Christ who is described in the book of Revelation.

> [6]The words of the LORD are pure words: as silver tried in a furnace of earth, **purified seven times. (Remember, Jesus shed his blood seven different ways or times—see the beginning of chapter 29 of this book.)**
>
> **[7]O LORD, you will keep us safe**
> **and protect us from such people forever. (NIV)**
> **(I am counting on this!)**

Looking at verse 7, I see the believer safely in heaven. protected forever from those who would want to harm him. In verse 8 below, only the wicked on earth remain and the vilest of men are exalted. It will be a scary time.

> [8]The wicked walk on every side, when the vilest men are exalted.

2) **Micah chapter 7** is so prophetic **to me.** I am seeing a believer who came to faith in Christ after the rapture and now is **left behind and living** during the time of tribulation described in the book of Revelation. He is a Jewish believer, and he is waiting for the healing of his people and the Lord to return. It will happen on the Day of Atonement, the next feast that must be fulfilled prophetically. I believe the prophet Micah describes perfectly what it will be like for a Jew who was lost at the start of the tribulation but did not take the "mark of the beast" and now is left behind after the rapture of the church has happened. I will highlight its important teachings that I see:

> [1]**Woe is me!** for I am as when they have gathered the summer fruits, as the grapegleanings of the vintage: there is no cluster to eat: **my soul desired the firstripe fruit.**

Jesus is our Firstfruits. I cannot help but think back to **Isaiah 53: 5;** "with **his stripes** we are healed."

> [2]**The good man is perished out of the earth: and there is none upright among men: they all lie in wait for blood**; they hunt every man his brother with a net.

During the tribulation, there will be people who are saved and it will cost them their heads. **Revelation 20: 4** I saw the souls of them **that were beheaded for the witness of Jesus**, and **for the word of God**, and **which had not worshipped the beast,** neither **his image**

> [3]**that they may do evil with both hands earnestly**, **the prince** asketh, and **the judge asketh for a reward**; and the great man, he uttereth his mischievous desire: so they wrap it up.

Corruption in government will be everywhere, officials and judges wanting their bribe money.

> [4]The best of them is as a brier: **the most upright is sharper than a thorn hedge**: the **day of thy watchmen and thy visitation cometh**; now shall **be their perplexity**.

Sounds very evil to me, no righteous persons left and the day of their punishment and the Lord's return is coming.

> [5]**Trust ye not in a friend**, put ye not confidence in a guide: **keep the doors of thy mouth from her that lieth in thy bosom**.

You will not be able to trust a friend or your wife.

> [6]For **the son dishonoureth the father**, the **daughter riseth up against her mother**, the daughter in law against her mother in law; **a man's enemies are the men of his own house.**

You cannot even trust your sons and daughters.

> 7Therefore I will look unto the LORD; **I will wait for the God (Elohim—allows for the Trinity.) of my salvation: my God will hear me.**
> 8Rejoice not against me, O mine enemy: when I fall, **I shall arise**; when I sit in darkness, **the LORD shall be a light unto me.**

This man is a believer who is all alone with no one to trust, but he rejoices in God for his salvation—**He knows he will rise again!**

> 9I will bear the indignation of the LORD, **because I have sinned (All have sinned!) against him, until he plead my cause**, and execute judgment for me: he will bring me forth to the light, and **I shall behold his righteousness.**

He knows Jesus is his intercessor and will plead his case, and he will see the Lord.

> **13Notwithstanding the land shall be desolate because of them that dwell therein, for the fruit of their doings.**

Desolation of the land is a good description for what will occur during the tribulation.

Skipping to verse 18, we see the God of the Bible who pardons sin. God will always have a remnant of his chosen people (the Jews) remaining, and he will turn again toward them in the later days and pardon and not remember their sins any longer. He will cast their sins in the depths of the sea. This will happen at the Day of Atonement, when Israel will recognize its Messiah, **Jesus Christ**:

> **18Who is a God like unto thee, that pardoneth iniquity, and passeth by the transgression of the remnant of his heritage?** he retaineth not his anger for ever, because he delighteth in mercy.

> [19]**He will turn again, he will have compassion upon us; he will subdue our iniquities; and thou wilt cast all their sins into the depths of the sea.**
>
> [20]**Thou wilt perform the truth to Jacob, and the mercy to Abraham,** which thou hast sworn unto our fathers from the days of old.

God's chosen people will finally see the truth and be saved! God will have compassion for his chosen people in the last days; and, like all who accept Jesus Christ as Lord, their sins will be forgiven.

There is so much in **Micah chapter 7**, so much prophecy. God is going to show his great wonders as he did when the Israelites came out of Egypt. This time, all nations will be ashamed, not just Egypt.

At the second coming of the Lord, it is important that you see that **he stands on earth when he comes.** He comes to make atonement with his chosen people. He will not stop in the air to meet them, but he comes in the same way he ascended into heaven. People on earth will witness his return, and **his feet will touch the ground**. Old and New Testaments bear this out:

> **Job 19: 25** [25]For **I know that my redeemer liveth**, and that **he shall stand** at the latter day **upon the earth**:

The ancient patriarch Job understood somehow that Jesus, his redeemer would stand on the earth in the last days.

> **Acts 1: 9-11** [9]And when he had spoken these things, **while they beheld, he was taken up**; and a cloud received him out of their sight.
>
> [10]And while they looked stedfastly toward heaven as he went up, behold, two men stood by them in white apparel;
>
> [11]Which also said, Ye men of Galilee, why stand ye gazing up into heaven? **this same Jesus, which is taken up from**

you into heaven, shall so come in like manner as ye have seen him go into heaven.

In the Old Testament, in **chapter 14 of Zechariah**, written between 520 and 518 B.C., the prophet foresees the Lord God being King over all the earth, and that he will fight one final battle against all the nations at Jerusalem. When this occurs, **Jesus will be standing** on the Mount of Olives and **he will bring with him his holy ones—his saints. This will be the Lord's second coming!**

> Excerpts from **Zechariah 14:** 3Then shall **the LORD** go forth, and **fight against those nations**, as when he fought in the day of battle.
>
> **4And his feet shall stand in that day upon the mount of Olives, which is before Jerusalem on the east...**
>
> **Verse 5:** and **the LORD my God shall come, and all the saints with thee.**

Look at Verse 5 above. The saints will be coming with Jesus! The apostle John in **chapter 19 of Revelation** confirms this is true:

> Excerpts from **Revelation 19:** 11And I saw heaven opened, and behold a white horse; and **he that sat upon him was called Faithful and True**, and in righteousness **he doth judge and make war.**
>
> 13And he was clothed with a vesture **dipped in blood**: and his name is called **The Word of God. (No doubt about it, this is Jesus! See John 1: 1-2)**
>
> 14And **the armies which were in heaven** followed him upon white horses, **clothed in fine linen, white and clean.**

Zechariah 14 and Revelation 19 are describing the same event. In both instances, it is the saints who are with Jesus. Clothing of fine linen, white and clean is what the saints are adorned in—**It is the clothing of the saints and saints are believers.** These armies of saints are already with him in heaven **(verse 14)** when he comes down.

Then who are these saints with Christ at his second coming?

Some important New Testament verses that point to the pre-tribulation rapture:

Just as I see Old Testament verses pointing to the rapture of the church before the tribulation, I see New Testament verses giving us hope for the rapture of the church to occur first, before the wrath of God comes during the seven-year tribulation.

We have to look at more scripture to see who **these saints might be**. Scripture is built upon scripture, and so we can find out who these saints are by reading more scripture. Some of the clearest scriptures written are by the apostle Paul who always gives us much hope. Two of his writings give me great hope for the pre-tribulation rapture of the church. Some of the saints of Jesus Christ who form this army that Zechariah and Revelation speak of will come from the rapture. Scripture speaks not only of the dead in Christ that form his army in the final battle, but also **those who never experienced death!**

> **1 Thessalonians 4: 13-18** 13But I would not have you to be ignorant, brethren, **concerning them which are asleep (dead in Christ!),** that ye sorrow not, even as others which have no hope.
>
> **14For if we believe that Jesus died and rose again,** even so them also **which sleep in Jesus will God bring with him.**
>
> 15For this we say unto you by the word of the Lord, that **we which are alive and remain unto the coming of the Lord** shall not prevent them which are asleep.
>
> 16For **the Lord himself shall descend from heaven with a shout**, with the voice of the archangel, and **with the trump of God**: and **the dead in Christ shall rise first:**

I must pause and reflect on what I just read. **Most important is verse 16.** If you can see that God is using the **seven feasts** as his timetable for fulfilling all the prophecies of Jesus (Proof is that the first four feasts have already been fulfilled.), I want you to see this could be the prophetic **rapture** of the church and is done in the same way the Israelites enter their **Promised Land** at **Jericho**—with a blast of the **trumpet** and a **shout.** The rapture will be fulfilled in the same way as the Feast of Trumpets began when Jesus lived on earth. It is the same as in **Matthew 24: 40** when Jesus told of his coming being as two men working in the fields—one would be taken and the other one left in the field. Remember, Jesus was using an example his apostles would understand. As Zola taught me in his video series on the feasts, in Jesus' day, the custom was to start the Feast of Trumpets with the blast of the trumpet. Immediately, the Jews would stop their work and rush to the temple to worship God. The ones that remained and continued working in the fields were the Gentiles or non-believers.

Verse 16 says this time it will be **Jesus descending with a shout, with the voice of the archangel and the trumpet of God.** This time, it is the believers who will go to be with the Lord to worship in heaven, **not a man made temple**, and the non-believers will remain for the tribulation. We know this must be the rapture and not the Lord's second coming because of what the apostle Paul continues to say in verse 17 below:

> **17 Then we which are alive and remain shall be caught up together with them in the clouds, to meet the Lord in the air: and so shall we ever be with the Lord.**

Verse 17 is the Rapture! Jesus has not touched the ground on earth, as he will at his second coming when his feet will land on the Mount of Olives as foretold in Zechariah 14 when he comes for the remnant of Jewish believers, and sets up his kingdom. Instead, **we have gone up in the air to meet him!** This reminds me of Enoch and Elijah who never died. Verse 17 definitely is speaking of **believers who are still alive**, going to be with Jesus in the air; and **it will last forever!**

> [18]Wherefore comfort one another with these words.

The scripture above does comfort me. **It gives me hope I will not be here for the tribulation.** Let us look at other scripture that may point to the rapture.

> **1 Corinthians 15: 51-52** [51]Behold, I shew you a mystery; **We shall not all sleep (die!), but we shall all be changed,**

Look at the scripture above. God is showing us a mystery. **We will not all die**, but we all will be changed. I again see the rapture. What will be the change?I believe we will be changed in a split second and receive our heavenly bodies that will never know sickness or death again.

> [52]In a moment, in the twinkling of an eye, **at the last trump**: for **the trumpet shall sound**, and the dead shall be raised incorruptible, and **we shall be changed.**

Again, the trumpet will sound! It is without a doubt the same trumpet Paul talked about in **1 Thessalonians 4: 17**. Just as the **Festival of Trumpets** is pointing prophetically to the rapture of the church where those in Christ will go to worship the Lord and celebrate in heaven. Those who are not of Christ will remain here on earth (the fields) for the tribulation.

Also; a well-known prophecy written by the apostle John, gives great hope to believers in a pre-tribulation rapture of the church.

> **Revelation 4: 1** [1]After this I looked, and, behold, a door was opened in heaven: and the first voice which I heard **was as it were of a trumpet talking with me**; which said, **Come up hither**, and I will shew thee things which must be hereafter.

The first three chapters of Revelation deal with the church. The start of chapter 4 starts with "**come up here**" and you never hear about the church again. This event takes place with the **trumpet** again, but this time the apostle John describes it as being able to speak. From this point forward in the book of Revelation, the **"Great Tribulation"** begins. This very well could point to the rapture of the church before the tribulation begins.

Another of Paul's writings goes like this:

> **1 Thessalonians 1:10 10And to wait for his Son from heaven,** whom he raised from the dead**, even Jesus, which delivered us from the wrath to come.**

The wrath the apostle Paul is speaking of that Jesus delivers us from **could be** the great tribulation. I believe it is. The book of Revelation describes in detail God's wrath he has for an unbelieving, unrepentant mankind, his righteous anger he has held back for thousands of years, **since the days of Noah** when he first punished **all evil** because there was no one left who was righteous—**except one**.

> **Genesis 6: 5-8** 5And **God saw that the wickedness of man was great in the earth**, and that every imagination of **the thoughts of his heart was only evil continually.**
>
> 6And it **repented (regretted)** the LORD **that he had made man on the earth**, and **it grieved him** at his heart. **(How God must hate evil. Man became so evil He regretted He created him and grieved over what man had become.)**
>
> 7And the LORD said, **I will destroy man whom I have created from the face of the earth**; both man, and beast, and the creeping thing, and the fowls of the air; for it repenteth me that I have made them.
>
> **8But Noah found grace in the eyes of the LORD.**

Certainly, we can see the evil man is doing in the world—Why has God held back his anger for so long this time?**Simple—because he loves us!**

2 Peter 3: 9 9The Lord is not slack concerning his promise, as some men count slackness; **but is longsuffering to us-ward, not willing that any should perish, but that all should come to repentance.**

God does not want anyone to perish, he wants you to come into repentance, and he wants to save you from the wrath to come. The wrath may not be the Great Tribulation foretold about in the book of Revelation, but there is one thing I am certain of—**Jesus definitely saves us from the wrath of hell!**

God has given us many signs when Jesus may return for his children. There is so much prophecy in both the Old and the New Testaments and almost all has been fulfilled already. The Lords return could be very near: the trumpet could be sounded at any time.

Matthew 24:43 43But understand this: If the owner of the house had known at what time of night the thief was coming, **he would have kept watch** and would not have let his house be broken into. **(NIV)**

Only Father God knows the day and hour for Christ's return. We will see in chapter 34 that this is also shown in the parable of the ten virgins that Jesus taught, using the customs of the Jewish marriage to explain his second coming. Again, it would be a teaching the Apostles could relate to, being Jews themselves. The lesson is plain, we are to keep watch and be ready for his return.

1 Thessalonians 5: 4- 6 4But ye, brethren, are not in darkness, **that that day should overtake you as a thief.**

5Ye are all the children of light, and **the children of the day**: we are not of the night, nor of darkness.

6Therefore let us not sleep, as do others; but **let us watch and be sober.**

Even though the Bible commands we do not predict the day or hour of his return, he does tell us to watch for the signs and the season of his return.

> **Revelations 3:3** [3]Remember therefore how thou hast received and heard, and hold fast, and repent. **If therefore thou shalt not watch, I will come on thee as a thief, and thou shalt not know what hour I will come upon thee.**

Summary: The most important reason I believe in the rapture before the tribulation is this—God is a God that always provides a **way out for persons of faith when he is going to bring destruction and judgment.**

1) He provided a way for the Jewish people at Passover through the blood of the lamb.
2) God provided a way out for Noah, Daniel, Jonah, and Lot.
3) In the tribulation period, some of the judgments are a lot like the plagues given against Egypt during the Israelites captivity, **only much worse.** The Jewish people were spared the torments that Egypt was afflicted with by God. I have hope we will be spared in the same way by what Jesus did on the cross and his shed blood.
4) God provided a sacrificial Lamb that was given to all **believers** as a way out from **eternal damnation** for our sins. **Jesus took our quilt and our punishment as his own.**

> **John 3: 16-18** [16]For God so loved the world, that he gave his only begotten Son, **that whosoever believeth in him should not perish, but have everlasting life.**
>
> [17]For God sent not his Son into the world to condemn the world; but that **the world through him might be saved.**
>
> **[18]He that believeth on him is not condemned: but he that believeth not is condemned already, because he**

> **hath not believed in the name of the only begotten Son of God.**

Another reason I believe that there is a pre-tribulation rapture is because of this study on the seven feasts of Israel. Prophetically, the seven feasts are **God's timetable** when **all the feasts must and will be fulfilled.** The first four feasts have been prophetically fulfilled already, **all in their proper order**. With the Feast of Trumpets and two more festivals after it approaching (and none yet prophetically fulfilled), we know it is not the time for Jesus' to establish his kingdom on earth yet. The Feast of Trumpets must be fulfilled first before the next two feasts can be fulfilled. The next feast we will study, the Day of Atonement, will be the fulfillment of Israel recognizing their Messiah—the suffering Messiah, the one they had pierced, prophesized by the prophet Zechariah. I have faith the last three festivals will be prophetically fulfilled before and after the Great Tribulation, and all in their proper sequence.

I believe in God's prophetic timetable that it is late summer and we are approaching fall and the end of the summer harvest. It is day six, and we are nearing day seven when Christ returns. We could be looming near the end of the Church Age, what is in reality to God, the harvesting of the Gentiles. Before the Feast of Trumpets comes, believers should be working the fields to harvest souls—Jews and Gentiles alike—for the Lord's kingdom. Share the good news with someone that **God is love**, and he has provided a way out through his Son Jesus Christ **so we all can have eternal life!**

God loves you and so do I!

Feast 6 - Day of Atonement -Yom (Day) Kippur (Atonement) - falls on 10-13-2005- Leviticus 23: 26-32

Chapter 31

"**May you be inscribed into the Book of Life!"** The Jewish people say this to each other on this sixth festival of Israel. I, too, pray that we all have our names inscribed in the most important Book of Life. I can confidently say my name is written in the **"Lambs Book of Life!" Can you?**

Fulfilled Feasts:

1) **Passover**
2) **Unleavened Bread**—prophecy of the shed body and blood of Jesus and his burial.
3) **First Fruits**—prophecy of Jesus' resurrection.
4) **Pentecost**—prophecy the Holy Spirit will come.

We are now living in-between the spring/early summer feasts and the fall feasts. It has been nearly 2,000 years (2 days in God's time) since the Pentecost after Jesus' resurrection and today. We are living during the time of working in the fields, harvesting souls (the Church Age). We are looking forward to the time of fulfillment of the fall feasts and Christ's return.

5) **Feast of Trumpets (Rosh Hashanah)** – prophesizes Jesus will return for his church. The Church Age is completed.
6) **Day of Atonement (Yom Kippur)** — when the remnant of the Jewish people will meet their Messiah **(the Second Coming of Jesus Christ).**

To the Jewish People, **the Day of Atonement is the most awesome and holiest of days**. It is a day of affliction of the soul (confession). For twenty-four hours, you must reflect of every sin you committed in the past year and seek forgiveness. You must forgive those that have harmed you and seek forgiveness from those you harmed. It is said to be the longest day of the year because the Jews stay up all night and day.

There are three things a Jewish person must do during this time of Yom Kippur.

1) **T'shuvah** (repentance: its meaning is more about returning to the right path). What a great description of what we should all be doing!
2) **Tefillah** (prayer)
3) **Tzedakah** (charity)

> The reason for this festival is given in **Leviticus 16: 30**
> 30For on that day **shall the priest make an atonement for you**, to cleanse you, that ye may be **clean from all your sins before the LORD.**

Atonement is needed to deal with the **problem of sin**. One of the Hebrew meanings for atonement is **"to cover."** The High Priest of Israel could not take away the sins of Israel. He performed the sacrifice of blood of the bulls and goats, it was only able to cover sin, and **it was temporary**.

> **Only Jesus can takeaway sin. (John 1:29)**
> 29The next day **John seeth Jesus** coming unto him, and saith, **Behold the Lamb of God, which taketh away the sin of the world**.

Jesus has fulfilled the Day of Atonement for the believer. Compare the high priest of the temple with our glorious High Priest, **Jesus Christ.**

1) One High Priest: On the Day of Atonement, the high priest would go into the Holy of Holies of the Temple and offer a sacrifice to reconcile the people with God. He was their **only intercessor**, their **only mediator**. There is **only one high priest,** and only he could perform the sacrifice **(Leviticus 16:17).** Jesus is the fulfillment of the one and only true High Priest. **He alone is the one who could perform the ultimate sacrifice to take away sin forever.**

Hebrews 7: 24- 28 24but **because Jesus lives forever**, he has a **permanent priesthood.** 25Therefore **he is able to save completely those who come to God through him,** because **he always lives to intercede for them.**
26Such a **high priest** meets our need—**one who is holy, blameless, pure, set apart from sinners, exalted above the heavens.**

27Unlike the other high priests, he does not need to offer sacrifices day after day, first for his own sins, and then for the sins of the people. **He sacrificed for their sins once for all when he offered himself.**

28For the law appoints as high priests men who are weak; **but the oath**, which came after the law, **appointed the Son, who has been made perfect forever. (NIV)**

Verse 28 above refers to an **oath given to us by God!** It is a promise that God will not and cannot break. God has appointed the Son to be the perfect sacrifice for our sins.

Hebrews 8: 1-2 and verse 8. Jesus is The High Priest of a New **Covenant (The meaning of the word "Covenant" is pledge / promise / contract)**:

[1]Now of the things which we have spoken this is the sum: **We have such an high priest, who is set on the right hand of the throne of the Majesty in the heavens;**

Verse 1—Jesus is our High Priest who is sitting at the right hand of God.

[2]A minister of the sanctuary, and of **the true tabernacle (God's throne in heaven),** which **the Lord pitched**, and not man... [13]In that he saith, **A new covenant, he hath made the first old**. Now that which decayeth and waxeth **old is ready to vanish away.**

Jesus fulfills the high priest in Scripture. Just as the high priest is the only one who can perform the sacrifice for sin in the temple, only Jesus could perform what he did on the cross—become the sacrificial Lamb of God who took away the sins of the world for all who believe.

2) One time for sacrifice: Just as there was **only one high priest** who serves in the tabernacle of the temple, there was **only one time** in a year to receive atonement. Only once a year was the high priest allowed to enter the Holy of Holies. Every year this ceremony had to be performed because the sacrifices of the high priest **could not take away sin. Only the Lamb of God can! Jesus is our High Priest who took away our sins!** Jesus had to perform his **sacrifice only once because he did take away our sins and not just cover up our sins.**

Hebrews 9: 24-28 [24]For **Christ is** not entered into the holy places made with hands, which are the figures of the true; but **into heaven itself**, now **to appear in the presence of God for us:**

Do not miss what **verse 24** is saying above. Jesus is in heaven right now in the very presence of God interceding on our behalf.

> 25**Nor yet that he should offer himself often**, as the high priest entereth into the holy place every year with blood of others;
>
> 26For then must he often have suffered since the foundation of the world: **but now once in the end of the world hath he appeared to put away sin by the sacrifice of himself.**

Verses 25 and 26 above verify that Jesus had to offer himself **only once for our sin**. No longer would the annual shedding of animal's blood be required to cover sin.

> 27And **as it is appointed unto men once to die**, but after this the judgment:
>
> 28**So Christ was once offered to bear the sins of many**; and unto them that look for him shall **he appear the second time without sin unto salvation.**

Jesus bore our sins on the cross to bring us salvation and life everlasting. No other religion can demonstrate the love God has for us this way. No other religion has this story where it is God who frees us of sin for no other reason but for his love of humanity.

> **3) One Place:** Jesus is the only **High Priest**. There is only **one time** for the proper sacrifice. There is only **one place** of sacrifice that is acceptable. At first, it was in the tabernacle in the desert and later the temple in Jerusalem. Jesus bore our sins on the only acceptable place that would permanently eliminate sin—**at the cross!**

1 Peter 2:24 "[24]He himself bore our sins in his body on the tree, so that we might die to sins and live for righteousness; **by his wounds you have been healed**."**(NIV)**

Do not miss what the apostle Peter is saying. He bore all of mankind sins in his body so **we will not die to sin.** We are healed by what Jesus did on the cross for you and for me!

4) **Must be a Blood Sacrifice**: On the Day of Atonement, there had to be a **sacrifice of blood** made for the atonement of sin. **The shedding of blood is the only means for atonement**, whether we read about it in the Old Testament or the New Testament—it is the same.

Leviticus 17:11 [11]For the life of the flesh is in the blood: and I have given it to you upon the altar to make an atonement for your souls: **for it is the blood that maketh an atonement for the soul.**

In **Hebrews 9:22** we read: [22]And almost all things are by the law purged with blood; and **without shedding of blood is no remission.**

Jesus' shed blood is our everlasting atonement for our sins.

Hebrews 9: 14-15 [14]How much more shall **the blood of Christ**, who through the eternal Spirit **offered himself without spot (sin) to God**, purge your conscience from dead works to serve the living God?

[15]And for this cause **he is the mediator of the new testament,** that **by means of death, for the redemption of the transgressions** that were under the first testament, they which are called might **receive the promise of eternal inheritance.**

Because of Jesus' sacrifice, we have the promise of eternal life, for those who accept the blood offering by the Lamb of God—Jesus!

> **5) No work is allowed:** One last parallel between the high priest and Jesus is found in **Leviticus 23:27-28,** and it is the same thing as taught in the New Testament, **the people were required to do no work!**
>
> **Leviticus 23:27-28** [27]Also on the tenth day of this seventh month there shall be a **day of atonement**: it shall be an holy convocation unto you; and ye shall afflict your souls, and offer an offering made by fire unto the LORD.
>
> [28]And **ye shall do no work in that same day**: for it is a day of atonement, **to make an atonement for you before the LORD your God.**

The high priest did it all. The people had to **confess and repent of their sins** and **do no work**. That is the way of Jesus—**our High Priest**. It is by **God's grace and not by works we are saved.**

> **Romans 3: 24** [24]**Being justified freely by his grace** through the **redemption that is in Christ Jesus**:
>
> **Ephesians 2: 8-9** [8]**For by grace are ye saved through faith**; and that not of yourselves: **it is the gift of God:**
>
> [9]**Not of works**, lest any man should boast.
>
> **Titus 3: 5-7** [5]**Not by works of righteousness** which we have done, **but according to his mercy he saved us**, by the washing of regeneration, and renewing of the Holy Ghost;
>
> [6]Which he shed on us abundantly **through Jesus Christ our Saviour;**

> [7]**That being justified by his grace**, we should be made heirs according **to the hope of eternal life**.

The Day of Atonement, when given to Moses some 3,500 years ago to keep, foreshadowed future events that would be prophetically fulfilled:

1) The future atoning work of Jesus Christ at the cross for **all believers—Gentiles and Jews alike.** We have read above that **Jesus** did this as our High Priest. Jesus has already fulfilled this at the cross.
2) The future cleansing (salvation) of Israel **at the end of the Church Age**. There are many prophetic scriptures for the renewal of Israel.

The most important one in the Old Testament says it very well, and this will happen at Christ's return.

> **Zechariah 12: 10 through Zechariah 13:1** [10]And I will pour upon **the house of David**, and upon the inhabitants of Jerusalem, **the spirit of grace and of supplications: and they shall look upon me whom they have pierced,** and **they shall mourn for him, as one mourneth for his only son**, and shall be in bitterness for him, as one that is in bitterness for his firstborn.

> **Zechariah 13** [1]In that day **there shall be a fountain opened to the house of David and to the inhabitants of Jerusalem for sin** and for uncleanness.

The prophet Zechariah foresaw the crucifixion of our Lord Jesus Christ. He also saw that the chosen people would mourn for the **one they had pierced** and repent for having crucified Jesus; and they will be redeemed in the later days. This is confirmed in the book of Romans.

> **Romans 11: 26-27:** 26And **so all Israel shall be saved**: **as it is written,** There shall come out of Sion the Deliverer, and shall turn away ungodliness from Jacob:
>
> **27For this is my covenant unto them, when I shall take away their sins.**

God has made a covenant, an oath, that he will take away the sins of his chosen people—his remnant that is alive at his second coming, just as he did for the Gentiles during the Church Age. This will fulfill the ancient prophecies of **Isaiah 59: 20-21**, **Jeremiah 31: 33-34**, and **Isaiah 27: 9**. Paul teaches that it is by faith we are saved—for **both the Jews and the Gentiles alike.**

> **Romans 3: 28–30**: 28Therefore we conclude that a man is **justified by faith without the deeds** of the law.
>
> **29Is he the God of the Jews only?** is he not also of the Gentiles? **Yes, of the Gentiles also**:
>
> 30Seeing **it is one God, which shall justify** the circumcision **by faith**, and uncircumcision **through faith.**

What the scriptures are saying is that by faith and only faith are both Jews and Gentiles alike saved. It is not by our good deeds or works, but by grace alone. This is why I love God so much. When I made mistakes and got the wrath from my earthly father as a boy, how I loved him when he would give me grace and would forgive me. How much more our heavenly Father is willing to give us his grace and forgiveness! But you must trust in him to receive it.

Special interest: are the high priest's sacred garments. It amazes me how everything written in the Bible has purpose and meaning. Many times in scripture things are written that symbolize what God is doing in this world or showing us how great our God in heaven is. God has completely revealed himself to us in scripture in so many awesome ways. In **Exodus chapter 39** you can read about the garments made for Aaron and all future high priests and ultimately the greatest of all High Priests—**our Lord Jesus Christ.**

Starting from the high priest's head, the **sacred diadem** (headdress) was engraved with "**Holy to the Lord**." The robe of the Ephod was made entirely of **blue** cloth. Bells and pomegranates alternated around the hem of the robe. **Bells** symbolize blessings, and the **pomegranates** show fruitfulness.

The garments were made of colors. **Gold** is God's color. **Scarlet** is the color symbolizing sacrifice—the color of blood. **Blue** is the color for heaven—God's residence. **White is fine linen that saints will be dressed in when they go to heaven**—it symbolizes righteousness given to his saints.

The **Ephod** garment symbolizes the **glory of Christ**. The **breastplate** is the symbol of judgment. The breastplate had **12 precious stones**, one for each for the twelve tribes of Israel. It is over the heart showing **God's compassion and love for his people.**

The mounted **onyx stones** on the shoulders of the Ephod were for the twelve names of the sons of Israel. It also speaks of strength **and the Good Shepard who carries the lost sheep on his shoulders.**

> The mounted stones also go with the passage of **Isaiah 9: 6**
> **6For unto us a child is born, unto us a son is given: and the government shall be upon his shoulder**:

No question the first half of this passage is speaking of the Messiah. The passage reminds us that He will be an everlasting king. He will govern the Jews and the whole world at his coming. To the Jew it will be the Messiah's first and only coming. But to the believer it will be his second coming. This passage speaks of a child born **(a human).** But if you read on and complete this passage, this child is much more. **DO NOT MISS IT!** The scripture is speaking of the second person of the Trinity—**one God, the Son of God**.

> **Isaiah 9:6 continued;** ... and his name shall be called Wonderful, Counsellor, The **mighty God, The everlasting Father, The Prince of Peace**.

This is our **Jesus**. This is our **High Priest**. This is **the one and only God** I serve. In the last days, all of Israel will see Jesus as their Messiah. He will become their High Priest, and they will be saved as we are—by faith and the grace of God, not by works. When this happens, the Feast of Atonement will be prophetically fulfilled. **The Day of Atonement is for Israel only.** It is not for the Gentiles. When it is fulfilled, it will be the end of the great tribulation period and will be at the Lord's second coming. I pray for this day for our brothers and sisters of the Jewish race. From scripture, I can see a day for them when God will return and say unto them:

> **Numbers 6: 22-27** [22]And **the LORD spake unto Moses**, saying,
>
> [23]Speak unto Aaron and unto his sons, saying, On this wise **ye shall bless the children of Israel**, saying unto them, **24The LORD bless thee**, and **keep thee**:
>
> [25]**The LORD make his face shine upon thee**, and **be gracious unto thee:** 26The LORD lift up his countenance upon thee, and give thee peace.
>
> [27]**And they shall put my name upon the children of Israel, and I will bless them**.

God loves you and so do I!

Feast 7 -The Feast of Tabernacles (Sukkoth)- Full week Feast (10/17/05 to 10/24/05) Leviticus 23: 33-43

Chapter 32

Our Lord Jesus celebrated all the feasts of Israel, and the Feast of Tabernacles is no exception. In **John chapter 7,** you learn that Jesus taught in the temple at this feast even though the Jews in Judea were waiting to take his life.

> 1After these things Jesus walked in Galilee: for he would not walk in Jewry, **because the Jews sought to kill him.**
>
> **2Now the Jew's feast of tabernacles was at hand.**
>
> **5For neither did his brethren (Scripture is speaking of Jesus' half-brothers.) believe in him.**

Remember: Jesus had two half brothers- James and Jude who authored books in the New Testament. They did not become believers until after his resurrection

Jesus teaches at the feast:

> [14]Now about the **midst of the feast Jesus went up into the temple, and taught.** [15]And the Jews marvelled, saying, **How knoweth this man letters, having never learned?**
>
> [16]Jesus answered them, and said, My doctrine is not mine, **but his that sent me.**

I find this fascinating that the Jews knew Jesus well enough to know he had not been formally trained in the Torah, and yet they marveled at his teachings. When we get to heaven, Jesus will teach us things we can only imagine and I look forward to hearing him speak.

Fulfilled Feasts

1) **Passover**
2) **Unleavened Bread**—shed body and blood of Jesus and his burial.
3) **Firstfruits**—resurrection
4) **Pentecost**—Holy Spirit comes.

We are now living between the spring/early summer feasts and the fall feasts. It has been nearly 2,000 years (2 days in God's time) since the Pentecost at Jesus' resurrection and today. We are living during the time of working in the fields, harvesting souls (the Church Age). We are looking forward to the time of fulfillment of the fall feasts.

5) **Feast of Trumpets (Rosh Hashanah)**—when Jesus will return for his church. The Church Age is completed.
6) **Day of Atonement (Yom Kippur)**—when the remnant of the Jewish people will meet their Messiah (the second coming of Jesus Christ).
7) **Festival of Tabernacles**—the **harvest of souls** is completed, and Jesus sets up his Kingdom on earth to dwell among his people.

The Feast of Tabernacles is the last prophetic feast that will be fulfilled in the last days.

This feast was also called the "**Feast of Harvest**" since it was observed in conjunction with the fall harvest once the Israelites entered the Promised Land.

> **Exodus 23:16** [16]And the **feast of harvest**, the **firstfruits of thy labours**, which thou hast sown in the field: and the **feast of ingathering**, which is in the end of the year, when thou hast gathered in **thy labours out of the field**

It is the most joyous and public of all the seven feasts mentioned in **Leviticus 23**. It is a full week festival celebrated starting on the fifteenth day of the seventh month. It is a celebration and remembrance of their time spent in Sukkah (plural Succoth) which are make-shift shelters or huts **(booths)** in the desert. This feast is known by so many names. It is known also as the "**Feast of Booths**" **(Succoth).** Succoth commemorates the journey out of Egypt into the Promised Land and God's watchful protection over his chosen people, the Israelites. The booths were sanctuaries so that **God could dwell among his people.**

> **Exodus 25: 8- 9** [8]And let them **make me a sanctuary; that I may dwell among them.**
>
> [9]According to all that I shew thee, after **the pattern of the tabernacle,** and the pattern of all the instruments thereof, even so shall ye make it.

Wow! "Dwell among them." That is exactly what Jesus did in his first coming!

> **John 1: 14 "[14]The Word became flesh** and made his **dwelling among us. We have seen his glory**, the glory of the One and only, who came from the Father, full of grace and truth. **(NIV)**

I look forward to the time when he will build his permanent home (Tabernacle) in Jerusalem at the fulfillment of the Feast of Tabernacles at his second coming.

The booths emphasize their temporary nature. They were made of perishable things from the desert. Branches and twigs made up the booth and the roof was loosely thatched so that the sky showed through. They would decorate the booth by hanging fruits and other natural items to give color to it.

Today, during the feast, day three through day six are called Chol Hamoed while the seventh day is called Hoshanah Harabbah or the **Great Hosanna. At the time of Ezra**, an eighth and ninth day were added to this celebration. The eighth day was known as Shemeni Atzeret, the eighth day of solemn assembly; and the ninth day as Simchat Torah, which means Rejoicing in the Torah. A Hatan Hatorah or **Groom of the Torah** is chosen. The man chosen for this honor exemplifies love and practices the Torah faithfully. His good deeds are proclaimed while being escorted up to the Torah. Then the last chapter of **Deuteronomy** is read to show that the reading of the Torah is finished; but immediately after, the first chapter of **Genesis** is read to show the Torah is never done with. A **Groom of Genesis** (Hattan BeReshit) and **Groom of the Prophetic Reading** (Hattan Maftir) are also chosen. I wanted to bring this out because Yeshua **(Jesus)** the Messiah exemplifies and fills the requirements for all three grooms as no one else can:

> **1)** He is the **Groom of the Torah:** The Messiah **(Jesus)** exemplifies more love and perfection of the Torah than anyone that ever lived. He is worthy to read the scrolls.
>
> **Revelation 5: 1-10** [1]And **I saw in the right hand of him that sat on the throne a book written within and on the backside, sealed with seven seals.**
>
> [2]And I saw a strong angel proclaiming with a loud voice, **Who is worthy to open the book, and to loose the seals thereof?**

> [3]**And no man in heaven, nor in earth, neither under the earth, was able to open the book, neither to look thereon.**
>
> [4]And I wept much, because no man was found worthy to open and to read the book, neither to look thereon.
>
> [5]And one of the elders saith unto me, **Weep not: behold, the Lion of the tribe of Judah, the Root of David, hath prevailed to open the book, and to loose the seven seals thereof.**

Verse 5 above is describing the only person who could open the Book—**the Lion,** from the tribe of Judah, an heir of David—**Jesus Christ! He is now the triumphant Messiah, no longer the suffering Messiah—the lamb that was slain—**as verse 6 below points out.

> [6]And I beheld, and, lo, in the midst of the throne and of the four beasts, and in the midst of the elders, **stood a Lamb as it had been slain**, having seven horns and seven eyes, which are **the seven Spirits of God** sent forth **into all the earth**.

Verses 5 and 6 verify it is the Messiah. **He is the lamb that had been slain.** Verse 6 also describes the lamb that was slain—Jesus, who has the seven Spirits of God. This is taken right out of the Messianic passages of Isaiah chapter 11. The **seven Spirits of God** are the fruits from the Holy Spirit that rested on Jesus when he was baptized. Compare verses 5 and 6 above with what the prophet Isaiah wrote—**count the seven fruits**.

> **Isaiah 11: 1-4** [1]And there shall come forth a rod **out of the stem of Jesse**, and a **Branch shall grow out of his roots**:

> [2]**And the spirit of the LORD shall rest upon him**, the spirit of **wisdom** and **understanding**, the spirit of **counsel** and **might**, the spirit of **knowledge** and of the **fear of the LORD**;

The seven fruits are spirit of the Lord, wisdom, understanding, council, might, knowledge, and fear.

> [3]And shall make him of quick understanding in the fear of the LORD: and **he shall not judge after the sight of his eyes**, neither reprove after **the hearing of his ears**:
>
> [4]But with righteousness shall **he judge the poor**, and reprove with equity **for the meek** of the earth

I love verses 3 and 4 above. He is not going to judge us by what he sees or by what he hears—he is going to look into our spirit, at our faith and give justice to the poor and the meek.

Now continuing in Revelation 5 starting with verse 7:

> [7]**And he came and took the book out of the right hand of him that sat upon the throne.**
>
> [8]And when he had taken the book, the four beasts and four and twenty elders **fell down before the Lamb**, having every one of them harps, and golden vials full of odours, **which are the prayers of saints.**
>
> [9]And they sung a new song, saying, **Thou art worthy to take the book, and to open the seals thereof: for thou wast slain, and hast redeemed us to God by thy blood out of every kindred, and tongue, and people, and nation;**

Wow! Look at verse 9 above! The Messiah was slain and has redeemed us by his blood. We who are redeemed are from every kindred (family members), tongue, people, and nation. **In verse 10 below, look what we have to look forward to!** The saints will reign with him on earth. I love you Jesus.

> 10And hast made us unto our God kings and priests: and **we shall reign on the earth.**

Summary: Scripture above is saying **only Jesus** the Lamb of God that came into the world and was slain, is worthy to read the scrolls. Now he is a lion, a king; he has prevailed, and he is the only one able to open the book. Now all of heaven is singing praises to him and worshiping the one who has redeemed us with his own shed blood, saints from every kindred, tongue, people, and nation. In verses 8 and 9 above, all of heaven is worshiping Jesus. He is God; for only God can and must be worshiped, and there is only one God.

> **2)** He is the **Groom of Genesis,** for **he is our Creator**. Scripture verifies Jesus created the universe:

> **John 1: 1–3** 1In the beginning was the **Word**, and the **Word** was with God, and the **Word was God**.
>
> 2The same was in the beginning with God.
>
> **3All things were made by him; and without him was not any thing made that was made.**

Wow! Scripture is saying Jesus has always existed; He is the Second Person of the Trinity, and He is God! He is the one who created the universe and all that is in it. Nothing in the universe was made without him!

> **3)** He is the **Groom of the Prophetic Reading** because he fulfilled all Scriptures.

Jesus said in **Matthew 5: 17-18** [17]Think not that I am come to destroy the law, or the prophets: **I am not come to destroy, but to fulfil.**

[18]For verily I say unto you, Till heaven and earth pass, one jot or one tittle shall in no wise pass from the law, **till all be fulfilled.**

Wow! Scripture is saying Jesus **has not come to destroy the law, but to fulfill the law.** He and He alone will fulfill all that is written in Scripture.

We see Jesus fulfilling prophecy in another way. The palm branch is used in conjunction with prayer during this feast, and it is the symbol of peace. Jesus' triumphant entry into Jerusalem as recorded in the gospels was the exact fulfillment of prophecy.

Zechariah 9: 9 [9]Rejoice greatly, O daughter of Zion; shout, O daughter of Jerusalem: behold, **thy King cometh unto thee**: he is just, and having salvation; lowly, and **riding upon an ass, and upon a colt the foal of an ass.**

John 12:14 below is the exact fulfillment of this Old Testament prophecy above. Jesus presented himself in Jerusalem on an donkey colt!

John 12: 11-15 [11]Because that by reason of him **many of the Jews went away, and believed on Jesus.**

[12]On the next day much people that were **come to the feast (the week-long feast of Passover),** when they heard that **Jesus was coming to Jerusalem,**

[13]Took **branches of palm trees**, and went forth to meet him, and cried, **Hosanna: Blessed is the King of Israel** that cometh in the name of the Lord.

The way Hosanna was used here literally meant, **"The Son of David is our salvation!"**

> [14]And Jesus, when he had found **a young ass**, sat thereon; **as it is written, ("As it is written" always refers to the Old Testament writings.)**
>
> [15]Fear not, daughter of Sion: behold, **thy King cometh, sitting on an ass's colt.**

An important note I learned from Zola was that Jesus' triumphant entry **was not done on the Feast of Tabernacles**; it was done **4 days prior** to the **Feast of Passover, on Palm Sunday.** This is very important. This means the Feast of Tabernacles is still not prophetically fulfilled, and we still must wait for our Lords second coming to have the feast satisfied. **Jesus entered Jerusalem to fulfill prophecy in two ways:**

1) To fulfill **Zechariah 9: 9** with his coming on an ass, a colt to be worshiped as the Messiah.
2) His triumphant entry was done on the **exact day** the sacrificial lamb was presented to the high priest to show the lamb was unblemished and without flaws. **Exodus 12** gives the regulations for the Lamb:

> **Exodus 12: 3, 5-6** [3]Speak ye unto all the congregation of Israel, saying, In **the tenth day of this month** they shall take to them **every man a lamb, according to the house of their fathers**, a lamb for an house:
>
> **[5]Your lamb shall be without blemish, a male** of the first year: ye shall take it out from the sheep, or from the goats:

> [6]And **ye shall keep it up until the fourteenth day of the same month**: and the whole assembly of the congregation of Israel **shall kill it in the evening.**

In the same way, by doing this, Jesus fulfilled the requirements of the sacrificial lamb by presenting himself and showing that he was without blemish and flawless **(without sin).** He was presenting himself so all could see **he was the perfect Lamb of God**. Then 4 days later**, on the Feasts of Unleavened Bread,** Jesus sacrificed himself for all mankind **(for all have sinned and that includes me!**) as a one-time blood sacrifice for the sins of all humanity, **"It is finished!"**

One more interesting note: this Palm Sunday, was the only time while Jesus was on earth that he allowed his chosen people to worship him as the Messiah. It was the only time he acknowledged their worship. Jesus at no other time allowed them to worship him. He came into this world as a humble servant. This detail fulfills what the prophet Zechariah foresaw—the people of Jerusalem would shout and rejoice for their King who has arrived, and it was on this first Palm Sunday that they did. (**Zechariah 9: 9)**

The fulfillment of the Feast of Succoth (Tabernacles) is yet to come. It will be at his **second coming**. He will set up his kingdom in Jerusalem and all nations will celebrate the **Feast of Tabernacles** fulfilling this prophecy below:

> **Zechariah 14: 16** [16]And it shall come to pass, **that every one that is left of all the nations** which came against Jerusalem shall even go up from year to year to worship the King, the LORD of hosts, and **to keep the feast of tabernacles.**

At Jesus' second coming, his kingdom will be set up in Jerusalem, but first another prophecy must be fulfilled:

> **Zechariah 14: 3-9** [3]Then shall **the LORD go forth, and fight against those nations**, as when he fought in the day of battle.

> **4And his feet shall stand in that day upon the mount of Olives,** which is before Jerusalem on the east, and the mount of Olives shall cleave in the midst thereof toward the east and toward the west, and there shall be a very great valley; and half of the mountain shall remove toward the north, and half of it toward the south.

This time Jesus does touch the ground at the Mount of Olives. This is his **"second coming!"**

> 5And ye shall flee to the valley of the mountains; for the valley of the mountains shall reach unto Azal: yea, ye shall flee, like as ye fled from before the earthquake in the days of Uzziah king of Judah: **and the LORD my God shall come, and all the saints with thee.**

Wow! Scripture is saying Jesus; will come again with **all of his saints.** The saints are those that met Jesus in the sky at the rapture as Paul prophesized in **1 Thessalonians 4: 17.**

> 6And it shall come to pass in that day, that the light shall not be clear, nor dark:

> 7But it shall be one day which shall be known to the LORD, not day, nor night: but it shall come to pass, **that at evening time it shall be light.**

Verses 6 and 7 describe that there will be no more darkness. The glory of God will fill the darkness, and he will be our light.

> 8And it shall be in that day, that living waters shall go out from Jerusalem; half of them toward the former sea, and half of them toward the hinder sea: in summer and in winter shall it be.

> **9And the LORD shall be king over all the earth: in that day shall there be one LORD, and his name one**

Jesus will set up his kingdom, and there will be one Lord and one God over all. In that day to come, Jesus will sit at his throne among all the people and spread his sukkah (booth) over the entire world:

> **Revelation 7: 15-17** [15]Therefore are they before the throne of God, and serve him day and night in his temple: and **he that sitteth on the throne shall dwell among them.**
>
> **[16]They shall hunger no more, neither thirst any more;** neither shall the sun light on them, nor any heat.
>
> **[17]For the Lamb which is in the midst of the throne** shall feed them, and shall lead them unto living fountains of waters: and **God shall wipe away all tears from their eyes.**

Wow! Scripture is saying Jesus will sit on his throne in the Tabernacle and dwell with us. We will no longer hunger or thirst, and God will wipe away every tear. I am looking forward to this. This will fulfill what is prophesized in **Isaiah 25: 8:**

> **[8]He will swallow up death** in victory; and **the Lord GOD will wipe away tears from off all faces;** and the rebuke of his people shall he take away from off all the earth: for the LORD hath spoken it.

God's **dwelling place** at the fulfillment of the Feast of Tabernacles comes down from heaven so he can be with his people:

> **Revelation 21: 3–5**: [3]And I heard a great voice out of heaven saying, Behold, **the tabernacle of God is with men, and he will dwell with them,** and they shall be his people, and **God himself shall be with them, and be their God.**
>
> [4]And **God shall wipe away all tears from their eyes; and there shall be no more death, neither sorrow, nor**

> **crying, neither shall there be any more pain:** for the former things are passed away.
>
> [5]And he that sat upon the throne said, Behold, I make all things new. And he said unto me, **Write: for these words are true and faithful.**

Summary: We have the seven feasts of Israel given to us in **Leviticus 23**. We can look back at the first four feasts of spring/early summer and see Jesus has already fulfilled them. There are three more feasts remaining, and I anxiously await for their fulfillment.

There is nothing to fear for those who have Jesus Christ as their Lord and Savior. We can look forward to the time of his return when all tears will be wiped from our eyes. But, for those who do not know him, I would be frightened. Judgment day will have arrived, and there is no turning back.

When the last three feasts are fulfilled, it will happen relatively fast, just as the first four feasts were fulfilled quickly. I believe the Festival of Trumpets could be fulfilled just around the corner, maybe even in **our lifetime.** Then the Day of Atonement for God's chosen people will arrive at the Lord's second coming. Right after that, the Feast Of Tabernacles will be fulfilled when Jesus sets up his kingdom on earth.

When may Christ return?

There are Bible Prophecies that can give us a view of when **Jesus could return.** As I have shown in earlier chapters, my belief is the history of the Bible to date is approximately 6,000 years old. I believe we are in the **sixth day of history.** At the end of the sixth day, the Day of Atonement for the Jews will be fulfilled and at the start of the **seventh day**, the 1,000-year reign of Jesus Christ spoken of in **chapter 20 of Revelation** will begin.

I will show the math for my belief that we are in the sixth day and headed for the day of rest—the seventh day. From Adam to Abraham is approximately 2,000 years (2 days). Abraham to Jesus' first coming is another 2,000 years (2 days). Jesus to present day is close to another 2,000 years (2 days). This is where I get the history of the world being 6,000 years old.

Now remember what Peter said in the Bible concerning **time** to God.

> **2 Peter 3: 8-10** [8]But, beloved, be not ignorant of this one thing, that **one day is with the Lord as a thousand years, and a thousand years as one day.**
>
> **[9]The Lord is not slack concerning his promise**, as some men count slackness; but is longsuffering to us-ward, **not willing that any should perish, but that all should come to repentance.**
>
> [10]But **the day of the Lord will come as a thief in the night; in the which the heavens shall pass away with a great noise**, and the elements shall melt with fervent heat, the earth also and the works that are therein shall be burned up.

Now, keeping in mind that a **thousand years is like a day to God**, we can reread what I covered in other chapters, another prophecy of his second coming in **Hosea 6: 1-3.** It is a Messianic prophecy of the Messiah coming after the destruction of Israel. He will restore his people after **2 days (approx. 2,000 years),** and they will live in his presence on the **third day—"The Millennium." The scripture reads:**

> [1]Come, and let us return unto the LORD: **for he hath torn**, and he will heal us**; he hath smitten**, and he will bind us up.
>
> **[2]After two days (2,000 years!) will he revive us**: **in the third day** he will raise us up, and **we shall live in his sight.**

Prophecy says after two days 2,000 years, God will restore Israel; and on the third day they will be raised and they will live with God in his sight. The first part of verse 2 has already been fulfilled. We know from history books written, the temple was destroyed in **70 A.D.** by the Romans; and its entire people were scattered throughout the world **(nearly 2,000 years ago—2 days in God's time).** In 1948, Israel was restored; and in 1967, during the Six Day War, Israel reclaimed Jerusalem to **fulfill the prophecy of its restoration.**

> 3Then shall we know, **if we follow on to know the LORD**: his going forth is prepared as the morning; and **he shall come unto us as the rain**, as the latter and former rain unto the earth.

The Holy Spirit is going to come upon the children of Israel like rain for those who follow and know the Lord.

Now using 2 Peter 3: 8, we see that God has given us another way to track his timetable of history, and also confirms that a day is like a thousand years to God. In Hosea, scripture speaks of Israel destruction and exile and that it would last **2 days (approx. 2,000 years).** Then they would be restored on the **third day- it happened!** Now we await the complete fulfillment of Hosea when Jesus will return and live on earth with all mankind.

For Prophesy, remember also the Jewish calendar is different than our own. The way they count days, any part of a day is considered **one full day** (Example: from dusk to midnight would be counted as one full day. Also, from midnight to dawn would count as one full day). That is why Jesus' resurrection is counted as **three full days.** Even though it was from 3:00 P.M. Friday when his body was taken down from the cross, and it was dusk when he was buried, that was the first day. Saturday or the Sabbath day would be the second day. When Jesus arose from the grave on Sunday morning, it was counted as the third day.

We are waiting for God's timetable to **be completely fulfilled**, when Israel will recognize the **one they have pierced** (Jesus) as their Messiah and be completely restored. Then the Day of Atonement **will be fulfilled**. We are waiting for **the Feast of Tabernacles to be fulfilled** and his kingdom set up on earth in Jerusalem. We are waiting for Israel to live in his presence, as well as all believers from all nations. At the end of the dry bones vision in **Ezekiel 37,** it prophesizes the rebirth of Israel in the last days, It also tells us that God's dwelling place, his sanctuary, his tabernacle will be among his people **forever.**

> **Ezekiel 37: 27-28:** [27] My **dwelling place will be with them**; **I will be their God**, and they will be my people. [28] Then the nations will know that I the LORD make **Israel holy**, when **my sanctuary is among them forever**.' **(NIV)**

According to my understanding of God's timetable, the time of Jesus' return could be near. **Seven is the number for completeness**. It took six days of work for God to complete creation and then he took a day of rest—the **seventh day**. Our workweek is patterned on his example. We are to work six days, and on the seventh (**Sabbath**) we should rest **(Exodus 35: 2).** I believe God's six days of creation is also is a pattern for when he will return. Doing the math again, it was approximately **4,000 years (4 days)** of history written in the Bible from Adam to Jesus. It has been another nearly **2,000 years (2 days) from** Jesus' resurrection to the present. We are approaching the **seventh day** when Jesus may appear **to rule and reign forever**. The work will be completed for the harvest of souls, and we will celebrate the Feast of Tabernacles **for a thousand years (The Seventh day).**

Note: I am not making any predictions of when Jesus will return. I am setting no dates. I am only reading the signs that foreshadow the fulfillment of prophecy. Only God the Father knows the exact day and hour. I only pray that you are ready to meet him when he comes.

> **Matthew 24: 36:** [36]But of that day and hour knoweth **no man, no**, not the angels of heaven, **but my Father only.**

In the meantime, we are between feasts. It is the time of the harvest. We should be out in the fields to win souls for Jesus. Share Jesus with your loved ones and friends.

God loves you and so do I!

Feast 8 - The Feasts of Chanukah and Feast 9 - Purim

Chapter 33

The two feasts of Hanukkah and Purim were not demanded by God to keep, they were added much later for the Jews to remember what God had done for them. In reading the stories that inspired these two feasts, you will see they both point to the Messiah. It is another way God has revealed that Jesus Christ is real.

The Feast of Chanukah; Hanukkah; **Dedication**; Lights date back nearly 22 centuries and is a joyous celebration done in the month of December. It is celebrated with lights and gift giving (especially money) and charity for the poor. Chanukah dates back **to December twenty-fifth, 165 B.C**. It celebrates the triumph of the Jewish fight to worship their **one true God** when Antiochus IV, one of the lines of Syrian-Greek monarchs, ruled the northern branch of Alexander the Great collapsed empire. He imposed on the Jews the pagan religion Hellenism and made Judaism illegal.

The collapse of Alexander's empire was prophesized about in **Daniel chapter 8** between 605 and 530 B.C.

> 19And he said, Behold, I will make thee know what shall be in the last end of the indignation: for at the time appointed the end shall be.

[20]**The ram** which thou sawest **having two horns are the kings of Media and Persia (The kingdoms of Babylon and Persia).**

[21]And **the rough goat is the king of Grecia (Alexander the Great and his Empire)**: and the great horn that is between his eyes is **the first king (Alexander himself)**.

[22]Now that being broken, whereas **four stood up** for it, **four kingdoms shall stand up out of the nation**, but not in his power.

The scripture above reveals the first world kingdoms would be the kingdom of Babylon and the kingdom of Persia. After this the king of Greece would rule the world and it happened with Alexander the Great. With his death in 323 B.C. it was divided into five kingdoms and then finally into the four Kingdoms in 301 B.C., which fulfilled the prophecy Daniel foresaw hundreds of years earlier.

Jesus celebrated the feast of Chanukah:

John 10: 22-23: [22]And it was at Jerusalem the **feast of the dedication**, and it was winter.

[23]And **Jesus walked** in the temple in Solomon's porch.

When Antiochus IV imposed on the Israelites the pagan religion Hellenism and made Judaism illegal; history shows that Judah Maccabee and his band of Jewish fighters were impossibly outnumbered, yet they won one miraculous victory after another. In 164 B.C., they recaptured the temple in Jerusalem and cleansed, purified, and rededicated it to God. On the 25th day of the Jewish month of Kislev (December), the feast of Chanukah was born. The **Menorah** (candlestick), which symbolizes God's presence, was rekindled.

The festival is also known as the **"Feast of Dedication" or "Feast of Lights."** It celebrates the **miracle of 8 days**. At the lighting of the menorah, at the first dedication in 165 B.C., they did not have enough oil to keep the Menorah lit, which was required by God's law to always be burning. In fact, there was only enough to keep the Menorah lit for one day, and it took 7 days to make ready more oil. The miracle is that the menorah stayed lit eight days, giving enough time to make more.

One thing about the Menorah is that it is made up of eight smaller candles and one larger candle. The smaller candles symbolize the believers, and the larger center candle symbolizes Jesus.

> **John 1: 9:** [9]The **true light (Jesus) that gives light to every man** was coming into the world. **(NIV)**
>
> **John 8: 12:** [12]Then spake Jesus again unto them, saying, **I am the light of the world:** he that followeth me shall not walk in darkness, but **shall have the light of life.**

As believers, we should let our light shine and not keep it hidden:

> **Mathew 5: 14-16**: [14]Ye are the light of the world**. A city that is set on an hill cannot be hid.**
>
> [15]Neither do men light a candle, and put it under a bushel, but on a candlestick; and it giveth light unto all that are in the house.
>
> **[16]Let your light so shine before men,** that they may see your good works, and **glorify your Father which is in heaven.**

The miracle of the eight days is very prophetic. We know that it is recorded in scripture that God created everything in 7 days (six days of work and on the seventh day God rested). In **Exodus 20 verses 8–11,** God gives us our workweek modeled after his 7 days of creation. Seven is the number for completeness. I believe the eighth day will be the miracle of heaven and God dwelling with us. It will be when all prophecy will be made complete. The Millennial reign of Jesus on earth (the seventh day) will close, and Satan, who was bound during that 1,000 years, will have one last chance at the nations (mankind) who lived through the tribulation (**Revelation 20). It will last a short time, and then Satan will be thrown into the Lake of Fire forever! This will begin the eighth day that is everlasting, where time will no longer exist or have meaning.**

> **Revelation 20: 10** [10]**And the devil that deceived them was cast into the lake of fire and brimstone**, where the beast and the false prophet are, **and shall be tormented day and night for ever and ever.**

In day eight, after the "**Great White Throne Judgment**," the old will have passed away; everything will be made new, and **only believers will be there.**

> **Revelation 21: 1- 5** [1]And I saw **a new heaven and a new earth: for the first heaven and the first earth were passed away;** and there **was no more sea.**

The term "sea" is often referred to as "Gentiles" or "non-believers"—they will not be in heaven.

> [2]And I John saw the holy city, **new Jerusalem**, coming down from God out of heaven, **prepared as a bride adorned for her husband.**

Verse 2 and 3 describe a new heaven and a new earth. It will be a transformation where they will be joined together, and God will dwell with his people.

> [3]And I heard a great voice out of heaven saying, Behold, **the tabernacle of God is with men, and he will dwell with them, and they shall be his people, and God himself shall be with them, and be their God.**

> [4]And **God shall wipe away all tears from their eyes**; and **there shall be no more death**, neither sorrow, nor crying,

> neither shall there be any more pain: **for the former things are passed away.**
>
> 5And he that sat upon the throne said, Behold, **I make all things new**. And he said unto me, **Write: for these words are true and faithful.**

I look forward to that day when God wipes every tear from our eyes, and there will be no more sorrow, crying, or pain. How joyous a time it will be, and it will be everlasting—It starts on the eighth day in God's timetable.

The Feast of Purim

The Feast of **Purim** is "**The Holiday of Joy**." It is a time to dress up, drink, and be merry while remembering how the Jews in Persia narrowly escaped annihilation thanks to the bravery of **Queen Esther**. It is celebrated with noisemakers. The time to celebrate Purim is in Adar (twelfth month of the Jewish calendar—February or March) on the 14th and 15th, **the last full moon of the year.**

THE FOUR-MAIN MITZVOT (meaning "commandments") OF PURIM

1. **Megillat Esther**: Jews read the story of Purim in the evening and the next day. Whenever the evil character **Haman** is mentioned, they make as much noise as possible to **blot out his name and his memory!**
2. **Send gifts of food** to at least one friend or relative, because Purim is a time of love and friendship between Jews.
3. **Give money to the poor** because Purim is a time of sharing, caring, and helping.
4. **Eat a festive Purim meal** on the afternoon of Purim.

Purim is costume time. Purim tells of the story written in the **Book of Ester**. Almost 2,500 years ago, the Babylonian King Nebuchadnezzar destroyed the Holy Temple in Jerusalem. The Jewish people were sent away from the land of Israel and were forced to live in Babylonia. Fifty years later, Babylonia was defeated by Persia.

The story of Esther opens with the Persian King, Xerxes, hosting a wild celebration; and the drunken king began to brag about his queen Vashti and how she was the most beautiful woman in the kingdom. On the last day of the feast, he commanded her to come and dance before the crowd. But Vashti, was the proud granddaughter of the cruel Nebuchadnezzar, and refused to appear. In a fit of anger, Xerxes had her killed.

Now Xerxes needed a new queen. The king's personal attendants proposed a search for a beautiful young virgin to replace the fallen queen. The search began, and young virgins from across the empire were brought in to compete to be the new queen.

Now, there was a **Jewish exile named Mordecai** who had a lovely cousin named **Hadassah,** also known by the **Persian name Esther**. When Esther was made one of the chosen competitors, Mordecai forbid Esther to reveal her nationality. To make a long story short, **Esther becomes Queen**.

Later in the story, Mordecai saves the day when he uncovers a plot to kill King Xerxes. After this, a man named Haman was elevated to the highest of all nobles. By the order of the king, all were to pay homage to Haman; but **Mordecai refused**. By homage, the king's order was the same as to worship Haman. Mordecai could not worship a man, but only the one true God. He had no choice but refuse. Of learning this, Haman was outraged and persuaded the King to destroy all the Jewish people, **to wipe out the Jewish race from the land.** Haman had gallows built with the intention of hanging Mordecai for his offense of not honoring him.

Interestingly that, no matter where you look in history, including present day, the Jews are the most hated people in the world to ever have lived. This only makes sense to me because Satan hates the chosen people who brought us the Messiah, Jesus Christ.

Mordecai was able to learn beforehand of the king's edict to kill and annihilate the Jews, and convinced Esther, now the new queen, to help the Jews. Esther asked Mordecai to have the Jews in the city of **Susa** fast and pray for her for **three days**. During that time, Esther held a banquet for the king and Haman.

Esther had found much favor with the king, so much so, **that any request she would make, he would honor.** The time came when she made her request. She exposed her own nationality to the king **and asked him to spare her people** the Jews. She also exposed the vile **Haman as the real adversary.** At this, the king had Haman hanged on the gallows meant for Mordecai. According to Persian law, **it was impossible to change a decree stamped with the royal seal, so the king could not cancel the decree against the Jews. But Mordecai was given the royal signet ring to issue whatever new decrees he could think of to help save the Jews**. Mordecai wrote a new decree that gave every Jew the right to assemble and protect himself and to kill any enemy that might attack him. It also gave the right for the Jews to plunder the properties of their enemies. In the end, the Jewish people did **triumph** over all their enemies.

The book of Esther is the only book in the Bible **where God is never mentioned.** That does not mean **he is not there. I see God in this story, I see Jesus in this story.** I see a battle that was taking place in the spiritual realm, and once again God was revealing Jesus to us by using the true history of his chosen people. This is what I see in my spirit:

I see **Haman** representing our most vile enemy, **Satan**. He utterly seeks to destroy mankind completely. He has built spiritual gallows that he wishes to kill us by. The Bible speaks of Satan:

> **1 Peter 5: 8:** [8]Be sober, be vigilant; because **your adversary the devil**, as a roaring lion, walketh about, **seeking whom he may devour:**

Our Lord Jesus tells us the devil is real!

In the parable of the Weeds, Jesus explains in **Matthew 13: 38-39:** [38]**The field is the world**; **the good seed are the children of the kingdom**; but the **tares (weeds, symbolizing unbelievers.)** are the children of the wicked one;

[39]**The enemy that sowed them is the devil**; the harvest is the end of the world; and the reapers are the angels.

In the parable of the Sower,

Jesus explains in **Luke 8: 11-12:** [11]Now the parable is this: **The seed is the word of God.**

[12]Those by the way side are they that hear; **then cometh the devil, and taketh away the word out of their hearts, lest they should believe and be saved.**

I see King Xerxes representing the most powerful King. What he says goes. He cannot even undo his own decrees once He makes them law**. God the Father is the most powerful King**. He reigns in heaven. **What he says goes. In fact, his decrees cannot be broken, and they haven't.** His first decrees came in Genesis when he commanded Adam and Eve not to eat of the **"Tree of Knowledge."**

Why did God not want them to eat from this tree?First, God warned if you were to eat of it, **you would surely die!** Death came into the world because our first parents ate of the tree. Worse yet, mankind was changed. Satan lied to the woman Eve, telling her she would not die if she ate of the tree; but he told the truth that she would become like God, **knowing good and evil. God "NEVER" intended us to know "EVIL."** God was forced to drive Adam and Eve from the garden, or they could have continued eating from the Tree of Life and living forever **without God, NEVER AGAIN TO BE ABLE TO HAVE A RELATIONSHIP WITH THEIR CREATOR.**

Genesis 3: 22-23 [22]And **the LORD God (Elohim) said,** Behold, **the man is become as one of us, to know good and evil**: and now, lest he put forth his hand, and take also of **the tree of life, and eat, and live for ever**:

[23]**Therefore the LORD God sent him forth from the garden of Eden**, to till the ground from whence he was taken.

God had to kick mankind out of the garden. God cursed the entire universe he created because of our sin. He made this decree he could not change.

> **Genesis 3: 17-19** [17]And unto Adam he said, Because thou hast hearkened unto the voice of thy wife, and **hast eaten of the tree**, of which I commanded thee, saying, Thou shalt not eat of it: **cursed is the ground for thy sake; in sorrow shalt thou eat of it all the days of thy life;**
>
> [18]Thorns also and thistles shall it bring forth to thee; and thou shalt eat the herb of the field;
>
> [19]In the sweat of thy face shalt thou eat bread, **till thou return unto the ground; for out of it wast thou taken: for dust thou art, and unto dust shalt thou return.**

This decree is doomsday for all of us. God cursed us all to death for our sins. **But praise be to God; he made another decree just before this decree** that would have doomed us to everlasting death:

> **Genesis 3: 14- 15** [14]And the LORD God said unto **the serpent (Satan)**, Because thou hast done this, **thou art cursed above all** cattle, and above every beast of the field; upon thy belly shalt thou go, and dust shalt thou eat all the days of thy life:
>
> **[15]And I will put enmity between thee and the woman, and between thy seed and her seed; it shall bruise thy head, and thou shalt bruise his heel.**

God made this first decree against Satan that saves us. God cursed Satan first and prophesized that a seed of Eve would crush his head. **This seed is not of Adam.** As more and more scripture is revealed by God throughout the Bible, we know the seed that defeats Satan is the Messiah, and He is the Son of God; and scripture is fulfilled to show the Messiah is Jesus Christ. This is where Esther and Mordecai come in. They both represent what Jesus has done for us. God has allowed Jesus, just like King Xerxes allowed Mordecai, **to make a new decree to save us**. And like Esther**, Jesus is at the throne of God right now acting as our intercessor, our mediator.**

> **Hebrews 9: 15:** [15]And for this cause **he (Jesus) is the mediator of the new testament (The New Testament is our new decree that saves us and cannot be changed!)**, that by means of death, **for the redemption of the transgressions that were under the first testament (when God cursed Adam and all his offspring to die in Genesis 3: 17-19),** they which are called might **receive the promise of eternal inheritance.**

Just as Esther made intercession for her people to the king, Jesus sits at the right hand of God, as **our intercessor:**

> **Hebrews 7: 24-25** [24]**But this man (Jesus), because he continueth ever, hath an unchangeable priesthood**.
>
> [25]Wherefore **he is able also to save them** to the uttermost that come unto God by him**, seeing he ever liveth to make intercession for them.**

God, being righteous, judges sin harshly. His first decree told us exactly how he is going to deal with sin. **There is no escape. His decree was final!** Eternal separation from God, He decreed, was just punishment for our sins. The other nature of God is that He is also a merciful and loving Father. **This is the God I serve!** So he let his Son decree a new law. Just like Esther, **Jesus went to bat for us**. Jesus is the only one who could; there is no one else who could.

In the story of Esther, she was afraid to approach the king with her request, for it was forbidden to come before the king without being invited. To come uninvited was punishable by death. There was only one exception to this, and that was if the king was pleased with you and extended his scepter to you. Esther found favor with the most powerful king:

Esther 4: 11 [11]All the king's servants, and the people of the king's provinces, do know, **that whosoever**, whether man or women, **shall come unto the king into the inner court, who is not called, there is one law of his to put him to death, except such to whom the king shall hold out the golden sceptre**, that he may live:

See what God is saying to us above?If God does not call us, we will never be able to approach him. To try without being called is punishable by death—**it is the Law!** In order to approach God, we must be pleasing to God so that he will hold out his golden scepter to us. How can we get God to hold out his scepter to us?**Simple**—by believing in his Son that He resurrected from the grave after **three days.**

Esther 5: 1-3 [1]Now it came to pass **on the third day**, that Esther put on her royal apparel, and **stood in the inner court** of the king's house, over against the king's house: and the king sat upon his royal throne in the royal house, over against the gate of the house.

Look at the parallel story above with Jesus. Esther waited **three days** to approach the king. Jesus stayed in the grave and Sheol (Hades) for **three days** before he approached his Father. After his resurrection, Jesus put on his royal apparel and went up to meet Father God.

[2]And it was so, **when the king saw Esther the queen standing in the court, that she obtained favour in his sight: and the king held out to Esther the golden sceptre that was in his hand.** So Esther drew near, and touched the top of the sceptre.

[3]Then said the king unto her, What wilt thou, queen Esther? and **what is thy request?** it shall be even given thee to the half of the kingdom.

Esther has found favor with the king, She has been offered the king's scepter and now anything she asks of the king will be granted. In the same way, **our Lord Jesus found favor with God!**

> **Matthew 3:17** [17]And lo a voice from heaven, saying, **This is my beloved Son, in whom I am well pleased.**

And God, whose first decree condemned us all for our sins, has granted Jesus the power to make his new decree—we must be **"born again":**

> **John 3: 5-8** [5]Jesus answered, Verily, verily, I say unto thee, **Except a man be born of water and of the Spirit, he cannot enter into the kingdom of God.** [6]That which is born of the flesh is flesh; **and that which is born of the Spirit is spirit.**
>
> [7]Marvel not that I said unto thee, **Ye must be born again.**
>
> [8]The wind bloweth where it listeth, and thou hearest the sound thereof, but canst not tell whence it cometh, and whither it goeth: so is every one that is **born of the Spirit.**

Jesus declares we must be "BORN AGAIN!" We must be born of the Spirit of God. How do we become "born again?" We become born again when we do as **John 3: 16** states:

> [16]For God so loved the world, that he gave his only begotten Son, **that whosoever believeth in him should not perish, but have everlasting life.**

The ending of the chapter of Esther is fantastic. You can see God the Father paying tribute to God the Son in the closing chapter of Esther through the great King Xerxes paying tribute to Mordecai the Jew and making him **second in rank. Mordecai represents Jesus the triumphant Messiah being paid homage by believers who are represented by the Jewish people. He is the greatest, above**

everyone, and his followers worship him for the good work he has done for their welfare. See Jesus in chapter 10:

> [1]And the **king Ahasuerus (Xerxes—representing Father God)** laid a tribute upon the land, and upon the isles of the sea.
>
> [2]And all the acts of his power and of his might, and **the declaration of the greatness of Mordecai (representing Jesus, God the Father declares his greatness!)**, whereunto **the king advanced him**, are they not written in the book of the chronicles of the kings of Media and Persia?
>
> **[3]For Mordecai the Jew was next unto king Ahasuerus (Jesus is God the Son, second only to God the Father)**, and **great among the Jews (representing believers)**, and **accepted** of the **multitude of his brethren, seeking the wealth of his people**, and speaking peace to all **his seed. (Believers are the children of God!)**

God has given us endless ways to see him in scripture. He has done the same using the story of Esther and Mordecai. By using all of scripture, you can use many paintbrushes to see the picture God is painting. God loved us so much; He justified us by our having faith in his Son only. We cannot earn our way to heaven... **it is a free gift**. By believing in his Son, you can be **born again** into eternal life. Please take the offer of this free gift **while you can! It is God's new decree!**

God loves you and so do I!

Passover Re-Visited - Leviticus 23: 4-8

Chapter 34

Passover, according to Zola Levitt, is **"the Crown Jewel"** of all the festivals given by God for the Jews to remember and celebrate. The celebration tells the 3,500-year-old story of the Jewish people being brought out of slavery from Egypt and being planted into the Promised Land by God after they had wandered in the desert for forty years. You can read this great story of deliverance in the **book of Exodus**.

Jesus, while on earth**, celebrated this feast**. In fact, we read that it was on the last night of his life that he was celebrating Passover with his disciples. Christians around the world celebrate a part of the Passover meal every time we take communion. We do it in remembrance of Jesus and his **"Last Supper"** we read about in the gospels.

> **Matthew 26: 17:** [17]Now the first day of **the feast of unleavened bread** the disciples came to Jesus, saying unto him, Where wilt thou that **we prepare for thee to eat the passover?**
>
> **Luke 22: 19-20 [19]And he took bread, and gave thanks, and brake it, and gave unto them, saying, This is my body which is given for you: this do in remembrance of me.**

[20]Likewise also **the cup after supper**, saying, **This cup is the new testament in my blood, which is shed for you.**

The Jewish Passover meal has so many symbolisms in it. They are fully revealed as to what they symbolize in the New Testament. In this chapter, I will go through the Passover meal that Zola performed for me on video, and point out the parallels between the deliverance story of Passover and the deliverance story of Jesus Christ. **I pray you can see Jesus.**

It is interesting that the first Passover came after 400 years of silence from God. God was silent during the entire time of their captivity in Egypt. God spoke again at their deliverance through Moses. In the same way, Jesus came into the world for our deliverance after 400 years of silence from God. The Old Testament writings ended with the prophets proclaiming the coming of the Messiah around 450 – 400 B.C. The New Testament picks up with the gospels, which proclaim the Messiah (Jesus) has arrived.

1.) **The Passover meal begins with the lighting of the candles—by a woman.** The symbolism is this: just as the woman brings light to the Passover meal, a woman brought the "Light of the World" into being—her name was Mary.
2.) **The woman, after** lighting the candles sings this exaltation:

"Blessed art Thou O Lord our **God King of the Universe** who hast sanctified thy Commandments and bade us to kindle the Festival Lights."

3.) **Unleavened bread.** All leavened bread must be out of the house. Leaven symbolizes "sin," and it must be taken away during Passover. The unleavened bread symbolizes our Lord Jesus Christ who is pure and without sin.

> **1 Corinthians 7:** [7]**Purge out therefore the old leaven**, that ye may be a new lump, as ye are unleavened. For even **Christ our passover is sacrificed for us:**

4.) **Four cups of wine.** Each cup is used for something different in the meal. **The first cup** is for sanctification. The father of the house looks over the table and sees that everything is in its place and ready to begin the meal and sanctifies the table with the **first cup of wine**. It is now time to begin the meal.

5.) **Three loaves of unleavened bread.** The three loaves of unleavened bread are individually placed in compartment bags. After the father gives a blessing, the **middle loaf is taken out** and broken in two. It is then separated and hidden from the other two loaves. The middle loaf will be brought back later in the meal.

6.) **Why three loaves?** Why the middle loaf broken, placed in a bag, and hidden from the rest of the loaves?**This is a beautiful picture God is painting.** The symbolism God is using shows us **the Trinity**. Jesus, being the Second Person of the Trinity, is the middle loaf that is **being broken.** The breaking of the bread symbolizes the whipping, beating, and crucifixion he went through for our deliverance from sin. The middle loaf **is placed in a bag and hidden**. This points us to the time **Jesus was buried** and spent time in the tomb and Sheol for us. The middle loaf, when **brought back** later in the meal, symbolizes the resurrection of our Lord Jesus Christ.

At this time the youngest child sings out four important questions. He sings out and asks these four questions pertaining to: "Why is this night different than any other night?" The four questions are:

1) Other nights we may eat any kind of bread, why on this night must we eat **unleavened bread only**?
2) Other nights we may eat any kind of herb, why on this night must we eat bitter herbs only?
3) Other nights we dip not even once, why on this night must we dip twice?
4) Other nights we may eat while sitting or reclining, why on this night must we eat while reclining only?

After the child finishes the song, the father goes directly into the book of Exodus and begins teaching of the Israelites exodus out of the land of Egypt. Each question above pertains to part of the story the father is going to tell.

From **Exodus chapter 12**: This night is different than any other night because there is going to be a "**blood sacrifice.**" At the very first Passover, God told Moses and Aaron to have all of the households take a lamb that is a one-year-old male (prime of life), **without defect,** and slaughter the animal at twilight. Take the **blood of the lamb** and put it around your doorpost. God then instructed them to eat the meat roasted over fire with **bitter herbs and bread made without yeast** and eat it in haste, for it is the **Lord's Passover.** God told Moses on this night he will pass through Egypt and strike down every **firstborn** of man and animal. God is going to pass judgment on all the gods of Egypt... but when God sees the **blood, he will pass over you**; no destruction will touch you when God strikes Egypt. **THIS IS THE GOSPEL MESSAGE!**

Jesus is our sacrificial Lamb of God who became our Passover. He was in his prime of life when he began his ministry and offered himself at the cross for humanity's sin. Egypt symbolizes the entire world, which is sinful in God's eyes. At the first Passover, God judged and punished Egypt for its sins by slaying every **firstborn** son of Egypt. The **firstborn son of Egypt** symbolizes every sinful human being—man or woman, (All have sinned.) God in his great wisdom is prophesizing to tell us it will happen again at the **"end of times."** Every firstborn of Adam (**we all start here**) will be judged and cast down into the Lake of Fire **except for those who are "born again" of the Spirit.**

> **John 3: 5-7 [5]Jesus answered**, Verily, verily, I say unto thee, **Except a man be born of water and of the Spirit**, he cannot enter into the kingdom of God.
>
> [6]That which is born of the flesh is flesh; and **that which is born of the Spirit is spirit.**
>
> [7]Marvel not that I said unto thee, **Ye must be born again.**

Only those who are covered by the Lamb of God's blood by accepting Jesus Christ as Lord and Savior **have a guarantee** they will be saved and given eternal life.

Remember this, Jesus gave his life **for everyone**, not just Christians. **No one is born a Christian.** We are all born into this world as a son of Adam, with his sinful nature. You only become a Christian by being **born again through faith in Jesus**. There is no other way. My wife Helen tells our children they cannot make it into heaven on their parent's shirttails; they have to do it on their own and be born again by having faith in Jesus Christ. We all have a free will to accept or reject his free gift of salvation—it is up to each individual.

There is so much more to see in the love story that God is painting in the Passover meal. Let us continue to see what God is revealing to us.

The Passover Plate

The plate of Passover set before each person has items on it to help tell the story of Passover as well. There are two stories actually taking place in this meal. The first is for the Jew and his exodus out of Egypt, and the second is for the Christian believer, **our own Passover.**

1) **Unleavened bread. This night!** Leavened bread is made with yeast and causes bread to rise. Yeast symbolizes "sin" in scripture; and just as bread puffs up from yeast, our sins puff up our pride. **Jesus was without sin. He is the bread of life.** We must humble ourselves and take Jesus into our lives.
2) **Bitter Herbs. This night!** Bitter herbs symbolize the 400 years of captivity the Jews had suffered under the Pharaohs and the Egyptians. For the Christian it symbolizes the years we were captive in our sins, slaves to our bitter enemies—Satan and his demons, our life before Christ.
3) **Dipping. This night!** The Passover meal has two items to dip your food in. First, a bowl of **salt water** to symbolize the Red Sea, and second, **horseradish** that can bring tears to a man. The idea is to weep over the slavery in Egypt. On the Passover

plate, there is parsley that symbolizes young and green Israel. You dip the parsley once for Israel into the salt water, for they came out of the Red Sea by God's love and protection; and you dip again for the Egyptian army and then eat the parsley, for they were engulfed by the sea and drowned. For the Christian, dipping symbolizes the Christian baptism. We are dipped into the water, and we come out of it unharmed. It will happen again at our resurrection from the grave.

Dipping was done at the Last Supper. Jesus used this to show which disciple was going to betray him.

> **Matthew 26: 23-25** [23]And he answered and said, **He that dippeth his hand with me in the dish, the same shall betray me.**
>
> [24]The Son of man goeth as it is written of him: but **woe unto that man by whom the Son of man is betrayed!** it had been good for that man if he had not been born.
>
> **[25]Then Judas, which betrayed him, answered and said, Master, is it I? He said unto him, Thou hast said.**

4) **Reclining. This night!** Celebrating the Passover meal is to be reclining because it is a long night telling the story. It symbolizes that it was God who freed the Israelites from their Egyptian enslavement. It was not by their own work that they were set free. As Christians, we can see it as symbolizing the **grace of God! By grace and not by works we are saved.** It is hard to do work while reclining.

At this time, **the second cup of wine** is introduced. It is spilled more than it is drunk. It is spilled on a clean, white plate once for each of the plagues God sent on the Egyptians. It tells the sad story of the plagues, and the idea is the wine looks like blood. Blood will be shed—there will be death. For the Christian, **we will avoid the second death** that is everlasting, Halleluiah! But for the non-believer it will be like the Egyptians; this death will be **the second death** that is everlasting. Please heed this warning!

> **Revelations 21: 8** [8]But the fearful, and **unbelieving**, and the abominable, and murderers, and whoremongers, and sorcerers, and idolaters, and all liars, **shall have their part in the lake** which burneth with fire and brimstone: **which is the second death.**

On the Passover plate are many other symbols for the Jews and Christians alike.

1) The lamb shank bone for the Jew symbolizes the sacrificial lamb. For the Christian, it is the sacrificial "Lamb of God" who takes away the sins of the world.

   > **John 1:29** [29]The next day John seeth Jesus coming unto him, and saith, **Behold the Lamb of God, which taketh away the sin of the world.**

2) A mix of apples, nuts, and cinnamon is on the plate reminding the Jews when Pharaoh decreed them to make bricks without straw. For the Christian, it would remind us of when we did not have Christ in our lives and were trying to do things on our own without him.
3) Today, an egg is on the plate. This did not come from the ordinances of the Passover. It was added much later, during the time of the Babylonian exile. To the Ancient Babylonians, the egg symbolized fertility. An Easter day hunt is really looking to get pregnant. So is the Easter bunny, another pagan symbol for fertility that found its way into our celebration of the resurrection of Jesus that should be rightfully called **"Firstfruits"** instead of Easter.

Our word Easter came during the captivity of the Jews in Babylon. The Babylonians worshiped the goddess of "fertility" named **Ishtar,** and this is where we get the name Easter. Jesus is the **Firstfruits** that has risen from the dead; and as believers, where there is a first fruit, there will be a second, and a third, and then a forth, and so on. This is a better description for the resurrection.

> **1 Corinthians 15: 22-23** [22]For as in Adam all die, even so in Christ shall all be made alive.
>
> [23]But **every man in his own order**: **Christ the firstfruits**; afterward they that are Christ's at his coming.

Just as the egg has no symbolic meaning for the Jews, it does not have any meaning for the Christian.

On this special Passover plate is the entire story of their exodus out of Egypt and their coming into the Promised Land. For the Christian, our entire story of Salvation is on this special plate. The bitter herbs remind believers what they were like before we were saved and knew Jesus. The salt water is our coming out of baptism by the Holy Spirit, and now we walk in the desert of life where life can be hard; and we have troubles, but we are always relying on God and always marching forward toward our Promised Land—**heaven.**

Jericho, it is the place where the Israelites entered their Promised Land. It is a beautiful place and still is today. The leader of the chosen people at the crossing into the Promised Land was Joshua. **Joshua = Yeshua = Jesus.** The meaning for the name is **Salvation. Is it a coincidence that two leaders of the chosen people**—one, the leader of the Israelites into the Promised Land, and the other, the leader of the believers in **"Yeshua"** (Jesus), who will lead us into heaven, have the same name, and the **name means "salvation?"Or did God plan it that way?**

Just as Joshua had the priest sound the **trumpets** and the people **"shout"** when they entered Jericho (**Joshua 6: 15- 16**), Jesus will come for his children in the same way.

> **1 Thessalonians 4: 16** [16]For **the Lord himself** shall descend from heaven **with a shout**, with the voice of the arch-angel, and with the **trump (Trumpet) of God**: and **the dead in Christ shall rise first:**

The Middle Loaf is Brought Back

At the end of the Passover meal, the father brings back the **middle loaf** that was broken in two and hidden at the start of the meal. **It is the last thing eaten.** The two pieces from the middle loaf are taken out of the bag and broken into many pieces and eaten. This is the **"Last Supper"** we celebrate every time we receive communion. We are doing it in remembrance of our Lord Jesus Christ, and we are performing the last part of the Passover Meal that Jesus was performing the night he was arrested. As we partake of the bread, we can see that **in believers' God lives** and is in the most special place of our being—**our Holy of Holies**, our spirit. We are the temple, the tabernacle of God on earth during the harvesting of the Gentiles. His living in us is what separates us from the non-believers who do not have God living in them. This is important to know because when the Lord comes back for his church at the rapture, this will happen:

> **Matthew 24: 40-42** 40Then shall **two be in the field**; the **one shall be taken**, and the other left.
>
> 41**Two women shall be grinding** at the mill; the **one shall be taken**, and the other left.
>
> 42**Watch therefore: for ye know not what hour your Lord doth come.**

From the middle loaf being eaten, can you see the Trinity?

> **Matthew 26: 26** 26And as they were eating, **Jesus took bread**, and **blessed it**, and brake it, and gave it to the disciples, and said, Take, eat; **this is my body**.

Now **the third cup** of wine is introduced, it is called **"The Cup of Redemption."** What an appropriate name.

> **Matthew 26: 27-28** [27]And he took the cup, and **gave thanks,** and gave it to them, saying, Drink ye all of it;
>
> [28]For this is **my blood of the new testament**, which is **shed for many for the remission of sins.**

Here is something fantastic. The above scripture says Jesus **blessed the bread.** As Christians, many of us do not know what this blessing is until we realize that Jesus was a Jew, and he was following the law to the letter. He was celebrating Passover at the Last Supper, and the blessing he said over the bread was already being said for 1,500 years when he said it. The Jews have been saying this same blessing at Passover now for 3,500 years. The blessing Jesus gave at the Last Supper was:

> "Blessed art thou O Lord our God King of the universe **who bringths bread forth from the earth. "**

Wow! This blessing is so prophetic! The Jews unknowingly when they pray this blessing to God for his bringing bread forth from the ground are speaking of Jesus, who came out of the earth at his resurrection—He is **our bread of life**, who has been raised from the tomb and lives! Jesus is the Firstfruits of all who will be raised. Halleluiah, Praise God!

The same is true with the cup of wine. What is the "**prayer of thanks**" Jesus offers up to God at his last Passover meal? The Jews who celebrate Passover know! Jesus was praying this:

> "Blessed art thou O Lord of the universe, **Creator of the Fruit of the Vine."**

Wow! Jesus is thanking God for us—his believers! Believers (the church) are the fruit of the vine, and he is toasting us and giving thanks to God for us.

> **John 15: 5** [5]I am the vine, **ye are the branches**: **He that abideth in me**, and **I in him, the same bringeth forth much fruit**: for without me ye can do nothing.

The Cup of Redemption is our invitation to accept Jesus Christ. It is our choice. The cup is presented to us in the same way the Jewish invitation in marriage was practiced in the days of Jesus. The bridegroom would propose by placing a cup of wine in front of her. Jesus is making a proposal to us, through his body and shed blood.

> **John 14: 5- 6**: [5]Thomas saith unto him, Lord, we know not whither thou goest; and how can we know the way? **[6]Jesus saith** unto him, **I am the way, the truth, and the life: no man cometh unto the Father, but by me.**

In the Jewish custom, if she rejected the proposal, she would not drink from the cup and the bridegroom would go away—most likely rejected and sad... **never to return again for her**. But if she drank from the cup, he would go to his **father's house** and **prepare a place** for her. He would return for his bride only after **the father said the home was ready** for the bride. It was up to the Father, and **only he knew when** it was ready for the bridegroom to go get his bride.

> **John 14: 2** [2]In **my Father's house are many mansions**: if it were not so, I would have told you. **I go to prepare a place for you.**

> **Matthew 24:36:** [36]"No one knows about that day or hour, not even the angels in heaven, nor the Son, but **only the Father.**

When the father said it was time, the bridegroom would go get his bride, usually at night, making lots of noise so she would know and **be ready for his coming**.

Jesus teaches that his coming for his church is like a bridegroom coming for his bride in using the parable of the Ten Virgins.

> **Matthew 25: 1-4** [1]Then shall **the kingdom of heaven** be likened unto **ten virgins**, which took their lamps, and went forth to **meet the bridegroom**.
>
> [2]And **five of them were wise**, and **five were foolish.**
>
> [3]They that were **foolish took their lamps, and took no oil with them:**
>
> [4]But **the wise took oil in their vessels** with their lamps.

The oil that all ten virgins were to take for their lamps was the **Holy Spirit.** The five who were wise had **faith in the bridegroom (Jesus Christ)** and therefore took the oil of the Holy Spirit with them and were ready.

The five who were foolish **had no faith!** They refused the Cup of Wine the bridegroom offered them and therefore did not take the oil that comes by faith and were not ready for when the bridegroom would return. They symbolize the unbelievers who have **heard the salvation message of Jesus Christ but refused the cup of wine offered to them for their redemption.** Because of this, they do not have the Holy Spirit in them and are not ready for Christ's return. This is the state of the world today. Some are ready, and some are not.

> **Verse 6:** [6]And at midnight **there was a cry made**, Behold, **the bridegroom cometh**; go ye out to meet him.

Those who have faith and the oil (**Holy Spirit**) in them will go to meet the Lord. This will happen as it is written in **1 Thessalonians 4: 17.** Believers who take the oil and have the Holy Spirit in them will go to meet Jesus in the air. **This is the rapture of the church.** Those without faith are left behind.

> **Verse 8 & 9:** [8]And the foolish said unto the wise, Give us of your oil; for **our lamps are gone out.** [9]But **the wise answered**, saying, Not so; lest **there be not enough for us and you**

> **Verse 10:** [10]And while they went to buy, **the bridegroom came**; and **they that were ready went in with him to the marriage: and the door was shut.**

Verse 10 above and verses 11 and 12 below are important to understand. The five foolish virgins were left behind. They missed the rapture. They were not ready for Christ's return for his church, as were the ones who accepted his cup of wine. They symbolize the people who heard the word of God, but have rejected Jesus. They will have to go through the tribulation that the apostle John foresaw and gave us in the book of Revelation.

> **Warning: Verse 11 & 12:** [11]Afterward came also the other virgins, **saying, Lord, Lord, open to us.**
>
> [12]But he answered and said, Verily I say unto you, **I know you not.**

Now, when all is said and done, the five foolish virgins go to where the bridegroom has made his home (**heaven**) with the wise virgins (**believers**) and ask him to open the doors and let them in. What does the bridegroom (**Jesus**) say? Jesus says, **"I do not know you!" This means the five virgins represent unbelievers who never accepted the gospel message for salvation even though they heard it preached.** They never accepted the cup of wine Jesus offered when He shed his blood for mankind, and **NOW IT IS TOO LATE!**

> **Matthew 7: 22-23** [22]**Many will say to me in that day** (**day of judgment**), **Lord, Lord, have we not prophesied in thy name?** and in thy name have cast out devils? and in thy name done many wonderful works?
>
> [23]**And then will I profess unto them, I never knew you: depart from me, ye that work iniquity.**

Please do not miss your invitation; Jesus is offering it to you right now! You are reading this book; you can see what Jesus is offering—eternal life with him. There is going to be a great celebration in heaven you will not want to miss. Turn to **chapter 38** right now and accept his cup of wine.

> **Warning: Verse 13: [13]Watch therefore, for ye know neither the day nor the hour wherein the Son of man cometh.**

In this parable, you see the bridegroom, our Jesus coming for his bride—the church. It is the gospel message. Zola states, "Jesus came down from his Father's House to our house and offered us his Cup of Redemption." He spilled his blood on the cross and paid the highest price for his bride. For those who accept his cup and want to become his bride, he has left to go to his Father's house **to prepare a place for us.** Someday he is going to return for his bride, and when he does, those who are not ready will be left behind; and the **door to the kingdom will be shut.** When he comes for his bride, **he will come back with a shout!**

> **1 Thessalonians 4: 16-17** [16]For the Lord himself shall descend from heaven **with a shout**, with the voice of the archangel, and with the **trump (trumpet) of God**: and **the dead in Christ shall rise first:**
>
> [17]Then we which are alive and remain shall be caught up together with them in the clouds, to meet the Lord in the air: and so shall we ever be with the Lord.

It was the custom when the bride accepted the proposal of the bridegroom, to wear a veil to show that she is waiting for him to return. The believer's veil is his or her **"Faith."** Our faith is what makes our lamps ready and the oil full, and our lamps will not go out. **The oil comes from the Holy Spirit who fills us.**

The New Testament is our bridal contract. Jesus signed the contract with his blood.

Matthew 26: 28 [28]For this is **my blood of the new testament**, which is **shed for many for the remission of sins.**

One last thing, the **Fourth Cup in the Passover meal—what is it for?** The Jews are still waiting for Elijah to return. It is poured for the prophet Elijah.

Malachi 4: 5 [5]Behold, I will send you Elijah the prophet **before the coming of the great and dreadful day of the LORD: (Prophecy of the Messiah coming—to the Jew it will be his first coming, for the believer in Yeshua, his second coming!)**

This concludes our study of the "feasts of Israel" given by God to the chosen people to keep holy. This study only scratches the surface of what the word of God shows us in the feasts of Israel.

One thing I want you to go away with in this study is how Jesus fulfilled the prophecies of the Old Testament. One thing I hoped you picked up on was that Jesus did this **without being trained in the Torah**. In chapter 32, we saw that Jesus honored the Feast of Tabernacles. He did so even though there was a threat to his life if he were to show his face at the synagogue. He snuck in after he sent his brothers in to celebrate the feast. Once there, Jesus began to teach. All who heard him were amazed and in awe of his teaching. They could not understand how a man not taught in the Torah, a simple carpenter, could know so much. Do you wonder how Jesus could know scripture so well that he could not only teach it but also **fulfill all that was written about him in the Torah?See what they say about Jesus and his teachings:**

Jesus Teaches at the Feast – John 7: 14-16 [14]Now about the **midst of the feast Jesus went up into the temple, and taught.** [15]And the **Jews marvelled**, saying, **How knoweth this man letters, having never learned?** [16]Jesus answered them, and said, My doctrine is not mine, **but his that sent me.**

Matthew 13: 53-57 [53]And it came to pass, that when Jesus had finished these parables, he departed thence.

[54]And when he was come into his own country, **he taught them in their synagogue,** insomuch that **they were astonished**, and said, **Whence hath this man this wisdom, and these mighty works?**

[55]Is not this the carpenter's son? is not his mother called Mary? and his brethren, James, and Joses, and Simon, and Judas?

[56]And his sisters, are they not all with us? **Whence then hath this man all these things?**

[57]And they were offended in him. But Jesus said unto them, A prophet is not without honour, save in his own country, and in his own house.

Jesus fulfilled the prophecies of himself without formal training in the Torah! His knowledge did not come from man but from God!

One last word on our study of the feasts:

Much of the information presented in these chapters of the feasts came from studying God's word, and the video series that was presented by Zola Levitt Ministry. I urge you to go to his web site **www.levitt.com** and see all that he has to offer. **I am going to quote from Zola Levitt's book, "The Seven Feasts of Israel"**—pages 19 and 20 and titled "Some Conclusions." I love the insight this man has of scripture. May this bless you and help you to know Jesus is Lord over all and He is coming back.

"Now after looking over the feasts, it becomes very clear that God did a momentous thing here. He forecast the entire career of the Messiah, the Jews, the Church, and even other nations. He foresaw the tribulation period in all its agony, the presence of the

Jew and the Gentile together in the Church, and even the detail of leaving the corners of the fields for sustenance for the poor, including his Son and disciples." "He laid out the feasts in the calendar year in a manner that reflects in proportion the history of the Church. Indeed, those first three feasts, the crucifixion, burial, and resurrection, occurred very close together. Then there was the pause before the coming of the Holy Spirit. And then the long pause before the big harvest, **the Rapture of the Church." "The seven feasts reassure us about a pre-tribulation Rapture.** Surely the entire system would be wrecked if the Church were not to be rewarded at Trumpets, but would have to put in an unwarranted Day of Atonement with, unbelieving Israel in the tribulation period." "It is possible that **we can even pinpoint the day of the Antichrist's blasphemy** in the Temple at Jerusalem during the tribulation period. Since we saw that the tribulation period ends on the Day of Atonement (the Second Coming), then it must have started seven years before on the Day of Atonement. Since the Day of Atonement is on the tenth day of the seventh month, and since the Antichrist comes exactly in the midst of the tribulation period (**Daniel 9:27; Rev. 11: 1-3**), then the day of the blasphemy is at the exact 3 ½ year point, or the tenth day of the first month in the fourth year. Is there something significant about the tenth day of the first month?Well, **that is four days before Passover,** which is on 14th. God asked the Jews to select their sacrificial lamb in Egypt **exactly four days before Passover** (Exodus 12: 3), in order that they examine the lamb for blemishes before sanctifying it on Passover day. The Lord himself appropriately observed this detail, riding the donkey into Jerusalem on Palm Sunday, **four days before Passover**, so that the people might examine him before choosing Him as their lamb. **Thus we see the Antichrist will make the perfect counterfeit,** arriving at the Temple four days before Passover and **presenting himself as Almighty God.** The way we discern the true God from a false one is that Jesus Christ rode the donkey in Humility, and the Antichrist comes claiming that he is God Incarnate!" "...A working knowledge of this marvelous prophetic system builds the faith of any Bible reader, and certainly of the believers in Jesus Christ."

I want to thank Zola for his insight. The beauty of God's word is that scripture is always pointing the same way—**to Jesus!** I pray the evidence of this study of Jesus and his fulfilling the prophecies of the Old Testament and these festivals will strengthen your faith. I pray you have accepted Jesus' invitation and are hanging on to the new contract given to us by the Second Person in the Trinity—**our Lord Jesus Christ**.

As for now, we are between feasts—the Church Age. We should do what we can to win souls for Jesus Christ. We do this by sharing the word of God and by the example of how we live our lives—that means even when we are not perfect. When we are not perfect, we can lead others to Christ by admitting our mistakes (sins), seeking forgiveness from God and the one we have offended, and forgiving those who have hurt or offended us. Let Jesus shine through.

As for sharing the word of God, it can be difficult, especially time wise. The person who does not know Christ may not give you enough time to plant a seed. They would rather be left alone. This is where this book or something like it may help. They might not let you take the time to walk them through the Bible or even open it. But maybe, just maybe, they will read a few chapters of this book and be lead to Christ. Scripture teaches it is the Holy Spirit who is doing the wooing, the calling, the convicting, and opens the truth of the word of God to everyone. God has lead me to show scripture in so many ways throughout this book so everyone can see Jesus from the beginning to the end—from Genesis to Revelation. I pray there is a chapter that can make the difference that if you did not see Jesus before—you do now. May I leave you with examples of God's love for you!

> **Romans 8: 38-39** 38For I am persuaded, that neither death, nor life, nor angels, nor principalities, nor powers, nor things present, nor things to come,
>
> 39Nor height, nor depth, nor any other creature, **shall be able to separate us from the love of God, which is in Christ Jesus our Lord.**

1 John 4: 7-19 7 Beloved, **let us love one another: for love is of God**; and every one that loveth is born of God, and knoweth God.

9 In this was manifested **the love of God toward us, because that God sent his only begotten Son into the world**, that we might live through him.

10 Herein is love, **not that we loved God, but that he loved us,**

11 Beloved, **if God so loved us, we ought also to love one another**.

12 No man hath seen God at any time. **If we love one another, God dwelleth in us, and his love is perfected in us.**

13 Hereby know we that we dwell in him, and he in us, **because he hath given us of his Spirit.**

14 And we have seen and do testify that **the Father sent the Son to be the Saviour of the world.**

15 **Whosoever shall confess that Jesus is the Son of God, God dwelleth in him, and he in God.**

16 And we have known and **believed the love that God hath to us. God is love**; and he that dwelleth in love dwelleth in God, and God in him.

19 **We love him, because he first loved us.**

God loves you and so do I!

Let the Children speak

Chapter 35

My two children wrote this chapter. The first, my 14-year-old son wrote for his Bible class in school. The second is by my daughter Courtney. When she was twelve, she had a dream about her Grandmother. May these two writings speak to you.

Psalm 1
For the instructor of Bible Class
of Colin

How is it, O Lord?
That a simple mistake can turn into such a sin?
I come before you in confession, but I cannot let it go.
It is a "thorn in my flesh"
It haunts me day and night
Like a never-ending nightmare.
Some others mock me because of what I have done.
They leave me full of shame.
They will not let me forget, O Lord
Though I call upon your name.
It's a heavy burden to carry,
The mockers make it worse.
I try to forgive them, O Lord
But mocking me amuses them; to a point it's all they do.

I praise you, O Lord
You are my source of joy.
Though my fellow men will not forgive me,
You, with your **unconditional love, forget about my sin**
You forgive me and take me for who I am.
Thanks to you I can shout,
Thanks to you I can sing.
I love you Lord, you are my everything.
You have boosted my mood, and taught me a lesson.
Never again, may I sin in that way.
Never again, not another day!

By: Colin Kreh

3/4/2003

The Great Race

By: Courtney Kreh

On Monday night, April 5,2004 I had a dream that changed my life. It was the last day on earth. It was a race to Heaven. There were twelve hours until it was all over, if you did not make it to the finish line, you were going to Hell for eternity. Those who crossed the finish line, those who were saved, spent eternity with Christ. I was the second person to the finish line. The first person to reach the destination was a boy in my class named Brian. Brian, with one foot on his scooter and his helmet on, stood ready to cross the line. Pretty soon a ton of people began to arrive, but none of them crossed the line right away. They were all waiting behind to tell more people about Jesus, so that they would be in Heaven forever too. My mother and I went back to try to bring my Grandma, my mom's mother, to salvation. On our way back, we saw our neighbors and friends, Ruth and Doug, walking in the race. Ruth had her arm hooked around Doug's, who was wearing a gray pullover fleece. My mom and I went to talk to my Grandma, but she refused to accept Christ. A notice came over the P.A. System saying that there were three hours left until midnight, when the world would end and all that was left was Heaven and Hell. My mother and I had three hours to witness to my Grandma. First, I went to talk to my Grandma. She was sleeping in a bed and I woke her up to talk to her. I asked if she wanted to become a Christian and live forever in Heaven and she said no. After that, my mom and I sat on some bleachers and talked to a woman who was also sitting there. She tried to explain to us how to save my Grandma, but we did not understand what she told us. Then a younger girl, probably in her twenties, came to the bleachers.

She was pale and wore black clothes with her short, black hair. She slowly explained to us, step by step, how to witness to my Grandma. We understood what she told us, so we went to my Grandma again to attempt to save her. We went to my Grandma and did everything on the list that the young woman had told us, and Satan no longer blinded my Grandma. She accepted Jesus into her life with only a few hours left to cross the finish line into Heaven. My mother and I made it across the finish line, with my Grandma right beside us.

After that dream, nothing happened. I have not received any more dreams since the Holy Spirit sent me that one. A few months after that dream, I was in Bible class doing a worksheet. We had to look up verses throughout the Bible, and I looked up Acts 20: 24; unaware that that was not one of the verses we were supposed to look up. However, this was no accident; God led me to it to give me faith and to tell me something. Acts 20: 24 says, "However, I consider my life worth nothing to me, if only I may finish the race and complete the task the Lord Jesus Christ has given me- the task of testifying to the gospel of God's grace." **(NIV)**

It has been almost two years since the dream and the verse that God revealed to me. I have tried witnessing to my Grandma on a few rare occasions, but there was no luck. She is spiritually blinded, and by the way things are going, I believe that the only hope for her salvation is the way this dream went. I believe that God will open her eyes when she is on her deathbed and there is not much time left for her. I have faith that He will come and take her to Heaven in the end.

I had a little fun creating these words – I hope you enjoy them!

"You'll be in my heart"

Chapter 36

I did not know you for a long, long time.
I did things on my own with foolish pride.
And now I know you and things are different
You are here Lord you're here.
I am so small and you are so strong
Your arms of love keep me safe and warm.
The world will be able to see I am different
You are here Lord you're here
Because...
You'll be in my heart
Yes, you'll be in my heart
From this day on...
Now and forever more.
Yes, you'll be in my heart
No matter what they say
You'll be in my heart...
Always.
Why can't the world understand your ways?
They just don't have faith in what they cannot see.
I know I am different, deep inside me...
I pray that they could come to see...
That...
You are in my heart
Yes Lord you are in my heart

From this day on...
Now and forever more.
They do not listen to you
They do not know your words.
We need the Holy Spirit
To show them the way.
They'll see in time...
I pray.
When God calls you
You must obey.
He will lead you,
He will show you the way.
They'll see in time...
I know.
God will show them his love.
Because...
He'll be in your heart
(Invite him to come on in)
He'll be in your heart
(He will be there)
From this day on...
Now and forever more.
We'll sing, he is in our hearts
(We love you Jesus)
No matter what they say
(We thank you Jesus)
He is in our hearts...
Always.
Always...
God is with us
God will be there for us always
Always and always...
Just look all around you
Just look all around you
Just look all around you
He will be there...Always.

This is written to tell the story of a **new born again Christian who has found Jesus as his personal Savior.** The first part tells his witness of him coming to Jesus and how he will remain in his heart forever, no matter what is said to him or what happens to him.

The second part tells of his witness to others who do not know Jesus as his or her personal Savior and it is his prayer that he or she will come to know him.

Just invite him into your heart and Jesus will be there. This is my prayer for everyone.

God loves you and so do I!

Romans 3:23- All Have Sinned and Fallen Short

Chapter 37

Romans 3: 23 [23]For all have sinned, and come short of the glory of God;

Throughout the Bible, God's word teaches that **everyone has sinned and fallen short of the glory of God.** As human beings, can we ever change this?This chapter was written with this truth in mind- **we are all sinners.**

I have sinned against my God too many times. I am ashamed of my sins. I have taken a hard look at my self and see the sin; it is deep rooted in my human flesh. Outwardly, people can look at me and see a pretty good person. I love my wife and children. I do not use the Lord's name in vain. I am honest. I try to do what is right. People would say Ken Kreh is a decent person. But when I look deep down inside of myself, I can see the sin I have committed. I can see that I have not kept God's commandments. I see the filth. I see the dirt that has piled up through the years. There is sin in the past that I do not want anyone else to see. And yet, who am I kidding, God sees everything. He sees my sins and remembers them—**or does he?** We will get back to this.

Kirk Cameron, star from the TV hit "Growing Pains" and Evangelist Ray Comfort have combined forces to have a ministry called, "The Way of the Master." They have a great web site (**www.**

wayofthemaster.com) and a television program that is shown on Christian stations. Their ministry is all about sharing the Gospel message with unsaved persons, especially your own loved ones who might be the most difficult to approach about faith.

I could not learn to change and turn from my sin until I humbled myself and looked at my inward self that no one sees and admit—**I am a sinner! I have broken God's Law! I am unworthy.** I hated it when my parents, especially my father, caught me in something I knew was wrong. I feared the punishment it would bring, but more so the embarrassment it brought—especially disappointing my father who I loved so very much when I knew that **what I did was wrong! How good it felt to ask for forgiveness and because of his love for me... he did. Your heavenly Father wants to do the same, but on a much larger scale.**

The Way of the Master ministry is about showing people that we are all sinners; and having broken the commandments of God, we must turn to God for forgiveness. Once you can accept that you are a sinner, the gospel message of Jesus Christ will set you free from the burden sin causes.

The Law given to Moses—the commandments from God—are given to us in the book of **Exodus chapter 20. There are only ten!** We can put religion aside and still see if we can follow these simple commandments; what a difference it would make in everyone's life, for all of mankind.

Let us take the time together to go over all ten of God's commandments and see how well we are doing keeping his laws. Let's be honest with ourselves as we do our own personal inventory! I am going to be very honest with myself right now.

> **Commandment 1:** 1And **God spake all these words**, saying,
>
> 2I am the LORD thy God, which have brought thee out of the land of Egypt, out of the house of bondage.
>
> **3Thou shalt have no other gods before me.**

The first commandment says we shall have no other gods before the one, true God. In my own case, I had many gods; but my two worst were:

(1) I love to golf. I used to think about golf from morning to night. It was always on my mind. I always wanted to be golfing. From the time I was sixteen until the time Helen and I had our kids when I was thirty-five and beyond that, I would play golf every evening after work and most weekends; I would play at least once if not both weekend days. This did not change much after the kids were born either. I did cut back to about four times-a-week. Everything in my life took a backseat to my precious game of golf, including my wife and kids, (I hated to admit that.) Even after coming to Christ at the age of twenty-three, God did not remain first in my life. Golf remained **first**, cigarettes (see 2) were **second,** in **third place** were Helen and the kids, work was **fourth**, television fifth, and God, if he was lucky, was **sixth.**

(2) I loved to smoke. This was my second god. I was a two-pack-a day smoker for twenty years. I loved cigarettes from my coffee in the morning to my pop in the evening. Even after coming to Christ, cigarettes were my god. I would sometimes skip church on Sundays because I could not bear to be away from my precious cigarettes.

Did I keep the first commandment?Do you fair better than I?

> **Commandment 2:** [4]Thou shalt not make unto thee any graven image, or any likeness of any thing that is in heaven above, or that is in the earth beneath, or that is in the water under the earth.
>
> **[5]Thou shalt not bow down thyself to them, nor serve them: for I the LORD thy God am a jealous God,**

The second Commandment says not to worship false gods and make idols of anything or bow down to them. It is plain I had made golf and cigarettes an idol. I was devoted to them. I wanted to have fun—I definitely chased after worldly pleasures more than my God.

Did I keep the second commandment? Do you fair better than I?

> **Commandment 3:** [7]Thou shalt not take **the name of the LORD thy God in vain**; for **the LORD will not hold him guiltless that taketh his name in vain.**

The third Commandment states we should never take the name of God in vain. We should never use it in a vile and degrading way. Never use his name except in awe and praise. Do we not all want our names to be respected?How quickly we are up in arms if someone says something derogatory about our own name, our race, etc.

Now here is God, the Creator of the universe and all that is in it. **The one you owe your very being to**, and I do not even know how to count the number of times I hear people use his name in disrespect or to damn something or someone. I even hear people use his name derogatively to express when they are happy. I never have been one to use his name in this way. My parents taught me not to and my conscience would not allow it. But I must admit, I cannot say I never broke this commandment. I tried it out a few times to see how it felt; it never really felt good to me. In some form or another, I am guilty of breaking this law.

Also, in my anger, I have used profanity, words that should not come out of the mouth of a believer in Jesus Christ. My flesh takes over and in a split second, I sin against God.

Do you fair better than I?Have you ever use your Creators name in the wrong way? Have you used profanity?

> **Commandment 4:** [8]Remember the **sabbath day**, to **keep it holy.**

The forth Commandment is such a simple commandment, but does anyone keep it anymore?God is commanding us to take one day out of the week and remember him. Why did he make this commandment?He wants us to remember him as our Creator:

> **Exodus 20: 11 [11]For in six days the LORD made heaven and earth, the sea, and all that in them is,** and **rested the seventh day**: wherefore **the LORD blessed the sabbath day, and hallowed it.**

Did God literally mean he created the universe in six days?I will let you decide that for yourself. The Bible says further he rested from all his work in creation on the **seventh day and blessed it and made it holy. He asks us to remember this.** I must admit that many, many times I did not keep his Sabbath day holy or remember him as Creator. **I have broken this law many times.**

Do you fair better than I?Have you kept his Sabbath day holy?It is not a matter of if you agree with God that we should do this; the question to you is—**have you kept this commandment?**

Because I do believe in the God of the Bible, I always try to live my life the following way: **It is God that sets the rules and not man (me).** We are not a god who can say to the one, true God, "This is the truth of what I believe, and I do not care what your Bible says because I am right and I follow my rules and not yours."

You do not have the excuse that because the Bible does not make sense to you, or you do not agree with what it teaches that you will escape his commands; for someday we will all find out that it is truly God who sets the rules. **I choose God's word in the Bible as "absolute truth," and I believe it over what any man says, including a minister.** I filter everything said or written to see if it aligns with the Bible. If it does, I accept it as true. If it does not align with scripture, then I will reject it as false no matter who says it because man's thinking can be flawed.

Interesting Note: The Jewish Sabbath day is from sundown on Friday to sundown on Saturday because in Genesis chapter one, each day began at evening:

Genesis 1: 5 [5]And God called the **light Day**, and the **darkness he called Night**. And **the evening and the morning were the first day.**

Commandment 5: [12]**Honour thy father and thy mother**: that thy days may be long upon the land which the LORD thy God giveth thee.

The fifth commandment is easy. I broke this commandment of God so many times—**I am guilty. Do you fair better than I?**

Commandment 6: [13]**Thou shalt not kill.**

The sixth commandment I have not broken... **or have I?**As it is written, I have not broken God's law; but if I go with the intent of the law, I have broken it a few times.

Jesus, at his "Sermon on the Mount," tells us to what extent this law's true meaning is:

Matthew 5: 21- 22 [21]"You have heard that it was said to the people long ago, **'Do not murder**, and **anyone who murders** will be subject to judgment.' [22]But I tell you **that anyone who is angry with his brother will be subject to judgment.** Again, anyone who says to his brother, **'Raca (means worthless)**,' is answerable to the Sanhedrin. **But anyone who says, 'You fool!' will be in danger of the fire of hell. (NIV)**

Matthew 5: 43-44 [43]Ye have heard that it hath been said, Thou shalt love thy neighbour, and hate thine enemy.

[44]**But I say unto you, Love your enemies, bless them that curse you, do good to them that hate you**, and pray for them which despitefully use you, and persecute you;

According to Jesus, I have broken the sixth commandment. I have not always been kind to others, especially my enemies. I have called others fools. I have disliked the person who has wronged me. I have not loved others, as I should. I have not prayed for them. **I am guilty. Do you fair better than I?**

Commandment 7: [14]Thou shalt not commit adultery.

I love my wife very much. I have been married to her for 28 years now, and I have been true and faithful all these years. **The seventh commandment** I have not broken... **or have I?**As it is written, no—I have not broken God's law; but if I go with the intent of the law, I have broken this law many times.

Again, Jesus, at his "Sermon on the Mount," tells us to what extent this law's meaning is:

> **Matthew 5: 27-28** [27]Ye have heard that it was said **by them of old time, Thou shalt not commit adultery:**
>
> [28]But I say unto you, **That whosoever looketh on a woman to lust after her hath committed adultery with her already in his heart.**

Many men, including myself and probably women as well, think looking at another person other than her or his spouse and being attracted to her or him is not adultery. You would be correct. It is when you cross the line and undress this person in your mind and dwell on this person and enjoy doing it that you have committed **adultery in your heart.**

I know that psychologists would say hogwash. It adds spice to a relationship. There is nothing to feel guilty about when using your imagination in this way.

Now I have to make a choice. Do I believe a fellow human, a psychologist, and a learned and probably brilliant mind that has all these degrees and knows so much about human nature, or... **do I choose to believe God's word?**There is no way around what Jesus spoke about lusting after a person. In your heart, he says you have broken the seventh commandment. I have to believe my Savior over the person who says I have done no wrong. As one that has lusted in his heart over a beautiful woman and wants to be totally truthful to himself and God, I have to admit my guilt. **I am guilty. Do you fair better than I?**

> **Commandment 8: [15]Thou shalt not steal.**

I am guilty. Do you fair better than I?

> **Commandment 9: [16]Thou shalt not bear false witness against thy neighbour.**

The ninth commandment says we should not lie. **I am guilty. Do you fair better than I?**

> **Commandment 10: [17]Thou shalt not covet thy neighbour's house, thou shalt not covet thy neighbour's wife,** nor his manservant, nor his maidservant, nor his ox, nor his ass, **nor any thing that is thy neighbour's.**

The tenth and last commandment God gave us to keep. He wants us not to be jealous and desirous of what our neighbors have. It's hard not to be envious of others when they have more than you. It just doesn't seem fair. I do not dwell on what I do not have, but deep down I must admit **I am guilty. Do you fair better than I?**

In reviewing the Ten Commandments God has given us and doing my own personal inventory on how I have kept them, I have surely broken 9 out of the 10. It did not take me long to break the 9. But, it looks like I have broken them all, at least in my heart. I had broken most of them before I was out of high school. I am a repeat offender; I still struggle with some of the laws. **Do you fair better than I?**If we were at all honest with ourselves, for most of us the answer would have to be a resounding **no!**

If you have done your own inventory and looked at how your life stacks up to his laws, and if you have broken fewer of God's commandments than I have, **good for you... or is it?**

> **James 2: 10** [10]For whosoever shall keep the whole law, and yet **offend in one point, he is guilty of all.**

> **Romans 3: 23 [23]For all have sinned, and come short of the glory of God;**

If you believe the Bible is the word of God, then according to scripture, **all are guilty of breaking God's law!** So if we are all guilty, **how do we get forgiveness** from our Creator for the sins we have committed, and **why would we want to** or **need to?**

The Why:

> **Daniel 12: 2** [2]And many of them that sleep in the dust of the earth shall awake, **some to everlasting life, and some to shame and everlasting contempt.**

> **Matthew 10: 28** [28]And fear not them which kill the body, but are not able to kill the soul: but rather **fear him which is able to destroy both soul and body in hell.**

> **Matthew 25: 41** [41]Then shall he say also unto them on the left hand, **Depart from me, ye cursed, into everlasting fire, prepared for the devil and his angels:**

It is a stern warning from the word of God in the above scriptures. Here is the simple truth: **God will judge us by what we have done on this earth while alive. But here is the good news from scripture.**

The Why and the How and the Reward in only two verses:

> **John 3: 16–17** [16]**For God so loved the world**, that **he gave his only begotten Son, that whosoever believeth in him** should not perish, but **have everlasting life.**
>
> [17]For God sent not his Son into the world to condemn the world; but that **the world through him might be saved.**

The Why: Because God loves you! God loves everyone in this world so much. God wants to redeem everyone from sin. Jesus did not come into the world to condemn us to everlasting misery (hell). He came to save us so we can be with him always because he loves us. **The why, then, is because God is love!**

The How: By believing God. That God sent Jesus to die on the cross for our sins. That his blood sacrifice does take away all of mankind sins—making us acceptable to God. **The How then is Faith!**

The reward for those who believe: everlasting life! We can have eternity with God for having faith in him. Do not miss out on this great opportunity no matter what. There is no other message out there better than this. **The reward, then, is everlasting life!**

It doesn't get any better than this—**everlasting life that comes through faith in Jesus Christ!** There will be no more tears or sorrows. The best part of all, we will live forever with our God—our Savior ...who loves us so very much. This is the gospel message. If you are convinced you have sinned against God and are ready to seek his forgiveness, please turn to the very next chapter. It will explain how to begin this relationship with the God of the Bible—our Creator.

God loves you and so do I!

The Final Chapter

Chapter 38

This is the last chapter in this book. I have tried to present the truth and the hope taught in the Bible. It is my hope that you will give your life to Jesus Christ and let him be the Lord over your life.

I will never forget what a Christian friend said to me once. He stated he did not know the Bible very well, but he was going to hang onto the Bible passage found in John. **It is probably the best-known Bible passage in the world.** He told me he is going to trust in it until the day he dies. **This is his Bible verse:**

> **John 3: 16** [16]For God so loved the world, that he gave his only begotten Son, that **whosoever believeth in him** should not perish, but **have everlasting life.**

John 3: 16 says it all. It is the gospel message in its simplest form.

If you are ready to accept God's Son and have faith in him, here are the simple steps in becoming a child of God:

1) You must repent. You must admit you are a sinner; you have rebelled against a holy and loving God. There must be a change of heart—a genuine sorrow and shame for your sin.

2) You must have faith in Jesus Christ. You must accept Jesus is the Christ, the Son of the Living God; and Christ died for the ungodly and sinners. It means to believe in the power and love of Jesus to save you. It means trusting Jesus to make you right with God.

3) You must confess. The Bible says that if you confess with your mouth **"Jesus is Lord"** and believe in your heart that God raised him from the dead, you will be saved.

4) Pray. You are now able to speak to God as **your Father**, something that you have never been able to do.

One last thing; begin a relationship with fellow believers by attending church and getting involved in Christ's ministry and work. God does not promise life on earth will be made easier—He is not a genie in a bottle. But he promises to be there for you always. He promises you eternity where all tears will pass away. You will be truly blessed by seeking a strong relationship with your Savior, Jesus Christ. God has wonderful things awaiting us in heaven. Look at who you have now become in Christ Jesus!

Who You Are Now in Christ (God's Promises to You)!

1) **You are a child of God. John 1: 12** [12]Yet to all who received him, to those who believed in his name, **he gave the right to become children of God— (NIV)**
2) **You are a friend of Jesus Christ. John 15: 15** [15]Henceforth I call you not servants; for the servant knoweth not what his lord doeth: but **I have called you friends**;
3) **You are justified (as if you have not sinned). Romans 5: 1** [1]Therefore being **justified by faith, we have peace with God** through our **Lord Jesus Christ**:
4) **You will never be condemned! Romans 8: 1-2** [1]There is therefore **now no condemnation to them which are in Christ Jesus**, who walk not after the flesh, but after the Spirit. [2]For the law of the Spirit of life in Christ Jesus hath made **me free from the law of sin and death.**

5) **God loves you forever! Romans 8: 35 & 38-39** [35]Who shall separate us from the **love of Christ?** [38]For I am persuaded, that neither death, nor life, nor angels, nor principalities, nor powers, nor things present, nor things to come, [39]Nor height, nor depth, nor any other creature, **shall be able to separate us from the love of God, which is in Christ Jesus our Lord.**
6) **You will live in heaven! Philippians 3: 20** [20]But **our citizenship is in heaven**. And we eagerly await a Savior from there, the Lord Jesus Christ, **(NIV)**
7) **You are a saint. Ephesians 1: 1** to **the saints** which are at Ephesus, and **to the faithful in Christ Jesus:**
8) **You are redeemed and forgiven! Colossians 1: 14** [14]In whom we have **redemption** through his blood, even the **forgiveness of sins**:
9) **You are an adopted child of Christ! Ephesians 1: 5** [5]Having predestinated us unto **the adoption of children by Jesus Christ to himself**, according to the good pleasure of his will,
10) **God has prepared a special place for you! 1 Corinthians 2: 9** [9]But as it is written, **Eye hath not seen, nor ear heard**, neither have entered into the heart of man, **the things which God hath prepared for them that love him.**

This is only a sampling of what God has in store for you. Welcome to the kingdom of God!

God loves you and so do I!

Encore: The Parable of the Prodigal Son

Chapter 39

I wanted to finish my book with chapter 38, but God had a different plan. He wanted me to be as clear as possible who he really is. This parable is the best-loved story of all the parables. In using this parable, Jesus taught us we could see who God really is—**LOVE!** Most, if not all of my chapters have had the stern warnings our Father gives us throughout his scriptures. It is a good thing that he does. My earthly father would warn me that certain behavior would bring punishment and his wrath. I appreciate that he did this for me. I am sure he did this because of his love for me, and he found no joy in having to punish me. Our heavenly Father is no different.

So I write this chapter to make it as clear as I can, who **the one and only God** of the Bible teaches he is. **He is the most loving Father**. He died on the cross for our sins.

> **Isaiah 9: 6** 6For unto us **a child is born**, unto us **a son is given**: and the government shall be upon his shoulder: and his name shall be called Wonderful, Counsellor, **The mighty God, The everlasting Father**, The Prince of Peace.

> **John 3: 16** 16For **God so loved the world, that he gave his only begotten Son**, that whosoever believeth in him should not perish, but **have everlasting life.**

Now let's dig into the parable and see how Jesus used this parable to demonstrated God's love for us. I am taking the parable from chapter 15 of Luke:

> [11]And he said, A certain **man had two sons**:
>
> [12]And the younger of them said to his father, Father, give me the portion of goods that falleth to me. And he divided unto them his living.

The younger son wanted his inheritance early. He wanted his cake and eat it too. He wanted to enjoy all his money and enjoy all of what life brings. He had no concern for the future. He had no concern for eternity. He just wanted a good time. He certainly felt he did not need his father. Sound like anyone you know?

> [13]And not many days after the younger son gathered all together, and took his journey into a far country, and **there wasted his substance with riotous living.**

The younger son went away from his father to live the good life. He wasted all that his father gave him. The good times are about to end.

> [14]And when he had spent all, **there arose a mighty famine in that land**; and **he began to be in want**.
>
> [15]And he went and joined himself to a citizen of that country; and he sent him into his fields **to feed swine.**

The young man who had it all now had to go out and make a living for himself. He had to take menial jobs to survive.

> [16]And he would fain have **filled his belly with the husks that the swine did eat**: and no man gave unto him.

The pigs he took care of ate better then he. He longed to eat the vegetation the pigs ate of.

> 17And when he came to himself, he said, **How many hired servants of my father's have bread enough and to spare, and I perish with hunger!**
>
> 18**I will arise and go to my father**, and will say unto him, **Father, I have sinned against heaven, and before thee,**
>
> 19**And am no more worthy to be called thy son**: make me as one of thy hired servants.

The young man came to his senses and realized he had sinned. He realized he is not worthy to be called his son. He would rather be his father's servant than in the way he lived his life then. The young man humbled himself and declared he would go back to his father to become his servant. **God is looking for the same willingness in us.** God looks at the heart and wants us to come home to him.

> 20And he arose, and came to his father. But when he was yet a great way off, **his father saw him**, and **had compassion**, and **ran,** and **fell on his neck, and kissed him.**

Oh, how the father longed for this day. He recognized his son from a great distance; he ran to him, threw his arms around him, and kissed him in **absolute love**.

> 21And the son said unto him, Father, **I have sinned against heaven, and in thy sight,** and am no more worthy to be called thy son.

The Son humbled himself and confessed. He owned up to his mistakes. He knew he was not worthy, but he was seeking only mercy from his father and nothing more. **But his father gave him a great deal more!**

22But the father said to his servants, **Bring forth the best robe**, and put it on him; and **put a ring on his hand**, and **shoes on his feet**:

23And **bring hither the fatted calf**, and kill it; and **let us eat**, and **be merry:**

There is a party going on. It was the plan of the father.

24For this my son was dead, and **is alive again**; **he was lost, and is found**. And they began to be merry.

We are that prodigal son or daughter. When we are off and running, doing our own thing, never thinking about our Creator Father, he misses us. **He still very much loves us!** When we come back to him to seek his forgiveness, it is like we are raised from the dead (and we really are). God loves his lost children so much. God loves his disobedient children as much as his obedient children.

25Now **his elder son** was in the field: and as he came and drew nigh to the house, **he heard musick and dancing**.

26And he called one of the servants, and asked what these things meant.

27And he said unto him, **Thy brother is come**; and thy father hath killed the fatted calf, **because he hath received him safe and sound.**

28And **he was angry**, and would not go in: **therefore came his father out, and intreated him.**

When the elder son came home from the fields, he heard the music and dancing. When he found out the party was for his brother who came home after all these years, he was angry and jealous.

29And he answering said to his father, Lo, these **many years do I serve thee, neither transgressed I at any time thy commandment**: and yet thou never gavest me a kid, that **I might make merry with my friends**:

30But as soon as this thy son was come, which hath devoured thy living with harlots, **thou hast killed for him the fatted calf.**

The elder son was faithful and true all these years and did whatever the father commanded. He never got the party his brother is now getting. His younger brother sinned greatly and squandered his inheritance. He wanted to know why his father would do this.

31And he said unto him, **Son, thou art ever with me, and all that I have is thine.**

32It was meet that we should make merry, and be glad: **for this thy brother was dead, and is alive again; and was lost, and is found.**

God loves all his children very much. He loves all of us who are obedient to him, who keep his commandments, who love him. God loves the sinner also. He is concerned for his lost child and wants him to come home, to be found, to **become alive again**. God is **LOVE!**

This parable is a love story between a father and his son. The true meaning of this scripture is that it is a **love story between our Creator God and me. Between God and you.** All of us started out in life as that disobedient son or daughter. God is looking for us to return to him and come home.

I urge you if you are ready to come home to the Father who loves you just the way you are, turn back the pages to **chapter 38** and begin your relationship with your heavenly Father.

God loves you and so do I!

Notes:

Chapter 3 - "Gods Loving Arms"

Ergun Mehmet Caner and Emir Fethi Caner, *Unveiling Islam* (Grand Rapids, MI: Kregel Publishing), 2002, page 122.

Chapter 5 - Jesus spent time in "Sheol" "Hades" "Hell" "Grave"

William MacDonald, *Believer's Bible Commentary* (Nashville, TN: Thomas Nelson Publishers), 1995.

Preface and Chapter 8 - Zero in on the Right word!

Watchman Nee, *The Spiritual Man*, (New York, NY: Christian Fellowship Publishers, Inc.), 1977.

Chapter 14 - Job: Only God is God and I am man!

David Catchpoole, Giant Oysters on the mountain, (Creation Magazine, Volume 24) published March 2002, pages 54-55.

Dr. Carl Wieland, Still soft and stretchy, Dinosaur soft tissue find, Answers in Genesis web site, 25 March 2005.

Chapter 18 - Is God Pro-Choice?

"Fathers Love Letter" web site, www.fathersloveletter.com

Chapter 21 - "Hear o Israel: The Lord our God, The Lord is one."

Day of Discovery, *The Oneness of God parts one and two,*
Produced by RBC Ministries

**Chapters 24 and 25 - Evidence for Creation:
Week One and Week Two**

1) Answers in Genesis Video Series, produced by Master Books
2) John D. Morris PH.D., *The Young Earth*, (Green Forest, AR: Master Books), 2000.
3) Creation Ex Nihilo, Volume 23 No.1 February 2001, (www.AnswersInGenesis.org)
4) Answers in Genesis web site, www.AnswersInGenesis.org
5) Dr Bob Compton and Mike Riddle, *The Origin of Life: Equipping Course* Video Series, Christian Training & Development Services

**Chapters 27 thru 34 -
The Seven Feasts of Israel- Appointed by God**

1) Zola Levitt, *The Seven Feasts of Israel Video, Parts one and two*, Produced by Berg Productions
2) Zola Levitt, *The Miracle of Passover Video*, produced by Berg Productions
3) Bible Study: The Seven Feasts of Israel web site, www.brandonweb.com
4) Pentecost or Shavuot Overview web site, www.biblicalholidays.com
5) Succoth: The Feast of Tabernacles web site, www.amfi.org

6) *Easter Sunday or Ishtar Pagan Day web site*, www.retakingamerica.com
7) Zola Levitt, *The Seven Feasts of Israel*, (Dallas, TX: Great Impression Printing & Graphics, 1979, pages 19-20.

Recommended Reading and Web sites

1) Web site: www.AnswersInGenesis.org is a fantastic source for information on the question of Creation and Evolution. Their Creation Museum near Cincinnati, Ohio is scheduled to open in 2007.
2) Magazine: Creation, Published Quarterly by Answers in Genesis Ministries. The information presented is scientific, yet easy to understand and the full color pictures are fantastic. You may subscribe from their web site.
3) Web site: www.fathersloveletter.com. The Fathers love Letter is wonderful. See how God truly loves you!
4) The Genesis Record by Henry M. Morris published by Baker Book House; Grand Rapids, Michigan is a fascinating study of the entire Book of Genesis. It is a scientific and devotional commentary on Genesis.
5) The Case for a Creator by Lee Strobel, published by Zondervan, Grand Rapids, Michigan, presents the scientific evidence for a Creator. Lee was a one time atheist and reporter who investigate the truth of the Bible and came to faith. He has also authored the Case for Jesus and the Case for Faith which are also excellent reading.
6) Web site: www.wayofthemaster.com. The Way of the Master Ministry is an excellent resource to help our witness to non-believers become more effective.
7) The Spiritual Man by Watchman Nee, published by Christian Fellowship Publishers, Inc. I learned so much about God through this man who spent the last twenty years in prison in communist China for his faith. Thank God his teachings made it out into the free world. All of his books are excellent reading.

8) Web site: www.levitt.com is the start to learn the Jewish roots for our Christian faith. Zola Levitt is a Jewish believer who has great insight to God's word.
9) **Your Bible.** This is most important of all. Spend time reading and searching for God. Jesus and the love of God can be found when you open up your heart and mind. I pray that you find him if you haven't already.

God loves you and so do I!

I see Jesus everywhere! Whether I am in the Old Testament or in the New Testament**- the message is the same.** We all have a **Redeemer and an Intercessor** seated at the **Right Hand of God.** Through him, **all the sins of the world have been taken away.** Because of what Jesus has done for us, we all can receive the good news the gospel message brings-**ETERNAL LIFE!** This is the hope of everyone who **believes in the Son of God** and believes **God raised his Son from the dead.**

This is the message I always want to share with people... **especially my loved ones and friends.** It can be so very difficult. **Here we have the most important message anyone could ever share with someone,** and we can't find the words to bring it up in conversation, or we cannot get over the fear that we might offend this person. **When we are dealing with someone's eternity,** we have to find a way to share this great news. **Jesus paid the ultimate price (his life)... in order for us to have eternal life.**

I wrote this book for this very reason—**to share the good news of Jesus Christ**. I wanted everyone who reads this book to **see Jesus** I wanted to give fellow believers a way they might warn their loved ones and friends that **everyone is going to live forever.** The Prophet Daniel wrote over 2,500 years ago **there are two ways to go**—some will be awaken to **everlasting life** and others will awaken to **everlasting shame and contempt.**

My idea was to show in this book that **the Bible is the biography of Jesus Christ. Meno Kalisher, a Jewish believer states, "**Jesus did not just pop out of the Bible in the Book of Matthew and say, 'Here I am!'." **Jesus was there from the beginning, before creation. The**

plan of salvation was in place before God created the universe. Jesus is written about from the first chapter in Genesis to the last verse in the book of Revelation. I wrote this book so—**you can see Jesus;** maybe like you never have seen him before.

1 Corinthians, chapter 15 is what I call my Bible Chapter. It describes where all my hope is found. The apostle Paul writes that if Jesus has not been resurrected from the grave, than no one else will be either, and we will be still in our sins. But Paul assures us God indeed has raised Jesus and because He has been raised, **everyone who believes in Jesus and his resurrection will follow suit and be given eternal life! Let's spread the Good News!**

Printed in the United States
50292LVS00004B/55-144